POLITICAL AND SOCIAL CONTROL IN CHINA

THE CONSOLIDATION OF SINGLE-PARTY RULE

POLITICAL AND SOCIAL CONTROL IN CHINA

THE CONSOLIDATION OF SINGLE-PARTY RULE

EDITED BY BEN HILLMAN AND CHIEN-WEN KOU

Australian
National
University

ANU PRESS

Australian
National
University

ANU PRESS

Published by ANU Press
The Australian National University
Canberra ACT 2600, Australia
Email: anupress@anu.edu.au

Available to download for free at press.anu.edu.au

ISBN (print): 9781760466190
ISBN (online): 9781760466206

WorldCat (print): 1417301352
WorldCat (online): 1417259158

DOI: 10.22459/PSCC.2024

Cover design and layout by ANU Press

This book is published under the aegis of the Public Policy editorial board of ANU Press.

Contents

List of figures

List of tables

Acknowledgements

This book is published with support from the Institute of International Relations (IIR), National Chengchi University, ROC (Taiwan) and the Australian Centre on China in the World, The Australian National University, Canberra. It grew out of a conference, 'Changes in the Chinese Party-State in the Xi Jinping Era', held at the IIR on 24–25 October 2019. The editors are grateful for financial endorsement during the conference and the editorial process of the book from the Foundation on Asia-Pacific Peace Studies, the Institute of Political Science at Academia Sinica, Mainland Affairs Council, Taipei City Government, Taiwan Foundation for Democracy, the IIR at National Chengchi University, and the Australian Centre on China in the World at The Australian National University. Six chapters of this edited volume, which have since been revised and updated, first appeared in *Issues and Studies*, an English-language academic journal run by the IIR and published by World Scientific. The journal's reprint permission has been indispensable to this edited volume.

The editors would also like to thank several individuals for their assistance. Yi-Horng Chiang and Yu-Wei Hu provided outstanding logistical support for the conference and organised student volunteers from National Chengchi University. In addition, Megan Wu and Cathryn Game provided vital administrative and editorial support (respectively) during the editorial process. We also owe our appreciation to the two anonymous reviewers of the manuscript for their invaluable suggestions to improve the quality of the final version. Last but not least, we would like to thank our authors for their valuable contributions to this project.

Chien-wen Kou
Ben Hillman
Canberra, 2023

Contributors

Jean-Pierre Cabestan is Senior Researcher Emeritus at the French National Centre for Scientific Research (Centre national de la recherche scientifique), attached to the French Research Institute on East Asia (IFRAE) of the National Institute of Oriental Languages and Civilisations, and Professor Emeritus at Hong Kong Baptist University. He is also an associate research fellow at the Asia Centre, Paris, and at the French Centre for Research on Contemporary China in Hong Kong. His most recent publications include *China Tomorrow: Democracy or Dictatorship?* (2019) and *Facing China: The Prospect for War and Peace* (2023).

Ben Hillman obtained his doctoral (PhD) degree from The Australian National University. He is a director of the Australian Centre on China in the World at ANU and Chief Editor of the *China Journal*—the world's number one-ranked journal in China Studies. His primary research interests include Chinese politics and public administration, ethnic policy and politics, and local government. Ben is the author or editor of six books on China, including *Patronage and Power* (2014) and *Conflict and Protest in Tibet and Xinjiang* (2016).

Stefanie Kam Li Yee is an Assistant Professor with the China Programme, Institute of Defence and Strategies Studies at Nanyang Technological University, Singapore. She obtained her doctoral degree in political science and international relations at The Australian National University. Her research interests include Chinese politics and ethnic policy in Xinjiang. Her articles have appeared in *International Affairs* and *Asian Perspective*.

Chien-wen Kou obtained his doctoral (PhD) degree from the University of Texas at Austin. He is a Distinguished Professor in the Department of Political Science and the Graduate Institute of East Asian Studies (GIEAS) at National Chengchi University, Taiwan. He has been serving as Director of the IIR since August 2017. His primary research interests include

Chinese politics, political elites and comparative communist studies. His major articles have been published in *China Quarterly*, *China Journal* and *Issues and Studies*.

Wen-Hsuan Tsai obtained his doctoral (PhD) degree from the National Chengchi University. He is a research fellow at the Institute of Political Science in Academia Sinica (Taiwan) and Jointly Appointed Professor at the Graduate Institute of East Asian Studies in National Chengchi University. His main research is on Chinese political development, Chinese governance and innovation, comparative politics and comparative authoritarian regimes. He has recently published in *China Journal*, *China Quarterly*, *Critical Asian Studies*, *Journal of Contemporary China*, *Modern China*, *Asian Survey*, *China Review*, *China Information*, *China Perspectives*, *China: An International Journal*, *Journal of Chinese Political Science*, *Journal of East Asian Studies*, *Problems of Post-Communism*, *Journal of Contemporary East Asia Studies*, and *Issues and Studies*.

Hans H. Tung is a professor in the Department of Political Science and a faculty associate of the Behavioral and Data Science Research Centre and the Centre for Research in Econometric Theory and Applications at National Taiwan University. He serves on the editorial boards for *Humanities and Social Sciences Communications* (Nature Portfolio), *PlOS ONE* and the Cambridge University Press book series on Taiwan Studies. He is primarily interested in formal and empirical analyses of the political–economic dynamics under authoritarian rule at both macro and micro levels, and has written several articles in academic journals such as *Political Communication*, *Review of International Organizations*, *Nature Communications*, *Social Science and Medicine*, *Japanese Economic Review* and *Public Opinion Quarterly*.

Wei-Feng Tzeng obtained his doctoral (PhD) degree from the University of North Texas. He is an assistant research fellow of the Institute of International Relations at National Chengchi University, Taiwan. His primary research interests include comparative politics, democratisation, contentious politics, China politics and cross-strait relations. His major articles have been published in the *Journal of Chinese Political Science*, *China Review*, *China: An International Journal*, *Pacific Focus* and *Issues and Studies*.

Hsin-Hsien Wang obtained his doctoral (PhD) degree from National Chengchi University in Taiwan. He is a Distinguished Professor of the Graduate Institute of East Asian Studies and deputy director of the Institute of International Relations at NCCU. His primary research interests include comparative politics, political sociology, state–society relations in China, and cross-strait relations. His major articles have been published in the *China Journal, China Review, China: An International Journal, Pacific Focus, Journal of Contemporary East Asia Studies* and major academic journals in Taiwan.

Ray Wang obtained his doctoral degree in political science from the University of California, Riverside. He is an associate professor in the Graduate Institute of East Asian Studies (GIEAS) at National Chengchi University, Taiwan. He is currently executive editor of *Mainland China Studies* (TSSCI indexed). His primary interests include human rights, religious freedom, cross-strait relations and transnational activism in the East Asia region. His major articles have been published in the *Journal of Contemporary China, Chinese Political Science Review,* the *Journal for the Scientific Study of Religion* and more.

Wen-Chin Wu is a research fellow of the Institute of Political Science at Academia Sinica (IPSAS), Taiwan. His research focuses on comparative and international political economy, comparative authoritarianism and Chinese politics. He is particularly interested in the economic statecraft and media politics in dictatorships. Dr Wu received his BA from National Chengchi University, MA from National Chengchi University and Katholieke Universiteit Leuven, and PhD from Michigan State University. Dr Wu has published in *China Quarterly, International Studies Quarterly* and *Journal of Contemporary China,* among others.

Florence W. Yang is an assistant professor in the NCCU Program in Japan Studies, College of International Affairs at National Chengchi University, Taiwan. She received her master's degree from the Department of Law and Politics, Political Science, Keio University, and doctoral degree from Josef Korbel School of International Studies, University of Denver. Her research interests include Chinese and Japanese foreign and security policy, Sino-Japanese relations, and state–society relations in both states and their influence on foreign policy.

Shuyu Zhang is a PhD candidate at the School of Literature, Languages and Linguistics at The Australian National University. She received her MA in General and Applied Linguistics from ANU. Her research focuses on socio- and psycho-linguistic aspects of Chinese–English intercultural communication. With a background in journalism and linguistics, she conducts research and writes about Chinese internet language, the media landscape in China and censorship mechanisms under new media.

1

From soft to hard authoritarianism: The consolidation of one-party rule in China

Ben Hillman

Since 2012 the Communist Party of China (CPC) has strengthened its monopoly on political power and greatly expanded its control over Chinese social and economic life. The sustained expansion of political and social controls across multiple arenas indicates that politics in the People's Republic of China (PRC) is entering the second part of the cycle that some observers, including Chinese intellectuals, call the *fang–shou shiqi* (放收时期), or 'relaxing and tightening cycle'. Since the beginning of the post-Mao reform era in the 1980s, the party has oscillated between a more relaxed (liberal) posture and a tight (repressive) one. Relatively relaxed periods have been characterised by social, cultural, economic and intellectual liberalisation, including greater tolerance for free expression and criticism. We could refer to this mode of governance as 'soft authoritarianism'. However, when periods of openness have produced too much criticism or social unrest, as during the student-led protest movement of 1989, party leaders have sensed a threat to their grip on power and responded by clamping down on the threat—with the help of the army in 1989—and by tightening political and social controls more generally. We could refer to this mode of governance as 'hard authoritarianism'.

The violent resolution of the 1989 protests ended the period of loosening that began in the years following Mao's death in 1976 and the efforts of Deng Xiaoping, Zhao Ziyang, Hu Yaobang and others to steer China away from the totalitarian excesses of Maoism and towards a path of reform and opening to the world.[1] However, the post-1989 period of hard authoritarianism was relatively short-lived. Following Deng's southern tour in 1992, China returned to the path of reform and opening. China's reform-era political economy—described as 'socialism with Chinese characteristics'—accommodated liberalisation in the economic sphere to stimulate economic growth but rejected liberalisation in the political realm. The challenge for party leaders was to allow enough freedom of movement, association, communication and information to spur economic activity without threatening the party's grip on power. Finding the 'sweet spot' between relaxing and tightening has arguably been the most fundamental political challenge facing CPC leaders in the post-Mao era.[2]

With the benefit of hindsight, we can see that China experienced an extended period of soft authoritarianism from the mid-1990s through to the late 2000s when a new cycle of tightening began. Since the late 2000s, and most notably since 2012 when Xi Jinping came to power, the party has steadily tightened its grip on the state, economy and society. It has further centralised power by expanding its already considerable influence across government agencies and policy sectors from the regulation of big tech to film production. There is no longer debate about the appropriate separation of party and state (党政分开, *dang zheng fenkai*). The party directs government agencies through a suite of powerful new central organs such as the Central Commission for Comprehensively Deepening Reform.

---

1   There was also extensive oscillation between relaxing and tightening during the 1980s as China's leaders sought to balance political control with economic growth. For a comprehensive treatment of the politics of this period see Richard Baum (1994).

2   The idea of oscillation reminds us that political systems exist along a spectrum and that aspects of authoritarianism can be found in all systems. An even more extreme form of hard authoritarianism is totalitarianism. Under totalitarian rule, the state controls all aspects of people's lives and mobilises people to work towards specific state goals. All individual freedoms become subsumed by duty and obedience to the state. Under hard authoritarianism, individual freedoms can still exist, particularly in the economic sphere, but various forms of social organisation will be subjected to close state surveillance. Under totalitarian rule, very little activity takes place outside state direction and surveillance. Earlier periods of CPC rule, notably during the Mao era, can be described as totalitarian, but those who use the term to describe today's China oversimplify the fragmented nature of China's vast state and overlook the freedoms that are available to people in the social and economic sphere (in stark contrast to the Mao era). David Shambaugh (2018) discusses four possible political futures for China: neo-totalitarianism, hard authoritarianism, soft authoritarianism and semi-democracy. Shambaugh argues that China will stagnate if it stays on the path of hard authoritarianism, making a return to soft authoritarianism more likely.

These coordinating bodies, which are akin to permanent task forces and report directly to the party leadership, steer the ship of state. In the name of bureaucratic streamlining, government bureaus have been absorbed into the party apparatus. These include the Ministry of Supervision, which has been absorbed into the National Supervision Commission, and the Ministry of Public Sector Reform, which has been absorbed into the party's Organisational Department. The State Ethnic Affairs Commission and the State Administration for Religious Affairs have both been swallowed by the powerful United Front Work Department, the role of which is to secure the allegiance of important non-party constituencies at home and abroad, such as scientists, entrepreneurs and ethnic minorities in China as well as Chinese diasporic communities, while creating a positive image of China in media and political parties in foreign countries.

On the ideological front, the party has intensified training for party cadres and purged officials suspected of questionable loyalties, particularly those serving in security organs—a process likened to 'scraping the poison from the bone' (刮骨疗毒 *guagu liadu*). The party has used an anti-corruption drive to weed out officials who have placed their own interests ahead of the party's and the current leadership's, reminding local officials across the country that they serve only at the pleasure of the party. The party has also progressively imposed restrictions on universities to forbid research and teaching that deviate from the party's increasingly detailed script. Non-compliant academics have faced the sack and even jail. Thinkers and activists, including human rights lawyers, labour activists and feminists, who promote alternative agendas to that of the party have met similar fates. The same goes for neo-Maoists, who are perceived to lean too far to the left of the party. It has become highly risky for citizens to express divergent perspectives on a wide range of topics, including ruling party ideology, China's past, China's future or the party's mission to restore China's national greatness—the 'China Dream'. The fame, wealth or social media followings of tech entrepreneurs, sports stars and celebrities have proven no protection should they indulge in criticism of the party, its leadership or its direction. This is not to say that the party has squashed all forms of dissent in a totalitarian fashion, but it has greatly narrowed the scope for expressing dissent.

Fears of retribution have prompted a greater degree of self-censorship across regular and social media and in academia as well. Chinese academics are choosing to research 'safe' topics, steering clear of the growing list of taboo subjects, which now even includes criticism of Confucius or unfavourable comparisons of China with other countries on any grounds. During my visit to Kunming in 2019, Chinese anthropologists told me that many in their field were choosing to move their field research to South-East Asia to avoid the potential political risks associated with working on questions related to China's ethnic minorities. Observing and documenting the differences among China's various ethnic groups in any meaningful way could be seen to undermine the unity of the nationalities (民族团结, *minzu tuanjie*) demanded by the party.

Meanwhile, hordes of young party faithful sing the party's praises and go to war against its critics and enemies across multiple platforms. The genuinely fervent 'Little Pinks', as they are called, are different from the previous cohort of pro-party trolls known as the 'Fifty Cent Party' (五毛党, *wu mao dang*) (so-called because it was rumoured that they were paid 50 Chinese cents for every social media post praising the party or attacking its enemies) (Jaivin, 2021). It is hard to say what proportion of the Chinese population identifies as loyal to the party, especially when a characteristic of the hard mode of authoritarianism is a tightening of ideological discipline (Kuo, 2022). The party has narrowed the scope for public debate through censorship while expanding the space for propaganda and 'thought work' in media, culture and school curricula—including the promotion of a personality cult around President Xi himself. As of September 2021, all of China's elementary and middle schools were required to teach classes on 'Xi Jinping Thought on Socialism with Chinese Characteristics for a New Era' (Zhonghua Renmin Gongheguo Jiaoyubu, 2021). The youngest children now learn, among other things, that 'Grandpa' Xi Jinping's 'warm smile' is brighter than the sun (Chen & Lau, 2021). Online one can always find resistance to the party's propaganda and thought policing—often expressed as satirical humour, such as the Winnie the Pooh meme used to poke fun at Xi Jinping. But increased digital surveillance and restrictions on social media accounts have greatly increased the risks of making fun of the party. Images of Winnie the Pooh are banned and quickly deleted when they emerge. Satirical commentary is increasingly coded to evade censors.[3]

The party has also expanded its policing of thought and action through high-tech surveillance and online tools, including an app for the study of Xi Jinping Thought called 'Study to Strengthen the Country' (学习强国). Pronounced *xuexi qiangguo*, the app also sounds (and reads) like 'Study Xi

---

3   For a selection of recent online satirical posts, see chinadigitaltimes.net/china/political-satire/

to Strengthen the Country', and its use is mandatory for party members and some other groups. By 2022, the party was intervening in people's everyday lives in ways unprecedented since Mao's time. In 2021, the party limited the number of hours that students under the age of 18 may play video games each week and banned private tutoring (Zhongguo Zhengfu Wang, 2019, 2021). The male-led party wants married people to stay married, making it difficult for women who have reported domestic violence or abuse to obtain a divorce (He, 2021). To address the demographic crises caused by its own one-child policy, including a rapidly ageing population, it exhorts women to have three children—despite many young women expressing a desire to have no children at all. The party tells effeminate men to toughen up, to be less like K-pop boy band idols and more like Wang Jing, the hard-muscled he-man star of the patriotic action *Wolf Warrior* films (Bloomberg, 2021). Through such actions as punishing Muslims (most obviously Uyghurs) for expressing their faith by growing beards or wearing headscarves, and banning schooling in minority languages, the party exhorts—and ultimately forces—its citizens to forego individual ethnic and religious identities in favour of national unity and a singular 'Chinese' identity.

During the phase of tightening since 2012, the party has used its institutional and legal powers to curtail and repress civil society activism such as that carried out by human rights lawyers, labour organisers and feminists. During the summer of 2015, the party rounded up 300 legal professionals in a widespread crackdown on rights advocacy, popularly referred to as the '709 crackdown' after the date it began—July 9, 2015 (Nee, 2021). Lawyers were disbarred, placed under surveillance and in some cases jailed as punishment for taking on politically sensitive cases, especially those related to freedom of belief or freedom of expression. Outspoken critic and human rights lawyer Yu Wensheng received a four-year prison sentence for subversion of state power following a secret trial. In the two years leading up to his trial, Yu was placed in detention and prevented from meeting family members or lawyers. Seven years after the 709 crackdown in 2022, some of these detained lawyers, such as Xu Zhiyong and Ding Jiaxi, remain in pre-trial detention (Buckley, 2022).

The purpose of this chapter and the volume it introduces is not to deny the CPC's many significant achievements over the past few decades, including growing the economy to become the second largest in the world, raising Chinese citizens' incomes and living standards widely, and making great strides towards the eradication of rural poverty. However, many of these accomplishments were either made or were on the way to being made during the previous period of 'relaxed' governance, which spanned from approximately the mid-1990s to the end of the 2000s. If the party was able to achieve many of its successes during periods of soft authoritarianism, why then has the CPC leadership taken a recent turn to hard authoritarianism? What shape has this taken, and what have been and are likely to be the consequences? These are the questions that lie at the heart of this volume.

To understand the gradual but certain shift from *fang* to *shou*, we must look for factors that have threatened the confidence of party leaders in their grip on power. What convinced the party leadership that the period of social and cultural relaxation had gone too far? While there was no single protest movement in the 2000s as in 1989, civil society had mushroomed during the first part of the twenty-first century. Groups advocating for such things as workers' rights, consumer rights and better protections for land and property against developers and local government were becoming increasingly well organised and assertive in seeking policy change. In addition, there were many tens of thousands of local protests every year about such issues as forced land acquisitions or the industrial pollution of waterways and soil (Steinhardt & Wu, 2016). Online activism too had become a potent force by this time, and online debate and criticism were increasingly forthright. China was riding high following its successful hosting of the 2008 Beijing Olympics and its management of the global financial crisis. Yet the rise of independent social forces was beginning to test the party's grip on power, even if the activism and protests were generally issues-based and not explicitly anti-party.

Alongside social groups calling for change, however, emboldened Chinese intellectuals were also calling for political reforms to match the economic ones, including adaptation of universal notions of human rights and the rule of law. The writer and democracy advocate Liu Xiaobo helped to draft 'Charter '08', which commemorated the sixtieth anniversary of the signing of the Universal Declaration of Human Rights and was named in tribute to the Czech anti-Soviet Charter '77. Charter '08 called for, among other things, the end of one-party rule, elections for public officials, an independent legal system and freedom of association, assembly, expression and religion. Three hundred and three intellectuals, former and current government officials, civil society activists, lawyers and writers inside and outside of China put their names to the charter (Béja, Fu & Pils, 2013). Thousands of others subsequently signed it. It would have reminded party leaders of the snowballing petition movement to free political prisoners and more that helped to set the scene for the massive, nationwide student-led protests of 1989. Authorities immediately arrested Liu Xiaobo, sentencing him the following year to 11 years for inciting subversion of state power. He was awarded the Nobel Peace Prize in 2010 while in prison and died seven years later from cancer while still incarcerated.

In 2008 and 2009, China's western regions of Tibet and Xinjiang became engulfed in spiralling ethnic unrest. There had been cycles of dissent or uprising and suppression in both of these resource-rich and strategically important 'autonomous regions' since 1949. Following the extreme suppression of religious activities in the Mao period, the Reform Era witnessed both religious revival and political unrest in both Tibet and Xinjiang. By 1996, the party was so worried about the possibility of Uyghur separatism in the wake of the Soviet Union's dissolution and the rise of Central Asian states such as Kazakhstan on Xinjiang's borders that it called a meeting of the Politburo Standing Committee to consider the threat. In both Xinjiang and Tibet, the party upped its security and military presence while investing billions of yuan into economic development and encouraging mass Han migration to dilute their non-Han majority populations. Such actions only sparked further unrest. For example, significant numbers of Tibetans self-immolated in protest at its policies and presence in their homeland, and violent riots erupted in the Xinjiang capital of Urumqi, which gave expression to years of frustration and hostility. Several terror attacks were also carried out by Uyghur separatists, including a bomb attack while Xi Jinping was visiting the region in 2014. The party appeared to be incapable of exercising administrative, ideological or even physical control of vast swathes of China's territory. Internally, party strategists blamed liberal policies and foreign influences for rising ethnic consciousness among Uyghurs and Tibetans and fanning the flames of local nationalism, threatening the territorial integrity of the People's Republic (Hillman & Tuttle, 2016).

CPC concerns about ethnic unrest and civil society assertiveness were heightened by the appearance of colour revolutions across the states of the former Soviet Union beginning with the 2004 'orange revolution' in the Ukraine and the Jasmine Revolutions that spread across the Middle East beginning with Tunisia in 2010 and 2011. Party leaders would have noted the central role played by NGOs and activist groups in these 'revolutions'. David Shambaugh reports that Russian President Vladimir Putin warned CPC General Secretary Hu Jintao at a G7 summit in 2009 that China could expect its own colour revolution if the party did not get NGOs, especially foreign-funded ones, under control (Carson, 2018). Putin's view would have carried weight since the dramatic collapse of Communist Party rule in the former Soviet Union has never been far from CPC leaders' minds when they consider the political and social control settings needed to maintain their own monopoly on power.

The collapse of the USSR has also had a persistent influence on the *fang–shou* oscillations of Chinese politics. Liberal-leaning party leaders and intellectuals generally agree that Gorbachev was correct to embrace liberalisation but that his reforms came too late to save Communist Party rule. According to this thesis, the Soviet Union's command economy had already been rendered dysfunctional by corruption and inefficiency, leaving the party-led system beyond repair. The CPC had to avoid a similar fate by continuing to modernise and open up. Proponents of this view, who have been largely sidelined in Xi's China, are confident in the party's ability following Deng Xiaoping's direction-setting in the late 1970s and early 1980s to manage an increasingly liberalised society and economy. Conservatives, on the other hand, view the Soviet collapse as the result of an inherent incompatibility between liberalisation and Leninist one-party rule. Such conservatives feel that the party is threatened by the expression of social, religious, cultural and intellectual diversity and are inclined to reach for coercive tools to enforce unity.

The hardliners expanded their influence during Hu Jintao's second term (2007–12) and have dominated the upper echelon of power since Xi's ascension to power in 2012. Prominent party theorist and ideologue Wang Huning joined the Politburo in 2012 and was elevated to its standing committee in 2017. Wang has been a powerful advocate for a culturally unified China governed by a strong party. He is seen as the architect of recent ideological formulations that merge Leninist socialism with Confucian values to justify the continuation of Communist Party rule and cement the party's status as the saviour of the Chinese nation. Just as the party saved China from the degradations of Western and Japanese imperialism and ended the century of humiliation, the party presents itself as the only political force capable of restoring the Chinese nation to greatness. Wang is seen as the brains behind a new set of party-sanctioned core values that promote a distinctive Chinese mode of governance and civility in direct competition with Western liberal ideas that the current leadership sees as an existential threat (Lin & Trevaskes, 2019).

When Xi came to power in 2012, he led a team that set about accelerating the transition from soft to hard authoritarianism, deploying a diverse range of political and social controls. His priority was boosting organisational strength and discipline within the party itself. Official corruption was a side effect of the transition from a centrally planned to a market economy, but it had grown into a systemic and reputational risk for the party (Pei, 2016). The pro-democracy protests of 1989 began as anti-corruption protests with the slogan 'sell the Benzes and save the nation'; many people have forgotten this fact, but the party leadership has not. Corruption had grown hand in hand with the progress of economic reforms. The participation of party-state officials at all levels of economic activity was needed to drive China's transition from a centrally planned to a dynamic market-oriented economy. Economic performance became a criterion for the career advancement of officials across the nation, particularly regional leaders.

Economic success, however, also provided opportunities for spoils. At the beginning of the reforms, these could be relatively modest: banquets, the use of a luxury car, a junket abroad, or cash bonuses. Public officials were directly engaged with enterprise development, particularly at the village and township level where factors of production were collectively owned and coordinated. As the central government began to decrease transfers to public institutions ranging from film studios to hospitals, those institutions, like local governments, became responsible for their own bottom lines. They began to open side businesses to generate revenue. For example, an agency might use its spare floors for a restaurant or hotel or, in the case of cultural institutions, producing films, plays, books or exhibitions that would have commercial appeal rather than a politically didactic message. Profits would be shared among employees as bonuses or in the form of other benefits such as subsidised loans and access to housing at below market rates. Government agencies began to generate large amounts of off-book revenues, which officials often siphoned off as personal benefits. Over time, corruption became more egregious, including the rigging of tenders for public works, approving land deals, or offering preferential treatment in exchange for payments and gifts. That some of China's most popular television dramas of recent years have related stories of official corruption testifies to wide societal frustration and anger about the problem. China's officials had become pervasively corrupt, and the people knew it.

Yet eliminating corruption was no longer a matter of making an example of the odd local official. Corruption had become baked into the system from top to bottom (Wedeman, 2012). In a fragmented bureaucracy operating under unclear rules and struggling to keep up with dynamic economic change, local power brokers recruited kin and trusted allies into state jobs, building their own 'little kingdoms' (Hillman, 2014, 2010). There were big kingdoms, too, including in strategic centrally controlled sectors such as energy and communications. Networks crisscrossed party organisations and state agencies vertically and horizontally, influencing personnel appointments, decision-making and resource allocation. Operating in a relative ideological vacuum, officials shared few common goals except to get rich. Factions and patronage networks that used party-state institutions to serve private ends weakened and threatened the party's authority and inflicted damage on its reputation.

By the time he assumed the party's supreme office in 2012, Xi understood that many officials had a stronger allegiance to their personal networks than to the party. Xi Jinping naturally had built his own networks and allegiances while ascending through the ranks. As top leader of the party and state, he deployed them to consolidate his personal power and destroy his rivals and enemies.

Against the backdrop of ambient corruption, the party's slogans sounded hollow, anachronistic and divorced from reality. The party's slogans had often become the butt of jokes, including among officials. Jiang Zemin's year 2000 mantra of 'three represents' (三个代表, *san ge daibiao*) referred to what and whom the party represented: the 'development trend of China's advanced productive forces', 'the orientation of China's advanced culture' and 'the fundamental interests of the overwhelming majority of Chinese people'. Because the phrase was a homonym for 'three [people] wearing wristwatches', it also became a pun calling out the extravagant consumption and lifestyles of party-state officials at a time when owning a (good) watch was still considered a sign of wealth. Within the party itself, a far more serious but related argument about the 'three represents' erupted with those on the left arguing that if the party were to represent and admit capitalists, then it would have abandoned its class character and the rural and urban working classes it had previously claimed to represent. By 2012, the combination of growing corruption, ideological stagnation and the contradictory role of capitalists and capitalism within the system—the increasingly awkward marriage of Communist Party rule with swashbuckling capitalism—was turning into a crisis of faith.

Many officials moved their families and ill-gotten assets abroad for safety. The practice became so common that it acquired its own epithet: the naked official (裸体官员 *luoti guanyuan* or *luoguan* for short), which referred to the fact that officials retained no possessions in China aside from the shirts on their back. Systemic corruption had produced a legitimacy crisis for the party in the public eye and a loss of faith in the party's mission among the rank and file. Xi understood that the party's future demanded a fix: it was time to tighten the controls.

Xi began his crackdown on corruption soon after taking office, determined to ferret out corrupt officials while stamping out behaviour that the public found repugnant such as conspicuous consumption and abuses of power by officials. Xi also used the campaign to eliminate political rivals such as former security tsar and Politburo Standing Committee member Zhou Yongkang—at the time the highest-ranking member of the party to be taken down on such charges since the Cultural Revolution. Xi did not stop there, displacing other rivals and internal critics and replacing them with his own loyalists. In consolidating his personal grip on power, Xi purposefully unravelled the power-sharing norms of elite consensus that had been in place since the Deng era. He then set about strengthening the party's organisational discipline and his own unassailable position at its apex. With the help of Wang Huning, Xi also placed fresh emphasis on ideology and ideological discipline. Xi determined that the party and nation needed a new set of core values to live by—values that extolled the virtues of both socialism and China's Confucian heritage. Those values are encapsulated in the Chinese Dream: the idea of the great rejuvenation of the Chinese nation, which the party is destined to lead. Party leaders have determined that the ideological discipline, shared vision and unified cultural identity needed to realise the Chinese Dream demands tighter political and social controls.

It is the purpose of this volume not just to examine the concepts, themes and actions behind the consolidation of single-party rule in China but also to situate the China case within comparative political studies. In chapter 2, 'The reshaping of the Chinese party-state under Xi Jinping's rule: A strong state led by a political strongman', Chien-wen Kou examines how Xi moved to entrench his power as China's new supreme leader, the most powerful since Mao, paying special attention to his 'political personality' and beliefs. Kou provides original insights into Xi's world view, sense of mission and leadership style by searching for their roots in his early life experiences and political thought. He also documents how Xi has expanded the party's control over the state and the state's control over society. His chapter introduces the themes that subsequent chapters examine in detail. Grounded in the literature on comparative authoritarianism, the chapter notes how Xi's turn to strongman rule in defiance of power-sharing norms has placed China outside most theoretical understandings of authoritarian resilience.

In chapter 3, 'What can comparative authoritarianism tell us about China under Xi Jinping (and vice versa)?', Hans H. Tung and Wen-Chin Wu ask what further the comparative literature on authoritarian resilience can tell us about how Xi governs China and what contemporary Chinese politics can tell us about authoritarianism more generally. They point out that although Deng Xiaoping is best known for his program of economic reform, he also made important adjustments to the architecture of power that facilitated party-state stability. Deng institutionalised power in the form of a balanced 'trinity': the General Secretary of the CPC, the State President and the Chairman of the Central Military Commission. Although someone could occupy all three posts, in the past this person was considered *primus inter parus* within the Politburo Standing Committee, and major policy portfolios were shared among its members. The President was constitutionally subject to a two-term limit (10 years in total). The positions of General Secretary of the CPC and the Chairman of the Central Military Commission are also subjected to two-term limits by informal convention. An agreed retirement age of 68 years also helped to regulate leadership succession. Deng's formal and informal institutional design enabled stable power-sharing among elite factions. This in turn provided the foundations for China's economic reforms, which included decentralised economic management and led to decades of dynamic economic growth.

Over time, decentralised economic management created new problems for party leaders. Not only did officials take personal advantage of the reforms they oversaw but also the regions appeared to be slipping out of control. As the popular refrain goes, 'above they have policies, below we have countermeasures' (上有政策，下有对策, *shang you zhengce, xia you duice*). Xi Jinping's anti-corruption campaign dominated the headlines of his first term. Accompanying the campaign were less noticed institutional and legal reforms designed to strengthen the party's vertical control over state officials. This tightening of administrative control is the subject of chapter 4, 'Controlling the cadres: Dual elite recruitment logic and political manipulation under Xi Jinping', by Chien-wen Kou and Wen-Hsuan Tsai. The authors examine Xi's attempt to consolidate the party's power over officialdom by introducing new criteria for cadre recruitment at both senior and grassroots levels. For the former, Xi emphasises 'comprehensive qualities' and has relaxed age limits, enabling him wide discretion to appoint loyalists. At the grassroots, the focus is on rejuvenation: the promoting and training of young and talented officials. The chapter addresses long-running debates about political control in China, including the relative influence of formal institutional controls versus informal ties and patronage. The authors show us that the two forces are not mutually exclusive, as Xi seeks to consolidate power by promoting loyalty at the top and performance at the grassroots.

The CPC's rigorous new training regime for grassroots cadres emphasises ideological correctness and imbibing the 'party spirit' (党性意识, *dang xing yishi*) (Tian & Tsai, 2021). This applies to the academic realm, too. In April 2013, the party's 'Communiqué on the Current State of the Ideological Sphere', popularly referred to as Document No. 9, warned that the party was in an existential struggle with Western liberal values. Among the 'false ideological trends, positions and activities' listed in the document were 'constitutional democracy' (which would subject the party to the restrictions laid out in the basic law), 'civil society' (described as a threat to the party's leadership of the masses), the notion of 'universal rights', 'freedom of the press', 'historical nihilism' (essentially, reassessing Chinese Communist Party history as a series of destructive mistakes) and 'neoliberal economics', which advocates for a reduced role for the state in the economy.

In chapter 5, 'More stick than carrot? Xi's policy towards establishment intellectuals', Florence W. Yang describes the ideological crackdown on universities that began soon after Xi took power. Yang documents the mechanisms through which the party tightened its grip on academic research and teaching. The 'malicious ideas' identified in Document No. 9 became the 'seven banned subjects' (七不讲, *qi bu jiang*). Party directives put universities on notice, demanding that professors serve as models of political virtue not just in the classroom but also in social media. If they fail, they might be subject to demotion, dismissal, forced retirement and even arrest. At the same time, Yang observes that 'carrots' are dangled in front of academics who express party-sanctioned perspectives, including research funding. The government provides lavish support to universities to promote the study of Xi Jinping Thought for the New Era as well as key policies such as the Belt and Road Initiative.

The media plays a central role in the party's 'thought work'. A rule from early in the reform era held that official media should publish at least 80 per cent 'positive content', with another 20 per cent allowed to include critical reports and commentary. Shuyu Zhang observes in chapter 6, '"Positive energy": The party's new approaches to censorship and media control', that throughout much of the reform era, the party's oversight bodies focused on censoring content that was unflattering or threatening to party legitimacy. Under Xi, an aggressive campaign around the promotion of 'positive energy' began to harness digital media to its purposes as well, including promoting positive stories about him as leader. Official newspapers such as the *People's Daily*—officially described as the party's 'throat and tongue'— became active posters on Weibo (China's version of Twitter) where they have amassed large followings and opened official accounts on WeChat as well. Zhang examines the sophisticated ways in which the party exercises control of public discourse on digital media, including social media, with less need for censors to intervene directly. The party has established a largely self-managed media carefully calibrated to party-sanctioned perspectives.

Domination of the digital sphere has been a hallmark of the party's latest 'tightening' and its broader shift to hard authoritarian rule. As Jean-Pierre Cabestan highlights in chapter 7, 'The state and digital society in China: Big Brother Xi is watching you!', the party has harnessed new technologies to expand surveillance and control, including smart ID cards, social credit systems and facial recognition. Such technologies are designed to consolidate the party's control over society and facilitate its ongoing hold on power. Cabestan describes these developments as 'part of an ambitious Orwellian project to micro-manage and micro-control every aspect of Chinese society'. He suggests that social credit and other surveillance systems make Chinese citizens 'the object of information' rather than subjects of communication. He also notes that the system, although powerful, is imperfect and challenged by technological limitations as well as citizens' concerns about privacy and data breaches. In 2021, the party introduced a new digital privacy law that addresses citizens' concerns about data theft and access to data stored by private companies. However, the law does not apply to state agencies. The Cyberspace Administration of China will oversee the implementation and enforcement of the new law, in contrast to Europe where similar laws are enforced by independent regulators. Cabestan forecasts a 'somewhat fragmented digitalised society and surveillance system that is more repressive in some localities and more flexible in others, as is the case with the Chinese bureaucracy in general'.

In chapter 8, 'Building a hyper-stability structure: The mechanisms of social stability maintenance in Xi's China', Hsin-Hsien Wang and Wei-Feng Tzeng continue the analysis of the party's application of power in the digital sphere. They argue that the party has consolidated its rule by building a hierarchical 'hyper-stability structure' to surveil and identify potential threats and shape public behaviours in accordance with party-sanctioned norms. Wang and Tzeng explore how the party's formidable digital powers have institutionalised and consolidated its autocratic rule. The authors focus on the evolution of the legal and institutional architecture of stability maintenance (维稳, *wei wen*—policing in all its forms) to the point where few aspects of life are outside the party's purview. Beginning with Xi's 'holistic approach to national security', they document how Xi centralised domestic security operations, offline and on, via the 2015 National Security Law and the Cyber Security Law of 2016 as well as the establishment in 2013 of a new National Security Commission (NSC). The NSC brings all security agencies under one umbrella and under the direct control of Xi Jinping as its chairman.

The authors note how the Xi administration has used other laws to tighten political and social controls, including making it a crime to 'spread rumours', which could include any public or private communication that the party disapproves of. Chinese citizens have been sentenced to prison for sending text messages or posting to social media about protests or issues that the party wants to keep a lid on. Famously, when Wuhan doctor Li Wenliang raised an alarm in a medical WeChat group about a new viral outbreak, he was summoned by police and instructed to stop 'making false comments' that had 'severely disturbed the social order'. He was one of several doctors reporting on the novel coronavirus outbreak who were subsequently investigated for spreading rumours (Hegarty, 2020).

Arguably, the biggest victims of the party's repression have been Chinese citizens from ethnically and religiously diverse backgrounds who do not conform to party-sanctioned values, including that of a uniform Chinese identity (Bulag, 2021). The party's crackdown on Xinjiang is the subject of chapter 9, 'Maintaining stability and China's "dual-track" counterterrorism strategy in Xinjiang', by Stefanie Kam. Kam documents the internal and external forces that have shaped Xi Jinping's Xinjiang policy, one that has incorporated extreme measures of repression and applied them to an entire population. In her analysis, coercion is a greater force than co-optation. The incarceration of Uyghurs en masse and the increased restrictions on religious expression highlight the CPC's ruthless determination to unify and mobilise the entire population behind its goals and to eliminate any form of deviance from party-sanctioned values and norms of behaviour.

The party's tightening of controls on religion more generally is the subject of chapter 10, 'Sinicisation or "xinicisation": Regulating religion and religious minorities under Xi Jinping', by Ray Wang. Wang observes that the CPC under Xi is taking a different approach from his predecessors. Just as Xinjiang repression targets an entire population, new religious controls target all practitioners and not just pockets of resistance within religious groups. Wang argues that the 'ultimate goal is to constrain and shrink the space of civic activism by adding both legal pressure on religious practitioners and political pressure on [religious] administrators'. Since Xi Jinping came to power, he has launched a policy of 'religious sinicisation' (宗教中国化, *zongjiao zhongguohua*), which Wang links to Chinese 'ultra-nationalism that puts party loyalty above anything else'. It combines internal purges, tough regulations and a radicalised version of the work done by the United Front Work Department, which supervises religious and other non-party social organisations to ensure their loyalty to the party, but without the objective to sinicise. Wang explains that the crackdown on religious groups is motivated by a belief of Xi and his fellows that the 'colour' and 'jasmine' revolutions were 'sparked or facilitated by faith-based actors'.

Wang's study also notes how the CPC uses the policy of religious sinicisation to cleanse its ranks of members with divided loyalties. In chapter 11, 'Revolutionary-style campaigns and social control in the PRC: The campaign to Sweep Away Black and Eliminate Evil', Ben Hillman identifies a similar crossover between political and social control in the context of the biggest campaign of Xi's second term. Promoted as a crackdown on organised crime, the campaign to 'Sweep Away Black and Eliminate Evil' also targeted the gangs' 'protective umbrellas' (保护伞, *baohu san*) in government and law enforcement agencies, thus overlapping with the anti-corruption campaign. As with the anti-corruption campaign, Sweep Away Black attacked personal networks that presented competing bases of power in the regions. In 2019, the campaign's scope was expanded to include eliminating social disorder (乱, *luan*) as a core objective, giving local officials and law enforcement wide latitude to police people's behaviour. Among the types of *luan* targeted by the campaign are popular protests. The CPC employs terms like 'black hand' or 'evil force' to dehumanise and delegitimise its critics and frame them as enemies of the state, whether they are local gangsters, pro-democracy protesters in Hong Kong or Tibetans demanding autonomy.

The Sweep Away Black campaign has served as one tool among many for political and social control in the latest cycle of tightening in the era of Xi Jinping. Xi is convinced that loosening control, including in the ideological and cultural sphere, will result in the CPC losing authority and ultimately power. He is therefore determined to shape the citizenry into loyal, obedient subjects who conform to party-sanctioned norms, values and practices. As mentioned earlier, no one is exempt. Property mogul Ren Zhiqiang was ousted from the party in 2020 for the 'severe violation of discipline and law' as a result of personal and cutting criticisms he made of Xi Jinping. The following year, the famous actress and director Zhao Wei disappeared along with her movies, fan sites and public-facing social media. Whatever the issues that are raised—tax evasion, for example—the real message is that even the livelihoods of the rich and famous ultimately depend on the party's good graces. The party tolerates celebrity and privilege only among those who sing from its hymn book.

By the time of the 20th National Congress of the CPC in October 2022, it was clear that the PRC was deep into tightening mode. The contributions to this volume show how political and social control shore up the party's monopoly over domestic political power. What is less clear is whether the pendulum might at some point swing back to a softer authoritarianism. The prospects for such change seem unlikely so long as Xi Jinping remains China's supreme leader, and it is possible that he will remain in power for another decade or longer. Under Xi, liberal voices are being comprehensively silenced, and political debate has been stifled to such an extent that it is difficult to identify any coalition of actors that might advocate for liberal reforms, let alone drive them. Liberal-leaning technocrats were expunged in the 2022 Congress, leaving only Xi loyalists in the upper echelons of power. It is conceivable that the CPC might relax its grip over some areas of social and economic activity, especially if it needs to do so to avoid the kind of economic downturn that would threaten its legitimacy. Yet the administrative, coercive and technological controls that the party has put in place since 2012 have helped it to consolidate its rule and will likely remain attractive to its leadership even beyond Xi Jinping's reign.

References

Baum, R. (1994) *Burying Mao: Chinese Politics in the Age of Deng Xiaoping*. Princeton University Press

Béja, J.H., Fu, H., & Pils, E. (eds) (2013) *Liu Xiaobo, Charter 08 and the Challenges of Political Reform in China*. Hong Kong University Press

Bloomberg (2021) 'China targets "effeminate" men in Xi's mounting push for conformity.' September. www.bloomberg.com/news/articles/2021-09-20/china-slams-effeminate-men-in-xi-s-mounting-push-for-conformity

Buckley, C. (2022) 'Trial looms after seaside gathering of Chinese activists.' *Japan Times*, 9 January. www.japantimes.co.jp/news/2022/01/09/asia-pacific/crime-legal-asia-pacific/trial-seaside-gathering-chinese-activists/

Bulag, U. (2021) 'Minority nationalities as Frankenstein's monsters? Reshaping "the Chinese nation" and China's quest to become a "normal country."' *China Journal* 86 (July) 46–67. doi.org/10.1086/714737

Carson, B. (host) (2018) 'Jaw-Jaw' [audio podcast]. *War on the Rocks*, 11 December. warontherocks.com/2018/12/jaw-jaw-vicious-cycle-the-opening-and-closing-of-chinese-politics

Chen, S.W., & Lau, S.W. (2021) 'Little red children and "Grandpa Xi": China's school textbooks reflect the rise of Xi Jinping's personality cult.' *ABC News*, 25 November. www.abc.net.au/news/2021-11-25/chinese-school-textbooks-reflect-rise-of-xi-personality-cult/100640642

He, X. (2021) *Divorce in China: Institutional Constraints and Gendered Outcomes*. New York University Press

Hegarty, S. (2020) 'The Chinese doctor who tried to warn others about coronavirus.' *BBC News*, 6 February. www.bbc.com/news/world-asia-china-51364382

Hillman, B. (2010) 'Factions and spoils: Examining political behavior within the local state in China.' *China Journal* (64) 1–18. doi.org/10.1086/tcj.64.20749244

—— (2014) *Patronage and Power: Local State Networks and Party–State Resilience in Rural China*. Stanford University Press

Hillman, B., & Tuttle, G. (eds) (2016) *Ethnic Conflict and Protest in Tibet and Xinjiang: Unrest in China's West*. Columbia University Press

Jaivin, L. (2021) 'Little pinks and their achy breaky hearts.' *Inside Story*, 3 December. insidestory.org.au/little-pinks-and-their-achy-breaky-hearts

Kuo, K. (host) (2022) 'Sinica' [audio podcast]. *SupChina*, 7 January. supchina.com/podcast/personality-and-political-discontent-in-china-with-rory-truex

Lin, D., & Trevaskes, S. (2019) 'Creating a virtuous leviathan: The party, law and socialist core values.' *Asian Journal of Law and Society* 6(1): 41–66. doi.org/10.1017/als.2018.41

Nee, W. (2021) 'China's 709 crackdown is still going on.' *The Diplomat*, 9 July. thediplomat.com/2021/07/chinas-709-crackdown-is-still-going-on

Pei, M. (2016) *China's Crony Capitalism: The Dynamics of Regime Decay.* Harvard University Press

Shambaugh, D. (2018) 'Contemplating China's future.' *Journal of Chinese Political Science* 23(1): 1–7. doi.org/10.1007/s11366-017-9491-x

Steinhardt, H.C., & Wu, F. (2016) 'In the name of the public: Environmental protest and the changing landscape of popular contention in China.' *China Journal* 75(1): 61–82. doi.org/10.1086/684010

Tian, G. & Tsai, W. (2021) 'Ideological education and practical training at a county party school: Shaping local governance in contemporary China.' *China Journal* 85 (January) 1–25. doi.org/10.1086/711562

Wedeman, A. (2012) *Double Paradox: Rapid Growth and Rising Corruption in China.* Cornell University Press

Zhongguo Zhengfu Wang [中国政府网] (2019) 'Yange kongzhi wei chengnian ren shiyong wangluo youxi shiduan, shichang' [严格控制未成年人使用网络游戏时段、时长, Strictly control the periods and duration of the use of online games by minors]. 11 November. www.gov.cn/fuwu/2019-11/11/content_545 0800.htm

—— (2021) 'Zhonggong zhongyang bangong ting guowuyuan bangong ting yinfa Guanyu jinyibu jianqing yiwu jiaoyu jieduan xuesheng zuoye fudan he xiaowai peixun fudan de yijian' [中共中央办公厅国务院办公厅引发《关于进一步减轻义务教育阶段学生作业负担和校外培训负担的意见》, General Office of the Central Committee of the Communist Party of China and the General Office of the State Council issue the Opinion on further reducing the burden of students' homework and extracurricular training in compulsory education]. 24 July. www.gov.cn/zhengce/2021-07/24/content_5627132.htm

Zhonghua Renmin Gongheguo Jiaoyubu [中华人民共和国教育部, Ministry of Education of the People's Republic of China] (2021) 'Xijinping xin shidai zhongguo tese shehui zhuyi sixiang xuesheng duben yu jinnian qiuji xueqi qi zai quanguo tongyi shiyong' [《习近平新时代中国特色社会主义思想学生读本》于今年秋季学期起在全国统一使用, Xi Jinping Thought on Socialism with Chinese Characteristics for a New Era student reader will be used nationwide from this autumn semester]. 8 July. www.moe.gov.cn/jyb_xwfb/gzdt_gzdt/s5987/202107/t20210708_543195.html

2

The reshaping of the Chinese party-state under Xi Jinping's rule: A strong state led by a political strongman

Chien-wen Kou

Xi Jinping (习近平) has been reshaping the party-state and state–society relations in China since 2012 at the height of a recentralisation of power. Why did he do so, how did he succeed and what has it done to the regime? Studies of China and authoritarian states must seek out the nature, cause and impact of these changes.

This chapter claims that political changes in the Xi era can be summarised by three intertwined but distinguishable trends: (1) a return to strongman rule, (2) an expansion of the authority of the Communist Party of China (CPC) and (3) a reinforcement of state control over society. Each of these involves changes that herald the revival of a strong state led by a political strongman.

This chapter further argues that while environmental factors have affected his efforts to grasp power, Xi Jinping's political personality has been pivotal in his alteration of the party-state, and the literature has yet to address the psychology behind his decisions. Xi came to power under increasingly complicated international and domestic challenges that called for a strong leader. These included tensions between the United States and China, sovereignty disputes in the South and East China seas, declining economic growth, cadre corruption, social inequality and social unrest in Tibet and Xinjiang. The Wang Lijun (王立军) incident triggered an upheaval among the party's top leaders, while the waning influence of Jiang Zeming (江泽民) and Hu Jintao (胡锦涛) unbound Xi's structural constraints, all the more amplifying the influence of his political personality.

By conducting a text mining analysis of the use of the phrase *douzheng* (斗争, struggle) in his public statements, this chapter presents Xi's thinking on the conflictual nature of politics, his beliefs in his destiny in China's national rejuvenation and socialist construction, and his preference for strong leadership in the face of political challenges. His thinking and beliefs have driven him to violate power-sharing practices and to prefer political coercion over social co-optation, while the centralisation of power gives him the leverage to meet the nation's challenges and to crush his rivals. Naturally, this poses new risks to the regime.

This chapter is divided into seven sections. The first section 'China and comparative authoritarianism' summarises the most recent mainstream argument of the literature on comparative authoritarianism and argues for China's importance as a case. The second, third and fourth sections provide an overview of the political landscape in China under Xi's rule. The second section, 'A return to strongman rule', discusses the recentralisation of power under a single leader; the third section, 'The expansion of the CPC's authority', outlines how the CPC apparatus diminished the government's role in the political process; and the fourth section, 'The reinforcement of state control over society', focuses on state control over society. The fifth section, 'Xi's circumstances within and without the CPC', describes the context in which Xi came to power. The last two sections focus on psychological factors. The sixth section, 'Xi's world view, historic mission and leadership style', presents Xi's world view, perceived destiny and style of leadership, while the seventh section, 'The formation of Xi's political cognition and beliefs', explains how early life experiences have shaped his political thinking and beliefs.

China and comparative authoritarianism: From a typical to a deviant case

The recent literature on comparative authoritarianism claims that institutions serve to monitor the commitments of autocrats. Authoritarian regimes with greater political institutionalisation last longer and perform better economically (Boix & Svolik, 2013; de Mesquita et al., 2003; Gandhi,

2008; Magaloni, 2008; Slater & Fenner, 2011), challenging the idea that this can be done only with democratic institutions. Autocrats may arbitrarily withhold the personal freedoms and properties of the selectorate, those who participate in the selection of leaders, without institutional constraints. They may also do so to ordinary citizens, who are disenfranchised entirely from the process of selecting leaders. Nevertheless, autocrats are constantly threatened by rebellion among their allies and revolution among their citizens.

Some autocrats rely on power-sharing to avoid rebellion and social co-optation to avoid revolution (see figure 2.1). To acquire and retain power, they build a majority coalition in the selectorate by sharing power. Power-sharing institutions represent the commitment of autocrats to constrain their use of power, and the balance among various factions and bureaucracies makes for a non-zero-sum game between them and their allies. Autocrats can still employ coercion to punish selectorate members who oppose them or shape the atmosphere of severe external challenges to maintain coalition solidarity. Yet the over-centralisation of power in the hands of an autocrat will eventually break down these institutions, and elite politics will inevitably become those of a political strongman.

Autocrats also face the threat of revolution. Disenfranchised citizens might rise when resentment boils over from abuses of power and rampant corruption among political elites. In addition to coercing citizens, autocrats could win their support through social co-optation or collusion. This can be done by means of revenue allocation and personnel arrangements like fiscal subsidies, jobs, social welfare, investment from state-owned enterprises and political recruitments for all or specific social groups.

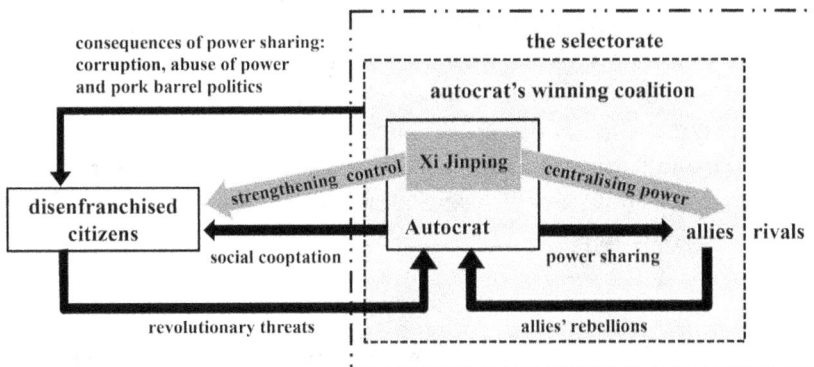

Figure 2.1: Xi's China and comparative authoritarianism: A deviant case
Source: Created by the author.

Owing to their limited resources, autocrats seldom fully implement both power-sharing and social co-optation for long. Some power-sharing practices like tolerating corruption and privileges among their cadres often result in strong social discontent. Accordingly, autocrats must still attend to their citizens to avoid revolution, sometimes at the expense of the selectorate. They must therefore constantly balance power-sharing and social co-optation to secure their rule.

The literature often treats post-1978 China as a successful case of power-sharing in single-party regimes (Gehlbach & Keefer, 2011; Svolik, 2012). Such practices within the CPC's top leadership—the Politburo and its Standing Committee (PBSC)—include collective leadership, age limits, term limits and term integrity, succession by echelon, step-by-step promotion and the exemption of serving and retired PBSC members from prosecution (Kou, 2010, pp. 267–357; Li, 2016, pp. 83–94). In the early 1980s, Deng and other veteran leaders upheld a combination of collective leadership and the division of labour with individual responsibility (集体领导与个人分工相结合, *jiti lingdao yu geren fengong xiangjiehe*) to prevent a return to the over-centralisation of power in the Mao Zedong (毛泽东) era. Power-sharing became institutionalised from Deng Xiaoping (邓小平) to Hu Jintao during a conversion from strongman to oligarchical rule that began in the 1980s.

The CPC oligarchy in Jiang's and Hu's eras was structured with the general secretary as a consensus builder and the first among equals. The vote of each leader carries equal weight when they cast votes to settle controversial issues (Lam, 2015, pp. xii–xiii). Consultation, negotiation and compromise are thereby necessary before a major decision is made, and any move on the part of the general secretary to monopolise power will run up against these structural constraints.[1] This explains how their rule was marked by new rules and precedents of power-sharing while cadre corruption, pork-barrel politics and the abuse of power became rampant at the same time. In this way, oligarchical rule maintains collective leadership as a power-sharing institution, and an increase in a single leader's power threatens the stability of collective leadership.

---

1   Jiang and Hu could not promote enough trustees to the PBSC and the Politburo to form a majority when they held the office of general secretary. One example of these limitations was Jiang's failed attempt in 1997 to establish a National Security Committee that was modelled after the National Security Council of the United States. When this was opposed by his colleagues in the top leadership, he instead established a National Security SLG (Takungpao, 2013a).

In the early 1980s Deng also called for a distinction between the responsibilities of the party and those of the government (党政分开, *dang zheng fenkai*). He held that the CPC should focus on long-range goals and planning, personnel recommendations, ideological indoctrination work and supervision while day-to-day governance should be left to professional administrators in the State Council and local governments. Its relationship with the judicial system, state-owned enterprises and mass organisations would follow a similar pattern. While the CPC stopped promoting this concept after the Tiananmen tragedy of 1989, its role continued to be one of political, ideological and organisational leadership. The State Council was instrumental in the socioeconomic policies of the 1990s and 2000s. Day-to-day decisions on these issues were made and implemented by the premier while the general secretary had the final say, as in the case of both Zhu Rongji (朱镕基) and Wen Jiabao (温家宝).

Political institutionalisation is a process whereby political actors come to accept the rules, norms and procedures of the allocation and transfer of power. The power structures might or might not reinforce the stability of these political institutions. A dramatic change in the distribution of power among major political actors can render enforcement ineffective and threaten institutions. Since 2012, Xi has begun to break down many of the aforementioned power-sharing practices and strengthen state control over society.

It should be noted that the CPC has been maintaining control through both repression and many forms of social co-optation, one of which is his policy of targeted poverty alleviation (精准扶贫, *jingzhun fupin*). Nevertheless, his relative preference for coercion differs significantly from Hu Jintao.[2] With this stark deviation from precedent, China has turned from a typical case like those described in the literature into a deviant one that stands in contrast to it.

---

2   The author would like to thank a reviewer for the suggestion that the CPC often takes advantage of self-censorship through fear to achieve political stability. In this case, the use of threats may be more effective than brutal coercion.

A return to strongman rule

Since 2012, Xi has taken three measures to concentrate power either in his own hands or in the office of the top leader, a trinity of party, state and military leadership.[3] His first measure was a series of large-scale personnel reshufflings by which his rivals were purged and his trustees rapidly came to occupy key positions. Although both Jiang and Hu had adopted similar strategies in moves such as the purge of Chen Xitong (陈希同) and Chen Liangyu (陈良宇) and the promotion of the Shanghai clique and Youth League affiliates, the oligarchical power structure at work during their time in office prevented them from achieving the centralisation of power to the extent that Xi has.

From December 2012 to May 2021, 392 high-ranking cadres and officers who were either retired or in service at the deputy minister (副部级, *fubuji*) or deputy group army levels (副军级, *fujunji*) and above were taken down either for corruption or violations of discipline (Zhang, 2021). Eleven Party and state leaders have been toppled between 1992 and the present, eight of whom were ousted after 2012.[4] The ousting of Sun Zhengcai, one of the two youngest 18th Politburo members and a frontrunner of post-Xi generation leaders, and Zhou Yongkang shows a lack of exemption from prosecution and succession by echelon, two common power-sharing practices in the PBSC.

After the 20th Party Congress in October 2022, four key Youth League affiliates were fully retired or transferred to less important posts. Li Keqiang (李克强) (premier) and Wang Yang (汪洋) (chairman of the National Committee of the Chinese People's Political Consultative Conference, NPPCC) were both 19th PBSC members and retired at the age of 67. Vice Premier Hu Chunhua (胡春华), the youngest 19th Politburo member, and Zhou Qiang (周强), president of the Supreme People's Court, were reassigned to be powerless vice chairmen of the NPPCC at the ages of 60 and 63, respectively. Li, Hu and Zhou were former first secretaries

---

3   The office of the top leader should be distinguished from Xi as an individual because, while positional power can transfer from one to another, this is not the case with personal authority.

4   They are Chen Xitong (removed in 1995), Cheng Kejie (成克杰, removed in 2000), Chen Liangyu (removed in 2006), Bo Xilai (薄熙来, fell in 2012), Zhou Yongkang (周永康, removed in 2013), Xu Caihou (徐才厚, removed in 2014), Su Rong (苏荣, removed in 2014), Ling Jihua (令计划, removed in 2014), Guo Boxiong (郭伯雄, removed in 2015), Sun Zhengcai (孙政才, removed in 2017) and Yang Jing (杨晶, removed in 2018).

of the Communist Youth League of China. Youth League affiliates usually belonged to Hu Jintao's faction because Hu served as head of the league in the early 1980s.

Meanwhile, several elite groups that had close ties with Xi at various stages in his life have been promoted to important posts. These connections include revolutionary family backgrounds and ties to a school, home province or organisation.[5] Within the 25-member 19th Politburo, two PBSC members and 12 Politburo members belong to one of these elite groups.[6] These 14 individuals include the party secretaries of Beijing, Shanghai, Chongqing and Guangdong; the heads of the Central Discipline Inspection Commission (CDIC), the Central Organisation Department, the Central Propaganda Department and the Central General Office; and the two vice chairmen of the Central Military Commission (CMC). Within the seven-member 20th PBSC, all of the four new members who were promoted in the 20th Party Congress had strong connections with Xi. They are Li Qiang (premier), Cai Qi (director of the Central General Office), Ding Xuexiang (executive vice premier) and Li Xi (secretary of the CDIC).

The career paths of Cai Qi and Wang Qishan (王岐山) indicate a weakening of power-sharing practices. Cai Qi received six appointments between November 2013 and October 2017, rapidly advancing from the deputy minister level to the deputy party and state leader level in violation of the common practice of step-by-step promotions. Cai is the third Politburo member after Tan Shaowen (谭绍文) and Ceng Qinghong (曾庆红) since 1978 who did not hold a Central Committee (CC) full or alternate membership for at least one term before obtaining the seat. His promotion to be a PBSC member in 2022 and appointment to head the Central General Office in 2023 made him rank higher than the heads of other functional departments of the CPC. He is likely to be the no. 2 person after Xi in handling party affairs. Wang Qishan's election as vice president of the PRC in March 2018 at the age of 69 weakened the practice of age restrictions whereby party and state leaders do not seek another term after reaching 68 years of age.

---

5   For more discussion of Xi's connections with his trusties, see Wu (2019).
6   They are Li Zhanshu (栗战书), Zhao Leji (赵乐际), Ding Xuexiang (丁薛祥), Wang Chen (王晨), Liu He ((刘鹤), Xu Qiliang (许其亮), Li Xi (李希), Li Qiang (李强), Yang Xiaodu (杨晓渡), Zhang Youxia (张又侠), Chen Xi (陈希), Chen Min'er (陈敏尔), Huang Kunming (黄坤明) and Cai Qi (蔡奇).

Xi's second measure was to reinforce the power of the top leader by strengthening the office of the general secretary through 'rule by leading small groups' (LSGs) (小组治国, *xiaozu zhiguo*). Capable of cross-bureaucratic coordination among the CPC central organs and the ministries of the State Council, central LSGs determine policy guidance for subordinate bureaucratic systems and dominate in policy-making. The expansion in the role and number of central LSGs has been a profound change to institutions under Xi's rule. Xi headed three ongoing central LSGs and seven newly formed ones (see table 2.1), four of which were upgraded to commissions in March 2018. This strengthened their decision-making power and endowed them with the authority to issue official documents and orders to government agencies (Wu, 2018). According to the latest reforms of party and state institutions in March 2023, the CPC will establish two new central commissions: the Central Commission for Technology and the Central Commission for Finance.

Table 2.1: Major central LSGs and commissions headed or likely to be headed by Xi

LSGs/commissions	Year of establishment	Year upgraded to commission
Central LSG for Taiwan Affairs	July 1954	
Central Commission for Financial and Economic Affairs	March 1980	March 2018
Central Commission for Foreign Affairs	1981	March 2018
Central Commission for National Security	November 2013	
Central Commission for Deepening Overall Reform (全面深化改革, quanmian shenhua gaige)	December 2013	March 2018
Central Commission for Cyberspace Affairs	February 2014	March 2018
CMC LSG for Deepening National Defence and Military Reform	March 2014	
Central Commission for Military–Civil Fusion and Development (军民融合发展, junmin ronghe fazhan)	January 2017	
Central Commission for Comprehensive Law-based Governance (依法治国, yifa zhiguo)	March 2018	
Central Commission for Auditing	March 2018	
Central Commission for Technology	March 2023	

Source: Created by the author.

By establishing work report institutions, Xi placed the general secretary in authority over other PBSC members. In October 2017, the Politburo passed the CPC Politburo's Regulations on Strengthening and Maintaining the Centralised and Unified Leadership of the Party Centre (中共中央政治局关于加强和维护党中央集中统一领导的若干规定, *zhonggong zhongyang zhengzhiju guanyu jiaqiang he weihu dangzhongyang jizhong tongyi lingdao de ruogan guiding*). The regulations required that all top organs of the party-state submit work reports to the Politburo and the PBSC annually. Politburo and PBSC members were urged to 'proactively report major issues to the Party Centre for deliberation' and to 'submit an annual written self-evaluation of their job performance to the Party Centre and the general secretary'. In March 2018, Politburo members vowed to uphold Xi's centrality as 'the supreme political principle' and 'the fundamental political protocol' in their first self-evaluations. Xi reviewed these evaluations and responded with his comments and requirements. In February 2019, the Politburo issued the Code on Seeking Instructions and Reporting on Important Matters (重大事项请示报告条例, *zhongda shixiang qingshi baogao tiaoli*), urging lower-level cadres and party organisations to consult the next higher-ranking party organisation before making key decisions. Owing to the broad definition of 'important matters', the code limited the discretion of lower-level cadres and party organisations (Pei, 2019, pp. 6–7).

The office of the CMC chairman has also been reinforced. In March 2014, Xi established and led the CMC LSG for National Defence and Military Reform. In late October 2014, the Chinese military's media began referring to the implementation of the CMC chairman responsibility system. In January 2016, the military command chain underwent a fundamental restructuring and stepped up checks and balances within the PLA, with 15 new CMC organs now under the direct command of the CMC.

In March 2018, Xi abolished the constitutional two-term limit on the state president. Although the president of the PRC is a titular head, it is the only post with a formal term limit among the top party, state and military positions. This amendment makes Xi eligible to serve a third term in 2022 and proves that he has been able to destroy formal power-sharing rules.

The third measure was to establish Xi's dominance in official ideology and political discourse. In communist systems, official ideology dictates the party line and acts as the arena for power competition. The insertion of Xi's ideas into official ideology has promoted his personal authority and helped to start a cult of personality. In October 2016, the CPC formally called on all party members 'to closely unite around Comrade Xi Jinping as the core of the CPC Central Committee'. While the CPC continues to mention collective leadership in official documents, Xi is more powerful than the other PBSC members because he is 'the core of the Party in thought, politics and actions' (Mingpao, 2016). Xi Jinping Thought was added to the Party Charter in October 2017 and the PRC Constitution in March 2018. Xi has become the third top leader of China to have his name written into official ideology and the second to achieve this while still in power.

The expansion of the CPC's authority

Although the CPC's dominion over political life is not a new development in China, it has been implemented under Xi's rule in a way that has been unprecedented since the 1990s. In the name of party–government integration, Xi created a new governance system in which the CPC absorbs government bodies and their policy jurisdictions. He has given clout to the CPC central organs in several ways while weakening the State Council. The first method was 'rule by LSGs', addressed in the previous section. This expansion in the role and number of central LSGs has both boosted the office of the general secretary and empowered the CPC central organs to participate directly in decision-making in wider policy domains.

Xi also broke down the division of labour between the CPC and the State Council. When he came to power in 2012, it became unclear who had the say in economic affairs when Xi and Premier Li Keqiang (李克强) offered different directions for the country's economic policies. For instance, 'Likonomics' (李克强经济学, *li keqiang jingji xue*) in 2013 seemed to run at odds with the 'New Normal' (新常态, *xin changtai*) in 2014. In May 2016, an article by a 'person of authority' again revealed contradictory judgements at the top leadership on economic conditions in China and the direction of its economic policies. All of these things indicated a weakening of the influence of Li and the State Council on economic issues (Naughton, 2016a, 2016b).

Meanwhile, Xi restressed the leadership of the CPC through legalisation and organisational restructuring. In January 2016, the PBSC emphasised that 'the party leads in everything' (党是领导一切的, *dang shi lingdao yiqie de*), and the principle was inserted in the Party Charter in October 2017. Issued in October 2020, the Work Regulations of the Central Committee of the Communist Party of China (中国共产党中央委员会工作条例,

zhongguo gongchan dang zhongyang weiyuanhui gongzuo tiaoli) specified the status and functions of CPC leading bodies and emphasised the importance of firmly safeguarding the Central Committee's authority and centralised, unified leadership.

In March 2018, the National People's Congress (NPC) approved the Plan to Deepen the Reform of Party and State Institutions (深化党和国家机构改革方案, *Shenhua dang he guojia jigou gaige fang'an*), which required increasing the CPC's control over major initiatives. It aimed to strengthen the leadership of CPC committees over other organisations at the same administrative level, task CPC functional departments with coordinating with other institutions in the same sector and even merge or work together as one office (合署办公, *heshu bangong*) while keeping separate identities. A major difference between the institutional reforms of 2018 and the previous seven from 1982 to 2013 has been the functional integration of governmental agencies into CPC departments, empowering the latter with a broader policy jurisdiction, bigger budgets and more personnel. The expansion of the CPC apparatus has further empowered the general secretary and weakened the premier.

For example, the jurisdictions of the CPC functional departments in charge of united front work, personnel and propaganda were all expanded after 2018. The Overseas Chinese Affairs Office and the State Bureau for Religious Affairs were merged into the CPC Central United Front Work Department and the State Ethnic Affairs Commission was placed under its leadership. The State Bureau of Civil Service was merged into the CPC Central Organisation Department. The State Administration of Press, Publication, Radio, Film and Television was reorganised into the State Administration of Radio, Film and Television while its jurisdiction in publication and film was transferred to the CPC Central Propaganda Department. As China's highest anti-corruption agency, the National Supervisory Commission has worked together with the CDIC as one office since its establishment in March 2018, giving the latter a legal channel to investigate officials without CPC membership.

The expansion of the CPC's authority continued after the 20th Party Congress in 2022. It appeared that the CPC under Xi's leadership treated the centralisation of power as a necessary instrument to face future international and domestic challenges. According to the Plan of the Reform of Party and State Institutions (党和国家机构改革方案, *Dang he guojia jigou gaige fang'an*) in March 2023, the CPC will establish two new central commissions for technology and finance, the Central Social Work Department, and the Central Hong Kong and Macau Affairs Office. In the meanwhile, the jurisdiction of Hong Kong and Macau affairs will be transferred from the State Council to the party. The CPC Central Social Work Department has a 'unified leadership' over the National Public Complaints and Proposals Administration of the State Council.

In the same month, the State Council issued a revised version of its working rules. The new version further consolidated decision-making power in the party apparatus while leaving execution and implementation primarily to the State Council (Zheng, 2023). The new working rules request the State Council to safeguard the authority of the party's leadership led by Xi, to implement the work laid out at the 20th Party Congress, to report and seek instructions from the party regarding major decisions, and to arrange special learning sessions to review Xi's latest speeches, instructions and requirements.

The reinforcement of state control over society

Xi has also sought to crush social collective action by removing its coordination networks, funding and information flows and content. This is because the principle that 'the party leads in everything' is challenged by the very existence of a civil society. The Xi era has seen much tighter state control over NGOs, the internet, mass media, education, ethnic minorities, religion and social protest than the Hu era.[7] The 709 crackdown begun on 9 July 2015 was a planned use of state violence to crush civil society. Since human rights lawyers are tasked with fighting arbitrary power for the protection of individual rights, they naturally turned to leaders of socio-legal activism and were perceived by the party-state as potential threats (Fu, 2018, pp. 554–5; Fu & Zhu, 2018).

The sinicisation of religion is another example. The CPC has rigorously constrained religious activities to ensure that they are patriotic and adaptive to socialist society (Madsen, 2019; Yang, 2021) The imperative of religious sinicisation and greater state supervision was formally presented in Xi's

---

7   Grassroots officials in the Hu era often made material concessions to pacify aggrieved people in labour, rights and property disputes by providing cash payments or urgent services and utilities (C.K. Lee & Zhang, 2013, pp. 1485–95).

speech at the CPC National Conference on Religious Work in April 2016. In April 2017, the State Council revised the Religious Affairs Regulations (宗教事务条例, *zongjiao shiwu tiaoli*) to exercise more sophisticated control. In February 2021, the State Religion Bureau issued the Measures on the Management of Religious Professionals (宗教教职人员管理办法, *zongjiao jiaozhi renyuan guanli banfa*), prohibiting religious preaching and teaching that endangers national security and the promotion of extremism and separatism. They have also required that clergy resist the infiltration of foreign forces through their religions.

The CPC has gone further to block overseas support to Chinese NGOs and social activists. The PRC's Law on the Management of the Activities of Overseas NGOs within the Territory of China (中华人民共和国境外非政府组织境内活动管理法, *zhonghua renmin gongheguo jingwai feizhengfu zuzhi jingnei huodong guanli fa*) of January 2017 required overseas NGOs to register with the Ministry of Public Security and disclose their sources of funding for activities in China. Several overseas NGOs stopped operating inside China as a result, and many local NGOs and activists lost their overseas financial support (Kojima, 2020, p. 9, fn. 7).

The control of the flow and content of information is another instrument to prevent the growth of civil society. The CPC began to attack Western democratic values and uphold socialism soon after Xi took power. In April 2013, a confidential document issued by the CPC Central General Office indicated seven political dangers in the ideological sphere and urged that the news media had to be controlled by those who closely sided with the CPC under Xi's leadership (Buckley, 2013).[8] Xi emphasised in the National Propaganda and Ideology Work Conference of August 2013 that ideological propaganda work was vital for the CPC and its goal was to secure the guidance of Marxism. Since then, the party has constricted the freedom of expression on the internet and elsewhere through a variety of legal and technological means.

For example, the Supreme People's Court released an official interpretation in September 2013 that any libellous posts or messages would be considered severe crimes if they were clicked on or browsed more than 5,000 times or forwarded more than 500 times. The Cyber Security Law (网络安全

---

8   The seven dangers were Western constitutional democracy, universal values of human rights, civil society, pro-market neo-liberalism, media independence, historical nihilism and scepticism towards the nature of socialism with Chinese characteristics.

法, *wanglu anquan fa*) of June 2017 legalised the CPC's call to defend its sovereignty in cyberspace by defining the security obligations of internet product and service providers, establishing a security system for key information infrastructure, regulating the transnational transmission of data from critical information infrastructures and establishing a real-name system for the internet. From 2017 to 2018, the government sequentially enacted the Internet News Information Service Management Regulations (互联网新闻信息服务管理规定, *hulianwang xinwen xinxi fuwu guanli guiding*), the Internet Comment Service Management Regulations (互联网跟帖评论服务管理规定, *hulianwang gentie pinglun fuwu guanli guiding*) and the Microblog Information Service Management Regulations (微博客信息服务管理规定, *weiboke xinxi fuwu guanli guiding*). The CPC has built up a complex and hierarchical management system with sophisticated procedures to censor cyber public opinion online (Tsai, 2016). It has also engaged in a participatory form of propaganda through a digital revamping of official media, the expansion of governmental Weibo and the official promotion of patriotic bloggers (Repnikova & Fang, 2018).

New technology has been adapted to control cyberspace and expanded to other parts of social control in such forms as the social credit system, DNA collection, the Skynet project, health codes and a grid-style social management system. Technological authoritarianism has gained the attention of China watchers. These projects are based on big data, cloud computing, artificial intelligence, biometrics and related technologies. While providing crime prevention and other public services, they also enhance the state's capacity to surveil society. Skynet, for instance, is an image surveillance system that incorporates GIS maps, image acquisition and other tools to perform real-time monitoring and information recording in a given region. The social credit system classifies citizens into various credit ratings, which offer them different treatment and restrictions.

Meanwhile, the CPC's penetration of organisations outside the government has been reinforced by requiring them to establish leading party groups (党组, *dangzu*) and party branches (党支部, *dangzhibu*). For example, the Plan to Deepen the Reform of Party and State Institutions in March 2018 called for strengthening CPC leadership over other organisations by writing the principle into their charters. The CPC passed a trial version of the Work Regulations on Leading Party Groups (中国共产党党组工作条例, *zhongguo gongchandang dangzu gongzuo tiaoli*) in June 2015 and revised them in April 2019. The regulations required that a leading party group be established in central and local state institutions and economic, cultural and social organisations with more than three CPC members in their top echelons. The CPC's Work Regulations on Party Branches (Trial) (中国共产党支部工作条例 (试行), *zhongguo gongchandang zhibu gongzuo tiaoli* [*shixing*]) of November 2018 required the establishment of party branches in enterprises where there were more than three CPC members working in any specific enterprise.

Xi's circumstances within and without the CPC

After describing these three political changes in the Xi era, this chapter now turns to their underlying causes. If power-sharing and social co-optation had once been self-reinforcing, why and how did their lock-in effects break down in the Xi era? Political leaders do not make decisions in a vacuum. The character, world view and personal style that comprise a leader's personality fit together, interacting with the power structure and national climate of expectations at the time the leader serves (Barber, 1992, pp. 4–7). Psychological factors are likely to be crucial to political outcomes (1) when institutional design or charismatic influence places power in the hands of political leaders; (2) when leaders have strong interests; or (3) when the nation is perceived to have become unstable so that past rules, practices and norms do not apply to its current circumstances (Greenstein, 1969, pp. 33–62).

Starting from the above studies, this chapter claims that an explanation of political changes in Xi's China should address three issues: first, whether China's past challenges created expectations for a strong leader; second, whether the power structure at the top leadership of the CPC had failed to constrain Xi's rise; and third, whether Xi's political thinking saw the recentralisation of power as the way to achieve his goals. The first two issues concern Xi's circumstances within and without the CPC while the last concerns his inner world. Xi's psyche has guided his choices while his circumstances have amplified his influence. This chapter shall begin with these circumstances and discuss his political personality in the sections to follow.

China faced more severe international and domestic challenges in 2012 than in 2002, and all emerged before the 18th Party Congress in October 2012. China experienced a structural transformation in US–China relations and the escalation of territorial disputes with Japan, the Philippines and Vietnam. The Obama administration began to announce a new strategy towards Asia in the fall of 2011, known as a 'pivot to Asia' or 'rebalancing towards the Asia Pacific' (Clinton, 2011; Obama, 2011). The United States made the shift in its strategy official in January 2012 (US Department of Defense, 2012). US–China relations have deteriorated throughout the Trump and Biden administrations and are now at the risk of falling into a Thucydides trap. The dispute over the Diaoyu/Senkaku Islands intensified after April 2012, and the Scarborough Shoal stand-off broke out in the same month. In June 2012, Vietnam repeated its sovereignty claims over the Paracel Islands and Spratly Islands by passing the Vietnam Maritime Law. While these territorial disputes have persisted for decades, it was uncharacteristic for these disputes to escalate almost at the same time as the CPC top leadership was undergoing a generational replacement.

China before the 18th Party Congress had also confronted domestic challenges like declining economic growth, social inequality, environmental pollution, food safety, cadre corruption and ethnic unrest in Tibet and Xinjiang. Many China watchers had noted these challenges in 2012 (Dyer, 2012; Naughton, 2012). These problems had triggered anti-rich (仇富, *choufu*) and anti-cadre (仇官, *chouguan*) sentiments in society (Aisixiang, 2011). Intellectuals were also divided over their causes and remedies (Chen, 2004; Shi, François & Galway, 2018). At the same time, the CPC's collective leadership under Hu Jintao became uncoordinated during his second term in office (Li, 2016, p. 14; Miller, 2012). While the institutionalisation of power-sharing helped keep the regime stable, a fumbling in both the top leadership and the bureaucracy hindered any major reforms. For example, bureaucratic interests hindered the integration of the Ministry of Railways into the newly established Ministry of Transport in 2008 despite the State Council having set a tone of 'giant department reforms' (大部制改革, *dabuzhi gaige*). Some called for installing a new organisation to coordinate them, while others went so far as to label the Hu era the 'lost decade' (S. Lee, 2017, p. 328; Li, 2016, p. 24).

The fear of chaos is central in Chinese political culture. Both the citizenry and high-ranking party elites expect their leaders to sustain national unity, stability and the survival of the regime (Dickson, 2016, pp. 243–4; Guo,

2019, pp. 4, 179, 318–19; Lampton, 2014, p. 59). The political turmoil brought by these challenges gave shape to a political climate that called for a strong leader who could put the country back on course.

Xi also faced a new power structure in which factional politics and retired elders had largely ceased to intervene, and radical changes in the balance of power among the party's top leaders had released the structure's hold on him. When Hu took over as general secretary in 2002, Jiang remained chairman of the CMC, and his trustees held a majority in the 18th PBSC. Hu's status as head of the CPC remained unchallenged nevertheless for, as long as the oligarchy endured, so did power-sharing practices and norms. This oligarchy had been fatally wounded by a series of political events by the eve of Xi's coronation in October 2012. The first of these, the Wang Lijun incident, had broken out in February of that year. As a close associate of Chongqing Party Secretary Bo Xilai, Wang once served as a vice mayor and the police chief of the city. He was also instrumental in Bo's campaign against organised crime. Feeling threatened by his falling out with Bo after the involvement of Bo's wife in a murder of British citizen Neil Heywood, Wang fled to the US consulate in Chengdu. The incident set off a sensational political scandal that toppled Bo in March.

Days after Bo's fall, the son of Ling Jihua died in a mysterious Ferrari crash. Ling, a close associate of Hu, headed the party's Central General Office. In exchange for his assistance in covering up the death of his son, Ling chose to cooperate with Zhou Yongkang, Hu's political rival and the PBSC member in charge of the party's legal and political system. Ling was politically sidelined in early September and placed under investigation two months later. When Xi mysteriously disappeared from the public from 1 to 15 September, it was reported that he was working behind the scenes during this period of silence to bargain for personnel arrangements that would follow the 18th Party Congress (Lam, 2015, pp. 7–8).

These events revealed a deep involvement of high-ranking leaders in murders, corruption, violations of discipline, abuses of power and political conspiracies. It is also highly likely that the crimes of Zhou Yongkang, Bo Xilai, Ling Jihua, Xu Caihou and Guo Boxiong were seized as excuses to purge them from power, as they were a serious threat to Xi's succession.[9] The weakening of the oligarchical power structure removed a major limitation

---

9   The CPC officially labelled them as arrivistes and conspirators (政治野心家，阴谋家, *zhengzhi yexinjia, yinmoujia*) in Wang Qishan's work report at the sixth plenum of the 18th CDIC in January 2016.

on the expansion of Xi's power. It also explains how he could so effectively remove threats to his power within the selectorate through a lasting anti-corruption campaign that began in December 2012. The campaign further boosted Xi's public support while he strengthened the party-state's political control to gain leverage in the suppression of his rivals.

Meanwhile, retired leaders interfered with Xi far less than with Hu. Hu did not intervene in Xi's decision-making after his full retirement in 2012. Jiang's physical strength was declining at the age of 86 in 2012, and his office in the CMC building was closed before the 18th Party Congress (BBC Chinese, 2012). Jiang requested the same rank as other retired leaders in the protocol ranking in January 2013 (Takungpao, 2013b). Both events point to the decline of his political influence in 2012.

Xi's world view, historic mission and leadership style: A textual analysis

Xi came to power at a moment when the political climate welcomed a strong leader and the CPC's oligarchy had become weakened. With this in mind, his political personality is crucial to understanding Chinese politics after 2012. The early experiences of political leaders shape a political psychology that affects their thinking and decisions in the later stages of their political careers, and understanding this psychology aids in explaining and predicting their behaviour (Barber, 1992, p. 4). Xi's moves to centralise power are strongly affected by three aspects of his political personality: his understanding of the nature of politics, his beliefs on the role of leaders and his preferred style of leadership. A leadership style is the habitual way in which political leaders perform their duties, while their understanding of the nature of politics relates to how they perceive their surroundings (Barber, 1992, p. 5).

Owing to the lack of direct access, this chapter instead examines Xi's political personality from a distance by analysing the use of the word *douzheng* (斗争) in his public statements.[10] *Douzheng* is chosen because it demonstrates Xi's

---

10   Content analysis is a widely used technique for measuring personality at a distance. Although leaders often rely on aides to prepare their speeches and written work, the speechwriter effect and image-shaping are not in fact obstacles to understanding their preferences or predispositions about politics by analysing their aggregated statements. See Crichlow (1998, pp. 689–90) and Suedfeld (2010, pp. 1677–9). For an overview of the literature, see Winter (2013, pp. 423–58).

unique characteristics and preferences. For example, he mentions *douzheng* 23 times in his report to the 19th CPC Party Congress whereas the word appears only four to nine times in any single report made by Jiang or Hu to the five preceding congresses.

There are two meanings of *douzheng* that are close but have certain notable differences. First, *douzheng* is often used in a conflict in which one attempts to triumph over rivals, often translated as 'to struggle'. Xi's frequent use of the word has caused public agitation owing to the negative legacy of class struggle and the Cultural Revolution. *Douzheng* can also be used to mean 'to strive', similarly to the word *fendou* (奋斗). Although there is less of a sense of rivalry in this usage, it does point to a leadership style defined by facing off risks and challenges rather than making concessions.

To gain more textual information through text mining, this chapter both calculates the total appearances of *douzheng* and examines its co-occurrence with other terms. The texts under analysis are three sources of public statements made from 15 November 2012 to 14 September 2021. They are (1) the Xi Jinping Xilie Zhongyao Jianghua Shujuku (习近平系列重要讲话数据库, Dataset of the Series of Xi Jinping's Important Speeches) in the *People's Daily* (jhsjk.people.cn); (2) *Xi Jinping Tan Zhiguo Lizheng* (习近平谈治国理政, Xi Jinping's talks regarding the governance of China), a three-volume book collecting Xi's important speeches (Xi, 2014, 2017, 2020); and (3) Xi's speeches cited in *Qiushi* (求是, Seeking Truth), an official magazine published by the CPC.

This chapter establishes a corpus of 789 texts after excluding unimportant texts such as congratulatory telegrams to foreign figures, letters to individual citizens and short talks during visits and inspections. Among these, 206 include the word *douzheng* at least once for a total of 922 times. Of these, *douzheng* is mentioned more than 50 times in Xi's opening remarks at the CPC Central Party School on 3 September 2019. It is overwhelmingly clear that the word has a unique value to him.

This chapter uses Quanteda, an R package for the quantitative analysis of textual data, to filter out 582 sentences that contain *douzheng* from the 206 texts, after which they are parsed into tokens. After conducting word segmentation, 10 tokens are extracted both before and after a single *douzheng* by making reference to the Standardised Terminology Database for Foreign Translation of Chinese Specialties and other similar corpora.[11]

The terms that co-occur with *douzheng* are classified into four categories of 'self', 'target', 'purpose' and 'significance' (see table 2.2). Those that cannot fit into any category are dropped. The procedure was implemented independently by two trained individuals with the final decision made by a third when a disagreement arose. The 'self' category contains terms denoting the actors engaging in *douzheng* or groups that the actors belong to in different contexts such as 'we' (我们, *women*), 'the Chinese people' (中国人民, *zhongguo renmin*), 'our party' (我们党, *women dang*) or 'the Chinese nation' (中华民族, *zhonghua minzu*). The 'target' category consists of targets to be defeated or overcome through *douzheng*. These include 'corruption', 'COVID-19' and 'risks and challenges'. Defeating corruption has obviously been Xi's priority target because he has mentioned the term much more frequently than the other two.

Table 2.2: The targets, purposes and significance of *douzheng* in Xi's statements

Category	Terms	Freq.
Self	we (我们)	85
	the Chinese people (中国人民)	54
	our party (我们党)	40
	the Chinese nation (中华民族)	30
	China (中国)	28
	the Party (党)	27
	cadres (干部)	26
	the CPC (中国共产党)	25
	the Party Central (党中央)	24
	leading cadres (领导干部)	16
Target	anti-corruption (反腐败)	125
	risk (风险)	35
	fighting the pandemic (抗疫)	34
	challenge (挑战)	29
	the Covid-19 pandemic (新冠肺炎疫情)	29

11   Zhongguo Tese Huayu Duiwai Fanyi Biaozhunhua Shuyuku (中国特色话语对外翻译标准化术语库; 210.72.20.108/index/index.jsp). This official terminology database is directed jointly by China Foreign Languages Publishing Administration (externally known as China International Communications Group) and China Academy of Translation.

Category	Terms	Freq.
Purpose	the party's style of work and the construction of clean government (党风廉政建设)	46
	military (军事)	41
	victory (胜利)	39
	great cause (伟大事业)	37
	great dream (伟大梦想)	31
	socialism with Chinese characteristics (中国特色社会主义)	28
	great project (伟大工程)	26
	pandemic prevention and control (疫情防控)	24
	great rejuvenation of the Chinese nation (中华民族伟大复兴)	23
	national liberation (民族解放)	16
Significance	great (伟大)	119
	dare to (敢于)	74
	conduct (进行)	71
	spirit (精神)	70
	persist (坚持)	67
	propel (推进)	54
	resolve to (坚决)	46
	prepare (准备)	44
	good at (善于)	41
	capability (本领)	38
	with many new historical features (具有许多新的历史特点的)	37
	strive for (争取)	31
	improve (提高)	29
	strengthen (增强)	28
	firmly (坚定)	27
	promote (发扬)	25
	put into practice (实践)	22
	unwavering (坚定不移)	21
	seize (夺取)	20
	endeavour (努力)	18
	continuously (不断)	16
	revolution (革命)	16
	overwhelmingly (压倒性)	16
	determination (决心)	15
	resist (抗击)	15

Note: Only terms with frequencies of 15 or greater are included. 'Great', 'great project', 'great cause' and 'great dream' are treated as four independent terms.

Source: Created by the author.

Terms regarding the purposes of *douzheng* are classified into the 'purpose' category. Some of these terms concern major CPC historic missions such as 'socialism with Chinese characteristics' (中国特色社会主义, *zhongguo tese shehui zhuyi*), 'the great rejuvenation of the Chinese nation' (中华民族伟大复兴, *zhonghua minzu weida fuxing*) and 'national liberation' (民族解放, *minzu jiefang*). Others, such as 'great project' (伟大工程, *weida gongcheng*), 'great cause' (伟大事业, *weida shiye*) and 'great dream' (伟大梦想, *weida mengxiang*), emphasise the greatness of related goals. These three sometimes co-occur with *weida douzheng* (伟大斗争) as 'the four greats'. The remainder are more specified goals such as the 'construction of clean government' (党风廉政建设, *dangfeng lianzheng jianshe*) and 'pandemic prevention and control' (疫情防控, *yiqing fangkong*). Clearly, the purposes of *douzheng* are all collective values. They reveal Xi's belief in his historic role as the top leader on the road towards national rejuvenation and socialist construction.

The most interesting finding here is the practical significance of *douzheng*. Xi highly praises its importance and value. Some examples include 'great' (伟大, *weida*), 'dare to' (敢于, *ganyu*), 'conduct' (进行, *jinxing*), 'spirit' (精神, *jingshen*), 'insist' (坚持, *jianchi*), 'propel' (推进, *tuijin*), 'resolutely' (坚决, *jianjue*), 'prepare' (准备, *zhunbei*), 'good at' (善于, *shanyu*) and 'capability' (本领, *benling*). However indirectly, these findings strongly reveal that Xi's cognition of politics is defined by conflict and that his preference is to face off risks and challenges. This is because *douzheng* denotes either a struggle for victory over rivals in a conflict or achieving a goal in difficult circumstances.

Moving further, this chapter also offers an examination of Xi's affective states towards *douzheng*. A sentiment analysis was conducted to create a sentiment lexicon via the aforementioned text data and procedures by referring to the Chinese Sentiment Analysis Library established by Dalian University of Technology (大连理工大学情感词汇本体库, Dalian Ligong Daxue Qinggan Cihui Benti Ku; ir.dlut.edu.cn/zyxz/qgbtk.htm). As table 2.3 shows, positive terms predominate (88.1 per cent) whereas negative ones hold only a small share (11.7 per cent). Most importantly, 'praise', 'happiness' and 'trust' jointly consist of 80.1 per cent of the total 2,171 terms. The results clearly show Xi's strong positive affection towards *douzheng* and his confidence and determination in overcoming difficulties.

Table 2.3: A sentiment analysis of *douzheng* in Xi's statements

Positive sentiment	Frequency (%)	Negative sentiment	Frequency (%)
happiness 快乐	242 (11.1%)	anger 愤怒	5 (0.2%)
love 喜爱	32 (1.5%)	sadness 悲伤	25 (1.2%)
surprise 惊奇	0 (0.0%)	fear 恐惧	31 (1.4%)
respect 尊敬	87 (4.0%)	hate 憎恶	22 (1.0%)
comfort 安心	38 (1.8%)	boredom 烦闷	33 (1.5%)
yearnings 思	1 (0.0%)	shyness 羞	0 (0.0%)
trust 相信	181 (8.3%)	guilt 疚	5 (0.2%)
praise 赞扬	1,318 (60.7%)	panic 惧. 慌	24 (1.1%)
wishes 祝愿	15 (0.7%)	disappointment 失望	3 (0.1%)
		jealousy 忌妒	0 (0.0%)
		suspicion 怀疑	13 (0.6%)
		derogation 贬责	96 (4.4%)
Subtotal	1,914 (88.1%)	Subtotal	257 (11.7%)
Total			2,171 (99.8%)

Note: Due to rounding, the total percentage is not equal to 100.

Source: Created by the author.

The formation of Xi's political cognition and beliefs: Early life experiences

On the basis of findings derived from the text analysis, this section discusses the influence of early life experiences on Xi Jinping's political personality. First, Xi's political thinking is defined by conflict. This world view further affects his beliefs on interpersonal relationships, which can be described as being 'harsh to enemies and warm to friends',[12] and his all-or-nothing mentality regarding political power. Xi grew up in an environment of difficult living conditions and hostility in the 1960s and early 1970s (Phoenix, n.d.; Reminwang, 2015a). These experiences taught him to survive on his own in an insecure environment. The Cultural Revolution through school and daily life also taught Xi and other young people of his generation that they had to weed out and eliminate the bourgeoisie enemy among their relatives, friends and neighbours (Mi, 2011, pp. 63–4, 328). This imprinted upon him the notion that politics is fraught with danger and that one should not

---

12   This chapter borrowed this term from Mi (2016).

be too quick to trust. In this mindset, politics is seen as having the potential to become a game of life and death. As such, the absolute control of political power is the optimal survival strategy, and no reconciliation with a political enemy can endure long. At the same time, Xi has cherished old friendships and loyalties, treating friends warmly and courteously and enjoying the sense of security this provides. He is also motivated by a strong need for power and achievement.

Xi's psychology regarding politics, self–other relations and political power helps to explain several tendencies in his political moves after 2012. He has rapidly promoted his protégés and continued to verify their loyalty, launched large-scale personnel reshufflings and used his dictatorship to crush his enemies. Xi has also reinforced his official power with an institutional restructuring of the party-state and the insertion of his ideas into official ideology.

Second, Xi believes in his historic destiny as the supreme leader of the CPC at a time of great national rejuvenation and socialist construction. Both his idealism and his affinity for collectivism are rooted in his revolutionary family life, middle-school education and sent-down experience in Shaanxi (Xinjingbao, 2016; Torigian, 2018, p. 9). Influenced in some way by his father's example, Xi followed in his footsteps in the cause of the communist revolution.[13] The generation of the Cultural Revolution had a passionate ambition to revitalise the Chinese nation (Mi, 2011, pp. 1, 82, 164). They were taught in school to uphold collectivist ideals over the individual by valuing the sacrifice of personal rights and interests for the greater good of the nation. Xi's studies in elite boarding schools also contributed to his collectivist thinking by emphasising discipline and team spirit (Mi, 2016). Many princelings were also ardent disciples of the bloodline theory (血统论, *xuetonglun*), believing it was their destiny to rule China because of their being born into the families of revolutionary veterans. This identity gave them a sense of superiority and a responsibility to further the revolution (Mi, 2011, pp. 82, 112, 121; Guo, 2019, pp. 4, 179, 318). This makes it highly unlikely that Xi is ever going to accept Western democracy. Rather he believes in reinforcing the leadership of the CPC as a necessary step to achieve his mission in history. He is also likely to sacrifice individual rights for the greater good.

---

13   In a TV interview in November 2003, Xi recalled that his father repeatedly told him and his siblings the stories about his part in the revolution and required that they join it in the future. Xi stated that the stories became imprinted on their minds (CCTV, 2003).

Third, Xi's self-assurance and reverence for strong leadership have been shaped by his early experiences. In 2002, Xi recalled his sent-down years (下乡, xiaxiang) in which he overcame the challenges of living in poor environments full of fleas (跳蚤关, tiaosao guan), eating meagre and unwholesome diets (饮食关, yinshiguan), performing hard manual labour (劳动关, laodong guan) and identifying himself as no different from the ordinary rural villagers (思想关, sixiang guan) (Reminwang, 2015b). In 2003, Xi wrote of his sent-down experience: 'First, I understood what real life is, what "seeking truth from facts" is and who ordinary people are. Second, I built up my confidence. When I encounter challenges later in life, I always think, why can't I achieve something at present if I could in the past in spite of hardships?' (Takungpao, 2014) This statement reveals that Xi believes in his ability to maintain control in the face of difficulties.

Xi's obsession with strong leadership also has its roots in the Cultural Revolution where Mao's strongman leadership offered him a model for political domination.[14] The generation of the Cultural Revolution worshipped authority but also dared to rebel (Mi, 2011, pp. 22, 38, 164, 329). They both followed and exercised authority as they organised the Red Guard movement to support Mao Zedong and persecute 'class enemies'. At the same time, they also enjoyed the upheaval of the existing order by challenging teachers, classmates and veteran cadres. Eventually, some questioned the political correctness of the Cultural Revolution itself.

Xi's self-confidence and the reverence for strong leadership in his psychology help to explain his leadership style and desire to weaken power-sharing practices and norms under his rule. He is both resilient and adaptable, keeping a low profile while seeking power to persevere in times of adversity. He also tends towards political domination in his exercise of power, being reluctant to reconcile with the opposition on major issues and insisting on his basic principles. As for the rules of the game that impede his destiny in history, Xi would rather rewrite them than adapt to them.

Conclusion

Xi has reshaped the Chinese party-state since assuming office in 2012. This chapter contributes to the field of China studies by explaining, through an examination of Xi's circumstances and political personality, why

---

14　For Mao's influence on Chinese political culture, see Qian (2012, pp. 13–21).

power-sharing institutions in China have become unsustainable. While structural factors have amplified his influence on these political changes, their direction has been guided by psychological ones. First, international and domestic challenges that had emerged before the 18th Party Congress created expectations among high-ranking CPC elites and citizens for a strong leader. Second, a series of political events before the Party Congress weakened the oligarchical power structure in the party's top leadership, an arrangement that had nurtured power-sharing institutions. This weakened the structural constraints on Xi's expansion of power. Third, Xi's choices in his bid to centralise power are shaped by his beliefs in the zero-sum nature of politics, his destiny in China's rejuvenation and socialist construction, and the necessity for strong leadership.

This chapter also contributes to comparative authoritarian studies in two ways. First, it reminds us that power-sharing institutions in single-party authoritarian regimes are sustainable only with a stable ruling oligarchy. Institutions and their environments influence one another, and, as a dynamic process rather than a static condition, institutionalisation can be reversed. While the literature has aptly noted that power-sharing institutions influence the economic performance and political stability of authoritarian regimes, they are also painfully vulnerable to dramatic changes in the external environment and balance of power among major political actors.

Second, both macro and micro factors should be taken into account when explaining the historical conjuncture of institutional changes. While structural factors are important to explain the collapse of power-sharing institutions in authoritarian regimes, the political personality and choices of a political leader are also crucial in the process. Xi's political personality was therefore pivotal in his reorienting of Chinese politics once two necessary conditions were met: the political climate welcomed a strong leader, and the CPC's oligarchy had become weakened. Xi would not have centralised power so dramatically had he believed in the virtues of collective leadership.

While the centralisation of power in Xi and the CPC has given him leverage to consolidate it as he deals with environmental challenges, it creates two political risks. The first is one of political succession: Xi's health and personal security have greatly preoccupied the party-state and a smooth transfer of power will be difficult after his personalistic leadership. If Xi were to become incapacitated, the return to a zero-sum game that would follow could create a severe power struggle in the CPC's leadership. With the practice of succession by echelon abolished, Xi's personalistic leadership could also hinder the smooth rise of a successor and result in great political uncertainty. There might also be a return to gerontocracy if he retires in good health.

The centralisation of power poses a second risk to the quality of China's governance. While Xi's personalistic leadership has overcome the clumsiness of the Hu era, it could lead to a lack of mechanisms to rectify errors, as was the case in the Mao era when no individual or institution could correct him. Furthermore, personalistic leadership does not solve the principal-agent problem caused by information asymmetry and discrepant interests between the principal and agents. Several ranking officials who obtained key appointments under Xi's rule have been relieved of duty or arrested owing to violations of discipline, corruption or incompetence in fighting the COVID-19 epidemic.[15] The centralisation of power might also discourage social forces and local officials from taking initiative in dealing with various governance issues as they are obliged to wait for Xi's personal instructions before taking action. The freedom of speech ensures that whistleblowers can give early warnings in a public crisis, but as the Li Wenliang (李文亮) incident shows,[16] the party-state often treats these as voices to be silenced.

References

Aisixiang (爱思想, 2011) 'Yu Jianrong: Choufu he chouguan shi yin bugongping, diceng baixing kanbudao qiantu' [于建嵘:仇富和仇官是因不公平，底层百姓看不到前途, Yu Jianrong: The hatred of the rich and officials is due to inequality, the common people cannot see their prospects]. 17 June. www.aisixiang.com/data/41472.html

Barber, J. (1992) *The Presidential Character: Predicting Performance in the White House.* 4th edn. Prentice Hall

BBC Chinese (BBC中文网, 2012) 'Rimei: Zhongguo junwei chexiao Jiang Zemin bangongshi [日媒：中国军委撤销江泽民办公室, Japanese media: China's Military Commission revokes Jiang Zemin's office], 1 November. www.bbc.com/zhongwen/trad/chinese_news/2012/11/121101_jiang_office.shtml

---

15   Two examples are Lu Wei (鲁炜) and Jiang Chaoliang (蒋超良). The former was placed under investigation for corruption in November 2017. The latter stepped down as party secretary of Hubei for his inability to control the COVID-19 epidemic in February 2020.

16   Li Wenliang was an ophthalmologist who warned his colleagues early on about COVID-19 infections in Wuhan. Local police admonished him and other doctors for making false comments on the internet about an unconfirmed SARS outbreak. He died from the disease in February 2020.

Boix, C., & Svolik, M. (2013) 'The foundations of limited authoritarian government: Institutions, commitment and power-sharing in dictatorships.' *Journal of Politics* 75(2): 300–16. doi.org/10.1017/s0022381613000029

Buckley, C. (2013) 'China warns officials against "dangerous" Western values.' *New York Times*, 13 May. www.nytimes.com/2013/05/14/world/asia/chinese-leaders-warn-of-dangerous-western-values.html

CCTV (2003) 'Shengwei shuji xilie zhuanfang: Zhejiang shengwei shuji Xi Jinping' [省委书记系列专访: 浙江省委书记习近平, A series of exclusive interviews with provincial party secretaries: Party secretary of Zhejiang Xi Jinping], 14 November. CCTV (中央电视台), news.sina.com.cn/c/2003-11-14/13312 136924.shtml

Chen, L. (2004) 'The debate between liberalism and neo-leftism at the turn of the century.' *China Perspectives* 55, 1–14. doi.org/10.4000/chinaperspectives.403

Clinton, H. (2011) 'America's Pacific century.' *Foreign Policy*, 11 October. foreign policy.com/2011/10/11/americas-pacific-century/

Crichlow, S. (1998) 'Idealism or pragmatism? An operational code analysis of Yitzhak Rabin and Shimon Peres.' *Political Psychology* 19(4): 683–706 doi.org/10.1111/0162-895X.00127

de Mesquita, B., Smith, A., Siverson, R., & Morrow, J. (2003) *The Logic of Political Survival.* MIT Press

Dickson, B. (2016) *The Dictator's Dilemma: The Chinese Communist Party's Strategy for Survival.* Oxford University Press

Dyer, G. (2012) 'Xi's got issues: China's new leader has 100 days to make his mark. Ready, set, go.' *Foreign Policy*, 12 November. foreignpolicy.com/2012/11/13/xis-got-issues

Fu, H. (2018) 'The July 9th (709) crackdown on human rights lawyers: Legal advocacy in an authoritarian state.' *Journal of Contemporary China* 27(112): 554–68. doi.org/10.1080/10670564.2018.1433491

Fu, H., & Zhu, H. (2018) 'After the July 9 (709) crackdown: The future of human rights lawyering.' *Fordham International Law Journal* 41(5): 1135–64. ir.lawnet. fordham.edu/ilj

Gandhi, J. (2008) *Political Institutions under Dictatorship.* Cambridge University Press

Gehlbach, S., & Keefer, P. (2011) 'Investment without democracy: Ruling-party institutionalisation and credible commitment in autocracies.' *Journal of Comparative Economics* 39(2): 123–39. doi.org/10.1016/j.jce.2011.04.002

Greenstein, F. (1969) *Personality and Politics: Problems of Evidence, Inference and Conceptualization.* Markham Publishing Company

Guo, X. (2019) *The Politics of the Core Leader in China: Culture, Institution, Legitimacy and Power.* Cambridge University Press

Kojima, K. (2020) 'Politics under Xi Jinping: Centralisation and its implications.' *Public Policy Review* 16(3): 1–21. ideas.repec.org/a/mof/journl/ppr16_03_02. html

Kou, C.W. [寇健文] (2010) *Zhonggong Jingying Zhengzhi De Yanbian: Zhiduhua Yu Quanli Zhuanyi, 1978–2010* [中共政治菁英的演变：制度化与权力转移，1978–2010, The evolution of Chinese elite politics: Institutionalisation and power transfer, 1978–2010] (3rd edn). Wunan

Lam, W. (2015) *Chinese Politics in the Era of Xi Jinping: Renaissance, Reform or Retrogression?* Routledge

Lampton, D. (2014) *Following the Leader: Ruling China, from Deng Xiaoping to Xi Jinping.* University of California Press

Lee, C.K., & Zhang, Y. (2013) 'The power of instability: Unraveling the microfoundations of bargained authoritarianism in China.' *American Journal of Sociology* 118(6): 1475–508. www.journals.uchicago.edu/doi/abs/10.1086/670802

Lee, S. (2017) 'An institutional analysis of Xi Jinping's centralisation of power.' *Journal of Contemporary China* 26(105): 325–36. doi.org/10.1080/10670564. 2016.1245505

Li, C. (2016) *Chinese Politics in the Xi Jinping Era: Reassessing Collective Leadership.* Brookings Institution Press

Madsen, R. (2019) 'The Sinicization of Chinese religions under Xi Jinping.' *China Leadership Monitor*, 61. www.prcleader.org/sinicization-of-chinese-religions

Magaloni, B. (2008) 'Credible power-sharing and the longevity of authoritarian rule.' *Comparative Political Studies* 41(4–5): 715–41. doi.org/10.1177/00104 14007313124

Mi, H. [米鹤都] (2011) *Xinlu: Toushi Gongheguo Tongling Ren* [心路：透视共和国同龄人, Insights: Insight into the peers of the PRC]. Central Party Literature Press

—— (2016) 'Dayuan wenhua yu hongweibing yundong qiyuan' [大院文化与红卫兵运动起源, The courtyard culture of official residences and the origin of the Red Guard movement]. *Phoenix* [凤凰网], 6 February. news.ifeng.com/a/20160206/47380745_1.shtml

Miller, A. (2012) 'Prospects for solidarity in the Xi Jinping leadership.' *China Leadership Monitor*, 47. media.hoover.org/sites/default/files/documents/CLM 37AM.pdf

Mingpao (明报, 2016) 'Guanfang cheng Xi "san hexin" shou ti "minzu fuxing yinlingzhe"' [官方称习「三核心」首提「民族复兴引领者」, Authorities describe Xi as 'three cores', mentioning the term 'the pioneer of national rejuvenation' for the first time]. 11 November. www.mingpaocanada.com/VAN/htm/News/20161111/tcab1_r.htm

Naughton, B. (2012) 'The political consequences of economic challenges.' *China Leadership Monitor*, 39. www.hoover.org/sites/default/files/uploads/documents/CLM39BN.pdf

—— (2016a) 'Supply side structural reform: Policy-makers look for a way out.' *China Leadership Monitor*, 49. www.hoover.org/sites/default/files/research/docs/clm49bn.pdf

—— (2016b) 'Two trains running: Supply side reform, SOE reform and the authoritative personage.' *China Leadership Monitor*, 50. www.hoover.org/sites/default/files/research/docs/clm50bn.pdf#overlay-context=publications/china-leadership-monitor

Obama, B. (2011) 'Remarks by President Obama to the Australian Parliament' (transcript). White House, 17 November. obamawhitehouse.archives.gov/the-press-office/2011/11/17/remarks-president-obama-australian-parliament

Pei, M. (2019) 'Rewriting the rules of the Chinese party-state: Xi's progress in reinvigorating the CPC.' *China Leadership Monitor*, 60. docs.wixstatic.com/ugd/10535f_c22e9e10b681444c93167478999e548c.pdf

Phoenix (凤凰网, n.d.) 'Xi Jinping nianpu—1954–1968 nian: Chushen hongse jiating, shaonian lijin zhengzhi fengbo' [习近平年谱—1954–1968年：出身红色家庭 少年历尽政治风波, The chronology of Xi Jinping from 1954 to 1968: Coming from a red family and experiencing tons of political turmoil]. news.ifeng.com/mainland/special/zhonggong18da/changwei/xijinping.shtml

Qian, L. [钱理群]. (2012) *Mao Zedong Shidai Yu Hou Mao Zedong Shidai: 1949–2009* [毛泽东时代与后毛泽东时代：The Mao Zedong era and the post-Mao Zedong era: 1949–2009]. Linking Publishing

Reminwang (人民网, 2015a) 'Xi Jinping yi Yan'an chadui: Ta jiao le wo zuo shenme' [习近平忆延安插队, 它教了我做什么, Xi Jinping recalls his living and working in the countryside in Yanan: It taught me what to do]. 14 February. politics.people.com.cn/BIG5/n/2015/0214/c1001-26566406.html

—— (2015b) 'Xi Jinping zishu: Yongyuan shi huang tudi de erzi' [习近平自述：永远是黄土地的儿子, Xi Jinping's self-statement: Always be a son of the yellow earth]. 14 February. politics.people.com.cn/n/2015/0214/c1001-26567403.html

Repnikova, M., & Fang, K. (2018) 'Authoritarian participatory persuasion 2.0: Netizens as thought work collaborators in China.' *Journal of Contemporary China* 27(113): 763–79. doi.org/10.1080/10670564.2018.1458063

Shi, A., François, L., & Galway, M. (2018) 'The recasting of Chinese socialism: The Chinese new left since 2000.' *China Information* 32(1): 139–59. doi.org/10.1177/0920203X18760416

Slater, D., & Fenner, S. (2011) 'State power and staying power: Infrastructural mechanisms and authoritarian durability.' *Journal of International Affairs* 65(1): 15–29. www.jstor.org/stable/24388179

Suedfeld, P. (2010) 'The cognitive processing of politics and politicians: Archival studies of conceptual and integrative complexity.' *Journal of Personality* 78(6): 1669–702. doi.org/10.1111/j.1467-6494.2010.00666.x

Svolik, M. (2012) *The Politics of Authoritarian Rule.* Cambridge University Press

Takungpao (大公报; 2013a) 'Jiang Zemin 1997 nian ceng tichu jianli guojia anquan weiyuanhui' [江泽民1997年曾提出建立国家安全委员会, Jiang Zemin proposed to establish a National Security Committee in 1997]. 13 November. news.takungpao.com/history/redu/2013-11/2035635.html

—— (2013b) 'Jiang Zemin qingqiu zai libin paiming zhong tong lao tongzhi pai zai yiqi' [江泽民请求在礼宾排名中同老同志排在一起, Jiang Zemin requests to rank with old comrades in the protocol ranking]. 23 January. news.takungpao.com/mainland/focus/2013-01/1401845.html

—— (2014) 'Xi Jinping 7 nian zhiqing chadui suiyue: Cunmin cheng mei ting qi jiao guo ku' [习近平7年知青插队岁月：村民称没听其叫过苦, Xi Jinping's seven years of living and working in the countryside as an educated youth: Villagers claim they never heard him complain]. 30 June. news.takungpao.com/history/redu/2014-06/2571385_6.html

Torigian, J. (2018) 'Historical legacies and leaders' world views: Communist party history and Xi's learned (and unlearned) lessons.' *China Perspectives* 2018(1–2): 7–15. doi.org/10.4000/chinaperspectives.7548

Tsai, W.H. (2016) 'How "networked authoritarianism" was operationalized in China: Methods and procedures of public opinion control.' *Journal of Contemporary China* 25(101): 731–44. doi.org/10.1080/10670564.2016.1160506

US Department of Defense (2012) *Sustaining US Global Leadership: Priorities for 21st Century Defense.* archive.defense.gov/news/Defense_Strategic_Guidance.pdf

Winter, D. (2013) 'Personality profiles of political elites.' In *The Oxford Handbook of Political Psychology*, ed. L. Huddy, D.O. Sears & J.S. Levy, 2nd edn, pp. 423–58. Oxford University Press

Wu, G. (2019) 'The king's men and others: Emerging political elites under Xi Jinping.' *China Leadership Monitor*, 60. www.prcleader.org/_files/ugd/10535f_da7effdfa8ad40979f17d561cb845a98.pdf

Wu, W. (2018) 'Shake-up in chain of command looms as Xi Jinping's leading group on economy is elevated.' *South China Morning Post*, 21 March. www.scmp.com/news/china/policies-politics/article/2138293/xi-jinpings-leading-group-economy-gets-more-heft

Xi, J. [習近平]. (2014, 2017, 2020) *Xi Jinping Tan Zhiguo Lizheng* (習近平談治國理政, Xi Jinping's talks regarding the governance of China), three vols, Foreign Languages Press

Xinjingbao (新京报, 2016) 'Dangxuan zongshuji qian, Xi Jinping zenme guo Chunjie?' [当选总书记前，习近平怎么过春节? How did Xi celebrate the Spring Festival before being elected as general secretary?]. 8 February. www.bjnews.com.cn/news/2016/02/08/393952.html

Yang, M. (2021) 'New Chinese decree tells religious leaders to "support the Communist Party".' VOA News, 24 April. www.voanews.com/a/east-asia-pacific_voa-news-china_new-chinese-decree-tells-religious-leaders-support-communist-party/6205013.html

Zhang, Y. (2021) 'Anti-corruption operations bring back 9,165 fugitives, recover 21.74 billion yuan.' *China Daily*, 14 July. global.chinadaily.com.cn/a/2021 06/28/WS60d97c35a310efa1bd65e67b.html

Zheng, W. (2023) 'New work rules for China's State Council put the party firmly in charge.' *South China Morning Post*, 28 March. www.scmp.com/news/china/politics/article/3215029/new-work-rules-chinas-state-council-put-party-firmly-charge

3

What can comparative authoritarianism tell us about China under Xi Jinping (and vice versa)?

Hans H. Tung and Wen-Chin Wu[1]

This chapter examines the previous two decades of literature on comparative authoritarianism to show how its conceptual innovations help us to better understand China under Xi Jinping and how this literature can be enriched by the Chinese case. A while after the end of the Cold War, scholars of comparative politics were puzzled by the robustness of some dictatorships and therefore began to investigate the conditions of their resilience in the face of democratising pressures from either domestic or foreign sources. In particular, the Chinese Communist Party's authoritarian rule seemed to be even more consolidated after it became richer and more integrated into the world economy, a fact that ran contrary to modernisation theory. Moreover, despite its façade of popular elections and other democratic components in its formal institutions since the early 1990s, Russian politics under Putin still exhibited strong authoritarianism in various aspects such as the regime's suppression of free speech and freedom of the press.

---

1   This chapter is a revised and updated version of the article that first appeared as H.H. Tung and W.C. Wu (2021) 'What can comparative authoritarianism tell us about China under Xi Jinping (and vice versa)?' *Issues and Studies* 57(4), Article 2150013. doi.org/10.1142/S1013251121500132. Reprinted with permission.

The continuing relevance of dictatorships to world politics has given rise to inter-disciplinary task forces to solve various puzzles ranging from their domestic politics to foreign behaviour.

Since the early 2000s, political scientists have developed two research agendas to cope with this issue of authoritarian resilience. The first one focuses on authoritarian power-sharing. According to this body of literature, authoritarian stability hinges on the way dictators share power with other political elites in their regimes. More critically, it shows both theoretically and empirically how authoritarian institutions like legislatures and political parties can make power-sharing arrangements credible.[2]

The second strand focuses on the informational problem facing dictators. Given their monopoly over power, dictators tend to have a strong incentive to censor information that might undermine their political control. On the one hand, they stifle any subversive news or messages from spreading and hurting the legitimacy of their autocratic rule. On the other, they also use propaganda to manipulate people's beliefs about the strength of the regime (Edmond, 2013). While both behavioural patterns are present in almost all dictatorships, there is still variation in the extent to which dictators enforce censorship on the freedom of expression. As a matter of fact, political scientists have found that the degree of media freedom among non-democratic regimes can vary widely. Depending on how desperately dictators need to improve the quality of their governance, some of them strategically grant a higher degree of media freedom to obtain local information inaccessible to their own private sources. In other words, to compensate for the loss of bottom-up information channels owing to the lack of democratic elections, dictators strategically allow for partial media freedom (Egorov, Guriev & Sonin, 2009; Gehlbach & Sonin, 2014; Lorentzen, 2014; Qin, Strömberg & Wu, 2017). Yet since dictators might not be able to commit credibly to media freedom, given their ability to punish media outlets ex post, we also discuss various related issues of self-censorship that have been largely ignored in the existing literature.

---

2   We would like to clarify that the main focus of this chapter is the role of domestic politics and institutions, so we decided not to engage with the literature on how external factors affect authoritarian regime changes. Meanwhile, there are also few studies in the field of Chinese politics that address this issue. Under the CPC's tight control of the Chinese state and society and its media censorship in particular, it is hard to imagine that external pressures would have brought about regime or institutional changes in China. Hence we do not engage with the literature on how foreign factors affect political changes.

Based on the two approaches summarised above, we then continue to show how their conceptual innovations can be applied to the case of China, especially for the Xi Jinping era, during which the structure of power-sharing among the dictator and elites has been broken and control over the media has been strengthened. China under Xi's rule in fact offers a good opportunity for scholars to advance the literature of comparative authoritarianism.

This chapter is structured as follows. The section 'Authoritarian power-sharing' offers a critical review of the authoritarian power-sharing literature in which we highlight its major conceptual, theoretical and empirical insights. The section 'Autocratic politics of information' then switches gear and delves into the literature on authoritarian responsiveness to discuss the autocratic politics of information. In the section 'China as a critical case', we turn to China as a case to show how we can understand the country's authoritarian politics through the lens of power-sharing and authoritarian responsiveness. This is accomplished through investigating political developments during Xi's first term to further develop both bodies of literature. We conclude the chapter by providing a conceptual pathway towards a dynamic theory of comparative authoritarianism.

Authoritarian power-sharing

Students of dictatorships have long noticed the importance of power-sharing arrangements or the distribution of patronage in authoritarian politics. As Bueno de Mesquita et al. (2003, pp. 28–9) summarise succinctly: 'Make no mistake about it, no leader rules alone. Even the most oppressive dictators cannot survive the loss of support among their core constituents.' In other words, just like their democratic counterparts, the leaders of authoritarian countries are not exempt from making compromises and cutting deals with their core constituents to form a ruling coalition. This is why roughly two decades ago, an earlier study on dictatorships by Wintrobe (1998, p. 336) made such an analogy: 'if democracy may be likened to a pork barrel, the typical dictatorship is a warehouse or temple of pork!'

Political scientists have developed different analytic frameworks for explaining how dictators distribute power and resources to themselves and their allies. For example, Bueno de Mesquita et al.'s (2003) selectorate theory defines two groups of people whose support is essential to the survival of political leaders: a winning coalition and the selectorate. According to them, dictators need to offer more public goods as their winning coalition grows in size. Ideally, a dictator should keep this winning coalition as small as possible.

Alternatively, Svolik (2012) takes a more theory-driven approach to the analysis of authoritarian politics. He contends that there are two problems of authoritarian rule: authoritarian control and authoritarian power-sharing. Specifically, the first problem centres on the political and economic conflicts between the authoritarian regime and the mass public. For instance, many studies have argued that distributive conflicts between the rich (regime insiders) and poor (regime outsiders) will trigger social unrest and revolutions. Dictators need to manage distributive issues properly to prevent democratic transitions from happening (Acemoglu & Robinson, 2005; Boix, 2003).

Meanwhile, historical data suggest that dictators are often overthrown by regime insiders and not the masses. Therefore another problem facing dictators is how they manage their relationships with other elites to sustain their political survival. According to Svolik (2012), one strategy dictators can adopt is to share their power and resources through institutionalisation. Institutionalised power-sharing within authoritarian regimes not only makes the rules of the game clear to all political actors but also constrains the political power of autocrats and keeps them from infringing on the rights and interests of others. As a result, elites are more willing to support the dictator as well as the regime.

Svolik's emphasis on the importance of power-sharing under dictatorships echoes previous studies on authoritarian institutions (Brownlee, 2007; Gandhi, 2008; Gehlbach & Keefer, 2011; Magaloni, 2008; Wright, 2008). According to the literature, authoritarian or seemingly democratic institutions can make an authoritarian regime very stable. For instance, Boix and Svolik (2013) point out that without any institutional arrangements to make other elites know how resources are divided, they might mistake a decrease in total benefits (e.g. a natural disaster) for the dictator's intentional violation of the political pact between them. Apparently, this misunderstanding can create a source of conflict among the incumbent's supporters and allow a challenger to switch their loyalty.

Hollyer, Rosendorff and Vreeland (2015, 2019) further illustrate the role of transparency in (de)stabilising authoritarian regimes. Using the proportion of economic data that are absent in reports from countries to international organisations as a proxy of transparency, Hollyer, Rosendorff and Vreeland

(2015) find that a higher level of economic transparency in autocracies leads to more protests. The puzzle is then why dictators are still willing to disclose such information that risks destabilising their regimes. The answer provided by Hollyer, Rosendorff and Vreeland (2019) is that since the public are more likely to act in concert to protest the regime once they have better information about its performance, economic transparency can actually be used by dictators to create a rally-around-the-flag effect and discourage their potential rivals from challenging them. Accordingly, other elites will stay in line instead of challenging their leadership. As the risk of initiating coups is much greater than that of mass mobilisation for most dictatorships, power-sharing and regime transparency become the survival strategies of authoritarian leaders.

More recently, the literature in this field has also endeavoured to extend this insight to understanding the politics of compensation in authoritarian countries. When dictators implement reforms that alter the initial power-sharing relationship between them and their supporters, this causes a disruption in authoritarian stability. As a matter of fact, even if such reforms are beneficial to the ruling coalition or the regime as a whole in the long run, they might nonetheless create immediate or prospective losers who no longer have any stakes in it ex post. For instance, Casper (2017) demonstrates that International Monetary Fund (IMF) programs facilitate coups in developing countries. Although lending from the IMF might be beneficial for economic recovery, the conditionality of IMF programs requires market reforms that makes political leaders less able to distribute patronage. Hence previously privileged elites might act against their leader to terminate these programs.

Similar cases have occurred in China and Russia. Although Deng Xiaoping's reform of party institutionalisation in the 1980s allowed China to attract 'investment without democracy', it 'eliminated lifetime tenure and instituted mandatory retirement for almost 20 million cadres' (Gehlbach & Keefer, 2011, p. 136) who lost certain perks enjoyed by predecessors. We can observe a similar, more recent case in Russia in which Putin tried to expand his party base (the United Russia) by changing the electoral rules between 2003 and 2007. This change made re-election more uncertain for several incumbent legislators of the party (Gandhi, Heller & Reuter, 2017). In the case discussed in this chapter, China's 2001 bureaucratic restructuring also created losers within the Chinese bureaucracy (i.e. the dissolved ministries) to facilitate the trade liberalisation needed for its accession to the World

Trade Organisation (WTO), an achievement that eventually would make the country one of the major trading powers in the world. Each of these different kinds of losers can pose a threat to the political survival of a dictator.

To sum up our discussions, dictators cannot rule alone but share power with other political elites who can challenge their authoritarian rule. These political elites face problems of collective action as well as the power of the dictator to break the promise of power-sharing. As a result, authoritarian leaders need to establish institutions that not only constrain the power of the dictator but also coordinate interests among the dictator and other political elites, including those who are included in the dictator's ruling coalition and those who are not. As a result, power-sharing under dictatorships helps authoritarian leaders to consolidate their regimes. Nevertheless, as this analytic view holds that the consolidation of authoritarian rule results from institutionalised power-sharing, it cannot explain why there are institutional changes among autocracies. In particular, why do some autocracies collapse but others do not? After experiencing a regime breakdown, why do some autocracies transition to democracies while others either remain unchanged or transition to other types of autocracies? In other words, this approach is too static to explain the changes and evolution of authoritarian regimes.

Autocratic politics of information

Although dictatorships have long been viewed as the antithesis of freedom of expression, the burgeoning literature on comparative authoritarianism has found a wide variation in freedom of speech and the press among non-democratic regimes. As the 'authoritarian resilience' thesis has it, the understanding of social problems is the first-order task for an authoritarian government's survival (Nathan, 2003, p. 14). When Mikhail Gorbachev tried to bring a new lease of life to the regime in the late 1980s, one of his major reforms was to lift media censorship. According to his former chief spokesman Gennadi Gerasimov:

> Hoping to use the media to help identify his nation's problems in order to solve them, Gorbachev gradually lifted Communist Party control of the mass media starting in 1985. In a matter of months, he introduced a degree of freedom unheard of before in the Russian press, or, to use his term, glasnost. He viewed this opening not only as a window on what was happening in the country, but also as a chance to ensure feedback as he tackled economic and political problems facing the nation. (Gerasimov, 1998, pp. 2–3)

In other words, while freedom of speech can sometimes be threatening to the survival of dictators owing to its potential to expose politically sensitive information, it can also be instrumental for them to acquire information that is elusive to their private sources (e.g. secret police). As a result, as long as the information asymmetry between the ruler and the ruled is severe enough, dictators will have an incentive to relax their control over the media 'to learn from bottom-up information and to address social problems before they become threatening' (Qin, Strömberg & Wu, 2017, p. 137). By pre-empting potential regime threats through addressing social problems in advance, dictatorships can also be responsive to the public and become more resilient to vicissitudes.

A number of comparative studies have investigated how dictators allow (partial) media freedom to overcome the information problem and become responsive to citizens. For example, Egorov, Guriev and Sonin (2009) demonstrate that resource-scarce dictators allow free media to improve their quality of governance. They show formally that media freedom is a mechanism for dictators (the principal) to ensure that bureaucrats (agents) have an incentive to implement good policies that are beneficial to their political survival. The incentive for dictators to use media freedom to induce good governance is stronger when dictators have tighter budget constraints, especially in countries that have a scarcity of natural resources. Lorentzen (2013) and Repnikova (2017) adopt a similar perspective to analyse China's censorship, arguing that the Chinese government strategically allows investigative reporting on local issues that include scandals and corruption to improve the quality of governance without facing the risk of being overthrown by the mass public.

In addition to the level of responsiveness and the quality of governance, other studies focus on the conditions rather than the goals for allowing freedom of the press. For instance, Chen and Xu (2017) demonstrate that dictators are more likely to allow freedom of speech if the policy preferences of citizens are more heterogeneous. In other words, media freedom helps dictators to 'divide and rule' citizens by suppressing the potential of collective action. Sheen, Tung and Wu (2022) also argue that a dictator whose power is less concentrated (i.e. less personalist) will allow more media freedom as a commitment to sharing their power with other elites.

While these studies have demonstrated that allowing partial freedom of expression and the media can be politically beneficial to dictators, one remaining question is how they at the same time tackle the potential risks of being overthrown by citizens who then have more opportunities to communicate with each other and organise rebellious collective action against the regime. In a series of papers, King and his co-authors find that while the Chinese government allows citizens and netizens to engage in online criticism of the government, it nonetheless censors online posts that have the potential to result in collective action (King, Pan & Roberts, 2013, 2014).

China as a critical case

After reviewing the two critical aspects of the literature on comparative authoritarianism during the first two decades of the twenty-first century, we proceed to observe how the literature aids in our understanding of China's political economy and to reflect on China's evolving political landscape since Xi's ascendancy to the top in late 2012. This enables us to enrich the literature with further theoretical insights into authoritarian politics. The subsections below begin with an analysis of the concept of power-sharing authoritarian institutions and its applications in the Chinese context.

Institutionalised authoritarian power-sharing and China's collective leadership during the reform era

While most people today remember Deng Xiaoping as China's 'chief architect of economic reforms', Deng's contributions to the formation of modern China certainly go beyond economics, at least before Xi Jinping's rise. After the Cultural Revolution ended, Deng created a political framework of collective leadership in an attempt to prevent Mao's cult of personality from returning to China's political landscape. One critical feature of this design was that for all top leaders after Deng, their power would be institutionalised in the form of a 'trinity': the general secretary of the CPC Central Committee, the president and the chairman of the Central Military Commission. Moreover, a two-term limit (10 years in total) was implicitly and explicitly imposed on all the three positions so that power would not be monopolised by a few individuals within the party.[3] In addition, an age threshold was also implicitly imposed on membership in the Politburo standing committee. Those older than 68 would have to bow

---

3   Before Xi lifted it, the only formal constraint was imposed on the position of the president; there were only implicit limitations on the other two.

out of the leadership. Lastly, while someone would hold the 'trinity' of the three key posts, this person was simply 'the first among equals' and had to share political power with other Politburo standing members. By means of these designs, Deng's formal and informal political engineering of collective leadership brought two decades of stability to China's elite politics, which was precisely what China's economic miracle was predicated on.

Analytically, Deng's institutional legacy was not fully appreciated until the recent rise of scholarly interests in authoritarian institutions. The early scholarship on Chinese politics was centred around the idea of 'fragmented authoritarianism' whereby China's policy-making process was basically understood as one driven by inter-ministerial bargaining among bureaucrats in different ministries (Lieberthal & Lampton, 1992; Lieberthal & Oksenberg, 1988; Shirk, 1993). In other words, while Deng's institutional designs are viewed as growth-enhancing by the more recent literature on authoritarian institutions, they were nonetheless regarded as the source of political conflict and policy contradictions in China by the earlier literature of fragmented authoritarianism.

This contrast between two generations of scholarship clearly shows how the literature on comparative authoritarianism has shone a new light on the field of China studies. While Deng's power-sharing institutional design did create additional coordination costs to China's political system, it also helped it steer clear of potential internal conflicts among elites. Before comparative authoritarianism scholars embarked on various empirical tests between different dictatorships, there was no way to know whether coordination costs or conflict absorption would be the dominant effect. As it turns out, the literature shows both theoretically and empirically that these institutions help make the regimes in these countries live longer, obtain higher economic growth rates and attract more investments (Boix & Svolik, 2013; Brownlee, 2007a; Gandhi, 2008; Gehlbach & Keefer, 2011; Svolik, 2012). While our coverage of the outcomes that have been studied in the literature so far might not be exhaustive, these findings imply that the presence of authoritarian institutions such as the People's Congress and the Communist Party in China's political system had contributed (causally) to its phenomenal political and economic performance.[4]

---

4   However, since the bulk of the literature is static by nature, it does not quite tell us much about the endogenous effects of some of the outcomes mentioned above. We will elaborate on this point in the next section.

If the period between Deng's reforms and Xi's political ascendancy in 2012 is a good case for confirming almost all the positive predictions made by comparative authoritarianism literature, the literature certainly also provides with us some guidance for where Xi's China is heading. While we will still have to wait for enough data to draw reasonable conclusions on the effects of Xi's political manoeuvrings, what personalising an authoritarian regime will bring to its survival and economic performance has been well documented in the literature (Geddes, Wright & Frantz, 2018). First of all, the decrease in the level of power-sharing among elites enfeebles the regime internally by reducing the stake that excluded elites have in it. This fragility also arises from a more severe informational problem. Sheen, Tung and Wu (2022) have shown empirically that personalisation in a dictatorship leads to a lower degree of media freedom and therefore less information for the regime to know what is happening on the ground.

Externally, personalist authoritarian regimes are also more likely to engage in international conflicts and lose credibility with their foreign partners (Weeks, 2014). The outbreak of the China–US trade war during the Trump era can also be understood in this context where Xi's concentration of power, especially the removal of the two-term limit previously imposed on the Chinese presidency, has made China's trading partners suspicious of its expansionist foreign policies (e.g. the Belt and Road initiatives).

Moreover, the dialogue between the bodies of literature on comparative authoritarianism and China studies is certainly not unidirectional. As a matter of fact, the recent discussion about succession politics in dictatorships has provided such an opportunity for the Chinese case to enrich the former. Some studies in the literature (Brownlee, 2007b; Frantz & Stein, 2017) contend that higher institutionalisation in authoritarian succession rules will make a dictatorship more stable. This argument, however, contradicts what we have observed in China's elite politics. For example, right after Hu Jintao succeeded Jiang Zemin, Jiang initially held on to his chairmanship of the CPC Military Commission for two additional years, and his informal influence lingered nearly throughout the Hu era. Jiang's lingering influence apparently hurt Hu's credibility and made it painfully difficult for him to discipline other factional followers. Although this tension did not eventually result in any observable political crises that fundamentally undermined the CPC regime during Hu's tenure as the supreme leader, it implied a shifting power-sharing relationship between Hu as the dictator and other elites.

More theoretically, Jiang's continuing influence during the Hu era means that if we focus instead on power-sharing between the incumbent and his successor, it becomes clear that, paradoxically, tensions between the two can take place more easily when succession is more institutionalised. In a non-monarchic context where the incumbent and his/her successor share nothing but interests in common, the effect of institutionalised succession turns out to be the opposite of that predicted in the current literature. When the incumbent has less control over succession and needs to transfer power to someone who might hold different preferences—for example when the transition in leadership is institutionalised—there will be certainly less trust between the incumbent and the successor. More critically, this distrust is definitely not unidirectional. The successor might also be haunted by his/her predecessor's remaining influence. In other words, the successor might have to share power not only with other members in the winning coalition but also with the predecessor. This constitutes a principal source of tension between them.

What has to be noted here is that while the literature on comparative authoritarianism does help us understand more about Chinese politics through providing new conceptual tools and empirical evidence, its static nature nevertheless makes it ill-positioned to explain the changes in China's authoritarian institutions we have witnessed since Xi became its supreme leader in 2012 (Minzner, 2018; Tung, 2019). For example, several prominent top leaders (including retired ones) were imprisoned and tried openly in court. A huge number of government officials and party cadres from upper and lower echelons of the Chinese bureaucracy were jailed and expelled from the party under the name of the anti-graft campaign. Furthermore, the government has also tightened up social control, both on- and off-line. These recent political developments therefore call for a new theoretical framework that is able to address the dynamics of authoritarian institutions.

Revisiting censorship, partial media freedom and authoritarian responsiveness in China

As we have pointed out above, a number of recent empirical studies in the literature on comparative authoritarianism have shown that China's censorship strategy reflects responsive authoritarianism, a critical principle of governance. According to this idea, the Chinese government responds to social demands expressed through channels that are both institutional—

for example the People's Congress at the central (Truex, 2016) and local (Manion, 2016) levels—and non-institutional: media reports, online requests (Chen, Pan & Xu, 2016; Distelhorst & Hou, 2017) and protests (Lorentzen, 2013). This instrumentalist perspective on the freedom of media or speech under dictatorships has nonetheless assumed that information providers such as media outlets and microbloggers are non-strategic actors. As a result, as long as the government allows a high degree of freedom of speech, the information will be available immediately. It is therefore blind to cases in which an authoritarian government explicitly allows for the freedom of speech ex ante, but the fear of being punished ex post still causes them to self-censor.

As Wintrobe (1998, p. 20) mentioned early on, there is a difference as to 'whether the population genuinely worships them or worships them because they command such worship'. While the commands of dictators are met with obedience on the surface, the truth on the ground—for example the true level of people's support for the regime or real problems of their governance—might still elude them if self-censorship prevails. In other words, unless dictators are able to make a credible commitment to not censoring any news reports, the non-sustainable freedom of speech policy is unable to quench their thirst for information. As a result, it should be noted here that such an informational theory of authoritarian resilience is actually predicated on the fact that dictators are able both to avoid and to induce self-censorship among their citizens.

To address these theoretical questions on self-censorship, Sheen, Tung and Wu (2018) derive the conditions under which the dictator can (or cannot) induce truth-telling. Specifically, they show that even if the dictator requires truthful reporting ex ante, the media might not 'tell the truth'. Dictators suffer from more severe information insufficiency when society is rather stable or when they are more capable of manipulating information. Neglecting self-censorship in analysis leads to an underestimation of the amount of missing information in autocracies and an overestimation of an autocrat's level of tolerance of criticism and authoritarian responsiveness. In other words, scholars of authoritarian media politics should consider the role of self-censorship when they investigate how dictators strengthen or loosen their control on media outlets. Sheen, Tung and Wu (2018) also provide empirical predictions as a way for this literature to calibrate the magnitude of China's responsiveness while empirically investigating the self-censorship of citizens against their benchmarks.

Conclusion: Towards a dynamic comparative authoritarianism

In this article, we critically review the two decades of literature on comparative authoritarianism and how its insights can be applied to China. First of all, our review of the literature on authoritarian power-sharing helps make it clear how this literature explains post-Deng Chinese politics before Xi Jinping came to power. The paired case study on China above illustrates how political institutionalisation during Deng's era made power-sharing and succession among China's elite more stable. In addition, we also point out that this theoretical heuristic will have to be extended into a more dynamic theory so all the institutional and political changes brought by Xi Jinping to China's political landscape can be properly accounted for. Second, the chapter also reviews the politics of information under dictatorships and authoritarian responsiveness. As the literature nicely illustrates, the informational perspective helps explain China's partial media freedom for both traditional and social media, a situation in which reports and discussions about local corruption are allowed if reporters and netizens shy away from corruption involving the top leadership. What should be noted here is that this largely applies to pre-Xi Chinese politics alone.

More importantly, the key takeaway from our critical review is that the resilience of China's authoritarian regime definitely does not imply any stasis in its institutional foundations. Xi's various political manoeuvrings for personalising Chinese politics has ushered in a new chapter of China's political history, and it certainly behoves both political scientists and China scholars to figure out the political logic behind all these changes. It calls for a more dynamic understanding of how this stability was maintained and why certain (institutional) changes arose. The literature on comparative authoritarianism has so far mainly focused on identifying static effects of authoritarian institutions without paying much attention to their evolution. This review therefore would like to raise the attention of our colleagues to this important issue through investigating China's changing political landscape. This lacunae in the current literature not only provides new avenues for future research on China's post-Xi political developments but also allows the Chinese case to enrich the general literature on comparative authoritarianism. More specifically, we have witnessed in the 20th Party Congress how Xi's power manoeuvring culminated in his status as an unchallenged supreme leader inside the party. The various factors examined in this chapter have shed light on how he accomplished this.

It can also be expected that after Xi further recentralises political power in his hands, media freedom in China will be further reduced as the media can no longer serve as an information mechanism for stabilising the power-sharing structure among elites. In other words, the CPC would rely more on the state apparatus to collect information. However, there is a critical danger for the regime to depend on private information to govern the country, since the top political leaders still face a challenge of inducing their subordinates to tell the truth and respond to citizens' needs promptly and properly. Although the rise of digital authoritarianism might help the CPC to monitor society tightly, it might not always be able to afford the cost of maintaining such a giant surveillance system. Even if the CPC succeeds in staying in power with digital authoritarianism, it also strengthens entrenched groups in charge of the state censorship and surveillance. As a result, the CPC might not be able to secure correct information to govern the country as it keeps tightening its grasp.

References

Acemoglu, D., & Robinson, J.A. (2005) *Economic Origins of Dictatorship and Democracy.* Cambridge University Press

Bates, R.H., Greif, A., Levi, M., Rosenthal, J.L., & Weingast, B.R. (1998) *Analytic Narratives.* Princeton University Press

Boix, C. (2003) *Democracy and Redistribution.* Cambridge University Press

Boix, C., & Svolik, M.W. (2013) 'The foundations of limited authoritarian government: Institutions, commitment and power-sharing in dictatorships.' *Journal of Politics* 75(2): 300–16. doi.org/10.1017/S0022381613000029

Brownlee, J. (2007) *Authoritarianism in an Age of Democratisation.* Cambridge University Press

Bueno de Mesquita, B., Smith, A., Siverson, R.M., & Morrow, J.D. (2003) *The Logic of Political Survival.* MIT Press

Casper, B.A. (2017) 'IMF programs and the risk of a coup d'état.' *Journal of Conflict Resolution* 61(5): 964–96. doi.org/10.1177/0022002715600759

Chen, J., Pan, J., & Xu, Y. (2016) 'Sources of authoritarian responsiveness: A field experiment in China.' *American Journal of Political Science* 60(2): 383–400. doi.org/10.1111/ajps.12207

Chen, J., & Xu, Y. (2017) 'Why do authoritarian regimes allow citizens to voice opinions publicly?' *Journal of Politics* 79(3): 792–803. doi.org/10.1086/690303

Distelhorst, G., & Hou, Y. (2017) 'Constituency service under nondemocratic rule: Evidence from China.' *Journal of Politics* 79(3): 1024–40. doi.org/10.1086/690948

Edmond, C. (2013) 'Information manipulation, coordination and regime change.' *Review of Economic Studies* 80(4): 1422–58. doi.org/10.1093/restud/rdt020

Egorov, G., Guriev, S., & Sonin, K. (2009) 'Why resource-poor dictators allow freer media: A theory and evidence from panel data.' *American Political Science Review* 103(4): 645–8. doi.org/10.1017/S0003055409990219

Frantz, E., & Stein, E.A. (2017) 'Countering coups: Leadership succession rules in dictatorships.' *Comparative Political Studies* 50(7): 935–62. doi.org/10.1177/0010414016655538

Gandhi, J. (2008) *Political Institutions under Dictatorship.* Cambridge University Press

Gandhi, J., Heller, A.L., & Reuter, O.J. (2017) 'Expanding the pie: Compensating losers in authoritarian regimes.' Paper presented at the Midwest Political Science Association Conference. Chicago, April 6–9. Mimeo, Memphis, TN

Geddes, B., Wright, J., & Frantz, E. (2018) *How Dictatorships Work: Power, Personalization and Collapse.* Cambridge University Press

Gehlbach, S., & Keefer, P. (2011) 'Investment without democracy: Ruling-party institutionalisation and credible commitment in autocracies.' *Journal of Comparative Economics* 39(2): 123–39. doi.org/10.1016/j.jce.2011.04.002

Gehlbach, S., and Sonin, K. (2014) 'Government control of the media.' *Journal of Public Economics* 118: 163–71. doi.org/10.1016/j.jpubeco.2014.06.004

Gerasimov, G. (1998) 'Russia's media revolution: From party control to money control.' *Asia Pacific Issues* 37: 1–8

Hollyer, J.R., Rosendorff, B.P., & Vreeland, J.R. (2015) 'Transparency, protest and autocratic instability.' *American Political Science Review* 109(4): 764–84. doi.org/10.1017/S0003055415000428

—— (2019) 'Why do autocrats disclose? Economic transparency and inter-elite politics in the shadow of mass unrest.' *Journal of Conflict Resolution* 63(6): 1488–516. doi.org/10.1177/0022002718792602

King, G., Pan, J., and Roberts, M.E. (2013) 'How censorship in China allows government criticism but silences collective expression.' *American Political Science Review* 107(2): 326–43. doi.org/10.1017/S0003055413000014

—— (2014) 'Reverse-engineering censorship in China: Randomized experimentation and participant observation.' *Science* 345 (6199): 1–10. doi.org/10.1126/science.1251722

Lieberthal, K.G., & Lampton, D. (1992) *Bureaucracy, Politics and Decision Making in Post-Mao China.* University of California Press

Lieberthal, K.G., & Oksenberg, M. (1988) *Policy Making in China: Leaders, Structures and Processes.* Princeton University Press

Lorentzen, P. (2013) 'Regularizing rioting: Permitting public protest in an authoritarian regime.' *Quarterly Journal of Political Science* 8(2): 127–58. doi.org/10.1561/100.00012051

—— (2014) 'China's strategic censorship.' *American Journal of Political Science* 58(2): 402–14. doi.org/10.1111/ajps.12065

Magaloni, B. (2008) 'Credible power-sharing and the longevity of authoritarian rule.' *Comparative Political Studies* 41(4–5): 715–41. doi.org/10.1177/00104 14007313124

Manion, M. (2016) *Information for Autocrats: Representation in Chinese Local Congresses.* Cambridge University Press

Minzner, C. (2018) *End of an Era: How China's Authoritarian Revival is Undermining Its Rise.* Oxford University Press

Nathan, A.J. (2003) 'China's changing of the guard: Authoritarian resilience.' *Journal of Democracy*, 14(1): 6–17. doi.org/10.1353/jod.2003.0019

Qin, B., Strömberg, D., & Wu, Y. (2017) 'Why does China allow freer social media? Protests versus surveillance and propaganda.' *Journal of Economic Perspectives* 31(1): 117–40. doi.org/10.1257/jep.31.1.117

Repnikova, M. (2017) *Media Politics in China: Improvising Power under Authoritarianism.* University Printing House

Rodrik, D. (ed.) (2003) *In Search of Prosperity: Analytic Narratives on Economic Growth.* Princeton University Press

Sheen, G.C., Tung, H.H., & Wu, W. (2018) 'Tell me the truth: (Un)committable media freedom in dictatorships.' Paper presented at the Annual American Political Science Conference, Chicago

—— (2022) 'Power sharing and media freedom in dictatorships.' *Political Communication* 39(2): 202–21. doi.org/10.1080/10584609.2021.1988009

Shirk, S.L. (1993) *The Political Logic of Economic Reform in China.* University of California Press

Svolik, M. (2012) *The Politics of Authoritarian Rule.* Cambridge University Press

Truex, R. (2016) *Making Autocracy Work: Representation and Responsiveness in Modern China.* Cambridge University Press

Tung, H.H. (2019) *Economic Growth and Endogenous Authoritarian Institutions in Post-Reform China.* Palgrave Macmillan

Weeks, J. (2014) *Dictators at War and Peace.* Cornell University Press

Wintrobe, R. (1998) *The Political Economy of Dictatorship.* Cambridge University Press

Wright, J. (2008) 'To invest or insure? How authoritarian time horizons impact foreign aid effectiveness.' *Comparative Political Studies* 41(7): 971–1000. doi.org/10.1177/0010414007308538

4

Controlling the cadres: Dual elite recruitment logic and political manipulation under Xi Jinping

Chien-wen Kou and Wen-Hsuan Tsai[1]

Political development in China seems to show signs of a step backward from the 'institutional layering' introduced under Jiang Zemin and Hu Jintao (Kou, 2010, pp. 79–91).[2] Many scholars have noticed a tendency towards autocracy since Xi Jinping assumed office in 2012 (S. Lee, 2017, pp. 325–36). Xi has disregarded norms set by his predecessors (Minzner, 2018), particularly in elite recruitment (Shirk, 2018, pp. 29–30). How can we better understand the way Xi is strengthening his power and ability to rule through adaptations of the cadre recruitment policy? How do these institutional changes affect Chinese politics? This chapter aims to answer these questions.

A great deal of research has been carried out into the CPC's cadre management systems. Some scholars argue that the CPC manages its cadres through characteristics such as their level of education or whether they occupy posts in the party or the government system (Walder, 1995; Zang,

---

1   This chapter is a revised and updated version of the article that first appeared as C.W. Kou and W.H. Tsai (2021) 'Dual elite recruitment logic and political manipulation under Xi Jinping.' *Issues and Studies* 57(4), Article 2150015. doi.org/10.1142/S1013251121500156. Reprinted with permission.
2   In the period 2000–12, most scholars believed that China's political system was going to be institutionalised (Bo, 2004, pp. 70–100; Zang, 2005, pp. 204–17).

2004). Landry, Lü and Duan (2018) identify two dimensions of economic performance and political loyalty, and they hold that the CPC has adopted a dual strategy in the management of its cadres. For local cadres who hold lower-level positions, performance in managing the local economy plays a greater role in their advancement in the party. For the recruitment of higher-level cadres, however, political connections and political allegiance become more important (Landry, Lü and Duan, 2018). These scholars have found that the CPC's cadre recruitment is based both on the nature of the jobs they hold and their political performance and connections.

Given the valuable opinions on elite recruitment in the CPC put forward by Landry, Lü and Duan (2018), we further argue that like his predecessors Jiang Zemin and Hu Jintao, Xi Jinping prefers to recruit his trustees to important positions. He has done so however by disrupting the system and particularly by not complying with age requirements for the appointment and removal of cadres.[3] This has mainly occurred in two situations: when cadres are appointed to important positions despite their exceeding the age limits and when they are allowed to continue in their posts despite having reached retirement age. These practices have resulted in a rise in the average age of senior officials.

As Landry, Lü and Duan (2018) suggest, the CPC attaches great importance to the performance of leading cadres in government at the grassroots level. Compared with previous leaders, Xi Jinping has paid more attention to local governance and the recruitment of grassroots cadres. He has repeatedly emphasised the need to recruit young and talented cadres as a way of strengthening the party's governance at the grassroots level.[4] However, these leading grassroots cadres have often become a 'tool' of governance. Although they might have been rapidly promoted to county-level leadership positions at an early age, they appear to stay at this level indefinitely. Even if they

---

3   Dictators typically recruit and appoint capable and loyal cadres to key positions. This study places special emphasis on the age factor in discussing the recruitment and appointment of senior cadres because, from the 1980s onwards, cadre rejuvenation has been a significantly critical criterion for personnel changes at all levels of Chinese elite politics. However, Xi Jinping has violated this principle in the recruitment and appointment of senior cadres and this bears relatively significant political implications. For relevant discussions on how dictators conduct political recruitment and appointment, please refer to Egorov and Sonin (2011).

4   The quality Xi Jinping values most in grassroots cadres is ability. This does not mean that Xi does not value their loyalty but that he considers grassroots cadres to be less important than senior cadres for the consolidation of his power. In this light, for the recruitment and appointment of grassroots cadres, this chapter argues that Xi wishes to promote young and capable cadres to county-level leadership positions to handle local governance properly. We will discuss this topic in the second section.

have a chance of being promoted to higher-level posts such as those at the department level (厅级, *tingji*), they might have ceased to be competitive in terms of age at this point. In other words, there might not be a strong correlation between experience as a grassroots cadre and the chance of promotion to a high-level post later in one's career.

To better capture the above characteristics of cadre management under Xi Jinping, we propose the concept of 'dual elite recruitment logic'. Here, 'dual' refers to political elites,[5] both at and above the provincial/ministerial level (senior cadres) and those at the grassroots and particularly the county level (县级, *xianji*).[6] During a speech on governance delivered in 2015, Xi stressed the importance of a 'key minority' (关键少数, *guanjian shaoshu*) of officials—provincial/ministerial level (省部级, *shengbuji*) leaders and county party secretaries—and the need to keep an eye on their recruitment and appointment to positions (Xinhua Net, 2020). The two sets of elites dealt with in this paper—high-level and grassroots officials—are exactly within the scope of this key minority. Therefore the concept of a key minority is critical for the study of contemporary CPC political elites.

The research methods used in this chapter are as follows. When discussing senior cadres, the main unit of analysis is the provincial/ministerial level official. The figures show that the average age of cadres at this level is indeed increasing under Xi Jinping. This paper also finds that under Xi, senior cadres do not fully abide by the age norms established under Hu Jintao. In other words, there are some cases where cadres who are unqualified in terms of age are promoted and those at the official retirement age do not retire. When discussing grassroots cadres, the main unit of analysis is the county party secretary. Since Xi came to power, many cadres have been appointed to this post while younger than 40, which was a rare occurrence

---

5   The concept of 'dual' has a particular meaning in the study of contemporary Chinese political elites. Walder (1995) put forward a theory of dual elite selection in which political credentials (party membership) are taken as an important variable. Zang (2004) identified a difference in the source and process of selection and the replenishment of party and government cadres as 'elite dualism'. In Landry, Lü and Duan (2018), the high/low administrative levels are used in a study of dual elite recruitment. Using an approach similar to that of Landry, Lü and Duan, this chapter discusses the differences in the selection process of senior and grassroots cadres.

6   The sources of senior cadres are mainly elites with special political advantage, such as the second-generation reds (红二代, *hongerdai*), leaders' secretaries, cadres of state-owned enterprises, or cadres of the Communist Youth League during the Hu period. The grassroots cadres are mainly elites who are promoted by means of civil service examinations. However, if these people do not have special political advantage or credit, it is difficult to be promoted to senior cadre positions at the provincial and ministerial levels. In other words, the sources of recruitment for senior and grassroots cadres may be different.

during the Hu Jintao period. From the 2015 list of 'National Outstanding County Party Secretaries' (全国优秀县委书记, *quanguo youxiu xianwei shuji*), we find that the cadres who received this award did not have age advantages over the others. This indicates that being officially recognised as an outstanding county party secretary does not guarantee promotion to a high-level post. This is likely due to a wish of the authorities to see county-level leading cadres contributing to grassroots governance for a comparatively long period.

This chapter is organised as follows. In the section 'The political functions of the two categories of cadres and Xi's manipulation', we discuss the political functions of these two categories of cadres and the adjustments that have been made to the 'rejuvenation' principle under Xi Jinping's leadership, proposing the concept of 'dual elite recruitment logic'. In the section 'Disregarding age limits and the rising average age of high-ranking officials', we show how Xi has disregarded age norms in the recruitment of high-level cadres and that the average age of high-level cadres is rising. In the section 'Xi Jinping's personal experience and the importance he attaches to the selection of grassroots cadres', we attempt to discern why Xi is emphasising the importance of grassroots governance. In the section 'County party secretaries: "Tools" for use in governing the grassroots?', we explore the function of the county party secretary and argue that for the CPC, grassroots cadres are being used as 'tools' for grassroots governance. Cadres with work experience as a county party secretary are not guaranteed a better chance of promotion to high-level positions. We then draw our conclusions.

A concept of analysis: Dual elite recruitment logic

In relation to the concept used in our analysis, we will discuss three issues in the following subsections. First is the way in which the two categories of elites—senior and grassroots cadres—serve to strengthen political power at the centre and the grassroots, respectively. Second is the way in which Xi Jinping has changed the method of recruitment for these two categories of political elites in a bid to achieve his goals of strengthening his personal political power and enhancing local governance. Finally, we conclude that Xi has adjusted the norms governing the rejuvenation of the cadre body according to a 'dual elite recruitment logic'.

The political functions of the two categories of cadre and Xi's manipulation

Provincial/ministerial level cadres and county party secretaries, the 'key minority' particularly valued by Xi, are the elites discussed in this chapter. These two categories of cadre possess different political attributes and perform different functions.

Promotion to a provincial/ministerial-level post indicates that a cadre has entered the inner circle of CPC politics. The paramount leader's main source of power is the 'selectorate', composed mainly of members of the CPC Central Committee, the majority of whom are cadres at or above the provincial/ministerial level (Shirk, 1993, pp. 86–7).

Cadres at or above the provincial level are required to have an overall view of political work. Professional qualifications are not the party centre's major concern when it is promoting cadres to these positions. It is more a matter of their 'comprehensive qualities' (综合素质, *zonghe suzhi*), including their overall views (全局观, *quanjuguan*). Under Xi, a 'sense of alignment' (看齐意识, *kanqi yishi*)—that is, whether their attitude is aligned with Xi's own—is highly valued as part of their 'comprehensive qualities' (Lin, 2020).

In order for high-level and grassroots cadres to fulfil their respective functions as outlined above, Xi Jinping has manipulated cadre recruitment rules. His current obsession with consolidating his political power may have its roots in the Cultural Revolution in which he was a target of 'political struggle' (T. Lee, 2018, pp. 473–97; Torigian, 2018, pp. 7–15). Xi's other goal is to 'modernise the national governance system and governance capabilities'. This might explain his enthusiasm for grassroots governance, which exceeds that of his predecessors Jiang Zemin and Hu Jintao. Xi's pursuit of these two goals has caused him to change the policy of 'rejuvenating' the regime's cadres, which has gradually evolved since Jiang Zemin's time in office (Kou, 2010, pp. 269–309). As such, the current criteria for selecting senior and grassroots cadres differ from those of the past.

When appointing cadres to full provincial/ministerial-level posts, Xi pays particular attention to political loyalty as it is essential for the consolidation of his power (Wang & Zeng, 2016, pp. 470–81). A large number of Xi's confidants have been recruited to positions at this level, and his excessive emphasis on political loyalty has resulted in many cadres nearing retirement age either remaining in office or being promoted. Rejuvenation has been halted, and the principle of age limits for promotion is no longer being adhered to.

County-level leading cadres, on the other hand, function differently. They are in charge of grassroots governance and situated far from the political power struggles of the CPC central leadership. In grassroots governance, county-level leaders have more discretionary power than provincial or prefecture-level city leaders. Governments above the county level are usually involved in laying down more abstract guiding principles, which county-level governments have to follow when they are devising detailed policies suited to local needs (Fan, 2008, p. 10; Heberer & Schubert, 2012, pp. 228–31).

Xi also wants to create a new cohort of grassroots cadres to strengthen local governance. To accelerate the promotion of grassroots cadres, several measures for 'exceptional promotions' (破格提拔, *poge tiba*) have been adopted. 'Exceptional promotion' refers to promotions within two years of appointment to a post (Hu, 2020). One common practice is the 'selected and transferred graduate' (选调生, *xuandiaosheng*) system under which local governments sign contracts with universities to select talented graduates on an annual basis for posts in grassroots governments. This system came into operation in 1986. *Xuandiaosheng* usually start their careers in section-level posts handling important tasks such as poverty alleviation and economic development. For grassroots cadres, serving as *xuandiaosheng* is a fast track to promotion. *Xuandiaosheng* take a relatively shorter time to be promoted from section-level to county-level positions compared to other civil servants.

Although the *xuandiaosheng* system was not established during the Xi Jinping era, Xi encouraged local governments to increase the number of *xuandiaosheng* serving as public officials through the assistance of Chen Xi (陈希), head of the CPC Central Organisation Department and a close confidant of Xi. Through this *xuandiaosheng* mechanism, Xi promoted a large number of outstanding and young cadres to serve in county-level leadership positions (Xiao, 2012). This has been a critical promotion avenue for grassroots cadres during the Xi era that enables them to advance to county-level positions at relatively younger ages. The CPC has recruited a large number of university graduates since Xi came to power to work at the grassroots level through such channels (Tsai & Liao, 2019).

Under Xi Jinping, detailed regulations have been formulated governing the 'exceptional promotion' (破格提拔, *poge tiba*) of grassroots cadres.[7] The aim is to cultivate a cohort of talented cadres to strengthen grassroots governance. In 2014, the CPC revised the 'Regulations on the Selection and Appointment of Leading Cadres of the Party and Government' (党政领导干部选拔任用工作条例, *dangzheng lingdao ganbu xuanba renyong gongzuo tiaoli*, hereafter referred to as 'the Regulations') ('Zhonggong Zhongyang Yinfa', 2019). Standards for 'exceptional promotions' are mentioned in Article 9 of the 2014 version. These specify that cadres who accomplish important tasks can be swiftly promoted or even leapfrog over people above them:

> [Cadres] who can withstand the test, have outstanding performance and make great contributions at critical moments or when they are undertaking urgent and risky tasks; those with outstanding work performance in regions or units with difficult conditions, in complex environments or in backward areas; and those who work earnestly and dutifully in their positions and whose work performance is particularly remarkable.

Rejuvenation of cadres revisited

In the above discussion, we have attempted to clarify the logic of cadre recruitment under Xi Jinping. The relevant policies introduced after Xi took office have indeed brought about major changes in the operation of Chinese politics (Brødsgaard, 2018; Doyon, 2018). To achieve his goals—namely, the consolidation of his political power and the strengthening of grassroots governance—Xi has changed the promotion criteria for both senior and grassroots cadres. The pace of rejuvenation has been slowed for cadres at or above the full provincial/ministerial level, and, by ignoring the rules on terms of office, Xi has sought to consolidate his power by promoting his confidants. For grassroots cadres (particularly county party secretaries), he has mandated the selection and promotion of young and talented officials and subjected them to rigorous exposure and training. This dual elite recruitment logic for cadres under Xi Jinping is summarised in table 4.1.

---

7   Some other 'exceptional promotion' methods have been adopted, such as that of 'college graduate village officials' (大学生村官, *daxuesheng cunguan*) (G. He & Wang, 2017) who occupy temporary positions (挂职, *guazhi*) (Tsai & Liao, 2020, pp. 52–5).

Table 4.1: Dual elite recruitment logic under Xi Jinping

	Priority goals	
Argument from the literature	Consolidating power among the political elite	Strengthening grassroots governance
Landry, Lü and Duan's suggestions	Political allegiance prioritised in the recruitment of high-ranking cadres	Administrative ability prioritised in the recruitment of grassroots cadres
Supplementary point of view argued by the authors	To senior cadres, Xi disregards age norms to promote his associates; Jiang Zemin and Hu Jintao had basically adhered to age norms to promote their associates	To grassroots cadres, Xi Jinping strengthened the use of 'exceptional promotions' to appoint young cadres as county party secretaries seen as 'tools' for governance and not necessarily intended for further promotions

Source: Compiled by the authors based on Landry, Lü and Duan (2018).

Xi Jinping prioritises political allegiance when recruiting cadres to provincial/ministerial-level posts, and in doing so he has to some extent disregarded age norms. As a result, the process of rejuvenation at this level has slowed and a large number of cadres from Xi's faction have been appointed. Through these practices, Xi aims to consolidate his power among the political elite. Concerning the system for recruiting county-level elites (this chapter mainly investigates the appointment of county party secretaries, 县委书记, *xianwei shuji*), the CPC aims to promote and train more competent young cadres (Schubert & Ahlers, 2012, pp. 67–86). In contrast to the situation under Hu Jintao, some cadres born since 1980 (the post-1980s generation who were younger than 40 in 2020) have been appointed to county party secretary posts. However, these young cadres are probably being used as tools by Xi. They are useful for improving governance at the grassroots but are likely to remain in county-level leadership posts for a long time without being offered promotions to provincial-level posts.

This dual elite recruitment logic on the one hand reflects the CPC's recent perception that 'rejuvenationism' (唯年轻化, *wei nianqinghua*) for senior cadres has gone too far and, on the other hand, Xi's desire to carry out 'modernisation of the national governance system and governance capabilities' (国家治理体系与治理能力现代化, *guojia zhili tixi yu zhili nengli xiandaihua*) (Xia, 2019). To consolidate his position in the party central and ensure the continuation of his political line, Xi has promoted cadres to full provincial/ministerial-level posts chiefly on the basis of their political loyalty. At the grassroots level, however, Xi recognises the necessity of training up a cohort of young, vigorous cadres capable of reinforcing the CPC's hold on local governance and responding to the demands of society (Oi et al., 2012, pp. 649–75).

Disregarding age limits and the rising average age of high-ranking officials

The main political function of high-ranking officials is to consolidate the power of the paramount leader. This has prompted paramount leaders throughout the history of the CPC regime to reserve provincial/ministerial-level posts for their associates. Jiang Zemin, Hu Jintao and Xi Jinping have all appointed trusted political cronies to key positions in the leadership, although they differ in their degree of adherence to age limit norms. There are two age limits: the mandatory retirement age and the age at which a cadre becomes ineligible for further promotions.[8] When cadres reach their mandatory retirement age, they are expected either to retire or to be transferred to 'second-front' posts. Both of these age limits originate from Deng Xiaoping's reform of the cadre system in the early 1980s, which involved the abolition of life tenure for leading posts (废除领导干部终身制, *feichu lingdao ganbu zhongshenzhi*) and the promotion of 'more revolutionary, younger, better educated and more professionally competent' (革命化, 年轻化, 知识化, 专业化, *geminghua, nianqinghua, zhishihua, zhuanyehua*) cadres. This system developed and became customary under Jiang Zemin and Hu Jintao.

Jiang and Hu promoted their close associates—members of the Shanghai clique in Jiang's case and cadres with a Youth League background in Hu's—to leading posts, but they did so in line with the above-mentioned age limits. In contrast, Xi Jinping is prepared to disregard these age limits, and the limits have lost their binding force for this reason. We examined records of 268 civilian cadres with CPC membership who were holding full ministerial or deputy state leader positions in central or provincial party organs or governments between November 2012 and October 2020. We found that 13 of these were in breach of the mandatory retirement age and that 40 had been promoted in violation of the age limit for promotion (see table 4.2). There have been more cases of the violation of age limits since Xi came to power than there were under Hu Jintao. For example,

---

8   For a discussion of changes in age limits since the 1980s, see Kou (2010, pp. 138–40, 188–91, 194–6, 271–3). For more discussion of the age at which cadres become ineligible for promotion, see Kou and Tsai (2014, pp. 156–7).

Wang Qishan (王岐山, born July 1948) retired from the CPC Politburo Standing Committee in October 2017 but was elected vice president of the PRC in March 2018. He would have been expected to retire at the age of 68.

Table 4.2: Retirement and promotion age limits for CPC cadres and violations of those limits, November 2012–October 2020

Position/rank	Age of ineligibility for promotion	Violation cases*	Mandatory retirement age	Violation cases*
State leader (正国, *zhengguo*)	n/a	n/a	68**	1 (0, 1)
Deputy state leader (副国, *fuguo*)				
Minister (正部, *zhengbu*)	64	0	65	10 (0, 10)
Deputy minister (副部, *fubu*)	58	41 (6, 35)	60	2 (0, 2)

* A case is defined as a violation if the cadre is promoted 12 months after reaching the age of ineligibility for promotion or remains in power 12 months after reaching the mandatory retirement age. The first number within the parentheses in the violation cases cell represents the number of violations during the Hu era, while the second number refers to cases during the Xi era.

** A leader should no longer seek re-election after the age of 68, although they can remain in office until the end of their term.

Source: Kou (2012). Cases were calculated and tabulated by the authors.

Under Xi Jinping, there have been 10 cases of cadres remaining in a provincial/ministerial post beyond the mandatory retirement age of 65. In late 2019, Luo Huining (骆惠宁, born October 1954) was appointed as deputy head of the Finance and Economic Affairs Committee of the National People's Congress, having previously been the party secretary of Shanxi Province. This is a typical personnel arrangement for newly retired cadres of full ministerial rank. However, his appointment as director of the Liaison Office of the Central People's Government in Hong Kong in January 2020 violates the age limit of 65 years. He Yiting (何毅亭, born 1952) continued to serve as executive vice president of the CPC Central Party School until December 2020 despite being over 65. No executive presidents of the Central Party School violated this rule while Hu Jintao was in power.[9] In another example, Chen Hao (陈豪, born February 1954) retired as party secretary of Yunnan province in November 2020 when he was approaching 67.

The mandatory retirement age for cadres at the deputy provincial/ministerial level is 60. However, Lin Duo (林铎, born March 1956) advanced to full ministerial rank as party secretary of Gansu province at the age of 61 in March 2017 after having previously held a deputy ministerial rank. Liu Kun (刘昆, born December 1956) retired as deputy minister of finance in December 2016 at the age of 60 and was transferred to the National People's Congress. In March 2018, however, he came out of retirement to take up a front-line position as minister of finance.

The rules on age limits for promotion have been significantly weakened since Xi Jinping came to power. For example, Fu Zhenghua (傅政华, born March 1955) was promoted to full ministerial rank in March 2015 as executive deputy head of the Ministry of Public Security. Yu Weiguo (于伟国, born October 1955) was appointed governor of Fujian province in January 2016, his first full ministerial-level post. These promotions all violate the age limit of 58 years for cadres at the deputy ministerial level. Other close associates of Xi Jinping have also been promoted in violation of the age limits, including Cai Qi (蔡奇), Liu He (刘鹤), Liu Cigui (刘赐贵), Wang Xiaohong (王小洪), Yang Xiaodu (杨晓渡) and Ying Yong (应勇).

The average age of full ministerial-level cadres has also risen under Xi Jinping compared to his predecessors. We have examined the age distribution of full provincial/ministerial-level cadres (including leaders of provincial party committees, provincial governments and the State Council) at the beginning of their terms of office over the past two decades. There are a total of 363 cases (see table 4.3). Another 42 individuals are excluded from the analysis because they concurrently held a post at deputy state leader level. For example, Beijing party secretaries are also members of the CPC Politburo. Their mandatory retirement age is 68 rather than 65, so they are older on average than their full provincial/ministerial-level colleagues.

The ages in these 363 cases averaged at 58.2 in 2003, 57.9 in 2008, 59.0 in 2013 and 59.8 in 2018. This means that ranking cadres in the Hu era could remain in service for seven years on average after advancing to full

---

9   Yu Yunyao (虞云耀) and Li Jingtian (李景田) both retired at age 65. Su Rong (苏荣) left the post and became party secretary of Jiangxi province before he was 65 years old.

ministerial rank, whereas they served for an average of five to six years under Xi Jinping. Two additional findings reveal an increase in the average age of ranking cadres. From the Hu era to the Xi era, the number of cases in the age range of 61–65 steadily increased from 2003 to 2018 while those in the age range of 56–60 decreased. The number of cases under 55 years of age also decreased under Xi Jinping. These findings are displayed in table 4.3.

Table 4.3: The ageing of full ministerial-level cadres from the Hu era to the Xi era

Age range						Cases	Average	Minimum	Maximum
Year	41–45	46–50	51–55	56–60	61–65	66–70			

Year	41–45	46–50	51–55	56–60	61–65	66–70	Cases	Average	Minimum	Maximum
2003	2	6	8	54	26	0	94	58.2	46.3	64
2008	0	2	19	37	32	0	92	57.9	44.8	64
2013	0	6	10	42	35	1	90	59.0	46.1	67.4
2018	0	1	12	29	44	1	87	59.8	49.1	65.5

*The ranking cadres under analysis are provincial party secretaries, governors and leading officials of full ministerial rank in the General Office of the State Council, constituent departments of the State Council (国务院组成部门, *guowuyuan zucheng bumen*), special organisations directly under the State Council (国务院直属特设机构, *guowuyuan zhishu teshe jigou*), organisations directly under the State Council (国务院直属机构, *guowuyuan zhishu jigou*) and the administrative offices of the State Council (国务院办事机构, *guowuyuan banshi jigou*).

**The data were accessed on 1 August 2003, 2008, 2013 and 2018. Forty individuals have been counted two or three times in different age ranges owing to the length of their terms of office.

Source: Kou (2012). The cases were calculated and tabulated by the authors.

Xi Jinping's personal experience and the importance he attaches to the selection of grassroots cadres

Another level of leadership discussed in this chapter consists of grassroots cadres whose political function lies mainly in local governance. Here we pay particular attention to the recruitment of county party secretaries. Xi Jinping has emphasised the importance of governance at the county level, something that might be attributable to his early experience as an official in Ding County, Hebei (河北定县, Hebei Dingxian) in the 1980s. A decade later, Xi penned an article on the importance of county party secretaries in which he wrote the following:

I once served as a county party secretary and whenever I talked with my colleagues, we always complained in much the same way: our ranks were not high, but neither were our responsibilities small. If the country is compared to a net, then the three thousand or so counties are like the knots (纽结, *niujie*) in this net. Once the 'knots' get loose, political unrest will occur in the country; if the 'knots' are strong and reliable, the political situation will be stable. No state decrees and ordinances would fail to be thoroughly implemented through the counties. Therefore, in view of the relationship between the whole and the part, the rise or fall and the safety or danger, of the country depends on whether work at the county-level is good or bad. (Study Group, 2015, p. 64)

An article on the People's Net website also underlines the importance that Xi Jinping attaches to the functions of the county party secretary (*Renmin Wang* [人民网], 2015a). Jiao Yulu (焦裕录) is one such party secretary who served in Henan province in the 1960s. He has been held up by Xi Jinping as a model (Zhongguo Gongqingtuan, 2016). Xi has been quoted as saying, 'to serve as a county party secretary, one has to be a Jiao Yulu–style county party secretary'. Xi launched a movement to learn from Jiao Yulu in 2014, and he is convinced that the experience a cadre gains while serving as a county party secretary forms the cornerstone of one's career.

Xi is opposed to party and government leaders rising to power through the Communist Youth League. In 2016, he issued regulations stipulating that Youth League cadres must have 'a clear orientation of not "becoming an official"'. Xi has therefore limited the role of the league, making it refocus on youth work so that it will never again serve as a springboard for career advancement.[10] Instead, cadres aspiring to rise through the ranks should first hone their governing skills through work as county party secretaries.

The Central Party School organised a series of 'county party secretary workshops' (县委书记研修班, *xianwei shuji yanxiuban*) in 2014, and by the end of 2017, every county party secretary in the country had attended this two-month course taught by heads of central government departments and commissions as well as by regular lecturers. One compulsory set text was *Xi Jinping on the Governance of China* (习近平谈治国理政, *xi jinping tan zhiuguo lizheng*), and Xi personally delivered an address at every graduation

---

10 Before Xi Jinping came to power, Communist Youth League cadres had to be transferred to party and government departments before they reached a certain age. As a result, when league cadres were transferred, they were usually younger than non-league cadres of the same level.

ceremony (Chu, 2015). Xi tried to make the acquaintance of as many outstanding county party secretaries as possible so that he would know who should be later promoted (*Renmin Wang*, 2015a).

Xi also values national awards for outstanding county party secretaries. These awards were introduced by the Central Organisation Department in 1995, although they lapsed after the first year. Xi revived them in 2015 when around a hundred outstanding county party secretaries were commended. Since then, he has presented the awards in person each year. In his speech at the 2015 award ceremony, Xi said that 'peace will descend on the country when the prefectures and counties are in order' (郡县治，天下安, *junxian zhi, tianxia an*) and that 'county party committees are the "first line of command" (一线指挥部, *yixian zhihuibu*) of our party in governing and rejuvenating our country and county party secretaries are the "first-line commanders-in-chief"' (*Renmin Wang*, 2015b).

There are presently several cadres who were born after 1980 (80后, *ba ling hou*) serving as county party secretaries. There were fewer cadres in their thirties holding similar positions under Hu Jintao (Tsai & Liao, 2019, pp. 951–4) or under Jiang Zemin (see table 4.4).

Table 4.4: County party secretaries in their thirties under Hu Jintao and Xi Jinping

Leader Cadre	Hu Jintao	Xi Jinping
Name, year of appointment, age	Dong Yuyi, 2012, 31	Yang Zunfeng, 2012, 32; Zhang Hui, 2013, 33; Zhou Senfeng, 2013, 33; Zhou Mi, 2014, 32; Li Teng, 2014, 32; Liu Kai, 2015, 32; Jin Li, 2015, 35; Wang Xiwei, 2016, 35; Yao Ning, 2019, 34; Zheng Shao, 2019, 39; Qiu Ling, 2019, 37; Su Jianjun, 2019, 38; Huang Xiuhang, 2020, 39; Ma Ju, 2020, 39; He Yefang, 2020, 34; Li Ming, 2020, 38; Hu Haiyang, 2020, 39; Hanxu, 2020, 38
Number	1	18

Source: Search engines Google and Baidu.

It is reasonable to expect that there are even more cadres in their thirties or even younger who presently serve as county governors or township leading cadres. Owing to a lack of data, we cannot precisely conclude that the average age of county-level leading cadres has been lower under Xi Jinping than when Hu Jintao was the CPC general secretary. What can be said with certainty is that more county party secretaries in their thirties have been singled out as model cadres in the Xi era and that this has encouraged regional governments to actively recruit younger cadres as county-level leaders (Zhang, 2016).

County party secretaries: 'Tools' for use in governing the grassroots?

While the CPC's emphasis on grassroots governance under Xi Jinping has encouraged the appointment of younger cadres to positions as county party secretaries, we argue that these cadres are not necessarily being promoted to higher-ranking posts. In short, the CPC is treating them as 'tools' for grassroots governance. As mentioned above, Xi Jinping has underlined their importance with the example of Jiao Yulu, a county party secretary from the 1960s. He has, however, asked cadres to 'focus on your contribution to the people instead of pursuing high-ranking posts' (*Renmin Wang*, 2020). In other words, he expects county party secretaries to dedicate themselves to grassroots governance instead of using their county posts as a springboard for promotion.

Cadres named as 'National Outstanding County Party Secretaries' tend to be older than expected (see table 4.5). No cadres in their thirties received the award in 2015; the average age is 50.21. Twenty-seven of the recipients were in their forties, including Zhang Xiaoqiang (张晓强, 40), Meng Lingxing (孟令兴, 41), Chen Junlin (陈俊林, 41, whereabouts uncertain), Zhang Xia (张霞, 42, female and an ethnic minority), Ji Jianjun (吉建军, 43), Zhang Dingcheng (张定成, 43), Hu Qisheng (胡启生, 44), Ren Houming (任厚明, 44), Yang Fasen (杨发森, 44), Chen Xingjia (陈行甲, 44, who later transferred to the private sector), Lin Hongyu (林红玉, 45), Li Junxia (李君霞, 45), Liao Guisheng (廖桂生, 45), Xiong Zhengyu (熊征宇, 45), Wang Xiaojiang (王晓江, 46), Sun Juxian (孙巨先, 46), Sun Jingmin (孙京民, 47), Liao Junbo (廖俊波, 47, later deceased), Zeng Yu (曾瑜, 47, female), Wang Hongbin (王洪斌, 48), Zheng Guangquan (郑光泉, 48), Nan Pei (南培, 48 and an ethnic minority), Li Jianfeng (李建锋, 49), Liu Xianwei (刘先伟, 49), Zhou Xin (周新, 49), Jiang Gang (蒋刚, 49) and Feng Zhendong (冯振东, 49, suspended from duty for corruption).

Table 4.5: Data on recipients of the National Outstanding County Party Secretaries Award, 2015

Rank in 2020 Content	County level	Deputy department level	Department level	Deputy provincial/ ministerial level	Other
Number of people	4	62	16	9	Suspended: 8 Deceased: 1 Transferred to the private sector: 1 Whereabouts uncertain: 1
The average age in 2015	50.21				

Source: Huanqiu Wang (2020); Google and Baidu.

Of the recipients of the award, nine now hold deputy ministerial-level posts. They are, however, relatively old, with one being 63, one 60, two 59, one 58, two 57, one 56 and one 55. Indeed, the recipients tended to be older than several other young deputy provincial/ministerial-level cadres in 2020, such as vice chair of the Tibet Autonomous Region Ren Wei (43); vice governor of Jiangxi province Wu Hao (48); vice chair of the Ningxia Hui Autonomous Region Lai Jiao (48); vice governor of Zhejiang province Liu Xiaotao (50); or Zhou Hongbo of the Guangxi Zhuang Autonomous Region (50). The youngest award recipient in 2015, Zhang Xiaoqiang (now 45), is the department-level party secretary of Shantou. He was not competitive in terms of age compared to other young department-level cadres in 2020, such as the general manager of the Lu'an Company, Liu Junyi (39), or party secretary of the Henan Province Communist Youth League Wang Yi (40, female).

Judging from the above, we suggest that the CPC uses county party secretaries as 'tools' for governing the grassroots and does not necessarily consider them as candidates for high-ranking posts. Although they might have been fast-tracked into county party secretary posts, their subsequent careers have generally slowed or even stagnated, indicating that the CPC plans to keep these cadres in low-level posts for the long term.

Another example of a county party secretary whose career has stalled is Zhou Senfeng (周森锋), a selected and transferred graduate (*Renmin Wang*, 2019) who was appointed to a deputy division-level leading cadre post at 28, promoted to the division head level at 29 and had become a district party secretary (equivalent to a county party secretary) by the age of 33. As of 2020, Zhou (40 years old) had been at the county party secretary level for six years. This is further proof that the CPC intends this group of cadres to continue in grassroots governance. As they are younger, they have the ability to remain in their posts until they achieve results. What is of greater importance is that these cadres might not be candidates for leading positions at or above the ministerial level. In particular, they are unlikely to be seen as future political successors (H. He, 2015, pp. 36–8).

Conclusion

Xi Jinping is trying to consolidate his power among senior cadres and strengthen grassroots governance using a new cadre recruitment policy shaped by dual elite recruitment logic. He has slowed down the rejuvenation of the leadership at or above the full provincial/ministerial level, interrupting the terms of office of cadres to prevent high-level ones from developing power bases and threatening his authority. In this way, Xi will be able to extend his term as general secretary beyond the 20th Party Congress, and, in an effort to strengthen grassroots governance, he has overseen the selection and promotion of young and spirited cadres to serve as grassroots leaders, particularly county party secretaries. However, it has been observed that while many county party secretaries were younger than 40 when they were appointed, they are unlikely to achieve a swift promotion to such positions as division head or bureau director. This seems to indicate that Xi wishes to keep them at the grassroots to solve local social and economic problems. Will these selected and transferred graduates be promoted to higher positions in the future? It is difficult to answer this question as Xi's cadre recruitment system began less than a decade ago, and more time must be devoted to observing its future development.

Xi Jinping's adoption of a dual elite recruitment logic may largely be explained by his determination to modernise China's governance system during his term of office. Although Jiang Zemin and Hu Jintao emphasised the importance of grassroots governance, they did not quickly promote a large number of outstanding young people to serve as county-level leaders in the way that Xi Jinping did, breaking certain conventions. In other words, a difference in the degree of intensity may be identified between Xi and his predecessors regarding the speed with which outstanding young people are selected to serve as grassroots leaders. In his recruitment policy for senior cadres, Xi Jinping acts fundamentally differently from Jiang and Hu. Xi Jinping values cadre loyalty above other factors, such as age. Xi Jinping has recruited some who are close to him, despite their being near or past retirement age, to important positions. This did not occur under Jiang Zemin and Hu Jintou.

Xi Jinping's particular practice has also caused Chinese politics under his administration to take a different path from the way it has tended to go in the past. Unlike Jiang Zemin and Hu Jintao, who are willing to give subordinates more power, Xi Jinping has a near monopoly on political authority. One factor influencing Xi's decision to dispense with the previous recruitment system has been his reluctance to make arrangements for a successor by allowing other leaders to share some of his power as his predecessors Hu Jintao and Jiang Zemin did. Some authorities hold that dictators seek to gain support from their colleagues by sharing power (Magaloni, 2008, pp. 715–41). However, this theory has been challenged in present-day China. Xi intends to extend his rule beyond the 20th Party Congress and purge any cadres who oppose him, thus treading a winner-takes-all path.

What, then, are China's political prospects? At least in the short run, the regime is likely to exhibit the characteristics of authoritarian resilience (Nathan, 2003, pp. 6–17; Shambaugh, 2008). However, if there arise serious unforeseen problems such as a threat to Xi's life or a deterioration in his health, the lack of an appointed successor could spark an intense power struggle at the top. Even if grassroots-level cadres perform exceptionally well, the overall political situation in China will still be seriously affected if the central leadership is destabilised. As Xi appears to have dispensed with the conventions and regulations governing political succession so that he can concentrate power in his own hands, his greatest mistake has perhaps been his failure to institutionalise any new procedures for succession.

References

Bo, Z. (2004) 'The institutionalisation of elite management in China.' In *Holding China Together: Diversity and National Integration in the Post-Deng Era*, ed. B.J. Naughton & D.L. Yang, pp. 70–100. Cambridge University Press

Brødsgaard, K.E. (2018) 'China's political order under Xi Jinping: Concepts and perspectives.' *China: An International Journal* 16(3): 1–17. doi.org/10.1353/chn.2018.0022

Chu, X. [储信艳] (2015) 'Jiemi zhongyang dangxiao xianwei shuji yanxiuban' [揭秘中央党校县委书记研修班, Revealing the secret of the County Party Secretary Workshop of the Central Party School]. Xinhua Net [新华网], January. www.xinhuanet.com/politics/2015-01/14/c_127385318.htm

Doyon, J. (2018) 'Clientelism by design: Personnel politics under Xi Jinping.' *Journal of Current Chinese Affairs* 47(3): 87–110. doi.org/10.1177/1868102618047 00304

Egorov, G., & Sonin, K. (2011) 'Dictators and their viziers: Endogenizing the loyalty-competence trade-off.' *Journal of the European Economic Association* 9(5): 903–30. doi.org/10.1111/j.1542-4774.2011.01033.x

Fan, H. [樊红敏] (2008) *Xianyu Zhengzhi: Quanli Shijian Yu Richang Zhixu* [县域政治：权力实践与日常秩序, County politics: The practice of power and order of the day]. China Social Sciences Press

He, G., & Wang, S. (2017) 'Do college graduates serving as village officials help rural China?' *American Economic Journal: Applied Economics* 9(4): 186–215. doi.org/10.1257/app.20160079

He, H. [贺海峰] (2015) '100 ming xian wei shuji de 20 nian' [100名县委书记的20年, 20 years of 100 County Party Secretaries]. *Juece* [决策, Decision-Making], Z1: 36–8

Heberer, T., & Schubert, G. (2012) 'County and township cadres as a strategic group: A new approach to political agency in China's local state.' *Journal of Chinese Political Science* 17(3): 221–49. doi.org/10.1007/s11366-012-9200-8

Huanqiu Wang (环球网, 2020) 'Zhonggong zhongyang zuzhibu guanyu biaozhang quanguo youxiu xianwei shuji de jueding' [中共中央组织部关于表彰全国优秀县委书记的决定, The CPC Central Organisation Department's decision on honoring national outstanding county party secretaries]. 4 November. china.huanqiu.com/article/9CaKrnJMBCk

Kou, C.W. [寇健文] (2010) *Zhonggong Jingying Zhengzhi De Yanbian: Zhiduhua Yu Quanli Zhuanyi 1978–2010* [中共菁英政治的演变：制度化与权力转移1978–2010, The evolution of CPC elite politics: Institutionalisation and the transfer of power, 1978–2010]. Wunan

—— (2012) Zhonggong Zhengzhi Jinying Ziliaoku [中共政治菁英数据库, Chinese political elite dataset]. Retrieved from National Chengchi University: cped.nccu.edu.tw/

Kou, C.W., & Tsai, W.H. (2014) '"Sprinting with small steps" towards promotion: Solutions for the age dilemma in the CCP cadre appointment system.' *China Journal* 71: 155–75. doi.org/10.1086/674558

Landry, P.F., Lü, X., & Duan, H. (2018) 'Does performance matter? Evaluating political selection along the Chinese administrative ladder.' *Comparative Political Studies* 51(8): 1074–105. doi.org/10.1177/0010414017730078

Lee, S. (2017) 'An institutional analysis of Xi Jinping's centralisation of power.' *Journal of Contemporary China* 26(105): 325–36. doi.org/10.1080/10670564 .2016.1245505

Lee, T. (2018) 'Can Xi Jinping be the next Mao Zedong? Using the big five model to study political leadership.' *Journal of Chinese Political Science* 23: 473–97. doi.org/10.1007/s11366-018-9540-0

Lin, Q. [林巧婷] (2020) 'Xi Jinping zai shengbuji zhuyao lingdao ganbu zhuanti yantaoban shang fabiao jianghua' [习近平在省部级主要领导干部专题研讨班上发表讲话, Xi Jinping's address to the special subject class of provincial level leading cadres]. Zhongyang Zhengfu Menhu Wangzhan [中央政府门户网站, Central Government Portal], 15 December. www.gov.cn/xinwen/2015-02/02/ content_2813544.htm

Magaloni, B. (2008) 'Credible power-sharing and the longevity of authoritarian rule.' *Comparative Political Studies* 41(4/5): 715–41. doi.org/10.1177/0010414 007313124

Minzner, C. (2018) *End of an Era: How China's Authoritarian Revival is Undermining Its Rise*. Oxford University Press

Nathan, A. (2003) 'China's changing of the guard: Authoritarian resilience.' *Journal of Democracy* 14(1): 6–17. doi.org/10.1353/jod.2003.0019

Oi, J.C., Babiarz, K.S., Zhang, L., Luo, R., & Rozelle, S. (2012) 'Shifting fiscal control to limit cadre power in China's townships and villages.' *China Quarterly* 211: 640–75. doi.org/10.1017/S0305741012000823

Renmin Wang (人民网, 2015a) 'Anhui shengwei fushuji Li Jinbin jieren Anhui daishengzhang' [安徽省委副书记李锦斌接任安徽代省长, Deputy Anhui Party Secretary Li Jinbin takes office as acting governor of Anhui]. June. politics. people.com.cn/BIG5/n/2015/0609/c70731-27123060.html

—— (2015b) 'Xi Jinping: Junxian zhi, tianxia an' [习近平：郡县治，天下安, Xi Jinping: Peace will descend on the country if the prefectures and counties are in order]. 1 July. society.people.com.cn/n/2015/0701/c136657-27233342.html

—— (2019) 'Dangzheng lingdao ganbu xuanba renyong gongzuo tiaoli' [党政领导干部选拔任用工作条例, Regulations on the selection and appointment of leading cadres of the party and government]. 18 March. cpc.people.com.cn/ BIG5/n1/2019/0318/c419242-30980036.html

—— (2020) 'Xi Jinping: Buqiu "guan" you duoda, dan qiu wukui yu min' [习近平：不求「官」有多大，但求无愧于民, Xi Jinping: Focus on your contribution to the people instead of pursuing high-ranking posts]. 23 November. theory. people.com.cn/n/2013/0705/c40531-22087040.html

Schubert, G., & Ahlers, A.L. (2012) 'County and township cadres as a strategic group: "Building a new socialist countryside" in three provinces.' *China Journal* 67: 67–86. doi.org/10.1086/665740

Shambaugh, D.L. (2008) *China's Communist Party: Atrophy and Adaptation.* University of California Press

Shirk, S.L. (1993) *The Political Logic of Economic Reform in China.* University of California Press

—— (2018) 'China in Xi's "new era": The return to personalistic rule.' *Journal of Democracy* 29(2): 22–36. doi.org/10.1353/jod.2018.0022

Study Group [学习小组] (2015) 'Xi Jinping: Guanyu xianwei shuji de "yi er san si"' [习近平：关于县委书记的「一二三四」, Xi Jinping: Some things concerning county party secretaries]. *Xianfeng* [先锋] 6: 64

Torigian, J. (2018) 'Historical legacies and leaders' worldviews: Communist Party history and Xi's learned (and unlearned) lessons.' *China Perspectives* 2018 (1–2): 7–15. doi.org/10.4000/chinaperspectives.7548

Tsai, W.H., & Liao, X. (2019) 'The impending rise of the "Tsinghua clique": Cultivation, transfer and relationships in Chinese elite politics.' *Journal of Contemporary China* 28(120): 948–64. doi.org/10.1080/10670564.2019.159 4106

—— (2020) 'Mobilising cadre incentives in policy implementation: Poverty alleviation in a Chinese county.' *China Information* 34(1): 45–67. doi.org/ 10.1177/0920203X19887787

Walder, A. (1995) 'Career mobility and the communist political order.' *American Sociological Review* 60(3): 309–28. doi.org/10.2307/2096416

Wang, Z., & Zeng, J. (2016) 'Xi Jinping: The game changer of Chinese elite politics?' *Contemporary Politics* 22(4): 470–81. doi.org/10.1080/13569775. 2016.1175098

Xia, J. [夏锦文] (2019) 'Guojia zhili tixi he zhili nengli xiandaihua de Zhongguo tansuo' [国家治理体系和治理能力现代化的中国探索, A Chinese exploration of the modernisation of the national governance system and governance capability]. *Renmin Wang* [人民网], 29 November. cpc.people.com.cn/BIG5/ n1/2019/1119/c430519-31462903.html

Xiao, G. [肖桂国] (2012) Xuan Diaosheng: Zhongguo Tese Ganbu Houbei Liliang [选调生：中国特色干部后备力量, Selected and transferred students: The strength of cadre reserves with Chinese characteristics]. World Book

Xinhua Net (2020) 'Xi Jinping yanzhong de "guanjian shaoshu" you shenme teshu hanyi' [习近平眼中的「关键少数」有什么特殊含义, What are the implications of the 'key minority' put forward by Xi Jinping]. 17 November. www.xinhuanet.com/politics/2016-02/03/c_1117976900.htm

Zang, X. (2004) *Elite Dualism and Leadership Selection in China*. Routledge Curzon

—— (2005) 'Institutionalisation and elite behaviour in reform China.' *Issues and Studies* 41(1): 204–17

Zhang, Q. [章强] (2016) '80 hou xianwei shuji xianzhang hen hanjian? Hubei yijing you zheme duo le' [80后县委书记县长很罕见？湖北已经有这么多了, Are county party secretaries and county governors born after 1980 rare? There have already been this many in Hubei]. Sohu Wang [搜狐网]. www.sohu.com/a/116378076_355684

Zhongguo Gongqingtuan [中国共青团, Chinese Communist Youth League] (2016) Gongqingtuan zhongyang gaige fangan [共青团中央改革方案, Reform plan for the Communist Youth League], August. www.gqt.org.cn/notice/201608/P020160809382774540571.pdf

5

More stick than carrot? Xi's policy towards establishment intellectuals

Relations between authoritarian governments and intellectuals are more complicated than relations between the government and general public. As information providers and opinion leaders on the one hand, intellectuals play an important role in promoting freedom of speech and challenging authoritarian social control. On the other hand, intellectuals may be recruited by authoritarian leaders as a mouthpiece for official policies and as providers of policy suggestions. Hence authoritarian governments are motivated both to repress and to co-opt intellectuals.

Chinese President Xi Jinping has tightened social and ideological control since his rise to power and subsequent centralisation of power in the Communist Party of China (CPC).[2] Xi announced that the Chinese media must serve the party in February 2016 (Xinhua, 2016). The publisher

1   This chapter is a revised and updated version of the article that first appeared as F.W. Yang (2021) 'More stick than carrot? Xi's policy toward establishment intellectuals.' *Issues and Studies* 57(2), Article 2150008. doi.org/10.1142/S1013251121500089. Reprinted with permission. The author would like to thank Professor Chien-wen Kou and Hans Hanpu Tung for their advice on the preliminary structure of this chapter, and Professor Titus C. Chen, Ben Hillman, Carl Minzner, Hsin-Hsien Wang and four anonymous reviewers for their valuable suggestions on its previous version. This article was subsidised by the Institute of International Relations, National Chengchi University (NCCU), Taiwan.
2   Zhao noted that 'Xi is trying to revive Communism as an official ideology' and his explanation for this is 'Communism's demise amid the reforms' (Zhao, 2016, p. 83).

and top editors of the liberal Chinese journal *Yanhuang Chunqiu* (炎黄春秋) were either dismissed or demoted in July of the same year. The liberal-leaning site Gongshi Wang (共识网, Consensus Net) was shut down that October after accusations of disseminating incorrect thinking. The upgrading of China's internet surveillance and the introduction of its 'social credit system' have been considered to be part of a series of comprehensive policies aiming at strengthening social control.[3] The same trend has also been reflected in the strengthening of ideological control over university education and establishment intellectuals.[4] Why then has the Xi administration decided to strengthen control over establishment intellectuals at this particular juncture?

This chapter observes the changes in China's political and social control under Xi Jinping from the Chinese government's policy towards establishment intellectuals, university teachers in particular. This chapter asks why and when an authoritarian state chooses to strengthen control over intellectuals. It focuses on the CPC's policy towards establishment intellectuals under Xi and explores the most applicable explanation for this policy shift.

This chapter consists of three sections: the first focuses on the CPC's existing social control system over institutions of higher education to observe how it has been able to control establishment intellectuals—university teachers in this case—and what institutional and policy changes have occurred under Xi. The second section investigates the methods of repression and co-optation that the CPC has employed towards establishment intellectuals during this period. The third section reviews previous research on the cyclical model of state–intellectual relations and proposes a new model of 'dual methods in state–intellectual relations' to explain shifting state–intellectual relations in China.

---

3   The 'social credit system' is a national reputation system developed by the Chinese government. The system was fully implemented in 2020 and manages the rewarding and punishment of citizens on the basis of their economic and personal behaviour. The social credit system has been described as the concretisation of the mass surveillance system depicted in *1984*, George Orwell's work of dystopian fiction.

4   Scholars have adopted the term 'establishment intellectuals' to distinguish intellectuals in the PRC from their Western counterparts, who are understood to be independent of state or commercial interests. Cheek and Hamrin (1986) defined establishment intellectuals as leading figures who were both high-level intellectuals and high-level party cadres. Scholars have continued to adopt this term, as Cheek (2015a) indicates, to reflect 'the focus on government service or at least working with the government that has characterised public activities of China's writers and thinkers into the 21st century'.

A system of social control over university education

It is true that the professionalisation, pluralisation and liberalisation of China's economy since the 1990s has allowed intellectuals to pursue careers in other industries and suffer less direct CPC control. Establishment intellectuals who work in universities, however, are still subject to CPC control from branches of the party stationed on campus and certain changes in state policy.

Chinese universities are managed very differently from those in Western countries. The basic principle of higher education is to emphasise 'a socialist higher education development with Chinese characteristics under the leadership of the Party committee' (Xu & Zhu, 2019, p. 39). The main management system in Chinese universities is the Presidential Accountability System under the leadership of the University Committee of the Communist Party (UCCP) with the UCCP playing a leading role in decision-making (Bao, 2010, p. 61, figure 1).

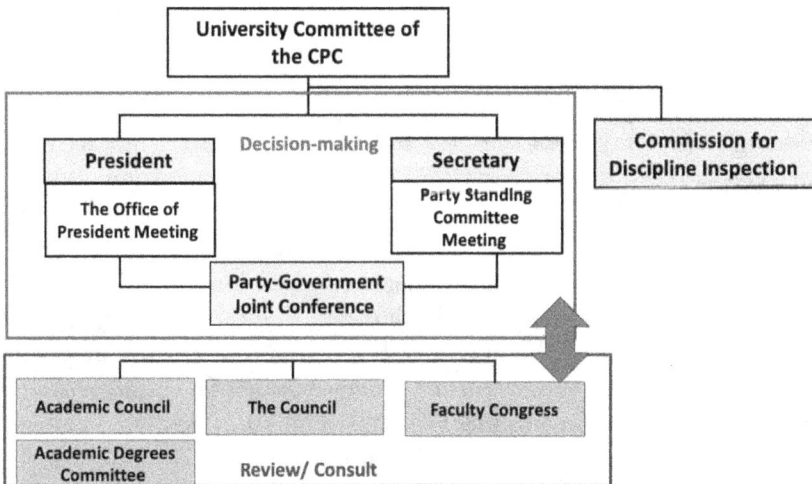

Figure 5.1: The system of decision-making in public Chinese universities
Source: Translated by the author from Bao (2010, p. 61).

Of course, the UCCP both determines and influences the management of university professors and administrators, including their recruitment, punishment and dismissal. Chinese economist Xia Yeliang (夏业良), for instance, was dismissed by the School of Economics at Peking University (PKU) in October 2013, and it was widely suspected that his dismissal had been politically motivated. University officials denied the charges and claimed that the decision was based entirely on Professor Xia's poor teaching evaluations. However, an email from Communist Party Secretary Zhang Zheng (章政) at the PKU School of Economics in August 2013 was sent to Xia warning him to withdraw his name from the petition in support of detained New Citizens' Movement activist Xu Zhiyong (许志永) and to write a written explanation for this matter. It did not include any mention of his teaching or scholarship. Although Zhang did not explicitly link Xia's signing of the petition to the faculty vote on his appointment, he did conclude the message by reminding him of the pending decision. Two months later, the faculty voted to dismiss Xia.[5] Another case also demonstrates the power of party officials on campus. Stephen Morgan had served as associate provost on the engineering faculty at the Ningbo branch of the University of Nottingham since 2016. Communist party officials at the school requested Professor Morgan's removal from the management board, saying an essay he had posted online that was critical of the 19th Party Congress had embarrassed the university (Feng, 2018a).

Although university presidents do share in school leadership to some degree, it should not be surprising that even the appointment and dismissal of university presidents is determined by the CPC. For example, the State Council and Central Committee of the CPC have the authority to appoint and dismiss university presidents under the supervision of the Ministry of Education (MoE) or other central ministries. The local government and CPC committees have the authority to appoint and dismiss university presidents under the supervision of provinces, autonomous regions and directly controlled municipalities (Bao, 2010, p. 50, table 2.5). Therefore it is highly likely that presidents carry out their responsibilities under the direction of the party committees.

---

5   The *Chronicle of Higher Education* obtained this email and published their correspondence (Fischer, 2014).

Overall, the leadership of the UCCP has demonstrated that 'in this structure, the political and ideological system of the Communist Party is integrated with the administrative and management structures at each level of the university' (Liu, 2017, p. 273).[6] In addition, informal pressures applied by party officials within universities (e.g. party 'loyalty checks') have also significantly dominated the decision process there (Hu & Mols, 2019, pp. 718–19). Accordingly, the CPC has been able effectively to extend its control over both institutions of higher education and establishment intellectuals.

Strengthening ideological control over the education system under Xi

Since Xi assumed office in 2012, Beijing has tightened its ideological grip over higher education. This section provides a brief description of institutional and policy shifts in the educational system under Xi.

Institutional changes and an emphasis on the leadership of the party

Since assuming the leadership of the CPC, Xi has emphasised strengthening party leadership and party construction in the education sphere. The CPC Central Committee issued a *Decision on Deepening the Reform of the Party and State Institutions* in March 2018, which included a decision to establish a new Central Leading Small Group for Education Work (中央教育工作领导小组, *zhongyang jiaoyu gongzuo lingdao xiaozu*) (LSGEW). The duties of the LSGEW include designing policies in education to strengthen party leadership over thought and ideological work; monitoring the national development strategy, medium- and long-term plans, principal policies and reform programs; and finally, coordinating and solving major problems. The LSGEW secretariat has been integrated with the MoE (Xinhua, 2018), indicating that the CPC has upgraded the priority of education work.

---

6   Liang (2017) reviews the rise and decline of the C9 as an advocacy group for China's elite universities and demonstrates the rigid regulatory environment of the university sector.

To strengthen party leadership, the General Office of the CPC Central Committee issued a document in October 2014 entitled *Implementation of Views on Sustaining and Improving the Presidential Responsibility System under the Leadership of the CPC at Universities*. The document defines the UCCP as the core of the university leadership system and clearly delineates its responsibilities:

> To carry out the policies of the CPC; to make decisions on the fundamental management system, important matters relating to reforms, teaching, research, human resources and other affairs that directly affect the interests of the staff; to lead the work of ideological, political and moral education; to strengthen the construction of the UCCP at a faculty level; to lead the discipline inspection within the Party, the Trade Union, the CYLO, Student Union and other mass organisations. (Zhonggong Zhongyang Bangongting, 2014)

In addition, the CPC Central Committee issued a revised *Chinese Communist Party Regulations on Basic Level Organisation Work in Ordinary Institutions of Higher Education* on 22 April 2021. The notice requires that party committees of all levels should put party-building in colleges and universities in a prominent position while upholding and strengthening the party's overall leadership over colleges and universities (Zhonghua Renmin Gongheguo Guofangbu, 2021).

Even joint ventures have not been excepted from the strengthening of party-building in universities. The MoE issued a directive from the CPC Organisation Department in October 2017 requiring that party secretaries in each education joint venture between Chinese and overseas universities be given vice-chancellor status and a seat on the board of trustees (Feng, 2017).[7] The Organisation Department oversees appointments to top party and government posts. It also issued a directive in 2018 mandating that foreign institutions include a clause that supports the establishment of internal Communist Party committees in any application to set up a joint venture university (Feng, 2018b). These are signs that the CPC has ordered foreign-funded universities to instal party units and grant decision-making powers to party officials.

---

7   Although joint venture administrators say the rules have not yet been formally implemented after they resisted, most joint venture branch campuses have in practice operated since their founding with a party secretary from their partnering Chinese university on their management boards (Feng, 2018a).

Policies related to ideological control over university education

These policies have also demonstrated that the CPC has not only overseen a drastic political tightening over Chinese schools but has also strengthened its ideological control over teachers and students on campus.

Beijing's policy of strengthening ideological control began in 2013. In April of that year, the General Office of the CPC's Central Committee issued *The Briefing on the Current Situation in the Ideological Realm*, also known as Document No. 9. According to the version released by *Mingjing Monthly* (明镜月刊), it specifically addresses seven issues that were seen as problems and needed to be eliminated. These included the promotion of Western constitutional democracy, universal values, civil society, neoliberalism, the West's idea of journalism and historical nihilism as well as questioning the reform and opening and the socialist nature of socialism with Chinese characteristics. The document was confidentially circulated to CPC cadres throughout China, and these seven topics were banned within universities. It was therefore also referred to as the 'seven banned subjects' (七不讲, *qi bujiang*). On 4 May, the Organisation Department, the Propaganda Department and the CPC Leading Group of the MoE issued *Opinions with Regard to Strengthening and Improving the Thought and Political Work on Young Teachers at Higher Education Institutions*. It declared, 'Some young professors confused in political and ideology belief have found their professional sentiments and ethics degraded, thus, they can't serve as a model of virtue' and stressed that the relative authorities at various levels must strengthen management and control (Quanguo Gaoxiao Sixiang Zhengzhi Gongzuo Wang, 2013).

During the National Propaganda and Ideology Work Conference held on 19 August 2013, Xi Jinping stated that 'ideological work is extremely important work for the Party', cautioning against weak ideological work by saying: '*The disintegration of a regime often starts from the ideological area* [emphasis added], political unrest and regime change may perhaps occur in a night, but ideological evolution is a long-term process.' On intellectuals, he remarked that 'there has been a tendency for a small number of people to drift away from the Party and the government and there are even a few people harbouring dissent and discord against the Party' (Xinhua, 2013). When Liu Yunshan (刘云山) spoke at the conference, Xi interrupted and added that 'a small number of reactionary intellectuals spread rumours around, attack and slander the Party's leadership, socialism and the regime. We must strike strictly' (Hai Tao, 2013).

According to the *New York Times*, the CPC issued a directive Document No. 30 in 2014 as a follow-up to Document No. 9. It demanded the cleansing of Western-inspired liberal ideas from universities and other cultural institutions (Buckley & Jacobs, 2015). In October 2014, the Central Committee issued a directive titled *Opinion Concerning the Further Strengthening and Reforming of Propaganda and Ideological Work at Universities under the New Circumstances*, which aimed at forcefully raising the ideological and political quality of teachers in higher education and demanded that universities 'firmly resist infiltration by hostile forces, closely grasp leadership and discourse power in higher education ideology work and work incessantly to consolidate the guiding position of Marxism' (Zhongguo Zhengfu Wang, 2015).[8]

In October 2014, Xi's comment to 'never allow eating the Communist Party's food and then smashing the Communist Party's cooking pots' began to appear on party and university websites in October (Buckley & Jacobs, 2015). During the 23rd National Work Conference on Party-Construction in Higher Education in December 2014, Xi called for better 'ideological guidance' in Chinese institutes of higher education, saying that universities should 'shoulder the burden of learning and researching the dissemination of Marxism' (Xinhua, 2014).

In January 2015, Chinese Education Minister Yuan Guiren (袁贵仁) wrote an article in the elite party journal *Qiushi* (求是, Seeking Truth) in which he indicated that 'young teachers and students are key targets of infiltration by enemy forces' and that 'some countries' fearful of China's rise 'have stepped up infiltration in more discreet and diverse ways'. Hence Yuan called for a ban on textbooks that promote Western values and ordered universities to add classes on Marxism and socialism (Yuan, 2015).

---

8   This opinion was circulated in October 2014 but made public in January 2015.

The CPC Central Committee and the State Council issued the *Opinions on Strengthening and Improving Ideological and Political Work in Colleges and Universities under the New Situation* on 27 February 2017, emphasising the party's leadership of colleges and universities, strengthening ideological and political work and underscoring the need to improve the ideological and political quality of teachers (Xinhua, 2017c).

To ensure that these policies were executed correctly on campus, the Central Commission for Discipline Inspection (CCDI) toured 31 of the best universities across China for a 'political check-up' from 28 February to 27 April 2017 (Xinhua, 2017a). The report accused 14 of ideological weakness for not making the effort to teach and defend Communist Party rule (Denyer, 2017). The CCDI published 'rectification reports' on eight top-tier universities in August, and seven have set up a 'teachers' affairs department' under their Communist Party committees with the aim of improving 'ideological and political work among teaching staff' (Gan, 2017). Tsinghua University did not mention the party department in its report but said that it had set up a leading group on ideological and political work among teachers headed by its party secretary (Zhonggong Zhongyang Jilü Jiancha Weiyuanhui, 2017).

The party further issued the following policy documents aiming at intensifying the implementation of Xi Jinping Thought in universities: *Opinions on Accelerating the Construction of the Ideological and Political Work System in Colleges and Universities*, issued in April 2020 (Zhonghua Renmin Gongheguo Jiaoyubu, 2020), *Textbook of Xi Jinping Thought on Socialism with Chinese Characteristics for a New Era for Students*, issued in 8 July 2021 (Zhonghua Renmin Gongheguo Jiaoyubu, 2021a), *Notice of the National Textbook Committee on Printing and Distributing Guideline to Teaching Materials for the Course of Xi Jinping Thought on Socialism with Chinese Characteristics for a New Era*, issued in 21 July 2021 (Guojia Jiaocai Weiyuanhui, 2021a) and *Notice of the National Textbook Committee on Printing and Distributing the Guidelines for Teaching Materials of 'Party Leadership' Related Content into the Curriculum of Universities, Primary and Secondary Schools*, issued on 26 September 2021 (Guojia Jiaocai Weiyuanhui, 2021b). While the main purpose of these documents is to consolidate Xi's authority, they also reflect the party's strengthening ideological control over all levels of the education system.

The policies above demonstrate Xi's resolve to strengthen ideological control over university education and teachers in keeping with his remarks to the 19th Congress that 'Party, government, army, society and education—east and west, south and north, the party leads on everything' (Xinhua, 2017b).[9] In this context, the following section focuses on the CPC's approaches towards establishment intellectuals, instructors and academics in Chinese universities.

Policies towards intellectuals

As with most authoritarian states, the CPC has extended its control over intellectuals using methods that include both repression and co-optation. This section focuses on the implementation and policy changes of these methods under Xi.

Repression: Demotion or dismissal

Since the CPC began to emphasise ideological control over university teachers in 2013, university authorities have taken retaliatory actions against scholars. These have included investigations, suspensions, terminations and the revocation of credentials. Such consequences act as a warning to other members of the intellectual community to avoid the expression of certain values or inquiries into the current social and political climate.

As table 5.1 demonstrates, university academics suffered retaliation from university authorities for opinions articulated in class or on the internet. Several points can be noted from these cases.

9　This remark was written into the CPC Constitution (Xinhua, 2017d).

Table 5.1: List of dismissed or disciplined professors

Data/year	Professor	University	Punishment	Reason claimed by the university	Suspected reason
Oct 2013	Xia Yeliang (夏业良)	PKU (北京大学)	Dismissal	Inadequate teaching evaluations and substandard research	Co-author of Charter '08 and outspoken liberal scholar
Dec 2013	Zhang Xuezhong (张雪忠)	East China University of Political Science and Law (华东政法大学)	Dismissal	Conduct such as spreading his political ideas to colleagues and students, violation of the moral norms of teachers	Called for constitutionalism; defended members of the New Citizens' Movement; revealed the 'seven banned subjects'
Nov 2015	Liang Xinsheng (梁新生)	Lingnan Normal University (岭南师范学院)	Removed from his post (行政撤职)	Publishing 'radical opinions' on his Weibo account that had been a 'bad social influence'	[Unspecified]
Jan 2017	Deng Xiangchao (邓相超)	Shangdong Jianzhu University (山东建筑大学)	Forced into retirement	'Mistaken comments online'	Posted controversial comments about Mao Zedong online
Jul 2017	Tan Song (谭松)	Chongqing Normal University (重庆师范大学)	Dismissal	'Regular adjustments (正常调整)'	Research into CPC land reforms in the 1950s (challenging official CPC historiography)
Aug 2017	Shi Jiepeng (史杰鹏)	Beijing Normal University (北京师范大学)	Dismissal	'Mistaken comments online which have a negative impact on society'	Called Mao Zedong a 'devil' and the CPC 'bandits' on social media
Aug 2017	Li Mohai (李默海)	Shandong Institute of Industry and Commerce (山东工商学院)	Suspended from his position	'Mistaken comments online which have a negative impact on society'	Criticised government propaganda and patriotic netizens via his Weibo account

Data/year	Professor	University	Punishment	Reason claimed by the university	Suspected reason
Mar 2018	Cheng Ran (成然)	Xiangtan University (湘潭大学)	Demoted and demerited	Reported by students for 'inappropriate speech' in class that had a negative impact	Used information and pictures from foreign media; criticised the CPC and the leader of the nation in class
May 2018	Zhai Juhong (翟桔红)	Zhongnan University of Economics and Law (中南财经政法大学)	Dismissal	Reported by students for 'inappropriate speech' in class that had a negative impact	Criticised the abolition of term limits
May 2018	Xu Chuanqing (许传青)	Beijing University of Civil Engineering and Architecture (北京建筑大学)	Administrative penalties	Reported by students for 'inappropriate speech' in class	Complained that students did not work hard enough and compared them with a Japanese student she had taught
Jun 2018	You Shengdong (尤盛东)	Xiamen University (厦门大学)	Dismissal	Reported by students for 'inappropriate political speech' in class	[Unspecified]
Jul 2018	Wang Gang (王刚)	Hebei Engineering University (河北工程大学)	Dismissal	His discourse violated the moral norms of teachers	Frequently criticised government on WeChat
Jul 2018	Christopher Balding	PKU's HSBC School of Business (北京大学汇丰商学院)	Discontinued appointment	'A normal academic employment decision'	Criticised Chinese censorship and lobbied Cambridge University Press to unblock articles it had censored at Beijing's request
Aug 2018	Yang Shaozheng (杨绍政)	Guizhou University (贵州大学)	Suspended, then dismissed	'Mistaken political comments online'	Published an article estimating the cost of maintaining the CPC's apparatus

Data/year	Professor	University	Punishment	Reason claimed by the university	Suspected reason
Sep 2018	Zhou Yunzhong (周运中)	Xiamen University (厦门大学)	Dismissal	'Mistaken political comments online'	Made inflammatory comments about the Chinese nation and Confucianism online
Sep 2018	Hu Hao (胡浩)	China University of Labour Relations (中国劳动关系学院)	Dismissal	Reposted information about the Hong Kong 'Occupy Central' demonstration on Weibo and 'promoted the idea of the liberalisation of capitalism, the rule of law system and democratisation' in the classroom	As claimed by the university
Oct 2018	Zhao Siyun (赵思运)	Zhejiang Uni. of Media and Communications (浙江传媒学院)	Severe internal party warning	'Inappropriate speech' in a welcoming ceremony, which had a negative impact	Resurrected and defined the concept of the 'public intellectual' in a welcoming ceremony for new students
Mar 2019	Xu Zhangrun (许章润)	Tsinghua University (清华大学)	Suspended his research and teaching credentials	[Unspecified]	Posted an article titled 'Our current fears and expectations' [我们当下的恐惧与期待, Women dangxia de kongju yu qidai] criticising the abolition of term limits and the restoration of a cult of personality
Mar 2019	Tang Yun (唐云)	Chongqing Normal University (重庆师范大学)	Stripped of teaching credentials and demoted	Reported by students for his speech in class, which was deemed by the authorities to be 'injurious to the country's reputation'	[Unspecified]

Data/year	Professor	University	Punishment	Reason claimed by the university	Suspected reason
Aug 2019	Zheng Wenfeng (郑文锋)	University of Electronic Science and Technology of China (电子科技大学)	Suspension from teaching for two years	Reported by students for his 'incorrect' comments on social media, saying 'ancient China did not have substantial innovations'	As claimed by the university
Oct 2019	Cao Jisheng (曹继生)	Shanxi University of Finance and Economics (山西财经大学)	Administrative penalties	His 'inappropriate remarks' in a WeChat group violated the 'Ten Guidelines for Professional Behaviour of College Teachers in the New Era' ('Ten Guidelines')	[Unspecified]
Oct 2019	Liu Yufu (刘玉富)	Chengdu University of Technology (成都理工大学)	Teaching certificate revoked	For his 'inappropriate remarks' on social media and in class	His criticisms in a QQ group about Xi ending term limits
Dec 2019	Li Zhi (李志)	Sichuan University of Science and Engineering (四川轻化工大学)	Administrative penalties	His 'inappropriate speech' violated the Ten Guidelines	[Unspecified]
Feb 2020	Chow Pui Yee (周佩仪) (from Hong Kong)	University of Chinese Academy of Social Sciences (中国社会科学院大学)	Dismissal (immediate termination)	Students reported her 'inappropriate remarks' on a WeChat group, which violated the Ten Guidelines	Claimed that China's political system caused the mishandling of COVID-19
Jun 2020	Liang Yanping (梁艳萍)	Hubei University (湖北大学)	Stripped of her CPC membership and suspended from teaching	For her 'wrong remarks' about Japan and Hong Kong	Voiced support for Fang Fang, the author of Wuhan Diary

Data/year	Professor	University	Punishment	Reason claimed by the university	Suspected reason
14 Jul 2020	Xu Zhangrun* (许章润)	Tsinghua University (清华大学)	Dismissal	For the accusation of soliciting prostitution and his articles violating the Ten Guidelines	For his article 'Imminent fears, immediate hopes', criticising government's handling of COVID-19 and the rule of the CPC
17 Aug 2020	Cai Xia (蔡霞)	Central Party School (中央党校)	Stripped of her CPC membership and her retirement pension cancelled	'There are serious political problems in her discourses which maliciously smeared the image of the country'	Criticised Xi and the CPC
28 Apr 2021	Li Jian (李剑)	Hunan City University (湖南城市学院)	Suspended from teaching	Reported by students for his 'hasty generalised remarks' about Japan and his conduct that violated teacher ethics	His remark that 'the Japanese strive for excellence' in the classroom

* The media reported that Xu was under house arrest after he published an essay entitled 'Viral alarm: When fury overcomes fear' condemning the Chinese government's response to the COVID-19 outbreak. He was detained on 6 July 2020 for one week for the accusation of soliciting prostitution. Tsinghua University used this accusation as excuse to dismiss him.

Source: Compiled by the author from media reports and information provided by the Twitter account Zhongguo Wenziyu Shijian Pandian (中国文字狱事件盘点) @speechfreedomcn.

First, cases where academics were dismissed or disciplined by university authorities have increased since 2017. Among the 26 cases investigated, two occurred in 2013, one in 2015, four in 2017, nine in 2018, six in 2019 and four in 2020.[10] Around two-thirds of these happened in 2018, and two reasons may explain the difference. First, political changes often provoke discontent among intellectuals. 'Xi Jinping Thought on Socialism with Chinese Characteristics for a New Era', simply known as Xi Jinping Thought, was affirmed as a guiding political ideology of the CPC in its 19th Congress in October 2017. At its closing session on 24 October, the 19th Party Congress approved the incorporation of Xi Jinping Thought into the Constitution of the CPC. Since then, the CPC has further urged Chinese universities to intensify ideological education with an emphasis on the study of Xi Jinping Thought. On 11 March 2018, the National People's Congress passed a constitutional amendment that lifted term limits on the presidency. Many scholars were concerned about these political changes, and some of them expressed their grievances and worries about the change. Hence the leadership of the CPC and Xi Jinping faced more criticism in 2018. Moreover, in October 2017, the head of the Propaganda Department was changed from Liu Qibao (刘奇葆) to Huang Kunming (黄坤明), an official considered to be a close associate of Xi.[11] While Liu Qibao was still in office, inspectors from the disciplinary commission had issued a report on 9 June 2016 that publicly berated the Propaganda Department for not taking firm enough control of the internet, the media, the arts and the nation's universities. It is reasonable that the Propaganda Department began to strengthen ideological control over universities after Huang Kunming assumed its leadership.

Second, professors were dismissed or disciplined in seven cases because their students had reported them to university authorities. This relates to surveillance and monitoring methods on campus. Methods include closed-circuit television (CCTV) and student informants. Some universities have installed CCTV systems in lecture halls and other facilities, claiming that they would be used as tools to improve teaching, learning and student behaviour. Scholars, however, expressed concerns about the system being used to restrict their lectures and classroom discussions (Scholars at Risk [SAR], 2019, p. 26). CPC officials in universities and state security bureaus have used student informants to monitor and report scholars and students

---

10   Refer also to 'Table of Incidents' in the appendix in *Scholars at Risk* (2019).
11   Huang had worked with Xi in Fujian province where Xi served as governor. When Xi was appointed party committee secretary in Zhejiang, Huang moved there as well. When Xi rose to become party leader, Huang was again transferred from Zhejiang to the party centre as deputy head of the Central Propaganda Department.

who cross the line (SAR, 2019, p. 26). According to a *Global Times* report, Shandong Normal University employs one student as a student information officer for each major, and these student information officers monitor education quality and collect the opinions of students about their teachers. Student information officers who do their jobs well are given material and spiritual encouragement (Zhang, 2018). Student information officers might also have the prospect of a future in politics (Ng & Sing, 2018). Student informants are recruited in various ways. For example, at Wuhan University of Science and Technology, officials recruit student informants on the basis of their academic performance and ideology while officials at Dezhou University in Shandong province work with the Domestic Security Department to recruit and train student informants (Xi et al., 2019; Xiao, 2010). It is clear that throughout China, the lectures of university teachers have been under strict surveillance and monitoring.

Third, professors were dismissed or disciplined in nine cases because they supported social movements, advocated liberal ideas or criticised the CPC or Mao Zedong on social networks such as Weibo and WeChat. Although some of them did not use their real names, it has been easy to track their identities through the introduction of the Real-Name System (实名制, *shimingzhi*). In addition, the Chinese government has increased its capabilities for internet surveillance in order to heavily restrict and monitor internet activity. Authorities have not only employed staff at Chinese social media and internet companies but have also made use of advanced technology systematically to monitor popular social media platforms and blogging sites and review content across China's web space (PEN America, 2018, pp. 33–4; SAR, 2019, p. 26). Professors in these cases were mostly reported by overzealous netizens or staff employed by the authorities. Some Weibo accounts of prominent government critics were closed. For example, the public WeChat and Sina Weibo accounts of PKU law professor He Weifang (贺卫方) were blocked, and he was banned from applying for new ones. He announced in May 2017 that he would no longer resist these bans by 'reincarnating' (Wade, 2017).

Fourth, the number of forbidden topics has increased since the CPC strengthened its ideological control. Forbidden topics formerly included the 'three Ts' (the autonomy of Tibet, Taiwan's status and the Tiananmen Square protests), democratisation, the rule of law and criticism of the government. From the cases of Deng Xiangchao, Xu Chuanqing and Zhou Yunzhong, it can now be seen that even criticising Mao Zedong, the Chinese nation or Confucianism, or comparing China with other nations can be reported by netizens or students. In Zhao Siyun's case, he had declared that China's education system had failed to nurture creativity, innovation and concern for society in its students, calling for students to think independently and embrace the concept of the 'public intellectual'. Although they did not advocate democracy or criticise the regime, these remarks are now taboo as well.

Moreover, several universities explicitly mentioned that the remarks of the teacher had violated the 'Ten Guidelines for Professional Behaviour of College Teachers in the New Era' (Ten Guidelines), a regulation released by the MoE in November 2018. These remarks most likely violated two rules in the guideline that require a teacher's behaviour to '[a]dhere to the guidance of Xi Jinping's new era of socialism with Chinese characteristics, support the leadership of the Communist Party of China and implement the party's educational policy' (Rule 1) and 'not to publish and forward wrong opinions through classrooms, forums, lectures, information networks and other channels, or to fabricate false information and bad information' (Rule 3) (Zhonghua Renmin Gongheguo Jiaoyubu, 2018).

Fifth, the strengthening of repressive policies against intellectuals has been sustained for longer under Xi. In the 1980s, the government alternated between relaxation and the repression of intellectuals in its policy, with periods of repression being shorter than those of relaxation. Since Xi came to office, the CPC has been strengthening its repressive policies. Although Xi softened his remarks on intellectuals in 2016,[12] the government actually ramped up its repression of university teachers in 2017 and 2018. The current policy adjustments on repression might have become a new standard: the CPC has drawn a new 'red line' and there may be no relaxation, at least not to the degree before Xi's rise to power.[13]

Sixth, the most recent target of censorship has been criticism of the CPC's handling of COVID-19. As shown in table 5.1, Chow Pui Yee maintained that China's political system was responsible for the slow response to COVID-19 and predicted that it would inevitably result in more social problems. Liang Yanping came under attack online after voicing support for Fang Fang (方方), the author of *Wuhan Diary*. Moreover, retired Hainan University professor Wang Xiaoni (王小妮), who has shown support

---

12 Xi demanded that party committees and the government 'reduce interference in intellectuals' creative work and allow them to concentrate their efforts on their job' (Xinhua, 2016a).
13 The strengthening of repressive policies under Xi has upset some returnee Chinese intellectuals who have opted to leave China and go overseas again (Kennedy, 2019, p. 1051).

for Fang Fang and Liang, is under investigation by the university. Chen Zhaozhi (陈兆志), a retired professor at the University of Science and Technology Beijing, had stated that COVID-19 was not a 'Chinese virus' but a 'Chinese Communist Party virus' and was arrested by Beijing police on 14 April. Additionally, legal scholar Zhang Xuezhong was arrested on 10 March (and released in May) for his open letter saying that 'the outbreak and spread of the COVID-19 epidemic was a good illustration of backward Chinese governance' (AsiaNews, 2020; Sharma, 2020).

Co-optation: Linking research funding with political loyalty

The distribution of research funds may serve as one of the methods employed by the CPC for its co-optation of intellectuals.

The encroachment of the CPC and its networks into research funding dynamics is significant in China. National research funding is distributed to research projects that speak directly to the party's vision and needs or to applicants showing loyalty to the CPC. The National Planning Office for Philosophy and the Social Sciences (NPOPSS) has been the highest authority in the funding of social science research and provides the largest and most prestigious grants. As figure 5.2 shows, the NPOPSS is directly within the orbit of the CPC propaganda system and is run by the head of the Propaganda Department, a member of the Politburo (Holbig, 2014, pp. 17–18).

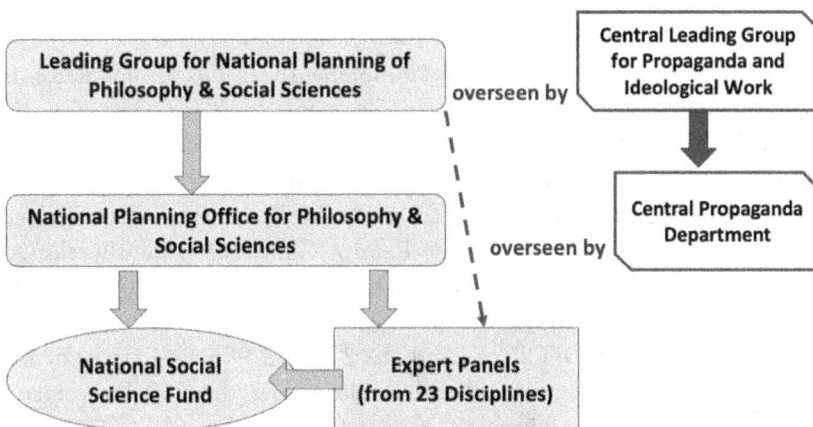

Figure 5.2: Social science research funding inside the propaganda apparatus
Source: Holbig (2014, p. 19).

The selection of research proposals is based on a review of expert panels. However, the recruitment of expert panel members has received criticism for its lack of transparency, and final decisions might be dominated by considerations of the institutional and personal backgrounds of the applicants (Holbig, 2014, pp. 20–1). Academics in elite universities have complained that 'too many research enterprises are controlled by administrators and governmental officials who are sometimes one and the same, given that Chinese universities are run to a great extent by the government' (Jarvis & Mok, 2019, p. 34).[14] In addition to a lack of transparency in research funding, academics have also expressed their grievances about their inability to pursue a full range of research and publishing options in terms of academic freedom and entrenched hierarchies typically based on seniority, party connections or *guanxi*, as opposed to academic merit (Jarvis & Mok, 2019, p. 34). Moreover, funding schemes may serve as a factor contributing to self-censorship at universities. Elizabeth Perry pointed out that the CPC's lavish funding of elite public institutions of higher education 'is surely a key reason for the notable quiescence of the Chinese academy' (Perry, 2015, p. 28). Furthermore, the party may also withdraw research funding as punishment. The media reported the withdrawal by the NPOPSS of funding granted to Yin Zhenhuan (尹振环), a professor at the Communist Party School in Guizhou Province, because authorities found that the research results of his publication on Laozi had serious political problems (Ding, 2019).

The utilization of research funding as a method of co-optation has become even more serious under Xi.

On 18 August 2015, the Central Comprehensively Deepening Reforms Commission passed *The Comprehensive Plan of Overall Development of the World First-Class University and World First-Class Discipline Construction*, designed to develop a group of elite Chinese universities into world-class institutions by 2050. In September 2017, the MoE, the Ministry of Finance and National Development and the Reform Commission jointly released a list of select universities and disciplines. Through this 'Double First-Class University Plan' (DFCP) (双一流, *shuang yiliu*]) or 'Double Top University Plan', the DFCP replaced the 211 and 985 Projects launched in the 1990s, incorporating all universities under the 985 Project and introducing Yunnan University, Xinjiang University and Zhengzhou

14 Originally from Rhoads et al. (2014).

University. The institutions for the new plan were selected after a process of peer competition, expert review and government evaluation, and selected universities will receive dynamic monitoring and management (*China Daily*, 2017). Once universities and disciplines are nominated, the government grants significant resources 'to support university activities along with more intensive oversight to monitor progress' (Jarvis & Mok, 2019, p. 33).

The resources offered by the DFCP and the reassertion of party ideology have led various universities to develop disciplines or research projects that are preferred by the CPC. The Chinese Academy of Social Sciences, China's largest funder of humanities research, has also featured Xi Jinping Thought at the top of its list of approved topics for several consecutive years (Hancock, 2017). A 2019 call for proposals from the NPOPSS, for example, sought research that heavily focused on Xi Jinping Thought and the 'spirit of the 19th National Congress of the Communist Party of China' (Quanguo Zhexue Shehui Kexue Gongzuo Bangongshi, 2018). According to Qiao Mu (乔木), a former professor at Beijing Foreign Studies University, scholars who apply with research proposals related to Xi Jinping Thought find it easier to obtain state funding, and many of his former colleagues are manipulated by this and other government 'perks', which include high incomes and better housing (SAR, 2019, p. 16).

Moreover, universities have established research centres dedicated to Xi Jinping Thought to accommodate the new trends. Renmin University, an elite DFCP university, established the first research centre dedicated to Xi Jinping Thought on 25 October 2017. In 2018, the government announced the founding of 10 research centres and institutes on 'Xi Jinping Thought on Socialism with Chinese Characteristics for a New Era' at Tsinghua University, Peking University, the municipalities of Beijing, Guangdong Province, the municipalities of Shanghai, the National Defence University of the People's Liberation Army, the Chinese Academy of Social Sciences, the Ministry of Education and the CPC Central Committee's Party School (Xinhua Net, 2017). In 2021, the government announced that seven new research centres had been set up in the National Development and Reform Commission, the Ministry of Ecology and Environment and the China Law Society, as well as in Jiangsu, Zhejiang, Fujian and Shandong provinces (Xinhua Net, 2021). The research centres at Renmin University of China, Tsinghua University and Peking University were reorganised into institutes (研究院). On 22 November 2021, the Institute of Xi Jinping Thought on Socialism with Chinese Characteristics for a New Era at Peking

University announced the establishment of four centres for Xi Jinping Thought in the dimensions of economics, law, foreign policy and ecology (Ning, 2021). In addition to these institutes officially announced by the central government, many research centres and institutions on Xi Jinping Thought have been established in universities in local provinces (Z. Chen, Hou & Sang, 2018).

Furthermore, Peking University, Fudan University and many others have set up undergraduate majors in Marxist theory since 2018. Renowned teachers funded by the Support Plan for the Development of Marxist Disciplines have jointly undertaken 41 national and 125 provincial-level scientific research projects (Global Times, 2020). The MoE announced in December 2020 that the total number of full-time and part-time teachers of ideological and political courses in colleges and universities across the country had reached 106,411, surpassing 100,000 for the first time (Zhongguo Zhengfu Wang, 2020).

The CPC Leading Group of the MoE issued an *Outline of Implementing the Project of Improving the Quality of Ideological and Political Work in Colleges and Universities* in December 2017. The outline urged 'improving the mechanism of teacher appointment' and that 'the evaluation of teaching, professional titles and special awards should set *political thought performance* [emphasis added] and teaching competence as the top priority' (Quanguo Gaoxiao Sixiang Zhengzhi Gongzuo Wang, 2017). The Teachers Law is also under revision—Minister of Education Huai Jinpeng said that the revision will focus on strengthening the party's leadership over the work of teachers and ensuring their correct political direction (Zhonghua Renmin Gongheguo Jiaoyubu, 2021b). Hence the appointment and evaluation of teachers will be dominated by their record of political ideas; that is, whether they are adhering to the CPC's ideology.

Borrowing Qiao Mu's words, '[t]he government buys scholars and intellectuals' (SAR, 2019, p. 16). If scholars follow the party's rules, they gain abundant research funding and receive appointments without difficulty. On the other hand, scholars who are perceived by the party as troublemakers find it difficult to gain research funding and might lose their jobs due to their poor political thought records. The CPC under Xi has constructed a new 'red line', a mechanism with co-optation that is more tempting and repression that is more threatening.

It is also evident that the methods employed in co-optation and repression have undergone changes. With gradual pluralisation and professionalisation in China, intellectuals have had more professional choices outside the government-provided establishment. The CPC therefore needs to invest more resources to co-opt establishment intellectuals in the name of its new national development projects. For instance, the Xi administration has proposed the DFSP to replace the 211 and 985 Projects. In addition, the development of the internet and information technology industries has given intellectuals many channels to express their ideas and attract the attention of the public. Therefore the CPC is determined to develop its internet censorship methods and punish the unfavourable online discourses of establishment intellectuals.

The rationale behind Xi's policy towards establishment intellectuals

In this section, we first review the existing literature on state–intellectual relations and the 'cyclical model' in particular. On the basis of the explanation provided by these works, we propose a new model of 'dual methods in state–intellectual relations' to explain shifts in the CPC's policy towards intellectuals.

The cyclical model

Among the literature on relations between the CPC and intellectuals in China, studies on the cycles of relaxation and repression are most related to our discussion on recent changes in CPC policy. A number of explanations have been provided for the original cyclical model and the more recent changes from relative relaxation to repression.

Cotton argued that the main factor driving the repression–relaxation cycle was power struggles within the party (Cotton, 1984, pp. 176–7). When there are disagreements among party leaders over a certain issue and conflicts cannot be settled, political debate spreads from the decision-making circle to a wider one. Two groups of leaders manipulate intellectuals into discourse battles, and these intellectuals become the protagonists at the front of the stage with their patrons at the back. The debate continues until a clear political victory is achieved by one side. The losing faction and its combatants, the intellectuals, are suppressed, after which an apparent ideological consensus emerges. This explanation is highly related to the patron–client approach for its assumption that intellectuals involved in debates are supported by political elites.[15] It might, however, face two problems in a contemporary context. First, it overemphasises the ability of elites to manipulate intellectuals. Second, the role of political debate among intellectuals has become less significant in the policy-making process (Ma, 1998, p. 449).

The second explanation is also based on power struggles between two groups. Hamrin (1987, p. 278) observed state–intellectual relations in the 1980s and argued that three factors also contribute to the cycle of relaxation and repression. These are the shifting balance of power among leaders with different policy preferences, competition for influence among groups of intellectuals with different interests, and the linkage between cultural and other policy arenas. In the 1980s, conservative and reformist groups took different stances on the degree of economic reforms and the lessening of ideological control. Reformist elites proposed new reforms, and their intellectuals showed their support with discourses while conservative elites and intellectuals opposed them. As a result, both sides settled on an ambiguous compromise in which reformist elites conceded on ideological issues in exchange for compromises on economic reforms. This accordingly brought a period of repression and the strengthening of ideological control. Hamrin (1987, p. 285) concluded that '[t]he length of the "lulls" between rounds varies, as reformers regain momentum for another surge'.

The difficulty with Hamrin's explanation is that it is based on state–intellectual relations in China in the 1980s, when the struggle between reformist and conservative factions focused mainly on the correct path for development and trade-offs between different policy arenas were therefore more likely. Moreover, the dynamics between state and society, elites and intellectuals, and intellectuals and the public were different in the 1980s from other periods in the history of the People's Republic. Intellectuals in the 1980s were more outspoken about Western values and more negative towards the Chinese nation and its culture. This was partially because they had learned from the Cultural Revolution that self-censorship might result

---

15 Ma (1998, p. 448) provides a definition of clientelism by citing Caciagli (1991): 'Clientelism refers to a relation of exchange in which a person with higher status (the patron) takes advantage of his or her authority and resources to protect and benefit somebody with an inferior status (the client) who reciprocates with support and services'. Regarding the patron–client approach, Ma provides a detailed literature review.

in more serious consequences when a nation goes down the wrong path and partially because reformist elites had intentionally removed ideological constraints on intellectuals.

The third explanation is that there is a certain amount of ambiguity in the policies of party leaders. Merle Goldman argues that the party utilises intellectuals to explain their policies, construct theoretical foundations and provide policy suggestions on the one hand while at the same time fearing that their criticism of policies and the system will threaten the stability of the regime.[16] Hence the party tightens its control until the intellectuals appear reluctant to produce, then relaxes its controls until its political authority appears threatened. In intervals of relative relaxation, the party permits intellectual debate, Western influence and criticism of the bureaucracy or corruption in order to gain information on veiled social problems. When discussion moves beyond to criticise the system and suggest alternatives, the regime represses with varying degrees of intensity (Goldman, 1993, pp. 286–7; see also Goldman, 1985). However, Goldman's explanation does not clarify exactly when the party adopts a policy shift and does not provide theoretical indicators.

Another problem in the cyclical model is its singular emphasis on repression, as the period of relaxation is seen as one in which repression is either diminished or non-existent. This model tends to overlook co-optation and other methods adopted by the party. The cyclical model was reasonable at the time because it had been developed from the patron–client approach and observations on state–intellectual relations in the Mao and Deng eras.[17] However, professionalisation and pluralisation in society have since given intellectuals more professional choices and spaces for expression, and the party has an increasing need to utilise co-optation methods to manage their behaviour.

16   Merle Goldman is a distinguished historian known for a series of studies on Chinese intellectuals and their relations with the CPC. She adopted the patron–client approach when studying the role of intellectuals under the rule of Mao Zedong and later turned to an approach focusing on the role of dissident intellectuals in China's democratisation after the late 1980s. Regarding Goldman's contributions, Timothy Cheek provides a review and critique (2007).

17   As nearly all institutions were owned by the party-state in the Mao era, most intellectuals accepted appointments and worked within them. Hence the party-state had various methods to control its intellectuals. Moreover, intellectuals tended to seek affiliation with political elites (i.e. patrons). Co-optation was therefore less emphasised in the cyclical model.

The dual methods in state–intellectual relations model

To solve the problems above by introducing the method of co-optation, we develop the 'dual methods in state–intellectual relations model' (the dual methods model) to explain the contemporary policy towards establishment intellectuals in China. In other words, the dual methods model can be viewed as an extension and enhancement of the cyclical model and Merle Goldman's explanation. In addition, most of these explanations are provided by historians who have observed the Chinese party-state's intellectual policies in a wider historical context. On the basis of these explanations, this chapter further explores and attempts to observe the CPC's strengthened control over intellectuals in the context of the existing literature on comparative authoritarians.[18] The dual methods model could serve as an explanatory framework to analyse why and when an authoritarian government decides to strengthen control over intellectuals.

The dual methods model includes three main arguments. First, the party state adopts dual methods, 'repression' and 'co-optation', while adopting more 'repression' on Role B and more 'co-optation' on Role A. As figure 5.3 demonstrates, the roles of an intellectual may be roughly divided into Roles A and B. Those in Role A tend to accept government co-optation and become the mouthpiece of the state, helping to articulate state ideology to the general public. Those in Role B tend to focus on existing social and political problems and urge the government to enact political reforms. Those in Role B tend to be more outspoken and have a greater influence on the general public by pointing out social and political problems in the current political system and advocating institutional reforms or even democratisation. Those in Role B have the potential to lead public opinion and encourage the public to adopt collective action to pressure the government for political reforms.

---

18 Bueno de Mesquita et al. (2003) and Bueno de Mesquita and Smith (2011) provided a comprehensive theory on the survival of authoritarians. This theory covers many important issues such as a leader's preference for increasing 'the selectorate' and decreasing the winning coalition, the decision to use oppression, and a comparison between authoritarian and democratic regimes.

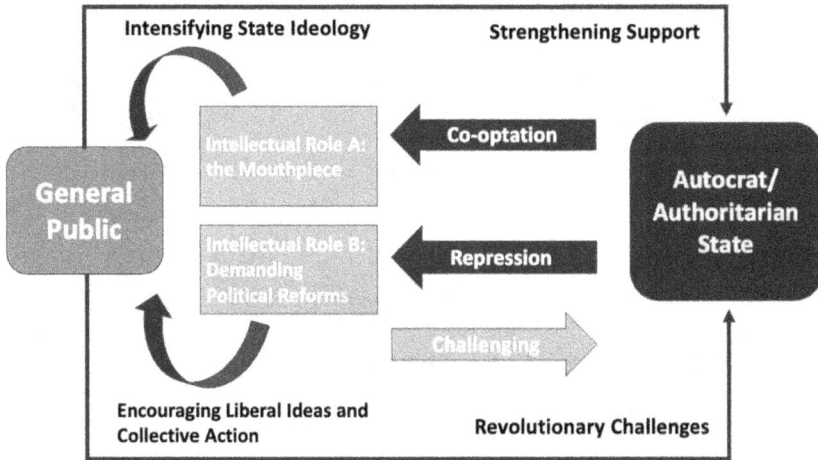

Figure 5.3: The dual methods in state–intellectual relations model
Source: Created by the author with reference to Kou (2019).

As this chapter demonstrates, the government employs dual methods towards intellectuals. It employs co-optation towards those in Role A in various ways that include defining their professions as 'first-class disciplines' (e.g. Marxism studies), granting more research funding and rewarding better treatment or higher salaries. Should these intellectuals show the right amount of loyalty, the government may recruit them into the 'selectorate' or even into the 'winning coalition'.[19] On the other hand, the government uses repression against those in Role B when it judges that their discourses have crossed the 'red line' and called for collective action from the general public. The government can use co-optation and repression interchangeably for both roles, although it might not be quite as effective.

Second, the main goal of the party-state's policy towards intellectual is to train 'loyal' or at least 'self-disciplined' intellectuals. When the government perceives there are too many outspoken intellectuals in Role B and that their influence on society might result in revolutionary challenges or a threat to the state, it strengthens its policy of repression. If not, the government continues its co-optation and recruits loyal intellectuals.

---

19   Bueno de Mesquita and Smith (2011, p. 2) specified that 'the (real) selectorate' is the group that actually chooses the leader. In China, it consists of all voting members of the Communist Party.

The Party State's Goal

Role B

Role A

Demands for
Political Reform

Self-Discipline

Loyalty to
state ideology

Role C

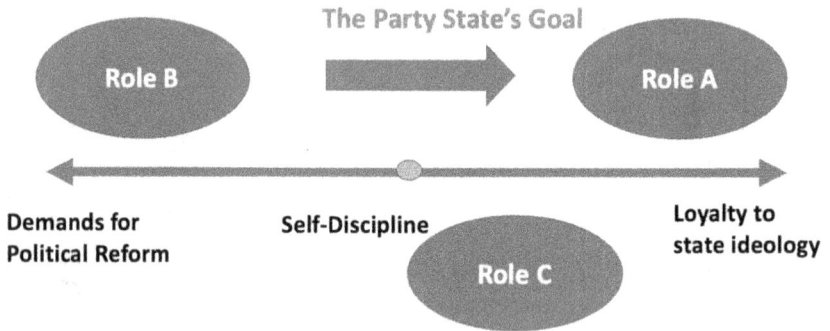

Figure 5.4: The typology of intellectual roles
Source: Created by the author.

Intellectuals may change their roles, and most of them move back and forth in the spectrum between becoming a mouthpiece and demanding political reforms, as figure 5.4 illustrates.[20] In between the two, those in intellectual Role C tend to exercise self-discipline and keep themselves within the government's red lines. Very few intellectuals exclusively demand political reforms, maintain self-discipline or accept social co-optation throughout their careers. Most choose to call for political reforms in periods of relaxation and choose self-discipline or co-optation in periods of repression. The goal of the party-state's policy of strengthening control is to convert those in Role B to adopt Role A or at least Role C.

Third, echoing the repression–relaxation cycle model, when the party-state perceives that the increasing Role B intellectuals start to pose a challenge to the party-state and co-optation alone cannot control Role B intellectuals' behaviour, the party-state intensifies the scope and degree of suppression. It can be viewed as the period of suppression. On the other hand, if the party-state perceives that co-optation alone can train 'self-disciplined' intellectuals, the party-state adopts few suppression measures or restrictions on specific intellectuals or in specific cases, it can be viewed as the period of relaxation.

The suppression itself is not the goal but more a result that reflects the government's lack of confidence that co-optation alone is not alluring enough to dissuade Group B from demanding political reform. Additionally, as the lesson learned from the Cultural Revolution, a long period of ruthless

---

20   The author would like to thank Professor Ben Hillman, Chien-Wen Kou, Titus C. Chen and two anonymous reviewers for suggestions about the typology of intellectual roles.

suppression with extreme scope and degree might also give intellectuals a serious sense of frustration, which leads to their losing confidence in the socialist political system. Therefore, once the party-state perceives that those in Group B have silenced themselves, it tends to loosen suppression and return to the period of relaxation, which forms a cycle of suppression and relaxation. This framework is applicable to most periods in PRC history.[21]

Questions in this research can be discussed in terms of this framework: when and why does an autocrat or authoritarian state choose repression and tighten ideological control over intellectuals in this case? While co-optation and repression have been used simultaneously on intellectuals adopting different roles most of the time, a leader decides to strengthen ideological control and the level of repression over intellectuals when they perceive that their legitimacy is externally or internally under threat from the criticism of intellectuals and the collective action that they inspire.

Applying this model to Xi's policy over ideology and establishment intellectuals, it can be explained that he increased repression and co-optation (or initiated a period of repression, as the cyclical model argues) in order to urge intellectuals to restrict their discourse and adopt Role A or C. The fundamental reason is that Xi perceived threats from the outspoken behaviour of intellectuals, their advocating of liberal thought and their influence on college students. As Xi's remarks above demonstrate, the CPC is concerned that while political unrest and regime change may perhaps occur overnight, the gradual disintegration of a regime begins from the ideological sphere. The Tiananmen Incident began with college student demonstrations. Yuan's remarks also indicate that the CPC suspects that enemy countries in the West who are fearful of China's rise will step up their infiltration of young teachers and students. The peaceful evolution conspiracy has long been a concern of the CPC. Hence the goal of repression is to prevent possible challenges from society by setting up a new 'red line' or warning intellectuals when they have crossed it.

---

21   The dual methods of co-optation and suppression can also be observed in state–intellectual relations in Japan in the 1930s and 1940s. Although many pro-socialist intellectuals were arrested under the provisions of the Peace Preservation Law, many of them were coerced to 'ideological conversions'. In the latter half of the 1930s, the Cabinet Research Bureau frequently hired these former leftist converts.

Conclusion

This chapter focuses on the Chinese Communist Party's policy towards establishment intellectuals under Xi Jinping and explores the most applicable explanation for this policy shift. On the basis of existing literature on this cyclical model, we have proposed a new model of 'dual methods in state–intellectual relations' to explain shifting state–intellectual relations. This model demonstrates that the CPC has employed dual methods of repression and co-optation towards intellectuals adopting different roles. Leaders choose repression when they perceive that their legitimacy is externally or internally under threat from the criticism of intellectuals and the collective action that they inspire.

This is a preliminary attempt to develop a framework that explains state–intellectual relations in China, and there are still some issues left for future research. First, repression might have varying degrees of intensity. What factors influence the degree of repression used by the state? Second, it would be difficult in practice to predict when a leader perceives a threat and decides to repress intellectuals since different leaders can have different notions of what constitutes a threat while also differing in their level of distrust towards them.

To be specific, several factors should be investigated to answer the question of why Xi perceived a threat in the discourses of intellectuals. Were Xi and the CPC intimidated by China's unprecedented integration with the world and its ability to engage Chinese intellectuals and the public with foreign ideas?[22] Do Xi and the CPC perceive any threat or enmity from the international environment? Do Xi and the CPC perceive there to be increasing pressure for political reform or democratisation from society? Was Xi concerned about the response of intellectuals to his centralisation of political power and therefore intent on repressing those who might utter criticism? Psychologically, does Xi distrust intellectuals, or is he simply more sensitive to the encroachment of Western ideology? Further research could help to define what indicators are able to identify a leader's perception of a threat to the regime.

---

22 Cheek (2015b, p. 319) indicates that although Chinese intellectuals have engaged with foreign ideas for more than a century, their current degree of integration with the world is unprecedented.

References

AsiaNews (2020) 'Chen Zhaozhi arrested for denouncing the "Chinese Communist Party virus".' 5 May. www.asianews.it/news-en/Chen-Zhaozhi-arrested-for-denouncing-the-'Chinese-Communist-Party-virus'-49997.html

Bao, W. [鲍威] (2010) 'Chūgoku ni okeru kōtō kyōiku seido to daigaku no setchi keitai' [中国における高等教育制度と大学の設置形態, The establishment style of universities and the higher education system in China]. In *Daigaku No Setchi Keitai Ni Kansuru Chōsa Kenkyū* [大学の設置形態に関する調査研究, Investigation and research on the establishment style of universities]. Kunitachidaigaku zaimu keiei sentā kenkyū hōkoku [国立大学財務・経営センター研究報告, National University Financial/Management Centre Research Paper], 13: 41–72

Buckley, C., & Jacobs, A. (2015) 'China's Maoists are revived as thought police.' *New York Times*, 4 January. www.nytimes.com/2015/01/05/world/chinas-maoists-are-revived-as-thought-police.html

Bueno de Mesquita, B., & Smith, A. (2011) *The Dictator's Handbook: Why Bad Behaviour is Almost Always Good Politics*. Public Affairs

Bueno de Mesquita, B., Smith, A., Siverson, R.M., & Morrow, J.D. (2003) *The Logic of Political Survival*. MIT Press

Caciagli, M. (1991) 'Clientelism.' In *Blackwell Encyclopedia of Political Science*, ed. V. Bogdanor. Oxford University Press

Cheek, T. (2007) 'New Chinese intellectual: Globalized, disoriented, reoriented.' In *China's Transformations: The Stories Beyond the Headlines*, ed. L.M. Jensen & T.B. Weston, pp. 265–84. Rowman & Littlefield

—— (2015a) 'Establishment intellectuals.' Oxford Bibliographies in Chinese Studies. www.oxfordbibliographies.com/view/document/obo-9780199920082/obo-9780199920082-0118.xml

—— (2015b) *The Intellectual in Modern Chinese History*. Cambridge University Press

Cheek, T., & Hamrin, C.L. (1986) 'Introduction.' In *China's Establishment Intellectuals*, ed. C.L. Hamrin & T. Cheek, pp. 3–20. M.E. Sharpe

Chen, Z. [陈振凯], Hou, K. [侯颖], & Sang, S. [桑珊珊] (2018) 'Zhongyang pizhun de 10 jia xijinping xin shidai zhongguo tese shehui zhuyi sixiang yanjiu zhongxin (yuan) xiangji chengli' [中央批准的10家习近平新时代中国特色社会主义思想研究中心（院）相继成立, 10 research centres (institutions) of Xi Jinping Thought on Socialism with Chinese Characteristics for the New Era approved by the central government have been established one after another]. *Renmin Wang* [人民网, People's Daily Online]. 18 April. theory.people.com.cn/BIG5/n1/2018/0418/c40531-29932832.html

China Daily (2017) 'Shuangyiliu daxue' [双一流大学, Double top university plan]. 25 September. www.chinadaily.com.cn/opinion/2017-09/25/content_32446664.htm

Cotton, J. (1984) 'Intellectuals as a group in the Chinese political process.' In *Groups and Politics in the People's Republic of China*, ed. D.S.G. Goodman, pp. 176–93. M.E. Sharpe

Denyer, S. (2017) 'Chinese universities scramble to open centers to study President Xi Jinping Thought.' *Washington Post*, 1 November. www.washingtonpost.com/world/chinese-universities-scramble-to-open-centers-to-studypresident-xi-jinping-thought/2017/11/01/a845e664-bed8-11e7-af84-d3e2ee4b2af1_story.html

Ding, L. (2019) 'Laozi Xiang Jun Shang de Jianyan bei chexiao, "yingshe shixue" chonglai?' [《老子向君上的建言》被撤销，「影射史学」重来？ Lao Tzu's Advice to the Lord is revoked and 'innuendo history' is back?]. VOA Chinese, 19 April. www.voachinese.com/a/chinese-scholar-history-political-implication-20190419/4882774.html

Feng, E. (2017) 'Beijing vies for greater control of foreign universities in China.' *Financial Times*, 19 November. www.ft.com/content/09ecaae2-ccd0-11e7-b781-794ce08b24dc

—— (2018a) 'China tightens party control of foreign university ventures.' *Financial Times*, 2 July. www.ft.com/content/4b885540-7b6d-11e8-8e67-1e1a0846c475

—— (2018b) 'China tightens grip on foreign university joint ventures.' *Financial Times*, 7 August. www.ft.com/content/dbb7b87e-99f7-11e8-9702-5946bae86e6d

Fischer, K. (2014) 'Email suggests embattled Chinese scholar was fired for political views.' *Chronicle of Higher Education*, 3 January. www.chronicle.com/article/Email-Suggests-Embattled/143839

Gan, N. (2017) 'Chinese universities tighten ideological control of teaching staff.' *South China Morning Post*, 28 August. www.scmp.com/news/china/policies politics/article/2108597/china-universities-tighten-ideologicalcontrol-teaching

Global Times (2020) 'Marxist education and ideology strengthened in Shanghai', 17 December. www.globaltimes.cn/page/202012/1210302.shtml

Goldman, M. (1985) 'The zigs and zags in the treatment of intellectuals.' *China Quarterly* 104: 709–15. doi.org/10.1017/S0305741000033385

—— (1993) 'The intellectuals in the Deng era.' In *China in the Era of Deng Xiaoping: A Decade of Reform*, ed. M.Y. Kau & S.H. Marsh, pp. 285–329. M.E. Sharpe

Guojia Jiaocai Weiyuanhui [国家教材委员会, National Textbook Committee] (2021a) Guojia Jiaocai Weiyuanhui guanyu yinfa Xi Jinping xin shidai Zhongguo tese shehui zhuyi sixiang jin kecheng jiaocai zhinan de tongzhi [国家教材委员会关于印发《习近平新时代中国特色社会主义思想进课程教材指南》的通知, Notice of the National Textbook Committee on printing and distributing the Guide to teaching materials for the introduction of Xi Jinping Thought on Socialism with Chinese Characteristics for a New Era]. 21 July. big5.www.gov.cn/gate/big5/www.gov.cn/zhengce/zhengceku/2021-08/25/content_5633152.htm

—— (2021b) Guojia Jiaocai Weiyuanhui guanyu yinfa 'Dang de lingdao' xiangguan neirong jin da zhong xiaoxue kecheng jiaocai zhinan de tongzhi [国家教材委员会关于印发《'党的领导'相关内容进大中小学课程教材指南》的通知, Notice of the National Textbook Committee on Printing and Distributing the Guidelines for teaching materials of 'party leadership' related contents into the curriculum of universities, primary and secondary schools]. 26 September. www.moe.gov.cn/srcsite/A26/s8001/202110/t20211015_572633.html

Hai Tao [海涛] (2013) 'Renmin ribao chong chao malie, lilun zhengzhi zaiqi xiaoyan.' [人民日报重炒马列，理论争执再起硝烟, *People's Daily* revives Marxism and Leninism, arousing theory debates again]. VOA Chinese, 17 September. www.voachinese.com/a/china-daily 20130916/1750772.html

Hamrin, C.L. (1987) 'Conclusion: New trends under Deng Xiaoping and his successors.' In *China's Intellectuals and the State: In Search of a New Relationship*, ed. M. Goldman, T. Cheek & C.L. Hamrin, pp. 275–304. Harvard University Asia Centre

Hancock, T. (2017) 'Chinese universities race to embrace Xi Jinping's theories.' *Financial Times*, 30 October. www.ft.com/content/7002d916-bd47-11e7-b8a3-38a6e068f464

Holbig, H. (2014) 'Shifting ideologies of research funding: The CPC's national planning office for philosophy and social sciences.' *Journal of Current Chinese Affairs* 43(2): 13–32. doi.org/10.1177/186810261404300203

Hu, J., & Mols, F. (2019) 'Modernizing China's tertiary education sector: Enhanced autonomy or governance in the shadow of hierarchy?' *China Quarterly*, 239: 702–27. doi.org/10.1017/S0305741019000079

Jarvis, D.S.L., & Mok, J.K.H. (eds) (2019) *Transformations in Higher Education Governance in Asia: Policy, Politics and Progress.* Springer

Kennedy, A. (2019) 'China's rise as a science power: Rapid progress, emerging reforms and the challenge of illiberal innovation.' *Asian Survey* 59(6): 1022–43. doi.org/10.1525/AS.2019.59.6.1022

Kou, C. (2019) 'The evolution of the Chinese party-state in the Xi Jinping era: Trends, causes and impacts' (paper presentation). International Conference on Changes in the Chinese Party-state in the Xi Jinping Era, Taipei, Taiwan

Liang, J. (2017) 'The enduring challenges for collective lobbying: The case of China's elite universities.' *China Journal* 78(1): 81–99. doi.org/10.1086/690498

Liu, X. (2017) 'The governance in the development of public universities in China.' *Journal of Higher Education Policy and Management* 39(3): 266–81. doi.org/10.1080/1360080X.2017.1300122

Ma, S. (1998) 'Clientelism, foreign attention and Chinese intellectual autonomy: The case of Fang Lizhi.' *Modern China* 24(4): 445–71. doi.org/10.1177/009770049802400404

Ng, Y., & Sing, M. (2018) 'Government relies on student informants at China's universities.' Radio Free Asia, 14 June. www.rfa.org/english/news/china/government-relies-on-student-informants-at-chinas-universities-06142018114732.html

Ning, S. [寧韶華] (2021) 'Shenru xuexi guanche dang de shijiu jie liu zhong quanhui jingshen beijing daxue chengli Xi Jinping jingji sixiang yanjiu zhongxin, Xi Jinping fazhi sixiang yanjiu zhongxin, Xi Jinping waijiao sixiang yanjiu zhongxin, Xi Jinping shengtai wenming sixiang yanjiu zhongxin' [深入学习贯彻党的十九届六中全会精神 北京大学成立习近平经济思想研究中心、习近平法治思想研究中心、习近平外交思想研究中心、习近平生态文明思想研究中心, Deeply study and implement the spirit of the Sixth Plenary Session of the 19th Central Committee of the CPC, Peking University established Research Centre of Xi Jinping Economic Thought, Research Centre of Xi Jinping Rule of Law Thought, Research Centre of Xi Jinping Diplomacy Thought, Research Centre of Xi Jinping Ecological Civilization Thought]. Beijing Daxue Xinwen Wang [北京大学新闻网, Peking University News Network]. 22 November. news.pku.edu.cn/xwzh/5e2e46b86a8b467c9f9b815444810dce.htm

PEN America (2018) 'Forbidden feeds: Government controls on social media in China', March. pen.org/wpcontent/uploads/2018/06/PEN-America_Forbidden-Feedsreport-6.6.18.pdf

Perry, E.J. (2015) 'Higher education and authoritarian resilience: The case of China, past and present.' Harvard Yenching Institute Working Paper Series. harvard-yenching.org/sites/harvard-yenching.org/files/featurefiles/Elizabeth%20Perry_Higher%20Education%20and%20Authoritarian%20Resilience.pdf

Quanguo Gaoxiao Sixiang Zhengzhi Gongzuo Wang [全国高校思想政治工作网, National University Ideological and Political Work Net (NUIPWN)] (2013) 'Guanyu jiaqiang he gaijin gaoxiao qingnian jiaoshi sixiang zhengzhi gongzuo de ruogan yijian' [关于加强和改进高校青年教师思想政治工作的若干意见, Opinions with regard to strengthening and improving the thought and political work on young teachers at higher education institutions]. 4 May. www.sizhengwang.cn/jdwx/zcwj/2018/1227/1978.shtml

—— (2017) 'Gaoxiao sixiang zhengzhi gongzuo zhiliang tisheng gongcheng shishi gangyao' [高校思想政治工作质量提升工程实施纲要, Outline of implementing the project of improving the quality of ideological and political work in colleges and universities], 5 December. www.sizhengwang.cn/jdwx/zcwj/2017/1206/256.shtml

Quanguo Zhexue Shehui Kexue Gongzuo Bangongshi [全国哲学社会科学工作办公室, National Office of Philosophy and Social Sciences] (2018) '2019 niandu guojia shehui kexue jijin xiangmu shenbao gonggao' [2019年度国家社会科学基金项目申报公告, Notice on application for the projects of the 2019 National Social Science Fund of China], 25 December. www.npopss-cn.gov.cn/n1/2018/1225/c219469-30487263.html

Rhoads, R.A., Wang, K., Shi, X., & Chang, Y. (2014) *China's Rising Research Universities: A New Era of Ambition.* Johns Hopkins University Press

Scholars at Risk [SAR] (2019) 'Obstacles to excellence: Academic freedom and China's quest for world-class universities. A report of the Scholars at Risk Academic Freedom Monitoring Project', 24 September. www.scholarsatrisk.org/wp-content/uploads/2019/09/Scholars-at-Risk-Obstacles-to-Excellence_EN.pdf

Sharma, Y. (2020) 'Government targets academic critics of COVID-19 response.' *University World News*, 5 May. www.universityworldnews.com/post.php?story=20200512140730235

Wade, S. (2017) 'Law scholar He Weifang quits social media.' *China Digital Times*, 26 May. chinadigitaltimes.net/2017/05/law-scholar-weifang-quits-social-media

Xi, W., Han, J., Wong, S., & Lau, S. (2019) 'Chinese universities ordered to spy on staff, students in ideological crackdown.' Radio Free Asia, 8 April. www.rfa.org/english/news/china/universities-04082019144318.html

Xiao, Q. (2010) 'DSD police recruit and maintain informant networks among university students.' *China Digital Times*, 11 April. chinadigitaltimes.net/2010/04/dsd-police-recruit-and-maintain-informant-networks-amonguniversity-students

Xinhua (2013) 'Xijinping: Yishixingtai gongzuo shi dang de yixiang jiduan zhongyao de gongzuo' [习近平：意识形态工作是党的一项极端重要的工作, Xi Jinping: Ideological work is an extremely important work of the Party]. Xinhua, 20 August. news.xinhuanet.com/politics/2013-08/20/c_117021464.htm

—— (2014) 'Xi Jinping: Jianchi lide shuren sixiang yinling, jiaqiang gaijin gaoxiao dangjian gongzuo' [习近平：坚持立德树人思想引领，加强改进高校党建工作, Xi Jinping: Persist in the thought guidance in fostering virtue through education, strengthen Party-construction work in higher education]. Xinhua, 29 December. www.xinhuanet.com//politics/2014-12/29/c_1113818177.htm

—— (2016a) 'Xi Jinping: Zai zhishifenzi, laodong mofan, qingnian daibiao zuotanhui shang de jianghua' [习近平：在知识分子、劳动模范、青年代表座谈会上的讲话, Xi Jinping: Speech at the symposium of representatives of intellectuals, model workers and youth]. Xinhua, 30 April. news.xinhuanet.com/politics/2016-04/30/c_1118776008.htm

—— (2016b) 'Xinhua Xi Jinping: Jianchi zhengque fangxiang chuangxin fangfa shouduan, tigao xinwen yulun chuanboli yindaoli' [习近平：坚持正确方向创新方法手段，提高新闻舆论传播力引导力, Xi Jinping: Persisting in the correct orientation, innovating methods and means and raising the dissemination strength and guidance strength of news and public opinion]. Xinhua, 20 February. www.xinhuanet.com//politics/2016-02/19/c_1118102868.htm

—— (2017a) 'Xi Jinping zhuchi zhongyang zhengzhiju huiyi, shenyi "guanyu xunshi 31 suo zhongguan gaoxiao dangwei qingkuang de zhuanti baogao"' [习近平主持中央政治局会议，审议《关于巡视31所中管高校党委情况的专题报告》, Xi Jinping hosts the Central Committee of the CPC, reviewing the Report on the situation of party Committees in universities based on the tours of 31 universities]. Xinhua, 28 June. www.xinhuanet.com/politics/2017-06/28/c_1121227905.htm

—— (2017b) 'Xi Jinping: Juesheng quanmian jiancheng xiaokang shehui, duoqu xin shidai Zhongguo tese shehuizhuyi weida shengli—zai Zhongguo gongchandang di shijiu ci quanguo dabiao dahui shang de baogao' [习近平：决胜全面建成小康社会　夺取新时代中国特色社会主义伟大胜利—在中国共产党第十九次全国代表大会上的报告, Secure a decisive victory in building a moderately prosperous society in all respects and strive for the great success of socialism with Chinese characteristics for a new era—Full text of Xi Jinping's report at the 19th CPC National Congress]. Xinhua, 27 October. www.xinhuanet.com/politics/19cpcnc/2017-10/27/c_1121867529.htm

—— (2017c) 'Zhonggong zhongyang guowuyuan yinfa "guanyu jiaqiang he gaijin xin xingshi xia gaoxiao sixiang zhengzhi gongzuo de yijian"' [中共中央国务院印发《关于加强和改进新形势下高校思想政治工作的意见》, The CPC Central Committee and the State Council issue the Opinions on strengthening and improving ideological and political work in colleges and universities under the new circumstances]. Xinhua, 27 February. www.xinhuanet.com/2017-02/27/c_1120538762.htm

—— (2017d) 'Shouquan fabu: Zhongguo gongchandang zhangcheng' [受权发布：中国共产党章程, Authorized to issue: Constitution of the Communist Party of China]. Xinhua, 28 October. www.xinhuanet.com/politics/19cpcnc/2017-10/28/c_1121870794.htm

—— (2018) 'Zhonggong zhongyang yinfa "shenhua dang he guojia jigou gaige fangan"' [中共中央印发《深化党和国家机构改革方案》, CPC Central Committee issues the Decision on deepening the reform of the party and state institutions]. Xinhua, 21 March. www.xinhuanet.com/politics/2018-03/21/c_1122570517.htm

Xinhua Net (2017) '10 institutes established to study Xi's thought.' Xinhua Net, 14 December. www.xinhuanet.com/english/2017-12/14/c_136826404.htm

—— (2021) '7 more research centres established to study Xi Jinping thought.' Xinhua Net, 26 June. www.xinhuanet.com/english/2021-06/26/c_1310029353.htm

Xu, J., & Zhu, X. (2019) *Conceptualizing and Contextualizing Higher Education with Chinese Characteristics: Ontological and Epistemological Dimensions*. Springer

Yuan, G. [袁贵仁]. (2015) 'Bawo dashi, zhuoyan dashi, nuli zuohao xin xingshi xia gaoxiao xuanchuan sixiang gongzuo' [把握大势，着眼大事，努力做好新形势下高校宣传思想工作, Grasp the trend, focus on important things, work hard on propaganda and ideological work in universities under the new situation]. Qiushi [求是], 31 January. www.qstheory.cn/dukan/qs/2015-01/31/c_1114143901.htm

Zhang, Y. (2018) 'More students inform on teachers who make politically inappropriate remarks in class.' *Global Times*, 14 June. www.globaltimes.cn/content/1107000.shtml

Zhao, S. (2016) 'Xi Jinping's Maoist revival.' *Journal of Democracy*, 27(3): 83–97. doi.org/10.1353/jod.2016.0051

Zhonggong Zhongyang Bangongting [中共中央办公厅, General Office of the CPC Central Committee] (2014) 'Zhonggong zhongyang bangongting guanyu jianchi he wanshan putong gaodeng xuexiao dangwei lingdao xia de xiaozhang fuzezhi de shishi yijian' [中共中央办公厅关于坚持和完善普通高等学校党委领导下的校长负责制的实施意见, Implementation of views on sustaining and improving the presidential responsibility system under the leadership of the CPC at universities], 15 October. www.moe.edu.cn/publicfiles/business/htmlfiles/moe/s5147/201410/176026.html

Zhonggong Zhongyang Jilü Jiancha Weiyuanhui [中共中央纪律检查委员会, Central Commission for Discipline Inspection (CCDI) of the CPC] (2017) 'Zhonggong qinghua daxue weiyuanhui guanyu xunshi zhenggai qingkuang de tongbao' [中共清华大学委员会关于巡视整改情况的通报, Notice regarding rectification reports of the Party Committee at Tsinghua University]. 27 August. www.ccdi.gov.cn/yaowen/201708/t20170827_149188.html

Zhongguo Zhengfu Wang [中国政府网, www.gov.cn] (2015) 'Zhonggong zhongyang bangongting, guowuyuan bangongting yinfa guanyu jinyibu jiaqiang he gaijin xin xingshi xia gaoxiao xuanchuan sixiang gongzuo de yijian' [中共中央办公厅、国务院办公厅印发《关于进一步加强和改进新形势下高校宣传思想工作的意见》, The Central Committee Office and State Council Office issue Opinions concerning the further strengthening and reforming of propaganda and ideological work at universities under the new circumstances]. 19 January. www.gov.cn/xinwen/2015-01/19/content_2806397.htm

—— (2020) 'Quanguo gaoxiao si zheng ke jiaoshi renshu tupo 10 wan ren' [全国高校思政课教师人数突破10万人, The number of ideological and political teachers in colleges and universities across the country exceeds 100,000]. 3 December. big5.www.gov.cn/gate/big5/www.gov.cn/xinwen/2020-12/03/content_5566847.htm

Zhonghua Renmin Gongheguo Guofangbu [中华人民共和国国防部, Ministry of National Defence of the People's Republic of China] (2021) 'Zhonggong zhongyang yinfa "Zhongguo Gongchandang putong gaodeng xuexiao jiceng zuzhi gongzuo tiaoli"' [中共中央印发《中国共产党普通高等学校基层组织工作条例》, The CPC Central Committee issues the CPC regulations on basic level organisation work in ordinary institutions of higher education]. 22 April. www.mod.gov.cn/big5/regulatory/2021-04/22/content_4883794.htm

Zhonghua Renmin Gongheguo Jiaoyubu [中华人民共和国教育部, Ministry of Education of the PRC] (2018) 'Jiaoyubu guanyu yinfa "Xin shidai gaoxiao jiaoshi zhiye xingwei shi xiang zhunze", "Xin shidai zhong xiaoxue jiaoshi zhiye xingwei shi xiang zhunze", "Xin shidai youeryuan jiaoshi zhiye xingwei shi xiang zhunze" de tongzhi' [教育部关于印发《新时代高校教师职业行为十项准则》《新时代中小学教师职业行为十项准则》《新时代幼儿园教师职业行为十项准则》的通知, Notice of the ministry of education on printing and distributing Ten guidelines for professional behaviours of college teachers in the new era, Ten guidelines for professional behaviour of primary and secondary school teachers in the new era and Ten guidelines for professional behaviour of kindergarten teachers in the new era]. 8 November. www.moe.gov.cn/srcsite/A10/s7002/201811/t20181115_354921.html

—— (2020) 'Jiaoyu bu "jiaoyu bu deng ba bumen guanyu jiakuai goujian gaoxiao sixiang zhengzhi gongzuo tixi de yijian"' [教育部 '教育部等八部门关于加快构建高校思想政治工作体系的意见', MoE 'opinions on accelerating the construction of the ideological and political work system in colleges and universities']. 22 April. www.gov.cn/zhengce/zhengceku/2020-05/15/content_5511831.htm

—— (2021a) 'Xijinping xin shidai zhongguo tese shehui zhuyi sixiang xuesheng duben yu jinnian qiuji xueqi qi zai quanguo tongyi shiyong' [《习近平新时代中国特色社会主义思想学生读本》于今年秋季学期起在全国统一使用, The Textbook of Xi Jinping Thought on Socialism with Chinese Characteristics for a New Era for students will be used throughout the country starting this fall semester]. 8 July. www.moe.gov.cn/jyb_xwfb/gzdt_gzdt/s5987/202107/t20210708_543195.html

—— (2021b) 'Jiaoshi fa xiuding jiang jujiao qiang shi de ti menkan bao daiyu' [教师法修订将聚焦强师德提门槛保待遇, The revision of the Teacher Law will focus on strengthening teachers' ethics, raise the threshold and secure the treatment]. 22 October. www.moe.gov.cn/jyb_zzjg/huodong/202110/t20211022_574252.html

6

Xi's *dao* on new censorship: The party's new approaches to media control in the digital era

Shuyu Zhang

This chapter offers new insights into the Communist Party of China's (CPC) renewed determination and updated apparatuses to tame social media and control online discourse. Using Chinese President Xi Jinping's speeches on media control from 2013 through 2019 as points of departure, it explores several key themes in online censorship in China, which has become more internalised, systematic and far-reaching in the population under Xi's leadership. Xi's conceptualisation of censorship dictates continuities and shifts in the party's policies on media control: while state censorship is further confirmed on structural and legislative levels, it is now realised by a network of censorious agents, with the party and Xi himself at the apex of power. The CPC's authority and control over agencies and individuals largely occur through Foucauldian 'self-managing', where internet platforms and netizens alike are driven to become their own censors. The purpose, as Xi defines it in culturally ingrained terms, is to achieve a clear and uncontaminated online ecology filled with 'positive energy', a grassroots term manipulated to represent the CPC's ideology superiority and to clamp down on free expression online on the pretext that they embody only negativity unconducive to the nation's grand agenda.

New language for new censorship

Censorship practised in its strict sense often involves repressive intervention and/or the removal of undesired materials from transmission by an authoritative power (Müller, 2004, p. 4). The socialist media censorship system that came into existence after the founding of the People's Republic of China (PRC) in 1949 is of a similar repressive nature. It incorporates the Leninist conceptualisation of the media as 'the eyes, ears, tongue and throat of the party' (cf. Brady, 2017, p. 129) and remains largely effective to this day, as a result of the *nomenklatura* system it borrowed from its Soviet 'brother-in-arms': trusted cadres are appointed to senior management roles in propaganda departments and media organisations such as editorial committees in news agencies to facilitate the party's surveillance over what China's vast population read, watch and listen to.

In the face of the ideological confrontation between gradually commercialising media and the party-state since the 1990s, the party adjusted its approach to media control and began to focus on market incentives, institutional control and coercive mechanisms (Esarey, 2005; Hassid, 2008). In addition to these external control mechanisms, the party also obtained compliance from media actors through the pervasive practice of self-censorship (Chin, 2018), which is best captured in Perry Link's (2002) 'anaconda on the chandelier' metaphor: the party's manipulation of uncertainty over what is permissible and what is not keeps journalists on their toes and fearful of punitive actions from the censorial authority, or 'the anaconda's strike'.

Nonetheless, while traditional censorship in its repressive and coercive form—consisting mainly of the surveillance, prohibition and manipulation of information—remains alive in today's China, new censorship in the digital age needs to be contextualised to take into consideration how the internet has changed journalistic practices and the shaping of public discourse and censorship understood beyond the dyad of control and resistance, as an interplay of power negotiation among the public, local agents and the party-state.

The 50th Statistical Report on Internet Development in China recorded 1.051 billion internet users in China as of August 2022, accounting for 74.4 per cent of its total population and one-fifth of global internet users (China Internet Network Information Centre, 2022). The sheer volume and speed of information transmitted online make it impossible for any censor to remove every piece of information deemed politically sensitive or even regime-threatening (Xu, 2015; Zeng et al., 2019; S. Zhao et al., 2013). 'New media' also fundamentally transformed how people access and consume information, producing a burgeoning number of citizen journalists (Xin, 2010) as well as self-media (自媒体, *zimeiti*): internet-based, independently operated media accounts on social media (Sun & Zhao, 2022). The newly emerged forms of media are swift to fill the silence when traditional media are delayed or absent (Wu, 2018), especially during large-scale emergencies such as the 2017 Tianjin Explosion.

Meanwhile, state censors struggle to catch up, and thanks to the networking nature of social media, the viral spread of sensitive information can easily lead to online discourse management crises and social instability (Guo & Zhang, 2020; Han, 2018). The internet poses a challenge for authoritarian regimes because it empowers society to mobilise and exert a more active role in decision-making (Lilleker & Koc-Michalska, 2017). For example, the streak of anti-PX (Para-Xylene) rallies that went on from 2007 to 2014 in several Chinese cities represents one of the most successful offline protests mobilised and facilitated through social media (Lee & Ho, 2014).

The online mass has also become more adept at circumventing censorship. From VPN software to long picture texts (texts that are transformed into long pictures to evade word limits) and taboo words detection, the tools and measures constantly evolve, forcing the censorship mechanism to stay on par with technological advancements, such as artificial intelligence detection, which can now screen long pictures for censorable content with surprisingly high accuracy and efficiency. This applies to languages other than Chinese as well, from the author's experience. In less than 10 seconds after publication, the long picture containing a piece of text on 'political correctness in communist propaganda'—inverted, turned upside down and marked with random emojis/lines throughout as an effort to confuse the artificial intelligence detection—was censored and no longer accessible.

Language, in the form of homophones and memes, becomes the last resort for netizens to evade censorship in a witty and almost coded way, as exemplified in the cat-and-mouse race between the censors and people eager to find out Peng Shuai's allegation of being sexually assaulted by former vice president Zhang Gaoli. Her original post was deleted within 20 minutes and her name censored on Weibo and other social media platforms. Netizens first discussed the instances using 'PS' and 'ZGL', the first capital letters in the pinyin of their Chinese names and, when the shorthand was censored as well, created memes by referring to their respective equivalents in the American context: 'Have you heard about Serena Williams and Mike Pence?'

The internet and the new media that comes along with it have put traditional media and old censorship apparatuses—pre- and post-publication/posting censorship, the Great Firewall and keyword blocking—to test. Effective as they may be, the party-state headed by Xi Jinping recognises a pressing need to further tighten the clamp on the internet, which it sees as 'the biggest variant on the battleground of public discourse' and 'a thorn in our side planted by the West to bring down China' (China Digital Times, 2013). Propaganda and thought work have been elevated to an unprecedented status, as Xi warned top cadres and propagandists that 'the fall of a regime always starts from the head' and 'irreversible historical mistakes would bear upon us if the party lost its firm grip on the power to lead, manage and speak on ideological work'.

It is this view that has given rise to Xi's *dao* on new censorship, embodied in his series of talks on the party-state's media control, written into official discourse through legislatures and policies, practised by his propagandists at all levels and incrementally materialised into the digital reality that we see in China today. This chapter examines a corpus made up of Xi's six speeches, sourced from the National Propaganda and Thought Work conferences in 2013 and 2018, the Cyber Security and Digitalisation Work conferences in 2016 and 2018, the party's News and Propaganda Work Seminar in 2016 and the 12th Politburo Group Study Session in 2019. These speeches showcase how language as an embodiment of power and knowledge is used to 'maintain the status quo and to structure power relationships' (Lovell, 2014, p. 221).

Excerpts from the corpus are supplemented with ethnographical observations and readings of laws and policies to illustrate how Xi's rhetoric on media governance translates into strategies of media censorship and control, diligently implemented by various institutions and agents as guiding morals to shape the media landscape in China. This chapter proposes that the state as the 'external, coercive and repressive' censor is merely a secondary form of thought control (Bunn, 2015). It is internal to a much broader category of censorship by social institutions, realised through a communication network of censorious agents. The myriad of state and non-state actors involved in censoring contravening dissonance showcases a complex and nuanced censorship mechanism in China's digital society, whereby the reach of state censorship is greatly extended through delegated censorship, censorship through reporting and increasingly heightened self-censorship.

The new language around the party-state's renewed approach to censorship and media control, while reiterating the party's all-encompassing role in media control ('the party leads the media'), departs from the traditional lines on authoritarian censorship as top-down and repressive. Instead, the new language stresses censorship internalised in a network of 'self-managing' censorious institutions and agents ('firm control is the absolute rule'). Xi conceptualises a 'comprehensive governing system of China's online ecology', in which service providers, as well as average netizens, are driven to take a more proactive role in maintaining and guarding a 'clear and uncontaminated digital space', as delegated censors and moderators.

It is also a space imbued with 'positive energy'—a concept embedded in grassroots cultural language yet redefined to preach populist 'political correctness' in the Chinese context ('positive energy is the overarching principle'). Members of the digital society who hold contravening beliefs are expected to self-edit their expressions or self-silence altogether, while the party digitalises its own propaganda apparatuses in order to stay uplifting and advantaged in the increasingly liberalised battlefield of discourse.

The party leads the media

The key theme at the core of Xi's rhetoric on media control and censorship is that the party has a firm grip on the media. In his 2013 speech at the National Propaganda and Thought Work Conference, Xi revived two slogans on media control from the Mao era: 'the party leads the media' (党管媒体, *dang guan meiti*) and 'the politicians run the newspaper' (政治家办报, *zhengzhijia ban bao*):

> We must firmly hold onto the principle of the party leading the media and the politicians running the newspaper, the publications, the TV stations and the news websites. We must have enhanced Marxist values in news. Whatever we insist on or resist, whatever we say or do must fall in line with the party's interests and requirements. Be resilient and reliable. [要坚持党管媒体原则不动摇，坚持政治家办报、办刊、办台、办新闻网站，加强马克思主义新闻观教育. 坚持什么、反对什么，说什么话、做什么事，都要符合党的要求，过得硬、靠得住。]

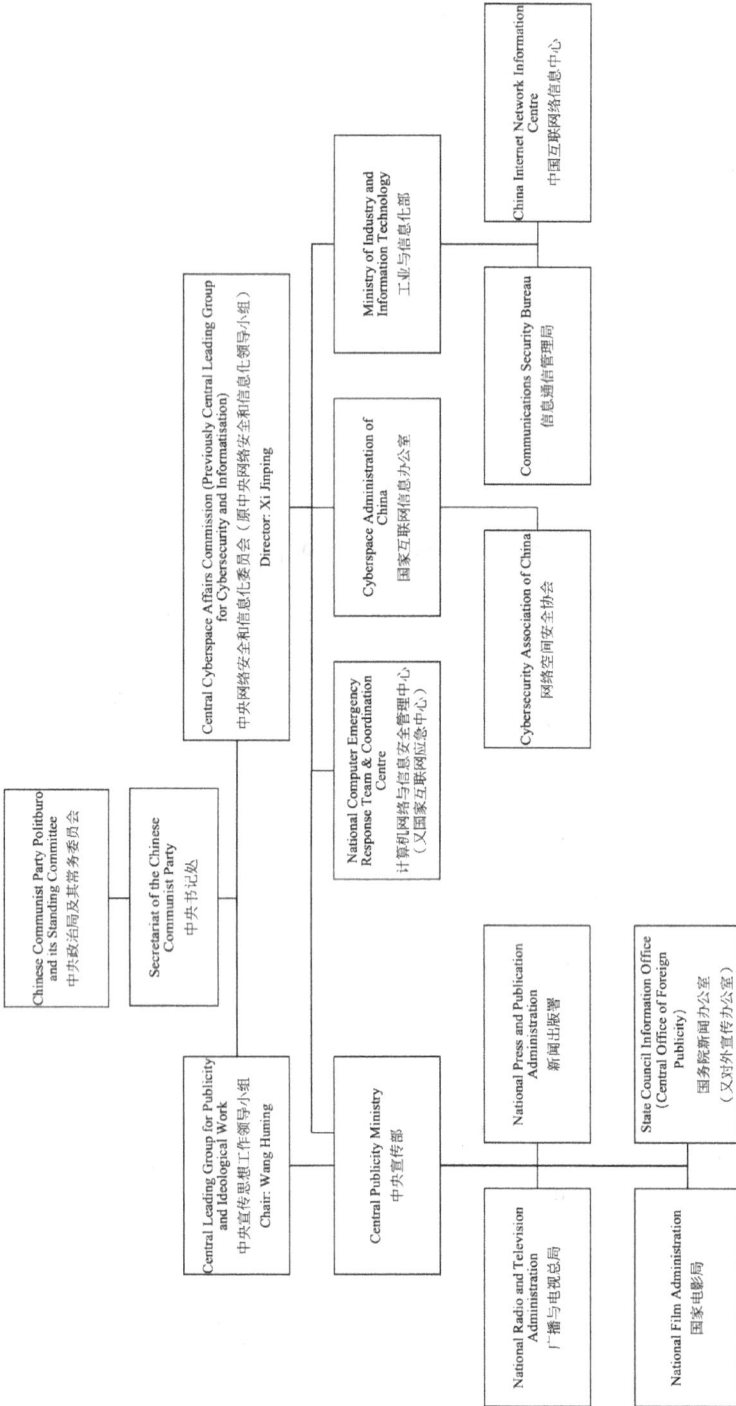

Figure 6.1: Organisational structure for media control and censorship following CPC institutional reforms of 2018
Source: Created by author.

While repetitively calling on his propagandists to resist 'temptations' and 'nihilism' with 'Marxism' and 'party character' (党性, *dangxing*), Xi sees the dire need to supervise their demeanour through 'centralised leadership on cybersecurity and information' at the state level. As shown in figure 6.1, this is realised through the centralisation of power in the party's organisational matrix, with the Politburo Standing Committee at the apex of oversight over multiple powerful bureaus and departments, coordinating with one another in media control and censorship. The structure consolidated power to the Leading Small Groups at the top of the hierarchy: (1) the Central Leading Small Group for Propaganda and Thought Work, headed by Politburo Standing Committee member Wang Huning, and (2) the former Central Leading Small Group for Internet Security and Informatisation, now the Central Cyberspace Affairs Commission, headed by Xi Jinping himself.

Together, the Leading Small Group and the Central Cyberspace Affairs Commission develop and issue guiding principles on all matters related to propaganda and information media policies, as well as supervise their implementation. However, since the party's 2018 institutional reform of its organisational structure, the two bodies have had different points of focus in their objectives and distribution of power. The Leading Small Group for Propaganda and Thought Work now directly harnesses both old and new media through the Central Publicity Department. It administers control over radio, television, film, the press, publications and the like—traditionally referred to as 'old media'—as well as some forms of 'new media', including online publications, news and games.

Meanwhile, the Central Cyberspace Affairs Commission, under Xi's directorship, bears more authority over media control and censorship on the internet (Cheung, 2018, p. 316). The commission supplants the roles previously carried out by the State Council, coordinating the Central Publicity Department and the Ministry of Industry and Information Technology. Zhuang Rongwen, one of the eight deputy heads of the Central Publicity Department, leads the Cyberspace Administration of China (CAC).

As the enforcement agency for the commission, the CAC, along with its branch offices at the provincial, municipal and, on occasion, local levels, is responsible for the management of online services and internet security, as well as regulating and censoring content that is published online. It exercises control over online discourse through directives issued to social media platforms and major news portals, a measure traditional to the party's propaganda work that provides guidelines on information distribution and agenda-setting on specific social issues, especially those of a sensitive nature or relevant to national interests, such as China's stance on the Russian invasion of Ukraine.

Moreover, under the aegis of Xi, the CAC is further empowered to 'legalise the internet' through CAC-issued legislatures and CAC-led joint law enforcement with other ministries and government bodies, which Xi envisaged in his talks as an essential component of 'governing under the rule of law' (依法治国, *yifa zhiguo*): 'Rule the internet, operate the internet and use the internet by law. And ensure that the internet operates in a healthy manner on law-abiding tracks' (要推动依法管网、依法办网、依法上网，确保互联网在法治轨道上健康运行).

As shown in table 6.1, this vision was subsequently materialised into a comprehensive and ever-growing list of laws, regulations, provisions, rules and CPC decisions on telecommunications and internet use, all either drawn up or revised after 2012, the year Xi took office. A majority of those that concern internet control were issued by the Cyberspace Administration of China or the State Internet Information Office, which are both under the supervision of the Xi-led Central Cyberspace Affairs Commission.

Table 6.1: Laws and regulations on information control through telecommunication (inclusive of media content)

Name — Chinese	Name — English	Issuing authority
全国人大常委会关于加强网路资讯保护的决定	Decision of the Standing Committee of the National People's Congress on Strengthening Information Protections on Networks	Standing Committee of the National People's Congress, 2012
中华人民共和国电信条例	Regulations on Telecommunications of the People's Republic of China	Issuing and revision authority: The State Council (issued in 2000, revised in 2014 and 2016)
中华人民共和国网路安全法	Cybersecurity Law of the People's Republic of China	Standing Committee of the National People's Congress, 2016
互联网群组资讯服务管理规定	Provisions on the Administration of Internet Group Information Services	Cyberspace Administration of China, 2017
互联网跟贴评论服务管理规定	Provisions on the Administration of Internet Comment Posting Services	Cyberspace Administration of China, 2017

Name — Chinese	Name — English	Issuing authority
互联网新闻消息服务许可管理实施细则	Detailed Rules for the Licensed Management of Internet News Information Services	State Internet Information Office, 2017
微博客信息服务管理规定	Provisions on the Administration of Microblog Information Services	Cyberspace Administration of China, 2018
网路资讯内容生态治理规定	Provisions on Ecological Governance of Network Information Content	Cyberspace Administration of China, 2019
中国共产党宣传工作条例	Regulations on the Party's Publicity Work	Central Committee of the Chinese Communist Party, 2019
互联网资讯服务管理办法	Provisions on the Administration of Internet Information Services (Draft Revisions for the Solicitation of Public Comments)	Issuing authority: the State Council, 2000 Revision authority: Cyberspace Administration of China, 2021

Source: Authors' summary.

The rules provide legal grounds for censorship and online discourse management on the whole. For example, the *Provisions on Ecological Governance of Network Information Content* (2021) dedicates an entire section to topics that internet content creators are encouraged to produce, replicate and publish, including those that promote Socialism with Chinese Characteristics in the New Era, in other words, Xi Jinping Thought (习近平思想, *Xi Jinping sixiang*). Conversely, there are also topics that content creators should not engage in or should take preventative and boycotting measures against; that is, topics that are censorable or even punishable under the 'rule of law', such as those that 'threaten the honour and interests of the nation' or 'distort, defame, insult or deny stories and spirits of national heroes or martyrs'.

The legislative arm extends to every aspect of online discussion, casting a wide legal dragnet over anyone who voices their opinion online. For one, the *Provisions on the Administration of Internet Comment Posting Services* made real-name registration a prerequisite for commenting online, be it in the form of 'texts, emoticons, emojis, pictures or *danmu* [bullet comments commonly used in animation, comics and gaming websites]'. Even discussions taking place in private chat groups are not free from scrutiny, and in-group members may be subjected to 'warnings, suspension from posting, or group termination', according to the *Provisions on the Administration of Internet Group Information Services*.

Joining the forces from other government agencies—specifically, that of the public security system—the CAC and its local branches are able to govern most of the internet censorship, effectively silencing and deterring dissonance online and offline. Depending on the scale of harm that the information might have caused in the online sphere, further prosecution in reality could follow. This can be as simple as a 'chat over a cup of tea' (请喝茶, *qing he cha*), a phrase that refers to informal questioning or detention by public security (Han, 2018, p. 43), or as serious as imprisonment.

This was what happened to Wuhan doctor Li Wenliang after he published information about a 'suspected new virus outbreak' in a private WeChat group to warn his university classmates who also worked as doctors in December 2019. He was summoned to the local public security bureau and reprimanded for 'publishing untruthful speech and seriously disturbing social order', after screenshots of his in-group post were disseminated to the wider public on Weibo. A similar fate was shared by investigative journalist Luo Changping, one of the latest to join the growing list of journalists and commentators who have been detained and imprisoned for questioning China's role in the Korean War on Weibo (Myers & Chien, 2021). His original Weibo post was censored and his social media accounts 'permanently terminated' on the grounds that he 'defames national heroes'. Furthermore, Luo was detained by public security and later sentenced to seven months in prison, a 'voluntary donation' of ¥80,000 (equivalent to A$18,000) to the Memorial of the War to Resist US Aggression and Aid Korea, and a public apology.

Beyond the Great Firewall, Chinese living and studying overseas have become new targets of state censorship as their social media behaviour on international platforms such as Twitter (now X) is closely scrutinised by Chinese authorities. However mild or facetious it may be, any negative portrayal of the country or content considered to be 'reactionary' or 'national interest threatening' could lead to their families in China being harassed and monitored or to the original poster being summoned to the local Public Security Bureau and reprimanded once they return to China (Xiao & Mozur, 2021).

Nonetheless, the ultimate role of the CAC resides in not only tackling individual dissidents but also reining in the internet as a whole and ensuring the party's unyielding lead on the new media. In addition to the ongoing Operation Qinglang (清朗行动) to 'cleanse and de-contaminate the online space', taking its name from Xi's quote 'returning a clear and uncontaminated sky to the online space', the CAC further chaired or engaged in cross-ministry law enforcement campaigns against specific 'chaos in the cyberspace', including fandom fights, rigged algorithms, internet water armies and commentators paid by commercial interests to manipulate public opinion through news, gossip and disinformation (also known as marketing accounts; 营销号, *yinxiaohao*). In its most recently announced campaign in September 2022, the CAC is going to collaborate with nine other ministries, including the Department of Public Security and the Supreme People's Court, in sweeping away 'internet Black and Evil crimes'.

These campaigns established the CAC as the overlord that, despite the dispersion and perversion of power in media control and censorship, rules over other state actors in exercising the party's will on controlling internet discourse through administrative and legislative means. The level of power centralisation also allows the CAC unprecedented control over internet service providers, which now assume a dual role. On the one hand, they are expected to act in coordination with CAC directives and follow suit in CAC-led campaigns to regulate and censor its users. In August 2022, Weibo reported censoring 18,000 accounts and more than 19 million posts as part of its response to the CAC Counter Cyberbullying campaign. Weibo further culled some 251 million accounts following the CAC's Counter Water Army campaign starting from December 2021.

At the same time, they are bound by law to become their own censors, enforcing state censorship as delegated censors. As clarified in the *Provisions on Ecological Governance of Network Information Content*, internet platforms are by law the 'main bodies to shoulder the responsibility of content management', which means promoting and recommending favourable content on trending topics or on their front page, while not featuring any 'inappropriate contents' that might adversely affect the internet ecology, such as inappropriate comments on large-scale emergencies. Internet platforms are driven to innovate and upgrade their own censorship apparatus to keep unfavourable content under control, while the party-state maintains its firm control on the platforms through administrative and punitive actions.

Firm control is the absolute rule

Despite its command of the control room, the party relies on a myriad of intermediary actors within a 'regime of truth' to implement the ambitions and visions of the upper echelon of media control and censorship at local levels (G. Yang, 2011, p. 1044). While the CPC's control of the new media and online discourse is absolute, the control apparatus is not monolithic. It involves a dynamic set of measures realised and internalised through various agents and institutions, or, in Xi's words, a comprehensive, multi-agent governing system: 'We need to improve on the capability to govern the internet comprehensively and form a comprehensive governing system that incorporates economic, legislative and technical measures, a system that is led by the party, administered by the government, delegated to responsible enterprises, supervised by the society and netizen's self-discipline' (要提高 网络综合治理能力，形成党委领导、政府管理、企业履责、社会 监督、网民自律等多主体参与，经济、法律、技术等多种手段相 结合的综合治网格局).

Xi calls on internet service providers to shoulder their 'social and moral responsibility' and take a more proactive role in bearing the cost and responsibility of censorship, all in the name of 'industry self-management' (行业自律, *hangye zizhi*) while the CAC remains the supervising body. This arrangement was confirmed by law, first in 2017 by the *Detailed Rules for the Licensed Management of Internet News Information Services* and again in 2019 by the *Provisions on Ecological Governance of Network Information Content*. The provisions clearly outline the responsibility of internet service platforms to censor published information and comments, as well as real-time surveillance (实时巡查, *shishi xuncha*) to identify potentially 'harmful' posts and first response to public opinion crises. They also make it compulsory for platforms to set up a designated role for the delegation of censorship or, consistent with the theme of Operation Qinglang, for 'internet ecology governance'.

Failure to perform proper and timely censorship leads to jurisdictional talks with the local branch of the CAC or, worse still, direct penalties. In December 2021, Weibo was fined an additional ¥3 million (equivalent to A$600,000) for 'repeatedly publishing illegal information', on top of 44 penalties—totalling ¥14.30 million (almost A$3 million)—imposed by the CAC from January to November that year.

Through its heavy-handed punitive actions, the party-state fosters a chilling environment in which internet platforms as delegated censors respond with excessive caution and enthusiasm, censoring any information that might catch the attention of higher authority and in turn trigger a penalty. This allows the party-state to remain less visible in the actual censorship process while remaining present in its control through the delegation of censorship. In fact, empirical data compiled by Sun Taiyi and Zhao Quanshan (2022) suggest that, of the 73 articles censored in their self-media account on WeChat, two-thirds resulted from delegated censorship rather than direct state censorship.

The majority of delegated censorship is carried out as prevention rather than mitigation as service providers are prompted to stay on the safe side and practise strict pre-posting censorship and swift post-posting censorship, rather than waiting for sensitive information to develop into potential public opinion crises.

In the case of Weibo, for example, pre-posting can take the form of the traditional blacklist of taboo words, as well as smarter technologies that attend to censorship evasion. Service or content providers constantly monitor the frequently updated list of taboo words (Vuori & Paltemaa, 2015). A list leaked in 2016 by a previous censor who worked for Leshi, an online video company, contains some 35,467 words or word combinations related to Xi. Some of the latest filtered words include the name and works of Xi's critics (China Digital Space, 2020). In just two days, Yan Geling, a renowned Chinese American novelist, was entirely wiped out on Chinese social media for calling out the Xi administration on its inert response and lack of transparency in addressing women's rights issues and human trafficking, following the astonishing story of the chained mother of eight (China Digital Times, 2022).

Online content containing a taboo word is automatically filtered and saved to a draft box, where it remains until the sensitive content has been removed. This often requires a trial-and-error process to determine which word is the culprit. The latest blacklisting nonetheless involves the creation of an echo chamber of one's own, where censorship takes place without the original poster even realising that it is in effect. The Weibo posts deemed to be 'inappropriate for public dissemination' or comments that contain 'inappropriate speech'—most likely in violation of Article 27 of Weibo's Community Management Regulations (Sina Weibo, 2021; see table 6.2), which cites extensively from *Provisions on Ecological Governance of Network*

Information Content—may appear to the original poster as successfully posted while in fact being subject to a 'cap on readership' (限流, *xianliu*), which limits its likelihood of being pushed to their followers' timeline, or downright 'screened' (过滤, *guolü*), that is, not readable to anyone but the original posters themselves.

Table 6.2: Article 27 of Sina Weibo's Community Management Regulations

Article 27: Users should not publish any information harmful to [discussion of] current affairs, which includes information that endangers national and social security under current laws and regulations. That is, information that:

1. Opposes the basic principles established by the constitution
2. Harms the unity, sovereignty, or territorial integrity of the nation
3. Reveals national secrets, endangers national security, or threatens the honor or interests of the nation
4. Promotes terrorism, extremism, or incites acts of terrorism or extremism
5. Incites ethnic hatred or ethnic discrimination, undermines ethnic unity, or harms ethnic traditions and customs
6. Undermines national policies on region, promotes evil teachings and superstitions
7. Spreads rumours, disrupts social order and destroys societal stability
8. Distorts, defames, insults, or denies stories and spirits of national heroes or martyrs
9. Promotes illicit activity, gambling, violence, or calls for the committing of crimes
10. Calls for disruption of social order through illegal gatherings, formation of organisations, protests, demonstrations, mass gatherings and assemblies
11. Has other content which is forbidden by laws, administrative regulations and national regulations.

Source: Sina Weibo Community Management Regulations, May 2020.

Weibo censors also actively surveil digital platforms, taking precautions by shutting down the comment sections, allowing only 'carefully picked comments' or no comments at all, on posts that are likely to draw public outcry. One of the latest such posts includes a one-liner posted by commentator/stand-up comedian Chen Di: 'For how long will this performance go on?' Posted on 18 September 2022, the day after the quarantine bus crash in Guizhou, in which 27 people on board were killed, Chen's post seems to have been interpreted by censors not as a reference to his own show business, in all likelihood, but as a criticism of the province's mass transportation policy, which sought to ship all confirmed cases and contacts to quarantine centres in order to meet its Zero-COVID deadline. First, comments to this post were made unavailable and subsequently the reposting function, as people reposted the original line and invited thoughts on possible interpretations of 'a performance'. Another instance involves the post by the official account of the Office of Foreign Spokesperson on 9 September 2022 that commended the CPC as 'people-centred and deeply loved by its people'. Unsurprisingly, only comments that resonate with this party-loving line were 'carefully picked' and made available in the comment section.

However, when sensitive information does slide under the radar, post-censorship through reporting needs to be involved. Weibo recruits its own service users as moderators (监督员, *jianduyuan*), or 'community volunteers', to help facilitate delegated censorship through reporting on posts that are 'violative of laws and regulations'. The active participation of netizens constitutes an integral element of the internet industry's effort to self-censor, or, as Xi remarks, 'self-discipline': 'We need to enhance the self-discipline of the internet industry, call on netizens to take an active part and mobilise all sectors to join forces in the governance' (要加强互联网行业自律，调动网民积极性，动员各方面力量参与治理').

As translated and included in table 6.3, the recruitment process, outlined in the official account of Weibo Community Volunteers, puts a strong emphasis on the applicant's ability to identify not only contents that are in violation of national laws and Weibo's own regulations but also the code used to encrypt such information and evade censorship. The moderators should preferably have prior experience of detecting and reporting sensitive information when automatic identification falls short.

Table 6.3: How to become a Weibo volunteer

Weibo users can apply to become a volunteer on a voluntary basis, providing that they:
Are older than 18 years of age;
Have a registered Weibo account for at least a year that is linked to a phone number;
Have Weibo Credit score higher than 120;
Must ensure the provision of factual and up-to-date personal information. They need to have some experience with reporting to correctly report on contents violative of laws and regulations;
Pass the ability test on identifying contents violative of laws and regulations. The test mainly examines the applicant's ability to identify contents violative of laws and regulations and reportable within their responsibility as moderators, such as those related to obscenity, gambling, evil teachings and martyr defamation. It also tests the applicant's familiarity with relevant regulations and requirements. Those who are unfamiliar with the basic features of these contents, including internet jargon, coded language and coreference, are not likely to pass the test.

Source: Official account of Weibo Community Volunteers, September 2022.

On top of the prior screening in recruitment to ensure their readiness for the job, Weibo moderators are further subsidised with self-enrichment incentives attached to the action of reporting, making them less compliant or merciful with discussions of sensitive social issues. Moderators are ranked monthly on the total number of their valid reports, or 'complaints', as well as the 'accuracy rate' of these reports. A subsidy of as much as ¥5,000 (approximately A$1,000 or US$760) per month is awarded to moderators whose total number of reports rank top 500, with an 'accuracy rate' of more than 99 per cent; that is, more than 99 per cent of their reported posts include information that may be considered 'harmful to the [discussion of] current affairs' (时政有害, *shizheng youhai*)—again quoting Article 27 in its Community Management Regulations on 'information that violates relevant laws and regulations'—and therefore censorable.

According to the official Weibo Moderators account, more than 2.44 million pieces of information (posts and comments) were taken down in August 2022 alone following complaints from 'volunteers'. Should a piece of information be determined to be 'harmful or dangerous', the account might be 'muted' (禁言, *jin yan*), suspended (停用, *ting yong*) or permanently terminated (封号, *feng hao*). Real-name registration also makes possible real, offline consequences for any virtual, online non-conformity, as enforced through the public security system. Paid 'volunteers' work hand in hand with Weibo censors to create the comprehensive governing network of censorious agents as envisaged in Xi's quote at the beginning of this section.

Positive energy is the overarching principle

The media's adherence to the CPC agenda is an integral means by which the party shapes public opinion and influences it in the desired direction. The party has long adopted a hegemonic approach to controlling media coverage of internal affairs. Chinese media are expected to 'accentuate the positive and minimize the negative' (Brady, 2017, p. 136), especially when news topics involve domestic politics, national unity or social stability.

At the same time, as Maria Repnikova (2017) observed in her seminal work on media politics in China, media policy before Xi recognised the crucial role of media in public opinion supervision (舆论监督, *yulun jiandu*), through which 'constructive criticism' could serve as a measure of accountability, especially at the local level. While not dropping the idea of 'positive reporting' (正面报道, *zhengmian baodao*) altogether, the Hu-Wen administration was not short of high-level statements in favour of the media's alternative role as the accountability and feedback channel, including the direct mentioning of the term 'public opinion supervision' in the 16th, 17th and 18th party congresses.

While the continuity is obvious in Xi's discourse on staying positive, in dire contrast to his predecessors is the scrapping of the term 'public opinion supervision' almost entirely from his speeches. The only mention of the term nonetheless comes together with 'positive propaganda': 'Public opinion supervision is in line with positive propaganda' (舆论监督和正面宣传是统一的).

The key to remaining critical and positive at the same time, according to Xi, rests in the renewed expression taken from the language of the grassroots: 'positive energy' (正能量, *zheng nengliang*), which could be roughly defined as 'any uplifting power and emotion, representing hope' (P. Yang & Tang, 2018).

Xi first adopted the term in his 2013 speech on propaganda and thought work and has since reiterated the importance of positive energy in multiple speeches. His redefinition of 'positive energy' closely aligns the concept with the party's political and ideological agenda, highlighting the positivity embodied in 'the achievements on reform and development, the economy and the improvement of the people's livelihood' and how these achievements essentially lay the foundation for the realisation of the great rejuvenation of the Chinese nation (中华民族伟大复兴, *Zhonghua minzu weida fuxing*) and the Chinese dream (中国梦, *Zhongguo meng*).

However, by reinforcing a sense of common duty for 'the greater good and the positive', it seeks to create a discourse that is itself hegemonic and functions as 'an impersonal form of control' (Bunn, 2015, p. 41). The semantic versatility of the catchphrase has been harnessed to reimagine the boundary of the 'speakable'. The phrase 'positive energy' has been used to preach 'correct political direction' (正确政治方向, *zhengque zhengzhi fangxiang*), or 'political correctness' in the Chinese context, despite the fallacy in logic in this new definition: conflating 'the positive' with 'the party' and 'the party' with 'the people': 'Only through reporting on positivity can we add positive energy to society. Mainstream media need to take active leadership in this. The "party character" is in line with the "people character". We must insist on the media's political stance and follow the correct direction' (要报道这

些正面积极的事情，这样才能给社会增添正能量。主流媒体在这方面要积极发挥引导作用。坚持党性和人民性相统一，就是要坚持讲政治，把握正确导向).

The 'political correctness' prescribes an intolerance of 'unpopular or critical opinions' and thus endorses the silencing of contravening voices riddled with 'negative energy' (負能量, *fu nengliang*). Meanwhile, the intentional vagueness in what is considered negative left anyone whose opinion varies from the party line susceptible to censorship. Delegated censors adopt similar vague rules in telling the negative voices from the positive ones.

Since 2020 Weibo has been censoring information 'harmful to [discussion on] current affairs', despite its not being specified in its Community Management Regulations, on the grounds that it contains 'negative information that breaches the boundaries set out by social morals or the institution' (制度底线, *zhidu dixian*). Followers of Lao Dongyan, a law professor and a policy critic, suspect that this was the reason her Weibo account was wiped clean on 17 September 2022, after she voiced concerns about the infringement of privacy and risks to personal information in big-data tracing and blanket surveillance. As China's Zero-COVID policy continues, it could well be that Lao's negative posts breached the boundaries set out by the party-state's determination to wipe out the virus entirely.

The conflation of the party and the people further adds a populist undertone to negative connotations attached to party critics, who, according to Xi, attack the party and the country 'with bias', 'for fame' or 'out of self-deprecation'. Recent years have seen critics being subjected not only to institutional censorship facilitated by the state or the platforms but also to online ostracism, compelling them to self-correct or self-censor. Unless they can verify their good intentions in providing 'normal, reasonable and kind criticisms and supervision'—deemed acceptable by Xi—they would have to hold back their opinion for fear of possible persecution offline, as well as attacks by the offended netizens online, who tend to question not the merits and validity of their criticism but their intention and identity.

Netizens were quick to question Luo Xiang, a criminal law scholar who garnered more than 250 million followers on Weibo for his humorous way of explaining legal cases to the general public, on the intention of his post, 'one should adhere to good virtues and not be enslaved by honour'. The post was made on 8 September 2020, the day when President Xi awarded the Medal of the Republic to respiratory expert Zhong Nanshan to commend his contribution to China's combat of COVID-19. The timing of the post led to speculations that Luo was mocking the celebration of the country's victory over the pandemic. Despite the denial of such ill intention, Luo was nonetheless attacked by netizens for this seemingly out-of-place 'negativity'. He announced on the same day that he would temporarily 'refrain from posting on Weibo' and subsequently aborted his Weibo account entirely in June 2021.

With the withering of contravening voices, Xi further calls on his propagandists to fill the void with 'positive energy', cancelling out the negativity online through adeptly steering propaganda and thought work through innovation and digitalisation. In the past, state-owned media was frequently ridiculed by the public for its archaic preaching, obtuse language and laughable attempts at astroturfing through its 'Fifty-cent Army' (五毛党, *wu mao dang*), who pose as spontaneous grassroots voices by extensively posting pro-party content online when they are in fact organised and sponsored by it (Benney & Xu, 2018; Han, 2015).

The party-state realised that to drown out the negative with the positive in the digital era, it needed a formidable 'internet army' (网军, *wang jun*) with insider knowledge of new media and online platforms to secure the ideological high ground with a form of speech that is charged with 'positive energy'. In a 2013 speech on propaganda and thought work, Xi stated: 'The internet is our latest battleground of public discourse. We need to fully appreciate the characteristics and art of this war and exert ourselves in building a force online. We need to form a strong internet army to stave off the one-foot-tall devil with ten-foot-tall virtues' (网上斗争，是一种新的舆论斗争形态。要深入分析网上斗争的特点和规律，精心组织网上斗争力量。要建设一支强大网军，做到魔高一尺、道高一丈).

The 'internet army' consists of barrages of official public accounts (公众号, *gongzhong hao*) and political accounts (政务微博, *zhengwu weibo*), increasingly present on all kinds of Chinese social media: Weibo, WeChat, even the Chinese TikTok, Douyin. By 2020, the number of agency and official Weibo accounts had risen to 164,522, a jump of 173 per cent compared to the number in 2012 (Sina Weibo Data Centre, 2021). The official public accounts are directly run by propaganda departments or official institutions at all geographical and administrative levels: central, provincial, municipal, county and township, contributing to the party-state's effort to shape the online media landscape into one of harmonious homogeneity and ensuring that party-endorsed news and information can reach as many recipients as possible and extend to a hyperlocal level.

These official accounts are further amplified as the favoured voices to pass on positivity in the supposedly pluralistic world of online expression through the party's whitelisting scheme (白名单, *baimingdan*), drafted and updated under the watch of the Cyberspace Administration of China (2021). Dividing online news service providers into three categories, the CAC grants only those in the first category—the 'whitelisted' category—the permission to report on current affairs, whereas the other two categories can reprint only content produced by those in the first category. In the latest revision of the list in 2021, hundreds of official public accounts on WeChat and Weibo were added to the whitelist, most owned by politically credible media outlets or directly run by propaganda departments at the national, provincial or prefectural levels. Meanwhile, several prestigious news agencies, including Caixin—known for its credible, in-depth, yet sometimes critical investigative journalism—were eliminated from the whitelist, ostensibly out of concern for their 'seriousness and credibility'. This move has been interpreted as Xi's strike on the negative voices that counter the positive voices in the realm of thought and public opinion.

These efforts result in the affluence of 'positive energy' online, produced by various official accounts and in all forms. In its 2021 round-up of top 500 'positive energy' paeans, the CAC listed the most 'positive' 100 pieces of online content across five categories: 'positive energy role models', 'positive energy writings', 'positive energy pictures', 'positive energy animation and audio-visual contents' and 'positive energy-themed activities' (results published on CCTV.com, 2021). Almost all are produced by official accounts, such as those affiliated with the Ministry of Public Security and state-run media, such as the *People's Daily* and *Global Times*. Topping the list was 'Learning in Progress' (学习进行时, *xuexi jinxingshi*)—*xuexi* as a homonym for both 'learning' and 'learning from Xi', a digital version of Xi's *Little Red Book*. Ran by the Xinhua News Agency, it was commended for its digital- and youth-friendly ways to propagate 'positive energy'—Xi's discourse—to the online population.

The 'positive energy' guards also contribute to the sanitation of stories that may contain 'negative energy' yet are redemptive through a positive spin. Official media were quick to jump on the story of the 'second uncle', an 11-minute video originally posted on the video-streaming website Bilibili, featuring a middle-aged village carpenter who remains optimistic and positive despite a life of poverty, disability and other suffering. Although the experience of the 'second uncle' represents an obvious failed case of the party's poverty alleviation campaign and social welfare scheme for the disabled population, it was nonetheless turned into a dose of 'positive energy' for China's youth, fraught with 'mental burnouts' and tired of the rat race.

A collective of official accounts and state media reposted the video on Weibo, as part of an information campaign to promote the 'correct' attitude and virtues in the face of hardships. As shown in figure 6.2, of the 2,092 media that reported on the 'second uncle', 1,912 were official-affiliated media at different administrative levels, attracting a staggering 630 million clicks on the 'positive energy' hashtag #Second Uncle Cured My Mental Burnouts#. Meanwhile, questions about the root causes of the 'second uncle's' adversity, as well as criticisms of institutional negligence and the official move to extol individual misery, were conveniently censored and received little publicity, let alone follow-up investigation or discussion.

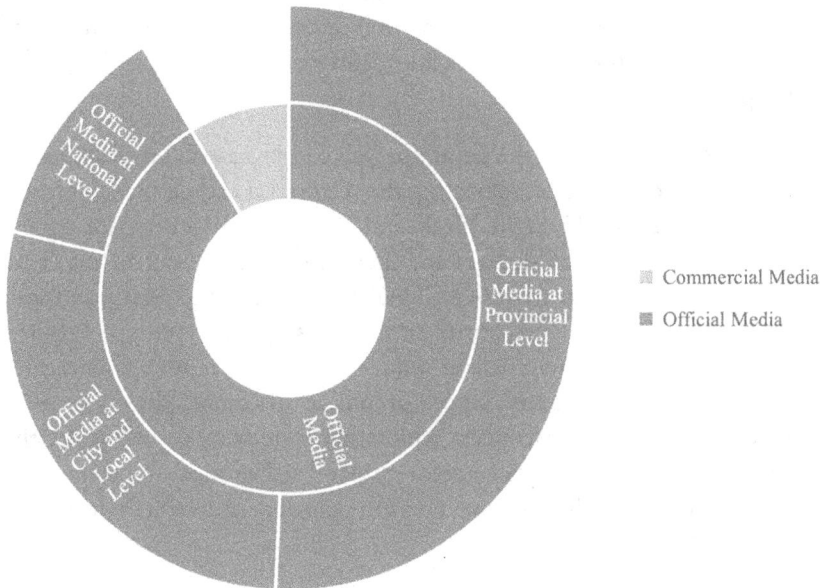

Figure 6.2: Percentage of official and commercial media that reported on the 'second uncle'
Source: Data extracted from Weibo trending topic and figure created by author.

By upholding 'positive energy' as the overarching rule, the media landscape under Xi's leadership was revamped drastically and its main functions were redefined: its function of supervising public opinion was strongly repressed in the name of 'political correctness', while its channelling function was placed in the hands of those who are trusted and endorsed to set the agenda in a direction favourable to the party—official accounts and state media.

Conclusion

Using Xi's speeches as a thread, this chapter examines the party-state's control and censorship of Chinese media during the time of Xi's leadership. While the censorship and media control apparatuses under Xi continue their repressive measures—recast in more technologically savvy forms to sift through sensitive information that has also evolved in its censorship evasion measures—it has become more 'productive' at the same time. This is reflected in its firmer control of internet platforms, which now have to shoulder the responsibility and cost, acting as their own censors through the delegation of state censorship, as well as censorship in 'new forms of discourse, new forms of communication and new genres of speech' (Bunn, 2015, p. 26).

Since 2012, when Xi took the helm, the party has reasserted its dominance of public discourse by establishing the Central Leading Small Group for Propaganda and Thought Work and the Central Cyberspace Affairs Commission. These CPC-led groups encroach on the power of the State Council to coordinate and oversee China's bureaucracy and administration, which is tasked with media control and censorship. Xi's vision to 'legalise' the Chinese internet materialised into a growing volume of laws and regulations that cover every aspect of online discourse, drawn up and enforced by the CAC in concert with other state actors, specifically the public security system. It provides a firmer legal ground for censorship and persecution, equally effective to whistleblowers and critics within and beyond the Great Firewall.

At the same time, rather than rule information with an iron fist as it did in the Maoist era, the party has adopted an increasingly subtle and indirect approach to media surveillance and censorship. The social power that this imposes on various institutions and agents serves to enforce censorship in a nuanced and internalised way. Internet platforms are now, by law, the censor of themselves, while the CAC stays behind the scenes while remaining in control through regular directives and administrative talks, as well as occasional heavy-handed penalties. Platforms as delegated censors are forced to draw up their own rules as guidelines for censorship, citing heavily from national laws and regulations and enforced with utmost caution to rule out any potential violation. Aside from active pre-censorship, manual censorship through reporting, where average netizens were made into accomplices in censorship, also contributes to the identification and silencing of sensitive or 'harmful' information.

The numerous control mechanisms introduced to tighten the party's grip on the media have been justified as a pursuit of 'positive energy'. The semantic versatility of this catchphrase has been exploited and appropriated as a guiding principle to suit the CPC's political agenda. 'Negative energy' embodied in dissonance and criticism is now subjected not only to state censorship and delegated censorship but also to heightened self-censorship. By aligning the positive with the correct and the people, the party acquiesced in online ostracism and cyber violence against negativity on populist grounds. Nonetheless, this is on the premise that the critics can speak loud enough on top of the deafening 'positive energy' to be heard in the first place.

The Xi administration has greatly improved its mastery of technology and discourse specific to digital-era propaganda and is successfully countering the grey and black forces that Xi Jinping identified as threats when he first came to power. Armed with updated knowledge of new media and guarded by a formidable 'internet army' of official accounts, the party is able to preach 'political correctness' in the Chinese context in a more digital-friendly way and drown out the negative voices through an overflow of 'positive energy', setting or even rewriting the agenda for the online population, which is subjected to the digital reality, modelled, recreated and heavily influenced by Xi's vision of a 'clear and uncontaminated space online'.

References

Benney, J., & Xu, J. (2018) 'The decline of Sina Weibo: A technological, political and market analysis.' *Chinese Social Media: Social, Cultural and Political Implications*, ed. M. Kent, K. Ellis & J. Xu, pp. 221–35, Routledge. doi.org/10.4324/9781315160214

Brady, M.A. (2017) 'Magic weapons: China's political influence activities under Xi Jinping' (paper presentation). Conference on the Corrosion of Democracy under China's Global Influence, Arlington, VA, 16–17 September. www.wilson center.org/article/magic-weapons-chinas-political-influence-activities-under-xi-jinping

Bunn, M. (2015) 'Reimagining repression: New censorship theory and after.' *History and Theory* 54(1): 25–44. doi.org/10.1111/hith.10739

Cheung, T.M. (2018) 'The rise of China as a cybersecurity industrial power: Balancing national security, geopolitical and development priorities.' *Journal of Cyber Policy* 3(3): 306–26. doi.org/10.1080/23738871.2018.1556720

Chin, S.J. (2018) 'Institutional origins of the media censorship in China : The making of the socialist media censorship system in 1950s Shanghai.' *Journal of Contemporary China* 27(114): 956–72. doi.org/10.1080/10670564. 2018.1488108

China Central Television (2022) '2021 zhongguo zhengnengliang "wuge yibai" wangluo jingping pingxuan jieguo jiexiao' [2021中國正能量"五個一百"網絡精品評選結果揭曉, Results revealed on top 100 internet content on Chinese positive energy in five categories]. January. news.cctv.com/2022/01/29/ARTIA8 heXcsrIhMzPytPvtCk220128.shtml

China Digital Space (2020) 'Guoxinban Xi Jinping min'gan ciku' [國新辦習近平敏感詞庫, Lists of censored words relevant to Xi Jinping (issued by State Council Information Office to Leshi)]. chinadigitaltimes.net/space/%E5%9 B%BD%E6%96%B0%E5%8A%9E%E4%B9%A0%E8%BF%91%E5%B9 %B3%E6%95%8F%E6%84%9F%E8%AF%8D%E5%BA%93

China Digital Times (2013) 'Xi Jinping Bayijiu jianghua jingshen chuanda tigang quanwen' [習近平"8.19"講話精神傳達提綱全文, Full text of Xi Jinping's speech on 19th August 2013], November. chinadigitaltimes.net/space/习近平 %228·19%22讲话精神传达提纲全文

—— (2022) 'Dearth of official information on Xuzhou's shackled woman spurs citizen journalists and online sleuths.' chinadigitaltimes.net/2022/02/dearth-of-official-information-on-xuzhous-shackled-woman-spurs-citizen-journalists-and-online-sleuths

China Internet Network Information Center (2022) 'The 50th Statistical Report on Internet Development in China.' www.cnnic.com.cn/IDR/ReportDownloads/ 202204/P020220424336135612575.pdf

Cyberspace Administration of China (2021a) 'Wangluo xinxi neirong shengtai zhili guiding' [網絡信息內容生態治理規定, Provisions on Ecological Governance of Network Information Content]. Retrieved 15 September 2022. www.cac. gov.cn/2019-12/20/c_1578375159509309.htm

—— (2021b) 'Zuixinban hulianwang xinwen xinxi gaoyuan danwei mingdan' [最新版互聯網新聞信息稿源單位名單, The latest internet news information source list]. www.cac.gov.cn/2021-10/18/c_1636153133379560.htm

Esarey, A. (2005) 'Cornering the market: State strategies for controlling China's commercial media.' *Asian Perspective* 29(4): 37–83. jstor.org/stable/42704523

Guo, L., & Zhang, Y. (2020) 'Information flow within and across online media platforms: An agenda-setting analysis of rumor diffusion on news websites, Weibo, and WeChat in China.' *Journalism Studies* 21(15): 2176–95. doi.org/10.1080/1461670X.2020.1827012

Han, R. (2015) 'Manufacturing consent in cyberspace: China's "Fifty-Cent Army".' *Journal of Current Chinese Affairs* 44(2): 105–34. doi.org/10.1177/18681026 1504400205

—— (2018) *Contesting Cyberspace in China: Online Expression and Authoritarian Resilience.* Columbia University Press

Hassid, J. (2008) 'Controlling the Chinese media: An uncertain business.' *Asian Survey* 48(3): 414–30. doi.org/10.1525/as.2008.48.3.414

Lee, K., & Ho, M.S. (2014) 'The Maoming Anti-PX protest of 2014: An environmental movement in contemporary China.' *China Perspectives* 2014(2014/3): 33–9. doi.org/10.4000/chinaperspectives.6537

Lilleker, D.G., & Koc-Michalska, K. (2017) 'What drives political participation? Motivations and mobilization in a digital age.' *Political Communication* 34(1): 21–43. doi.org/10.1080/10584609.2016.1225235

Link, P. (2002) 'China: The anaconda in the chandelier.' *New York Review of Books* 49(6): 1230–54. www.nybooks.com/articles/2002/04/11/china-the-anaconda-in-the-chandelier/

Lovell, M. (2014) 'Languages of neoliberal critique: The production of coercive government in the Northern Territory Intervention.' In *Studies in Australian Political Rhetoric*, ed. J. Uhr & R. Walter, pp. 221–40. ANU Press. doi.org/10.22459/SAPR.09.2014

Müller, B. (2004) 'Censorship and cultural regulation: Mapping the territory.' In *Censorship and Cultural Regulation in the Modern Age*, ed. B. Müller, pp. 1–31. Rodopi

Myers, S.L., & Chien, A.C. (2021) 'Chinese journalist detained after criticizing government-sponsored blockbuster.' *New York Times*, October. www.nytimes.com/2021/10/08/world/asia/luo-changping-china-battle-at-lake-changjin.html

Repnikova, M. (2017) *Media Politics in China: Improvising Power under Authoritarianism.* University Printing House

Sina Weibo (2021) 'Weibo Shequ Gongyue' [微博社區公約, Weibo shequ gongyue], May. service.account.weibo.com/roles/gongyue?from=10B5395010&wm=9006_2001&weiboauthoruid=7504817032

Sina Weibo Data Centre (2021) 'Weibo 2020 Yonghu Fazhan Baogao' [微博2020用戶發展報告, 2020 Official Report on Weibo Users]. data.weibo.com/report/reportDetail?id=456

Sun, T., & Zhao, Q. (2022) 'Delegated censorship: The dynamic, layered and multistage information control regime in China.' *Politics and Society* 50(2): 191–221. doi.org/10.1177/00323292211013181

Vuori, J.A., & Paltemaa, L. (2015) 'The lexicon of fear: Chinese internet control practice in Sina Weibo microblog censorship.' *Surveillance and Society* 13(3–4): 400–21. doi.org/10.24908/SS.V13I3/4.5404

Wu, X. (2018) 'Discursive strategies of resistance on Weibo: A case study of the 2015 Tianjin explosions in China.' *Discourse, Context and Media* 26: 64–73. doi.org/10.1016/j.dcm.2018.05.002

Xiao, M., & Mozur, P. (2021) 'A digital manhunt: How Chinese police track critics on Twitter and Facebook.' *New York Times*, December. www.nytimes.com/2021/12/31/technology/china-internet-police-twitter.html

Xin, X. (2010) 'The impact of "citizen journalism" on Chinese media and society.' *Journalism Practice* 4(3): 333–44. doi.org/10.1080/17512781003642931

Xu, D. (2015) 'Online censorship and journalists' tactics: A Chinese perspective.' *Journalism Practice* 9(5): 704–20. doi.org/10.1080/17512786.2014.982968

Yang, G. (2011) 'Technology and its contents: Issues in the study of the Chinese internet.' *Journal of Asian Studies* 70(4): 1043–50. doi.org/10.1017/S0021911811001598

Yang, P., & Tang, L. (2018) '"Positive energy": Hegemonic intervention and online media discourse in China's Xi Jinping era.' *China: An International Journal* 16(1): 1–22. doi.org/10.1353/chn.2018.0000

Zeng, X., Jain, S., Nguyen, A., & Allan, S. (2019) 'New perspectives on citizen journalism.' *Global Media and China* 4(1): 3–12. doi.org/10.1177/2059436419836459

Zhao, S., Gu, Y., Kang, L., & Dang, H. (2013) 'Circumventing the Great Firewall: The accommodation and defiance of Internet censorship among Chinese students.' Social Science Research Network. ssrn.com/abstract=2258659. doi.org/10.2139/ssrn.2258659

7

The state and digital society in China: Big Brother Xi is watching you!

Jean-Pierre Cabestan[1]

State–society relations in the People's Republic of China (PRC) have changed profoundly in the last 40 years. At the beginning of the reform era, there was no clear distinction between the party-state and society: whether they lived in a city or the countryside, most Chinese belonged to a work unit (单位, *danwei*), an extension of both the state and the Communist Party of China (CPC). Today, while the emergence of a full-fledged civil society remains aspirational, it is fair to say that Chinese society has gained genuine autonomy. At the same time, the state/society dichotomy is a misleading oversimplification, as most social scientists have highlighted the continuum between the party-state and society and the interpenetration of the two, underscored and embodied in many ways by enormous membership of the CPC, a figure that was more than 95 million in 2021 (Perry, 1994).

One of the most unexpected transformations in Chinese society has been its rapid accession to the digital era. Supported by unprecedented modernisation, the impressive development of China's digital economy has been an uncontested success. The digitalisation of Chinese society has had two opposite consequences: it has clearly simplified the lives of many

1   This chapter is a revised and updated version of the article that first appeared as J.P. Cabestan (2020) 'The state and digital society in China: Big brother Xi is watching you!' *Issues and Studies* 56(1), Article 2040003. doi.org/10.1142/S1013251120400032. Reprinted with permission.

Chinese, allowing them to remain in constant connection and facilitating a variety of business transactions and payments. At the same time, it has allowed the party-state to spy on citizens and maintain its control over society with greater efficiency.

On the one hand, the internet and other social media platforms have contributed to creating forums for discussion, new manifestations of citizenship and new means of resistance and criticism of the party-state. On the other hand, thanks to the new digital means of surveillance at their disposal, authorities have been able to remain ahead of the curve, tightly managing society and even pre-empting most of its potentially destabilising moves, particularly since Xi Jinping came to power in 2012 (Qiang, 2019). Since its outbreak in late 2019, the COVID-19 health crisis has both confirmed and enhanced this ability.

In order to explore the significance of this new phenomenon, this chapter aims to elaborate on the research of other scholars on the development of the Chinese internet (Boyle, 1997; Lessig, 1999; Tsui, 2003) and later its social credit system (SCS) as two new means of control (Chorzempa, Triolo & Sacks, 2018). This chapter offers Michel Foucault's panopticon metaphor and Jeremy Bentham's 'perfect jail', a perfect means of surveillance and discipline (Foucault, 1985). Bentham imagined the panopticon as a circular penitentiary designed to allow inmates to be observed (-opticon) by a single watchman without being able to tell whether or not they are being watched. As a result, inmates are compelled to regulate their behaviour.

In his famous book *Discipline and Punish* (1985), or *Surveiller et Punir* in French, Foucault viewed the panopticon as a symbol of the disciplinary society of surveillance and understood discipline as an 'apparatus of power' (p. 208).[2] With digitalisation and later the introduction of the SCS, Chinese citizens like Foucault's inmates are 'the object of information, never a subject in communication': 'He who is subjected to a field of visibility and who knows it, assumes responsibility for the constraints of power; he makes them play spontaneously upon himself; he inscribes in himself the power relation in which he simultaneously plays both roles; he becomes the principle of his own subjection' (Foucault, 1985, pp. 202–3).

---

2   And more generally Part III: Discipline, Section 3. Panopticism.

This chapter supposes that the CPC regime's multiple digitalised means of surveillance are forcing Chinese citizens (and netizens) to interiorise the new rules of the game and behave in such a way that they will not be caught.

This chapter will first present the major features of the digitalisation of Chinese society and the emergence of the internet and other social media in particular. The second section will describe the successive measures adopted by the party-state in order both to manage these new platforms and to better control society as a whole: the introduction of smart and digitalised identity cards, the strict surveillance of the internet and social media, and the recent introduction of the SCS and facial recognition technology. The final section will attempt to assess the efficiency and limitations of these technologies as well as their implications for the future of state–society relations and the political future of China in general.

The major features of the digitalisation of Chinese society

The internet landed in China around 1994–95 and has since developed very rapidly. In 2008, China became the country with the largest number of internet users in the world. It had 730 million netizens in July 2016, a figure representing 54 per cent of its total population at the time. In late June 2018, the number exceeded 800 million (802 million, or 57.7 per cent of the population), 98.3 per cent (or 788 million) of which were mobile users, preferring all sorts of tablets, generally smartphones, to a fixed computer (Russell, 2018). China had 1.011 billion netizens at the end of June 2021, which is 71.6 per cent of the population and more than the European Union and United States combined. Underscoring a narrowing of the gap between the cities and the countryside, 59.2 per cent of the rural population is also connected (China Internet Network Information Centre [CNNIC], 2021). These data underscore the penetration rate of the internet, how efficient the authorities have been in expanding network coverage and the multiple uses of the internet in China. The enthusiasm of Chinese consumers for digital tools has facilitated the expansion of the digital economy and innovation while at the same time persuading the government to take full advantage of this novel kind of dependence, if not addiction. In China as elsewhere, the 'magic tablet' is fast becoming a drug that people cannot live without (Reid, 2018).

A digital society can mean many things; a more connected society is not necessarily a more open, democratic and free one (Lessig, 1999). In China today, the internet and social media are generally used for shopping, obtaining administrative or commercial services, online gaming, connecting with family and friends, receiving and disseminating information, and recreation. Only a small fraction of Chinese netizens uses the internet for political purposes.

Authorities in the PRC continue to boast about how connected Chinese society is today. For example, many Chinese citizens go online to shop (80.3 per cent, particularly on Alibaba's platform Taobao) or order food, reserve bus or train seats, or book taxis. Some 87.8 per cent of Chinese netizens use short video applications such as ByteDance's popular Douyin app (抖音短视频, *douyin duan shipin*, known as TikTok outside China) (Yingzhi Yang, 2019). According to the same source, Chinese netizens are also using online government services more frequently: at the end of June 2018, the number of users of online government services reached 470 million and included 58.6 per cent of all netizens, 42.1 per cent of whom had obtained government services through the city service platforms of Alipay (支付宝, *zhifubao*) or WeChat (微信, *weixin*) (CNNIC, 2018, 2021).

The internet is clearly now a part of everyday life in China, and it can be argued that at least in its urban areas, Chinese society has become more digitalised than many other developed societies, including that of the United States and its roughly 313 million internet users. The internet has also changed state–society relations while facilitating access to information, the delivery of government services both to individuals and companies, and the emergence in China of a more business-friendly if not citizen-friendly e-government. China's e-government has been introduced as 'a vehicle intended to support economic development through an increasingly transparent and decentralised administration' (Ma, Chung & Thorson, 2005). Yet although China's appropriation of good practices in its e-government as defined by the United Nations since the mid-2000s is far from being able to solve all the tensions between the government and the governed, it has on the whole improved state–society relations, especially at the grassroots level (Schlaeger, 2013; Sodhi, 2016; Yao Yang, 2017).

This incredible expansion of digital communications and services has been stimulated by several well-known private companies such as Baidu, Alibaba and Tencent (BAT) that have helped move their country's digital economy ahead of others (Sacks, 2018; Woetzel et al., 2017). While benefiting from their close links to Chinese digital product hardware manufacturers, the BAT has also helped the expansion of this industry both in China and in the rest of the world. The best known example is Lenovo, which bought the American company IBM's PC business as early as 2005 and later IBM's server business. China's smartphone market has rapidly expanded and localised, giving first a large smartphone market share to Huawei (33 per cent in the second quarter of 2011), but then favouring other domestic producers against foreign ones. In the second quarter of 2021, Huawei controlled only 10 per cent of the market, Vivo 23 per cent, Oppo 21 per cent, Xiaomi 17 per cent and Apple 14 per cent (Team Counterpoint, 2021).

The Chinese government has been very supportive of this expansion, giving space both to digital players and manufacturers to innovate and win market share. It has only very gradually regulated the market, 'playing an active role in building world-class infrastructure to support digitalisation as an investor, a developer and a consumer' (Woetzel et al., 2017). Beijing's 2015 publication of the 'Made in China 2025' plan has confirmed the importance of information technology in the realisation of the country's economic ambition to become a 'manufacturing superpower' in the middle of the next decade (Wübbekke et al., 2016).

It is true that since the end of 2020, Xi Jinping has started to impose more restrictions on BAT and the other internet giants to prevent them from invading the banking sector and to weaken their monopoly on the market in terms of data collection and retention (see below). The Chinese government has never aspired to kill them, however. The strategic importance of this sector for the national economy and the CPC has also been underscored by the Chinese government's fierce and successful defence of Meng Wanzhou, Huawei's chief financial officer and the daughter of its founder, after the United States asked for her extradition from Canada in December 2018; she was eventually released after having accepted some vague charges in September 2021.

In other words, the leadership of the party-state has very early on identified both the economic and political importance of giving priority to the comprehensive digitalisation of China.

A party-state more empowered to manage and control society

While China's digitalisation has allowed society to improve both interactions with the government and daily life in general, it has also afforded the government the capacity not only to manage society but also to control and even micromanage it. As Foucault defines it, this surveillance capacity has developed in four distinct steps with an acceleration since the late 1990s when China began to truly enter the digital era. These four steps (described in the following subsections) are (1) the general use of smart identity cards, (2) the establishment of a Great Firewall aimed at strictly monitoring the internet and social media, (3) the government use of big data, (4) the testing and gradual introduction of the social credit system, and (5) the expansion of facial recognition technology.

The ubiquitous use of ID cards

As early as 1984, the Chinese government decided to compel every Chinese citizen over the age of 16 to apply for and possess a 'resident identity card' (君民身份证, *jumin shenfenzheng*) issued by the local Public Security Bureau. Chinese citizens have been required to carry these cards in public ever since. More importantly, after China's 'rubberstamp parliament', the National People's Congress (NPC), issued a new law on ID cards in 2003, all ID cards have been gradually computerised, containing an IC chip card and digital encryption (Xinhua, 2004; Law of the People's Republic of China on Resident Identity Cards, 2004). Resident identity cards have therefore become smart. The second-generation cards are machine-readable and more difficult to forge while also allowing the authorities quick access to a growing amount of data on each citizen. Today, ID cards are required in order to conduct business with the government: they are needed to obtain a residence permit, marriage registration or a driving licence. They are also required in a growing number of online and offline activities such as purchasing bus, train or plane tickets, registering a mobile phone number, opening an internet account or microblog, e-banking or entering an internet café. The activities requiring an ID card in China are arguably more numerous than in open, free and democratic societies. Since ID cards must be shown not only for airline travel but also to enter or exit all train stations, it has become much easier for authorities to locate people.

In 2017, the Chinese government began to issue digital ID cards to replace physical ones, working with Tencent's Wechat to host them. This allows Chinese citizens to use the digital ID stored on their smartphones instead of having to carry a physical card (Tao, 2018). In Guangzhou's Nansha District, for instance, residents can use smartphones and facial recognition technology to link their ID cards with their WeChat accounts. A few months later in May 2018, Alibaba announced that it would store the IDs of Alipay users who opt for a 'Web ID' by scanning their faces on its payment app. The project has been tested in three cities, including Hangzhou, where it has its headquarters (Corum, 2018).

While it makes the lives of many Chinese more convenient, the gradual use of digitalised ID cards can only expand the government's ability to keep tabs on them, as it has the potential to offer access to a larger set of data. More generally, the ubiquitous need for ID cards has served to compel citizens to 'normalise their behaviour', as Foucault has observed in the panopticon.

The Great Firewall

From the very beginning, China's internet and social media have existed under high political and moral surveillance (Griffiths, 2019a; Tsui, 2003). As early as the 1990s, the Chinese government set up what Geremy Barmé and Sang Ye termed as early as 1997 as the 'Great Firewall' with the help of technology companies like CISCO Systems (an American firm) and Huawei (Barmé & Ye, 1997). Aimed at keeping the blogosphere healthy and particularly clean of any pornographic content (a recurrent justification for censorship), the Great Firewall also partly seals the country from outside information. These limits are well known, although they might change in future. A great many websites, search engines, apps and email services are currently blocked and still inaccessible in China, among them Twitter, Facebook, Instagram, YouTube, Whatsapp, Snapchat, Google, Gmail and Netflix (Travel China Cheaper, 2021). Newspapers, magazines and information websites such as the *New York Times*, the *Economist*, Bloomberg, *Le Monde* and the *Wall Street Journal* are also censored. In October 2021, LinkedIn was added to the list.

Most Chinese are unaffected by internet censorship, as most of these websites and apps do not contain Chinese-language content. Moreover, China has developed its own local equivalents such as WeChat or Weibo (微博), a microblogging site launched by the state-owned Sina Corporation in 2009, which drew much of its inspiration from Twitter. Later, other Chinese internet companies such as Tencent (腾讯微博, *tengxun weibo*), Sohu (搜狐微博, *sohu weibo*) and NetEase (网易微博, *wangyi weibo*) developed their own microblogging services. Tencent's Qzone is one other such example.

Online activities have been more widely censored and monitored since Xi Jinping came to power in late 2012. In November 2013, Xi decided to establish the CPC Central Cybersecurity and Informatisation Leading Small Group (中央网络安全和信息化领导小组, *zhongyang wangluo anquan he xinxihua lingdao xiaozu*). This LSG has been instrumental in tightening control and management of the blogosphere. Highlighting its importance in the eyes of the Chinese leadership, the Cybersecurity and Informatization LSG was elevated to the rank of commission (中央网络安全和信息化委员会, *zhongyang wangluo anquan he xinxihua weiyuanhui*) in March 2018, a key position also enjoyed by the three LSGs tasked with deepening reforms, foreign affairs, and finance and the economy. This is part of a larger plan aimed at recentralising many capabilities of the State Council and central government in the party apparatus, particularly in the area of security and propaganda (Cabestan, 2019b). The LSG and now Commission Office (办公室, *bangongshi*) is headed by the director of the Cyberspace Administration of China (CAC) (国家互联网信息办公室, *guojia hulianwang xinxi bangongshi*), a State Council organ headed by Zhuang Rongwen (庄荣文) since August 2018. Close to Xi owing to having worked under him in Fujian, Zhuang is also deputy director of the Publicity (or Propaganda) Department of the CPC, underscoring the direct relationship between this powerful Central Committee bureaucracy and the CAC. The first director of both the LSG Office and the CAC from 2013 to 2016, Lu Wei (鲁炜), was investigated for corruption in 2017. The CAC includes 60,000 internet propaganda workers and 2 million others employed off-payroll as freelances (Cairns, 2015). Since 2020, it has also been tasked to better control the data collection and usage of Chinese internet giants, turning data into a national security matter (Li, 2021).

The primary mission of this colossal workforce is to direct discussion on social networks and snuff out content that is deemed noxious (King, Pan & Roberts, 2017). Labelled by critics as the Wumaodang (五毛党, the 50-cent Party) for the amount supposedly paid to them for each politically correct post, this force of 'internet police' initially numbered 40,000. Internet policing has since gone much further and now targets users accused of spreading 'rumours', whether they are of a political, economic or financial nature (Wu, 2016). Consequently, the number of 'inspectors' in charge of 'internet clean-ups' on behalf of administrations or private companies was estimated at 2 million in 2013 and has since sharply increased (Williams, 2017).[3]

The government began to maintain stricter control of Weibo in 2013, requiring that users register with their real names and closing many accounts, particularly the ones developed by the well-known public intellectuals referred to as the 'big Vs'. This has persuaded droves of Chinese to move to WeChat, where only shorter messages limited to 500 characters can be exchanged (Muncaster, 2013). WeChat's penetration rate was at 87 per cent in 2021 (FinancesOnline, 2021). As a result, the number of Weibo users dropped from more than 500 million in 2012 to 220 million in 2015. It had bounced back, however, to 573 million by the third quarter of 2021 (CIW Team, 2021), pointing to a gradual internalisation of the new rules of the game by most Chinese netizens. Here again, as in Foucault's panopticon, behaviour has been normalised.

The most significant turning point after 2012 was the adoption of the Cybersecurity Law of the People's Republic of China (2016) on 7 November 2016. The law's main objective is to control the internet better and more systematically, giving priority to defending state interests and securing critical infrastructures. Article 9 of the law states that 'network operators … must obey social norms and commercial ethics, be honest and credible, perform obligations to protect network security, accept supervision from the government and public and bear social responsibility'.

While the law also aims at protecting individuals against cybercrime and data theft, it does not establish any concrete mechanisms, let alone an independent institution that guarantees the privacy of information exchanged on the web. More importantly, the law removes internet anonymity: internet providers must now verify the identity of users when offering network access or data services and can be fined or closed if they do not. Moreover, data collected by domestic providers of 'key digital infrastructures' may now be stored only in China, triggering heavy criticism from foreign and particularly Western companies. Any export of data from the country must receive prior governmental authorisation (Schulze & Godehardt, 2017).

---

3   No figures have been officially published.

The Chinese authorities have intensified the crackdown in the years since. In October 2017, for example, China cracked down on VPNs (virtual private networks): networks that can be bought online and are widely used in China to bypass the Great Firewall and gain access to blocked websites or applications. In April 2018, the Chinese start-up ByteDance (字节跳动, *zijie tiaodong*, valued at $30 billion by investors) was ordered to shut down its app for sharing jokes and 'silly videos' after many 'honest citizens' had reportedly complained about its content. A few days earlier, its flagship app Jinri Toutiao (今日头条), a news aggregator that claims 120 million users, was pulled from app stores. It was in this context that ByteDance founder and chief executive Zhang Yiming (张一鸣) publicly apologised, indicating that '[Toutiao] content did not accord with core socialist values and was not a good guide for public opinion' (Russell, 2017; Zhong, 2018). In August 2018, Tencent was forced by the government to impose stricter rules and limits on its very popular online games, particularly in order to reduce the tendency for Chinese youth to become addicted to them (Deng, 2018a). Deriving two-thirds of its revenues from its games, Tencent was later forced to restructure (Deng, 2018b).

In the eyes of the CPC, censorship is not enough. It must be maintained with active propaganda that imposes the official narrative of China's history and its politics in particular, both inside and outside of the country. To accomplish this task, the party has mobilised a large number of people in addition to its 'internet police' whose status is hard to determine. Since 2016, for example, there has been a burgeoning nationalist 'troll army' referred to as the 'Little Pinks' (小粉红, *xiao fenhong*) voluntarily launching all-out attacks against anyone venturing to criticise the party or Xi's policies (Pedroletti, 2017). These nationalists have clearly been used by the regime to better disseminate and shield its propaganda. In that sense, they act as a part of the Great Firewall and the guards of Foucault's panopticon.

The CPC has also expanded its repressive objectives by targeting the users of Chinese Twitter, a social media platform popular among overseas political and human rights activists, for 'liking' posts accused of insulting the party leadership or even for simply opening an account (Shepherd & Yang, 2019). Likewise, an increasing number of Chinese 'trolls' are active on Facebook, conducting organised raids on accounts defending the causes and rights of Uyghurs. In January 2016, they launched an 'expedition' against Taiwanese President Tsai Ing-wen's own Facebook account shortly after her election (Griffiths, 2019b). The crackdown on VPNs has also intensified, underscoring both the fact that more educated youth are using them and that the CPC harbours ambitions to monitor the online behaviour of its citizens beyond the Great Firewall.

In a similar vein, ByteDance has made sure to wall off users of Douyin and TikTok in order to 'avoid having problematic content created outside of China viewed by its domestic audience', according to Samm Sacks (2018), a China digital economy expert with US think tank New America. This is in spite of the growing worldwide success of TikTok, which had more than 1 billion monthly active users in 2021 (Dean, 2021).

Control of online communication has recently witnessed a more micro-level development: in a growing number of universities, students are being asked to give their personal data to university authorities, including WeChat accounts, QQ numbers and email addresses.

As Roberts (2018) has shown, censorship has become subtler, making it difficult to access information that is critical of the government by diverting netizens to pro-government views. This has particularly been illustrated during the COVID crisis (Khalil, 2020).

The government use of big data

Similar to Russia and other authoritarian regimes, Chinese authorities have adopted a 'sovereignist' approach to the internet and social media, feeding a much-discussed Balkanisation of global cyberspace governance (Griffiths, 2019a). At the same time, however, the CPC has allowed Mainland China–based netizens some flexibility or 'breathing space' with the double objective of letting out their frustrations (or *bad qi* [气] in Chinese) and helping the government maintain a more accurate understanding of the mindsets of both Chinese society and resident foreigners. China's 'angry youth' (愤青, *fenqing*), for example, have been managed with a certain degree of tolerance by the cyber police.

By allowing debate and controversy on the web to develop to a certain point, China's cyber authorities can collect an impressive sum of big data that are constantly updated and directly help the government in managing and maintaining control over society. It improves governance and public policies, makes it possible to address the concerns of specific groups and allows the government more efficiently to repress and even pre-empt bad individual or company behaviour, social unrest or crime (Economist, 2016).

The Social Credit System

In 2014, the party-state decided to introduce the Social Credit System (SCS, 社会信用体系, *shehui xinyong tixi*), a new digitalised instrument aimed at maintaining better control over society. In June of that year, the State Council issued a circular that planned to fully establish such a system by 2020 (State Council of the People's Republic of China, 2014). Borrowed from Western credit institutions, it aims to assess and rate the reliability of citizens and companies with respect both to their ability to repay a loan and to a vast and varied set of activities, including such qualities as respect for the law or political, social and moral conduct. Citizens are rated in four main areas: administrative affairs, commercial activities, social behaviour and law enforcement.

One other often overlooked objective of the SCS is to better check on government officials and the judiciary and to improve the confidence of citizens in their institutions. Still, it is the former objective that has been the most noticed outside China. Individuals may be marked as asocial for not visiting their parents, behaving badly on public transportation, or jaywalking. Worse, they can be labelled as dissidents or dangerous for social stability should they participate in an underground church or a workers' rights NGO. Such cases could result in a negative rating and attract a certain number of sanctions or constraints: a ban on travel in public transportation such as high-speed trains or aircraft, the denial of access to social housing or public jobs, or being prohibited from leaving the area. This task is facilitated through the accumulation of an immense quantity of data on both individuals and organisations by the party-state and its security services (the aforementioned big data) as well as progress in artificial intelligence (AI).

The social credit system was first conceived in the early 2000s to keep businesses under control and compel them to show greater respect for their legal, economic and social obligations. This included adhering to rules and their own entrepreneurial engagements, tax returns, environment protection, energy-saving and other corporate social responsibilities. The system has gradually been set up through a series of local trials and was extended in 2014 to monitor not only citizens and companies but also government organs and courts. In December 2017, 12 cities, including Hangzhou, Nanjing and Xiamen, initiated local personal credit scoring systems. The smaller city of Rongcheng, Shandong, has also been included and is often promoted as a model (Mistreanu, 2018). Nearly 20 cities have created similar official systems since, and their numbers will continue to grow (Y. Zhang & Han, 2019).

Coordinated by the CPC's LSG and the Commission for Comprehensively Deepening Reforms since March 2018, the system is managed by the State Council's National Development and Reform Commission (NDRC), an organisation that keeps an official nationwide database and a China Credit website that regularly publishes information. Officially, the SCS was supposed to be fully in place in 2020 (Zhou, 2018). While this has not been the case owing to COVID-19, the pandemic has contributed to expanding the SCS. While the economic slowdown led the authorities to be provisionally more lenient regarding loan repayments, the rewarding and punishment of COVID-19–related behaviour by companies and individuals have been strengthened (Khalil, 2020).

As indicated above, the official objective of the social credit system has been to restore the faith of citizens in the government, the judiciary, economic actors and their fellow citizens. To some extent, the SCS attests to the high level of mutual distrust in Chinese society today (Ding & Zhong, 2021). Targeting both Chinese and foreign enterprises, the project also aims to reduce the cost of transactions and cut economic risks by compelling the government to gather a great deal of legal, financial and commercial information on firms. Currently, 75 per cent of this information has been made public, the rest being restricted mainly to government access (Meissner, 2017).

This new system links mechanisms for holding individuals responsible with social control methods. On the one hand, society is induced to take part in the system because it allows access to diverse services and advantages. On the other hand, society's implication in the SCS opens it to potential sanctions, thereby holding it responsible (Hoffman, 2017).

In June 2018, for example, the government released a list of 169 people who had committed misbehaviour such as provocations on flights, attempting to take a lighter through airport security, smoking on a high-speed train, tax evasion and failing to pay fines. Those on the list ended up being banned from buying train and plane tickets for a year. To shame them, they were also listed on the Credit China website (F. Tang, 2018). According to the

NDRC, some 10.5 million people by the end of April 2018 had been named and shamed by the courts, prompting a quarter of them to fulfil their obligations (F. Tang, 2018).

A year later, the NDRC published even more compelling figures that resulted in the blacklisting of 13.49 million people classified as 'untrustworthy'. In its report, the NDRC claims that the SCS has blocked the sale of 20.47 million plane tickets (including 17.46 million in 2018 alone) and 5.71 million high-speed train tickets (5.47 million) between 2014 and the end of March 2019 as punishment for failing to repay debts and other misbehaviour. The list of blacklisted people has been compiled by Chinese courts. Local authorities can also put pressure on untrustworthy persons by preventing them from buying premium insurance, wealth management products or real estate (H. He, 2019; A. Lee, 2019). In 2018, 3.51 million citizens and companies repaid their debts or paid off taxes and fines 'due to pressure from the SCS'. In addition, 3.52 million enterprises were added to the creditworthiness blacklist, banning them from various activities including bidding on projects, accessing the security market, taking part in land auctions and issuing corporate bonds. Further, 1,282 peer-to-peer lending platforms were also blacklisted because they could not pay back their investors or were involved in illegal fundraising (H. He, 2019).

In April 2019, NDRC spokesman Yuan Da indicated that the National Public Credit Information Centre, the NDRC unit that manages the social credit database, has started sharing the credit scores of individuals and enterprises with credit firms in various sectors such as gas, coal, travel and transport. The centre will also give priority to cracking down on fraud in the medical sector by establishing a blacklisting system targeting hospitals, doctors and insured persons (A. Lee, 2019).

Consequently, it appears that there is a close relationship between the development of the SCS and the establishment by the judiciary of an online inspection and control network (网络查控系统, *wangluo chakong xitong*) to implement its decisions. The 2019 Supreme People's Court report to the NPC sheds some light on the progress of the latter, which officially has been far from easy.

The Supreme Court claims that its network has been able to 'connect 16 units and more than 3,900 banking financial institutions, including the Ministry of Public Security and the Ministry of Natural Resources, covering 16 categories of deposits, vehicles, securities, real estate and network funds' and substantially improve the execution of court judgements as a result (L. Tang, 2019). In order to speed up the introduction of the SCS and improve the implementation of difficult court decisions, for example, the higher people's court of Shaanxi Province decided to improve its online inspection and control network of financial, construction and real estate sectors in October 2018 (Xinyong Zhongguo, 2018).

The introduction of the SCS has the potential to clean up the internal economic environment, improve the behaviour of economic actors, reduce corruption and regulate the market. As described above, however, the SCS also contains an Orwellian dimension that the growth of the internet can only enhance (Ding & Zhong, 2021). The SCS increases the party-state's right to oversee business activities, its interference in market mechanisms and its control over the private sector, including foreign companies. It confirms the CPC's intention to remain on top of the political system and the economy while thwarting the emergence of economic forces out of its tight leash. The SCS establishes above all a level of surveillance and micro-management of citizens that is particularly anti-freedom, ignoring among other things a respect for privacy and the right to be forgotten. It promotes a 'rule of trust' arbitrarily defined and carried out by the CPC to the detriment of the rule of law (Y.J. Chen, Lin & Liu, 2018). Finally, the SCS contributes to creating a new panopticon in which citizens are both inmates and guards, empowered to spy on their neighbours (see below).

For the time being, the SCS is in force only partially and is far from being fully centralised: much of the data are being held and managed by local governments, which draw their information from their own services, mobile payment companies that hold personal data, or court verdicts.

In any event, the social credit system seeks to reassure credit enterprises, consumers, parents and the government, highlighting the need for security and predictability with which Chinese society is preoccupied. This proclivity far outweighs individual freedoms or privacy at present. The system also confirms the low level of interpersonal confidence within Chinese society, the priorities of the majority of its members and its dominant political culture (Cabestan, 2019a, pp. 59–74).

Facial recognition

The most recent product of the digital surveillance of citizens, facial recognition has been presented in China first and foremost as a gem of domestic innovation. The true objective of this new technology, however, is to better monitor citizens and their movements and behaviour in public spaces.

Since 2017, facial recognition has been gradually adopted by local public security bureaus across China with the help of local companies such as Megvii and SenseTimes that have mastered the technology. They are part of what in China is called the 'Sharp Eyes' program, an important dimension of the country's 'Smart City' program (K. Lee, 2018). Facial recognition is a substantive component of the AI industry, another key target of Made in China 2025. The State Council expects that this industry will be worth around $150 billion by 2030 (C. Lee, 2018). The objective of local governments for using facial recognition is to 'run their cities more efficiently', meaning to keep them safe, stop street crime and protect residents from pickpockets. Similar to internet censorship, however, one perhaps less overt but equally crucial objective is social stability (Schmitz, 2018).

According to some reports, Chinese authorities have ambitious plans to use facial recognition and AI to track and monitor its 1.4 billion citizens. China is already the biggest market in the world for video surveillance—$6.4 billion in 2016—and has the highest number of security cameras, with 170 million currently in use for its Skynet surveillance system and 400 million on the way in the coming years. China was equipped with 623 million CCTV cameras by 2020, a stark increase from its roughly 200 million in 2019 (P. Zhang, 2019). Skynet is a national system aimed at fighting crime and preventing possible disasters. In March 2018, Beijing police started to use facial recognition and AI-powered glasses to catch criminals (Zhou, 2018).

Since 2018, Chinese security has introduced advanced facial recognition technology specially designed for tracking Uyghurs and other Turkic minorities. First used in Xinjiang when Beijing launched an unprecedented crackdown on the Uyghur ethnic group and threw more than a million into concentration camps, it has since been adopted by a growing number of provinces and cities. Developed by software companies such as Yitu, Megvii, SenseTime and CloudWalk, this racial profiling technology has also received investment from US companies such as Fidelity International,

Qualcomm Ventures and Sequoia and Sinovation Venture led by Kai-Fu Lee (李开复), a Beijing-based Chinese tech investor of Taiwanese origin (Mozur, 2018).[4]

It is the CPC leadership's ambition to turn China into a massive panopticon in which anyone can be constantly watched and citizens consequently regulate their behaviour in order to avoid being caught.

Thanks to digitalisation, the PRC party-state is today much better equipped to understand and maintain control of Chinese society as well as to predict any of its potential moves. It tightly manages the internet and social media with a degree of flexibility and pluralism purposefully employed as both a safety valve and an abundant source of information. These new technologies are a new source of power that is conducive to maintaining social stability and defending the interests of the CPC regime. The introduction of both the social credit system and facial recognition technology has added to the many ways in which the regime is able to maintain its control over society and the timely prevention of any social manifestations that could weaken or destabilise the regime in the foreseeable future.

The complicity of China's digital economy giants

The CPC has been able to mobilise many resources to these ends, including the support and cooperation of national champions such as Alibaba, Tencent and Huawei. In 2019, Sarah Cook reported that 'Dutch hacker Victor Gevers revealed that the content of millions of conversations on Tencent applications among users at internet cafés are being relayed, along with the users' identities, to police stations across China' (2019b). Tencent is currently expanding overseas, having bought the news aggregator Reddit in February 2019. As a result, Reddit has been inundated with pro-China accounts that have 'downvoted' links that are critical of China. Moreover, there has been evidence of politicised censorship and surveillance of WeChat conversations between overseas users and users based in China (Cook, 2019b).

---

4   Kai-Fu Lee, who earlier worked for Microsoft and Google, is known for his book *AI Superpowers: China, Silicon Valley and the New World Order* (2018), which predicts China surpassing the United States to gain global dominance in AI.

SenseNets is a Shenzhen-based Chinese firm founded in 2015 that offers facial recognition and crowd analysis technology. It has also been closely working with the police. The company is one of the world's leading suppliers of AI-powered video technology solutions in the security business. It has been part of China's Skynet Project and relies on more than 20 million cameras installed in public spaces. SenseNets has also helped the government track more than 2.5 million people in Xinjiang.

The perfect digital dictatorship and its weaknesses

The digitalisation of Chinese society has helped the CPC regime to establish an authoritarian political system that appears more and more totalitarian, has the means to control and even pre-empt the moves of its citizens, and cannot envisage its own demise. China is using digitalisation to achieve Stein Ringen's concept of a 'perfect dictatorship' (2016). Yet 'perfect' is an aspiration more than a reality, an ideal that by definition cannot be reached: Chinese society is in reality more complicated, diverse, hostile and reactive than any perfect dictator can imagine, including Xi Jinping. The complexity of society imposes significant limitations on a dictator's ambition to control and rule indefinitely, and these limits have important implications for the future of state–society relations in China.

Big Brother Xi is watching you!

The founding document of the Social Credit System clearly states the CPC leadership's objective: 'Allow the trustworthy to roam freely under heaven while making it hard for the discredited to take a single step' (使守信者处处受益、失信者寸步难行, *shi shouxinzhe chuchu shouyi, shixinzhe cunbu nanxing*).[5] The document is centred on the concept of 'trust' (诚信, *chengxin*), which is mentioned 143 times but remains more than vague about the legitimate authority or agency that can define it and adjudicate disputes about its interpretation. Seen by some as a 'gigantic social engineering experiment' (Dockrill, 2018), the SCS has been described by others as a

---

5   This is the most often cited translation ('Big Data and Government', 2016). Rogier Creemer's translation (at chinacopyrightandmedia.wordpress.com/2014/06/14/planning-outline-for-the-construction -of-a-social-credit-system-2014-2020/) is closer to the Chinese original version: 'Ensure that those keeping trust receive benefit in all respect and those breaking trust meet with difficulty at every step.'

'gamification of trust' because of its scary scoring system (Ramadan, 2018). As for the most interesting analysis of the SCS and the various aspects of the digitalisation of Chinese society discussed above, much has been done by Martin Chorzempa, Paul Triolo and Samm Sacks (2018). They argue that the goal of the PRC leadership is 'algorithmic governance', describing its approach as a panopticon in reference to Jeremy Bentham's perfect jail.

As demonstrated above, the CPC regime's multiple digitalised means of surveillance are forcing Chinese citizens (and netizens) to interiorise the new rules of the game and behave in such a way that they will not be caught. This means not only self-censorship and prudence on the web or in public debates and publications but also a temptation to denounce those who misbehave. The digitalisation of Chinese society has magnified Perry Link's famous 'anaconda in the chandelier' metaphor (2002) whereby a large snake does not need to move or intervene but only to be there and watch. At the same time, digitalisation has highlighted what Zuboff (1988, pp. 315–61) calls the 'dual nature of the information panopticon': participants may be under surveillance but may also use the system to engage in the surveillance of others by monitoring or reporting the contributions of other users. Thus the information panopticon is one in which everyone has the potential to be both a prisoner and a guard.

This is precisely how the CPC wants the web and the SCS to operate, and there are multiple signs that it will work in this way. In general, critics have deplored the lack of awareness in Chinese society of the dangers of these new surveillance systems (Carney, 2018). According to opinion surveys such as those in Bruce Dickson's *Dictator's Dilemma* (2016, pp. 71–3), while most Chinese internet users declare support in principle for freedom of expression online, a majority claim not to be affected by censorship: 72 per cent have never experienced blocked sites, 77 per cent have never seen their messages deleted and 91 per cent have never had their accounts closed. Should censorship happen to affect their online activity, they often react with resignation (49 per cent): 'it doesn't matter' (无所谓, *wusuowei*).

Another factor continues to feed attitudes of acceptance and resignation towards censorship: in China as elsewhere, new public spaces opened by the internet and especially social networks are becoming increasingly fragmented and ephemeral. This Balkanisation of the web has reached China and allowed netizens sharing the same ideas (e.g. new left or nationalist sites) or interests to gather among themselves, limiting pluralism in debates and comforting each other in their positions. Moreover, Chinese cyberspace has been truncated and distorted as 'liberal' sites and blogs that favour real political reforms are shut down one after the other. A mere 11 per cent of Chinese netizens (around 90 million) are known to use a VPN, a tool that would allow them to reach the global blogosphere. Consequently, most netizens in China are daily influenced by a highly distorted web. In any event, most Chinese who have not mastered another language are limited to reading local websites and blogs, and they do not find this particularly frustrating.

One should not neglect the attractiveness of the reward system for citizens who denounce the misbehaviour of their neighbours or colleagues (Ding & Zhong, 2021). A diverse array of incentives from the SCS points to monetary rewards being distributed to those who report on 'illegal' religious practices (by Uyghur or Falun Gong practitioners) or asocial behaviour (Y.J. Chen et al., 2018, p. 15; Cook, 2019a). In the same vein, the Ministry of State Security launched a new bilingual website in 2018 (www.12339.gov.cn) that offers 10,000 to 500,000 yuan (US$1,600 to US$79,700) for information on spies and Chinese officials who have taken bribes from their compatriots or foreigners (*South China Morning Post*, 2019).

Finally, many Chinese have another view of the SCS and facial recognition: they see these new systems not only as tools that can prevent misbehaviour and crimes by citizens and companies but also as a means to monitor their government and judiciary, to compel their improvement and to encourage greater transparency with more participation from citizens. Believing in CPC propaganda, they think that the SCS will contribute to enhancing society's trust in the government and the courts (Chorzempa, Triolo & Sacks, 2018, pp. 4–5). In other words, many Chinese citizens have enthusiastically become both the inmates and guards of Foucault's panopticon.

There is no such thing as a 'perfect digital dictatorship'

It is clear that Chinese society currently gives priority to security over liberty. By and large, it prefers to submit itself to the government's totalitarian means of surveillance and maintain the illusion of being more secure rather than to question these in the name of freedom or even the rule of law, acts that would cause it to feel less secure. Nonetheless, China's new system of digital surveillance faces two major limitations and weaknesses: no system of surveillance is either fully reliable or operational. In fact, some Chinese have begun to question and even challenge it.

First of all, the internet controls imposed by the authorities are not as effective as sometimes believed. Censorship is often erratic. Even under Xi, a substantial and increasing minority of netizens continue to have access to banned foreign sites by using increasingly sophisticated foreign VPNs. As we have seen, these VPNs are often tolerated because they are used by elites, researchers looking for cutting-edge technologies, or Chinese and foreign enterprises. There are also provincial variations: VPNs are having greater difficulty in penetrating the Great Firewall in Beijing, the regime's nerve centre, than in other cities.

Second, the widespread use of WeChat and the exchange of instant short messages on the web has forced the government to become more tolerant by closing the accounts of only the most persistent abusers and hoping that the threat of account closure is enough to persuade most netizens to restrain themselves and engage in self-censorship. For instance, multiple interviews with mainland Chinese students have confirmed that many rely on a VPN without being threatened by authorities. They use VPNs to gain access to independent news and are inclined to use coded language when they discuss politically sensitive issues, precisely to circumvent self-censorship (Arsène, 2011).

Third, the geometric increase of online payments has rapidly multiplied the risks of data leaks and privacy breaches. These leaks are often used by Chinese (or Taiwanese) cybercrime organisations established abroad, particularly in developing countries such as Cambodia, Kenya or the Philippines. They make money by extorting careless or naïve netizens. In September 2018, a Chinese Consumer's Association survey indicated that 85 per cent of people had suffered some sort of data leak such as having a phone number sold to spammers or one's bank account details stolen. PRC authorities have only very recently become aware of the magnitude of the problem and are now rushing to introduce 'data governance' regulations (S. Wang, 2017).

Baidu's chief executive Robin Li (李彦宏) presumed that contrary to Western consumers, Chinese consumers would be ready to 'trade privacy for convenience', but the opposite seems to be taking shape in China. As a result, the government is putting pressure on big internet companies to better enforce data protection rules (Yang, 2018). Both Alibaba and Tencent have pledged to meet the European Union's General Data Protection Regulation requirements introduced in May 2018 (Chorzempa, Triolo & Sacks, 2018, p. 8). While they have not done so, privacy rules have become stricter after the Personal Information Protection Law (个人信息保护法, *geren xinxi baohufa*) came into effect on 1 November 2021, forcing Tencent for example to suspend any upgrading of its apps or launching of new ones (China Briefing, 2021; Ye, 2021). However, it is also feared that the CPC will at the same time take advantage of the new regulations to better protect national security and its own interests to the detriment of citizens.

Recent studies have shown that there is a growing awareness of privacy among netizens, persuading more of them to reveal less about their own lives on the web or to use pseudonyms in many of their online transactions (see below). True, the COVID-19 pandemic seems to have put safety and health ahead of privacy and freedom (L. He, 2021). Nonetheless, the need for better privacy protection can also be felt. In Hangzhou, for example, authorities were compelled to crack down on the abusive use of facial recognition technology as a requirement to enter amusement parks or buildings (Dou, 2021). China is also undergoing a social media fatigue along with the rest of the world, leading netizens to become less active on the web (Z. Wang, 2019).

Fourth, more Chinese are becoming unhappy with the stricter controls and ideological surveillance imposed by the government since Xi Jinping came to power. For instance, many students have reacted negatively to requests from university authorities to provide their personal digital data and have tried to give away as little information as possible (Xi et al., 2019).

Fifth, facial recognition technology is not without limitations: cameras can only search a limited number of faces at the same time. Technological prowess has been purposefully exaggerated by the authorities in order to frighten potential lawbreakers and fulfil the CPC regime's ambitious objectives for social stability (Jacobs, 2018; Mozur, 2018).

Sixth, while Chinese hardware and software companies are required to cooperate with the government according to the Cybersecurity Law and others, they are sometimes negligent. In February 2019, Victor Gevers indicated that an online database belonging to SenseNets had been publicly available for months, compromising the personal data of millions of people (Tao, 2019). While this raises questions about the protection of privacy, it also shows that companies do not always operate according to the book.

Finally, more Chinese have started to express concerns about the intrusiveness and potential unfairness of the SCS. The SCS has already attracted heavy criticism for its attack on freedoms, the inconsistency of data gathered and the potentially arbitrary nature of the scoring system (Ding & Zhong, 2021). This criticism has come from both Chinese society in general and economic circles. There are also concerns about privacy and the way China's technology giants will be handling personal information. While many PRC citizens are happy to see powerful entrepreneurs and officials disciplined by this system, some are already worried about the lack of established procedures to challenge the decisions. The investigative journalist Liu Hu (刘虎), for example, was blacklisted by the SCS for 'speech crime' after he had accused a government official of extortion. As a result, his career was destroyed, his social media accounts were shut down (he had 2 million followers on WeChat and Weibo combined) and he has been in de facto house arrest in Chongqing (Carney, 2018). As with Liu Hu, many of the more than 10 million Chinese who have received bad scores in the dozen cities where SCS has been tested have been wrongly blacklisted and can do nothing about it. The fact that a growing number of Chinese netizens are leaving WeChat or using it more selectively because of privacy fears is not unrelated to this intensified repression (L. Chen, 2018).

The fact that 'most Chinese don't yet understand what's to come under the digital totalitarian state', as Liu Hu has said, is bad news for Chinese citizens but good news for the CPC. The system is run by a gigantic panopticon-like party-state, which maintains the exclusive right to decide the score of every citizen and company and the type of information to make public. The good news is that its full implementation has been postponed and will probably trigger many glitches and unforeseen problems, leading more Chinese citizens either to challenge the system or at least to question its sharpest angles (Horsley, 2018). To address some of the criticism, the NDRC and the People's Bank of China drafted two documents in July 2021 aimed at standardising and clarifying data collection as well as punishments related to the SCS (Koty, 2021). As Chorzempa, Triolo and Sacks remind us: 'The SCS is a herculean effort that will take many years to succeed' (2018, p. 4). The chances of having a full-fledged unified SCS remain limited. It might more likely be heading towards a fragmented system that is more repressive in some localities and more flexible or even non-existent in others, as is the case with the Chinese bureaucracy in general (Devdiscourse, 2021).

Conclusion

There is no question that China is ahead of many developed countries in terms of the digitalisation of its society and surveillance systems. It is also clear that new digital technologies such as the widespread use of ID cards, the Great Firewall, the accumulation of big data, the SCS and facial recognition have enhanced the capacity of the CPC to rule China, maintain its control over society and stay in power for a long time. These are not the only systems in place to manage Chinese citizens and managing them is not their sole purpose—the fight against COVID-19 has demonstrated that they can help keep this new virus in check. However, these systems have also been rightly seen as part of an ambitious Orwellian project to micro-control every move of the Chinese public and normalise the behaviour of its citizens (Qiang, 2019). As in Foucault's panopticon, these new technologies and institutions have turned Chinese citizens into both inmates and guards, as they have been given the means to check constantly on other inmates.

Clearly, these developments in China are going to inspire other authoritarian countries. In fact, with the help of big firms such as Huawei, ZTE, Alibaba, Tencent and others, the PRC has already offered and transferred its surveillance technology to many other countries.

Nevertheless, we have shown that a perfect digital dictatorship is unlikely to take shape in China. China's digital dictatorship is likely to remain fragmented owing to the sheer size of the country, the rivalry among the bureaucracies and telecommunications companies serving the party-state, the lack of discipline in these firms, the slow pace of SCS development and the growing awareness of privacy in society. Despite Xi Jinping's iron fist, China's authoritarian political system still appears fragmented (Cairns, 2016; Lieberthal & Oksenberg, 1988).

The digitalisation of any society presents both benefits and risks. While Foucault's prescient work far preceded the digital era, panopticon theory has witnessed a genuine revival precisely because of the growth of digital surveillance. This has inspired questions not only about China's recent innovations but also about the world's fascination for big data, algorithms, smart cities and technological surveillance 'solutions'. For example, Haggerty and Ericson (2006, p. 14) have demonstrated that increasingly visible data made accessible to organisations and individuals from new data-mining technologies has led to the proliferation of 'dataveillance', a mode of surveillance that aims to single out particular transactions through routine algorithmic production.

As such, the fundamental question for every democracy is whether China is showing the way. What kind of institutions and mechanisms can be put into place to protect transparency and the freedoms and privacy of citizens? Many democratic countries have already established independent institutions that are responsible for the protection of privacy and the prevention of the cross-utilisation of data by the state, the police, the secret service and other security bureaucracies. However, much remains to be done, as the Snowden affair has revealed. The digitalisation of Chinese society compels us to remain vigilant and see that the newest technological treasures do not evolve into nightmares.

References

Arsène, S. (2011) *Internet et politique en Chine* [Internet and politics in China]. Karthala

Barmé, G.R., & Ye, S. (1997) 'The Great Firewall of China.' Wired, 6 January. www.wired.com/1997/06/china-3

Boyle, J. (1997) 'Foucault in cyberspace: Surveillance, sovereignty and hard-wired censors.' *University of Cincinnati Law Review* 66: 177–205. scholarship.law. duke.edu/cgi/viewcontent.cgi?article=1552&context=faculty_scholarship

Cabestan, J.P. (2019a) *China Tomorrow: Democracy or Dictatorship?* Rowman & Littlefield

—— (2019b) 'Political changes in China since the 19th CCP Congress: Xi Jinping is not weaker but more contested.' *East Asia* 36(1): 1–21. doi.org/10.1007/s12140-019-09305-x

Cairns, C. (2015) 'Seizing Weibo's "commanding heights" through bureaucratic re-centralisation' (unpublished doctoral dissertation). Cornell University. www. chrismcairns.com/uploads/3/0/2/2/30226899/chapter_3_-_seizing_weibos_ commanding_heights_through_bureaucratic_re-centralisation_-_final_7.30. 15.pdf

—— (2016) 'Fragmented authoritarianism? Reforms to China's internet censorship system under Xi Jinping' (paper presentation). American Political Science Association Annual Meeting, Philadelphia. www.chrismcairns.com/uploads/3/0/2/2/30226899/cairns_-_fragmented_authoritarianism_-_reforms_to_chinas_internet_censorship_system_under_xi_jinping.pdf

Carney, M. (2018) 'Leave no dark corner.' ABC News. www.abc.net.au/news/2018-09-18/china-social-credit-a-model-citizen-in-a-digital-dictatorship/10200278?section=world

Chen, L. (2018) 'Why China's tech-savvy millennials are quitting WeChat.' *South China Morning Post*, 22 July. www.scmp.com/news/china/society/article/2156297/how-growing-privacy-fears-china-are-driving-wechat-users-away

Chen, Y.J., Lin, C.F., & Liu, H.W. (2018) '"Rule of trust": The power and perils of China's social credit megaproject.' *Columbia Journal of Asian Law* 32(1): 1–36.

China Briefing (2021) 'PRC Personal Information Protection Law (Final): A full translation', 24 August. www.china-briefing.com/news/the-prc-personal-information-protection-law-final-a-full-translation/

China Internet Network Information Centre (CNNIC) (2018) 'Di 42 ci "Zhongguo hulianwangluo fazhan zhuangkuang tongji baogao" fabu' [第42次《中国互联网网络发展状况统计报告》发布, Issue of the 42nd statistical report on the development of internet networks in China], 20 August. www.cnnic.net.cn/gywm/xwzx/rdxw/20172017_7047/201808/t20180820_70486.htm (page discontinued)

—— (2021) 'Di 48 ci "Zhongguo hulianwangluo fazhan zhuangkuang tongji baogao" fabu' [第48次《中国互联网网络发展状况统计报告》发布, Issue of the 48th statistical report on the development of internet networks in China], 23 September. www.cnnic.net.cn/gywm/xwzx/rdxw/20172017_7084/202109/t20210923_71551.htm (page discontinued)

Chorzempa, M., Triolo, P., & Sacks, S. (2018) 'China's social credit system: A mark of progress or a threat to privacy?' Peterson Institute for International Economics. Policy Brief 18–14. www.piie.com/publications/policy-briefs/chinas-social-credit-system-mark-progress-or-threat-privacy

CIW Team (2021) 'Weibo MAU grew to 573 million in Q3 2021.' China Internet Watch, 19 November. www.chinainternetwatch.com/31281/weibo-quarterly

Cook, S. (2019a) '"Social credit" scoring: How China's Communist Party is incentivising repression.' Hong Kong Free Press, 27 February. www.hongkongfp.com/2019/02/27/social-credit-scoring-chinas-communist-party-incentivising-repression

—— (2019b) 'Analysis: Worried about Huawei? Take a closer look at Tencent.' *China Media Bulletin*, 134. freedomhouse.org/china-media/china-media-bulletin-tencent-complicity-surveillance-upgrades-reddit-manipulation-no-134

Corum, C. (2018) 'Chinese digital ID comes to Alibaba's payment app.' *SecureIDNews*, 4 May. www.secureidnews.com/news-item/chinese-digital-id-comes-to-alibabas-payment-app

Cybersecurity Law of the People's Republic of China (2016). Enacted 7 November 2016, effective 1 June 2017. Dezan Shira & Associates. www.dezshira.com/library/legal/cyber-security-law-china-8013.html

Dean, B. (2021) 'TikTok user statistics (2021).' Blacklinko, 11 October. backlinko.com/tiktok-users

Deng, I. (2018a) 'Tencent launches strictest verification system yet to detect minors after Beijing's call for action on gaming.' *South China Morning Post*, 6 September. www.scmp.com/tech/article/2163015/tencent-launches-strictest-verification-system-yet-detect-minors-after-beijings

—— (2018b) 'Tencent restructures with eye on industrial internet as gaming business slows.' *South China Morning Post*, 1 October. www.scmp.com/tech/big-tech/article/2166540/tencent-restructures-eye-industrial-internet-gaming-business-slows

Devdiscourse (2021) 'China's Social Credit System is a fragmented experiment.' 29 November. www.devdiscourse.com/article/science-environment/1826212-chinas-social-credit-system-is-a-fragmented-experiment

Dickson, B. (2016) *The Dictator's Dilemma: The Chinese Communist Party's Strategy for Survival.* Oxford University Press

Ding, X., & Zhong, D.Y. (2021) 'Rethinking China's Social Credit System: A long road to establishing trust in Chinese society.' *Journal of Contemporary China* 30(130): 630–44. doi.org/10.1080/10670564.2020.1852738

Dockrill, P. (2018) 'China's chilling "social credit system" is straight out of dystopian Sci-Fi and it's already switched on.' *Science Alert*, 20 September. www.sciencealert.com/china-s-dystopian-social-credit-system-science-fiction-black-mirror-mass-surveillance-digital-dictatorship

Dou, E. (2021) 'China built the world's largest facial recognition system. Now, it's getting camera-shy.' *Washington Post*, 30 July. www.washingtonpost.com/world/facial-recognition-china-tech-data/2021/07/30/404c2e96-f049-11eb-81b2-9b7061a582d8_story.html

Economist (2016) 'Big data and government: China's digital dictatorship.' 17 December. www.economist.com/leaders/2016/12/17/chinas-digital-dictatorship

FinancesOnline (2021) '178 significant Wechat statistics: 2021 market share and data analysis.' FinancesOnline Review for Business. financesonline.com/wechat-statistics

Foucault, M. (1985) *Discipline and Punish: The Birth of the Prison*. Penguin

Griffiths, J. (2019a) *The Great Firewall of China: How to Build and Control an Alternative Version of the Internet*. Zed Books

—— (2019b) 'How Chinese internet trolls go after Beijing's critics overseas.' CNN Business, 19 April. edition.cnn.com/2019/04/18/tech/china-uyghurs-internet-trolls-facebook-intl/index.html

Haggerty, K.D., & Ericson, R.V. (eds) (2006) *The New Politics of Surveillance and Visibility*. University of Toronto Press

He, H. (2019) 'China's social credit system shows its teeth, banning millions from taking flights, trains.' *South China Morning Post*, 18 February. www.scmp.com/economy/china-economy/article/2186606/chinas-social-credit-system-shows-its-teeth-banning-millions

—— (2021) 'China is raising the alarm over corporate surveillance. But it's got a massive network of its own.' CNN, 19 March. edition.cnn.com/2021/03/19/tech/china-consumer-rights-surveillance-intl-hnk/index.html

Hoffman, S. (2017) 'Managing the state: Social credit, surveillance and the CCP's plan for China.' *China Brief* 17(11): 21–6. jamestown.org/program/managing-the-state-social-credit-surveillance-and-the-ccps-plan-for-china/

Horsley, J. (2018) 'China's Orwellian social credit score isn't real. Blacklists and monitoring systems are nowhere close to Black Mirror fantasies.' *Foreign Policy*, 16 November. foreignpolicy.com/2018/11/16/chinas-orwellian-social-credit-score-isnt-real

Jacobs, H. (2018) 'China's "big brother" surveillance technology isn't nearly as all-seeing as the government wants you to think.' *Business Insider*, 15 July. www.businessinsider.com/china-facial-recognition-limitations-2018-7

Khalil, L. (2020) 'Digital authoritarianism, China and Covid.' Lowy Institute Analyses, 2 November. www.lowyinstitute.org/publications/digital-authoritarianism-china-and-covid

King, G., Pan, J., & Roberts, M. (2017) 'How the Chinese government fabricates social media posts for strategic distraction, not engaged argument.' *American Political Science Review* 111(3): 484–501. doi.org/10.1017/S0003055417000144

Koty, C.A. (2021) 'China's Social Credit System: Scope, punishments amended.' *China Briefing*, 9 August. www.china-briefing.com/news/chinas-social-credit-system-scope-punishments-amended

Law of the People's Republic of China on Resident Identity Cards (2004). Enacted 28 June 2003, effective 1 January 2004. Central People's Government of the People's Republic of China. www.gov.cn/banshi/2005-08/02/content_19457.htm (English translation retrieved from www.npc.gov.cn/englishnpc/Law/2007-12/05/content_1381969.htm)

Lee, A. (2019) 'China's credit system stops the sale of over 26 million plane and train tickets.' *South China Morning Post*, 18 April. www.scmp.com/economy/china-economy/article/3006763/chinas-social-credit-system-stops-sale-over-26-million-plane

Lee, C. (2018) 'China identifies 17 key areas to make AI breakthroughs.' *ZDNet*, 19 November. www.zdnet.com/article/china-identifies-17-key-areas-to-make-ai-breakthroughs

Lee, K.F. (2018) *AI Superpowers: China, Silicon Valley and the New World Order*. Houghton Mifflin Harcourt

Lessig, L. (1999) *Code and Other Laws of Cyberspace*. Basic Books

Li, J. (2021) 'How China's top internet regulator became China's tech giants' worst enemy.' *Quartz*, 23 August. qz.com/2039292/how-did-chinas-top-internet-regulator-become-so-powerful

Lieberthal, K., & Oksenberg, M. (1988) *Policy Making in China: Leaders, Structures and Processes*. Princeton University Press

Link, P. (2002) 'China: The anaconda in the chandelier.' *New York Review*, 11 April. www.nybooks.com/articles/2002/04/11/china-the-anaconda-in-the-chandelier

Ma, L., Chung, J., & Thorson, S. (2005) 'E-government in China: Bringing economic development through administrative reform.' *Government Information Quarterly* 22(1): 20–37. doi.org/10.1016/j.giq.2004.10.001

Meissner, M. (2017) 'China's social credit system.' *Merics China Monitor*, 24 May. merics.org/en/report/chinas-social-credit-system

Mistreanu, S. (2018) 'Life inside China's social credit laboratory.' *Foreign Policy*, 2 April. foreignpolicy.com/2018/04/03/life-inside-chinas-social-credit-laboratory

Mozur, P. (2018) 'Inside China's dystopian dreams: AI, shame and lots of cameras.' *New York Times*, 8 July. www.nytimes.com/2018/07/08/business/china-surveillance-technology.html

Muncaster, P. (2013) 'China's "big Vs" disown selves online to avoid new gossip laws.' *Register*, 18 September. www.theregister.co.uk/2013/09/18/verified_accounts_weibo_unverify_rumour_crackdown/

Pedroletti, B. (2017) 'La Chine vaillamment défendue par son armée de trolls' [China vigorously defended by troll army]. *Le Monde*, 4 June. www.lemonde.fr/asie-pacifique/article/2017/06/04/la-chine-vaillamment-defendue-par-son-armee-de-trolls_5138582_3216.html

Perry, E.J. (1994) 'Trends in the study of Chinese politics: State-society relations.' *China Quarterly* 139: 704–13. doi.org/10.1017/S0305741000043113

Qiang, X. (2019) 'The road to digital unfreedom: President Xi's surveillance state.' *Journal of Democracy* 30(1): 53–67. doi.org/10.1353/jod.2019.0004

Ramadan, Z. (2018) 'The gamification of trust: The case of China's "social credit".' *Marketing Intelligence and Planning* 36(1): 93–107. doi.org/10.1108/MIP-06-2017-0100

Reid, A.J. (2018) *The Smartphone Paradox: Our Ruinous Dependency in the Device Age*. Palgrave Macmillan

Ringen, S. (2016) *The Perfect Dictatorship: China in the 21st Century*. Hong Kong University Press

Roberts, M.E. (2018) *Censored: Distraction and Diversion Inside China's Great Firewall*. Princeton University Press

Russell, J. (2017) 'Ambitious new media firm ByteDance is no longer a secret outside of China.' *Techcrunch*, 10 November. techcrunch.com/2017/11/10/what-exactly is-bytedance-and-toutiao

—— (2018) 'China reaches 800 million internet users.' *Techcrunch*, 21 August. techcrunch.com/2018/08/21/china-reaches-800-million-internet-users

Sacks, S. (2018) 'Disruptors, innovators and thieves: Assessing innovation in China's digital economy.' Centre for Strategic and International Studies. www.csis.org/analysis/disruptors-innovators-and-thieves

Schlaeger, J. (2013) *E-Government in China: Technology, Power and Local Government Reform*. Routledge

Schmitz, R. (2018) 'Facial recognition in China is big business as local governments boost surveillance.' National Public Radio, 3 April. www.npr.org/sections/parallels/2018/04/03/598012923/facial-recognition-in-china-is-big-business-as-local-governments-boost-surveilla

Schulze, D., & Godehardt, N. (2017) 'China 4.0: Party and society debate the digital transformation.' SWP Comments, 6. www.swp-berlin.org/fileadmin/contents/products/comments/2017C06_Schulze_gdh.pdf

Shepherd, C., & Yang, Y. (2019) 'China increases crackdown on Twitter users.' *Financial Times*, 16 April, p. 4

Sodhi, I.S. (2016) 'E-government in China: Status, challenges and progress.' In *Trends, Prospects and Challenges in Asian e-Governance*, ed. I.S. Sodhi, pp. 36–55. IGI Global

South China Morning Post (2019) 'China launches website to report foreign spies, corrupt officials.' 16 April. www.scmp.com/news/china/policies-politics/article/2141910/china-launches-website-report-foreign-spies-corrupt

State Council of the People's Republic of China (2014) 'Guowuyuan guanyu yinfa shehui xinyong tixi jianshe guihua gangyao (2014–2020 nian) de tongzhi' [国务院关于印发社会信用体系建设规划纲要 (2014–2020年) 的通知, State Council notice concerning issuance of the planning outline for the construction of a social credit system (2014–2020)], 14 June. www.gov.cn/zhengce/content/2014–06/27/content_8913.htm

Tang, F. (2018) 'China names 169 people banned from taking flights or trains under social credit system.' *South China Morning Post*, 2 June. www.scmp.com/news/china/policies-politics/article/2148980/china-names-169-people-banned-taking-flights-or-trains

Tang, L. [唐斓] (2019) 'Zuigao renmin fayuan gongzuo baogao' [最高人民法院工作报告, Supreme People's Court report]. *Xinhua*, 12 March. www.xinhuanet.com/politics/2019-03/19/c_1124253887.htm

Tao, L. (2018) 'A look at China's push for digital national ID cards.' *South China Morning Post*, 23 January. www.scmp.com/tech/article/2129957/look-chinas-push-national-digital-id-cards

—— (2019) 'Sensenets: The facial recognition company that supplies China's Skynet surveillance system.' *South China Morning Post*, 12 April. www.scmp.com/tech/science-research/article/3005733/what-you-need-know-about-sensenets-facial-recognition-firm

Team Counterpoint (2021) 'Chinese smartphone market share by quarter.' *Counterpoint*, 5 August. www.counterpointresearch.com/china-smartphone-share

Travel China Cheaper (2021) 'List of websites and apps blocked in China for 2021.' 1 November. www.travelchinacheaper.com/index-blocked-websites-in-china

Tsui, L. (2003) 'The panopticon as the antithesis of a space of freedom: Control and regulation of the Internet in China.' *China Information* 17(2): 65–82. doi.org/10.1177/0920203X0301700203

Wang, S. [王思北] (2017) 'Zhongyang wangxinban deng sibumen lianhe kaizhan yinsi tiaokuan zhuanxiang gongzuo' [中央网信办等四部门联合开展隐私条款专项工作, Central Cyberspace Affairs Commission and four other departments jointly launch dedicated privacy policy work]. Xinhua, 27 July. www.cac.gov.cn/2017-08/02/c_1121421829.htm

Wang, Z. (2019) 'When "WeChat" turns to "we tired": An empirical explanation on social media fatigue (SMF) by understanding perceived privacy' (paper presentation). 7th Global Social Sciences Graduate Student Conference, Hong Kong Baptist University, China, April. sosc.hkbu.edu.hk/sites/default/files/documents/2019conf/abstracts.pdf

Williams, I. (2017) 'China's internet crackdown is another step towards "digital totalitarian state".' NBC News, 6 September. www.nbcnews.com/news/china/china-s-internet-crackdown-another-step-towards-digital-totalitarian-state-n798001

Woetzel, J., Seong, J., Wang, K.W., Manyika, J., Chui, M., & Wong, W. (2017) *China's Digital Economy: A Leading Global Force.* McKinsey Global Institute. www.mckinsey.com/featured-insights/china/chinas-digital-economy-a-leading-global-force

Wu, M. (2016) 'China's crackdown on "internet rumours" and "illegal" internet publicity activities.' In *Governing Society in Contemporary China*, ed. L. Yang & W. Shan, pp. 41–56. World Scientific

Wübbekke, J., Meissner, M., Zenglein, M. J., Ives, J., & Conrad, B. (2016) 'Made in China 2025: The making of a high-tech superpower and consequences for industrial countries.' Merics Papers on China, No. 2. www.merics.org/sites/default/files/2017-09/MPOC_No.2_MadeinChina2025.pdf

Xi, W., Han, J., Wong, S.S., & Lau, S.F. (2019). 'Chinese universities ordered to spy on staff, students in ideological crackdown.' Radio Free Asia, 8 April. www.rfa.org/english/news/china/universities-04082019144318.html

Xinhua (2004) 'Beijing launches second-generation ID cards.' 8 April. www.china.org.cn/english/government/92519.htm

Xinyong Zhongguo [信用中国, Credit China] (2019) 'Shaanxisheng fayuan wanshan wangluo zhixing chakong xitong' [陕西省法院完善网络执行查控系统, Shaanxi Province Higher Court improves the online inspection and control network]. 16 October. www.creditchina.gov.cn/home/zhuantizhuanlan/aWeek/xinyongdongtai/201810/t20181016_128179.html

Yang, Y. [Yao] (2017) 'Towards a new digital era: Observing local e-government services adoption in a Chinese municipality.' *Future Internet* 9(3): 53. doi.org/10.3390/fi9030053

Yang, Y. [Yingzhi] (2019) 'Short video app TikTok extends reach in global markets, sees in-app purchases surge more than 200 per cent.' *South China Morning Post*, 16 April. www.scmp.com/tech/apps-social/article/3006319/short-video-app-tiktok-extends-reach-global-markets-sees-app

Yang, Y. [Yuan] (2018) 'China privacy outcry fuels calls for tighter rules.' *Financial Times*, 2 October, p. 4

Ye, J. (2021) 'China tech crackdown: Tencent's app update suspension seen as a shot across the bows of other app developers.' *South China Morning Post*, 25 November. www.scmp.com/tech/policy/article/3157395/china-tech-crackdown-tencents-app-update-suspension-seen-shot-across

Zhang, P. (2019) 'Cities in China most monitored in the world.' *South China Morning Post*, 19 August. www.scmp.com/news/china/society/article/3023455/report-finds-cities-china-most-monitored-world

Zhang, Y., & Han, W. (2019) 'In depth: China's burgeoning social credit system stirs controversy.' *Caixin*, 1 April. www.caixinglobal.com/2019-04-01/in-depth-chinas-burgeoning-social-credit-system-stirs-controversy-101399430.html

Zhong, R. (2018) 'It built an empire of GIFs, buzzy news and jokes. China isn't amused.' *New York Times*, 11 April. www.nytimes.com/2018/04/11/technology/china-toutiao-bytedance-censor.html

Zhou, J. (2018) 'Drones, facial recognition and a social credit system: 10 ways China watches its citizens.' *South China Morning Post*, 4 August. www.scmp.com/news/china/society/article/2157883/drones-facial-recognition-and-social-credit-system-10-ways-china

Zuboff, S. (1988) *In the Age of the Smart Machine: The Future of Work and Power.* Basic Books

8

Building a hyper-stability structure: The mechanisms of social stability maintenance in Xi's China

Hsin-Hsien Wang and Wei-Feng Tzeng[1]

Alongside institutional construction, elite interaction and state-market relations, state–society relations have long been a major subject of inquiry for students of comparative authoritarianism and the transitions of post-socialist states. The subject is primarily concerned with the rise of social power and the state's response (Petrova & Tarrow, 2007). China has witnessed a gradual rise in social power following the progression of its reform and opening up, which includes the development of non-governmental organisations (NGOs), the emergence of social resistance, the power of public opinion formed by various statements made on the internet, and even the advent of tensions between the government's desire to maintain stability and the protection of civil rights in various regions. This has also become the ideal perspective from which to observe changes in

1   This chapter is a revised and updated version of the article that first appeared as H.H. Wang and W.F. Tzeng (2021) 'Building a hyper-stability structure: The mechanisms of social stability maintenance in Xi's China.' *Issues and Studies* 57(1), Article 2150002. doi.org/10.1142/S1013251121500028. Reprinted with permission.

China's state–society relations. As such, this chapter aims to explore changes in the state's 'stability maintenance' that have occurred since Xi Jinping assumed power.[2]

Using Mann's distinction between despotic and infrastructural power (Mann, 1993),[3] China's coercive state authority continues to be far greater than its infrastructural power, especially with the reinforcement of social control during the rule of President Xi. However, we have also witnessed the occurrence of several large-scale protests in recent years, including the protests of military veterans, truck driver strikes, the Jasic (佳士, *jiashi*) labour rights conflict and the #MeToo movement, all of which have presented a certain threat to the state. First, there have been several noteworthy instances of interregional mobilisation. One example is the veteran protests of October 2016 in which thousands of veterans from more than a dozen provinces surrounded the Bayi Building (八一大楼, *bayi dalou*). This was further illustrated by incidents in 2018, where protests in Luohe City of Henan Province, Zhenjiang of Jiangsu Province and Zhongjiang County of Sichuan Province had to be suppressed by local governments, while protests in other provinces were supported by military veterans. China's capacity for inter-provincial mobilisation has been illustrated both by the 2018 Truck Drivers' Strike and the Shan Xin Hui (善心汇) Incident of 2017, where more than 10,000 investors gathered in Beijing to petition against an MLM organisation. Second, 'professional activists' have begun to emerge. Protests have seen the involvement of notable figures such as Peking University graduate Yue Xin (岳昕) and Guangzhou labour activist Shen Mengyu (沈梦雨) in the #MeToo movement, the Jasic labour rights conflict and a number of other protests. Third, a certain collaboration across class lines has begun to take place. The main body of protests usually consisted of specific groups in the past, and inter-class incidents were relatively uncommon. However, the Jasic Incident witnessed a rare combination of young workers and several university Marxist societies nationwide.

---

2   'Stability maintenance' refers to 维护稳定 or 维稳. The definition of stability might be vague in different contexts. While practitioners, including the Chinese government, consider the absence of social turmoil as stability and minimising social unrest as stability maintenance, some scholars believe persistence of the regime is the sign of stability. For the purpose of this chapter, we use the official definition of stability as the basis for analysing the mechanism of stability maintenance in China.

3   Despotic power refers to the state's capacity to direct policies coercively while infrastructural power refers to its capacity to enforce policies effectively throughout its entire territory while consulting with society.

The phrase 'political security' has appeared with increasing frequency in the speeches of Xi Jinping and other officials of the Communist Party of China (CPC) since 2017. The concept has also grown in prominence under the pressure of the US–China trade war (from 2018) and a domestic economic downturn. Xi Jinping's speech at the Provincial and Ministerial Level Leading Cadre Seminar on 21 January 2019 emphasised the need for bottom-line thinking to prevent major risks in all aspects and areas and to ensure the security of politics, ideology, economics, science and technology, society, the external environment and party building. The minister of public security at the time, Zhao Kezhi (赵克志), also emphasised at the annual Meeting of National Public Security Bureau Chiefs that the 'prevention of political risks' must be a top priority, with a focus on guarding against 'colour revolutions'. Moreover, Xi Jinping has signalled a growing sense of insecurity in China by emphasising a 'comprehensive view of national security'. While the term 'security' was mentioned 36 times during Hu Jintao's report to the 18th Party Congress, this increased to 55 in Xi's report to the 19th Party Congress in 2017. Thus it is evident that the CPC is facing tremendous pressure to maintain stability. It has consequently been exerting increasingly strict social control in recent years by reinforcing its control over online speech; suppressing NGOs, rights protection lawyers and home churches; charging teachers with 'speech crimes' in classrooms; and making intensive adjustments to the party committee secretaries and presidents of more than 20 universities under the direct administration of the Chinese Ministry of Education, including Peking University.

While there has been a surge in both social power and the protection of civil rights, we also can see an increase in the intensity of measures to maintain stability. Numerous studies have noted that the CPC has strengthened its control over society since Xi Jinping took office as he consolidated his personal power in the party (Dickson, 2021; Fewsmith, 2021; Saich, 2021). Following previous insights, this chapter contributes to current literature by identifying the specific changes that have occurred in the CPC's mechanisms of stability maintenance. What adjustments have been made at the institutional and practical levels? What is the significance of these changes for the CPC regime?

On the basis of these questions, the following discussion will begin by noting the relevant research on comparative authoritarianism and the CPC regime. Next, the concept of institutional autocratisation will be proposed, followed by a discussion of the changes in China's stability maintenance mechanisms since Xi Jinping took office from the perspectives of institutions and actions. While the institutional part of this concept indicates that Xi has strengthened his hold on power through the institutionalisation of autocratic governance, this alone does not guarantee the compliance of society. To make society comply with authoritarian rule, the government has found it necessary to utilise information technology and other more sophisticated measures for social control. Finally, this chapter will analyse and evaluate the tension between an increasingly diverse society and the ever-strengthening coercive power of the state.

Varieties of authoritarianism in China

As the PRC was founded during the height of the Cold War and information from China was opaque, China studies initially applied the concept of totalitarianism that was used to observe the Soviet Union (Friedrich & Brzezinski, 1956). Most researchers believed that the CPC mobilised the country in support of the new regime's policies and controlled resource allocation by means of a planned economy, thereby ensuring the full penetration of state mechanisms throughout society (Barnett, 1960; Lewis, 1963; Schurmann, 1966). Yet despite the CPC's monopoly over political power, nearly four decades of reform and opening up have brought about institutional diversification, the weakening of ideology, the introduction of a market economy and the relative autonomy of society within the regime. Hence it is generally acknowledged that China has long since moved away from totalitarianism and begun to move towards post-totalitarianism or authoritarianism (Linz, 1975, 2000; Linz & Stepan, 1966).

According to Nathan (2003), China's continued authoritarianism has been largely due to the resilience of its authority, which has been accomplished through a high degree of institutionalisation. In addition to the institutionalisation of its political succession and the recruitment of its political elite, China's authoritarian resilience is also based on institutionalisation that is both multi-level and multi-faceted. In terms of literature, this can be divided into its three aspects of structure, organisation and policy orientation. Several theories have been developed to explain how each of these aspects is able to effectively maintain authoritarian rule (Lee & Zhang, 2013; Mertha, 2009; Nathan, 1992; Teets, 2013; Wright, 2010).

First, the decentralisation of overall regime power has become a key structural feature in the maintenance of the CPC regime. Lieberthal and Oksenberg (1988) suggested that the CPC's internal policy formulation involves complex bureaucratic bargaining processes among different levels and different departments, or 'fragmented authoritarianism'.[4] Mertha (2009), on the other hand, believes that policy entrepreneurs such as the media and NGOs have emerged in China with the development of social diversification. These have the ability to engage in issue-framing, making it necessary for governmental departments to form alliances with them in order to promote policies, known as 'fragmented authoritarianism 2.0'. In addition, Landry (2008) proposed the concept of decentralised authoritarianism to explain how the central government controls local officials, safeguards organisational integrity and reduces political risks through organisational and personnel appointments despite the substantial budgetary and political power held by local governments.

Second, organisations developed by the Chinese regime require a certain level of flexibility that enables them to evolve alongside social changes and coordinate with the legitimacy of Chinese authoritarian rule. Specific examples include the introduction of direct elections in grassroots social organisations such as residents' committees and village committees, making them into foundations of the legitimacy of the Chinese authoritarian regime. In addition, Chinese governmental organisations also cater to various social needs with timely adjustments to governmental mechanisms and functions in order to meet the current needs of Chinese society. In high-level elite political organisations, various deliberative bodies have been established to consolidate different elite opinions. This not only reflects the characteristics of the CPC's democratic centralism but also reduces the chances of an elite coup. From an organisational point of view, many scholars have described China as being in a state of flexible or adaptive authoritarianism from which its authority derives its resilience (Wright, 2010).

Finally, there was a high degree of opinion absorption in the policy orientation under Hu Jintao. For example, Wright (2010) used the intertwined effects of state-led development policies, market forces and socialist legacies to explain how the CPC regime enabled people from all levels of society to tolerate and even accept single-party rule within the context of economic openness and political closure—a state she called 'accepting authoritarianism'. Teets (2013) examined the development of civil society in China and suggested 'consultative authoritarianism' to describe the situation in which organisations assist in the local governance

---

4   Also see Lieberthal (1992).

of grassroots communities. Similarly, Lee and Zhang (2013), after four years of in-depth field research, used the term 'bargained authoritarianism' to describe how the Chinese grassroots state reached agreements with society after negotiations and further incorporated these agreements into its policy formulation to avoid future social resistance. Among these characteristics of policy orientation, the policy responsiveness of the Chinese government is a key aspect in the avoidance of large-scale social opposition.

The above-mentioned terms demonstrate that China is an 'authoritarianism with adjectives'. China's party-state system adapts itself in response to changes in the external environment, creating a balance between the state and society and between the state and the market. This is also why Nathan (1992, 2003) believes that the CPC regime possesses sufficient resilience for its survival and can compensate for its own institutional defects. Shambaugh (2008) also argues that, unlike other post-communist and authoritarian states, the CPC has an ability to adapt and learn that endows it with the potential for long-term governance. On the basis of the literature analysis above, the state's internal 'fragmentation', the relative autonomy of society and the responsiveness of government policies under the rule of Hu Jintao have allowed China's authoritarian regime to maintain stable rule (see figure 8.1).[5]

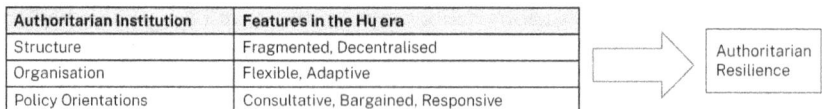

Authoritarian Institution	Features in the Hu era
Structure	Fragmented, Decentralised
Organisation	Flexible, Adaptive
Policy Orientations	Consultative, Bargained, Responsive

Authoritarian Resilience

Figure 8.1: Institutional features of authoritarianism in the Hu era
Source: Authors' summary.

Nevertheless, most of these views have described the political situation before Xi Jinping came to power, especially during the Hu Jintao administration. It is questionable whether the adjectives used to describe the structure, organisation and policy orientation of the CPC continue to be appropriate after Xi Jinping's taking office in light of the changes that have occurred in

---

5   It is worth noting that Nathan's argument that institutionalisation has strengthened the longevity of the CCP's authoritarian rule is not unquestionable, and it has been challenged by several alternative explanations. For instance, Fewsmith contended that China's authoritarian rule is consolidated not by institutionalisation but by the reassertion of party norms in the central leadership, a phenomenon that goes against institutionalisation (Fewsmith & Nathan, 2019). In this chapter, we incorporate both perspectives and argue that the CCP leaders can change current institutions and organisations and then institutionalise those changes to strengthen its power. For their debate, see Fewsmith and Nathan (2019) and Fewsmith (2021).

the face of pressure from recent social developments. We believe that the above understanding of the CPC's party-state system is overly optimistic. Although 40 years of reform and opening up has led to its modernisation, China has not moved towards a more open and democratic government as the liberalists expected but has instead retained its communist traditions. Some researchers have called this 'neo-authoritarianism' (Petracca & Xiong, 1990). Walder (1986) emphasised that there is an essential difference between this type of neo-traditional image and totalitarianism or pluralism. Although it has been characterised by totalitarian organised political control, there continues to be an exchange of interests through social networks and interpersonal relationships in return for political loyalty.

This chapter contends that after Xi Jinping took office, he did not follow the approaches adopted by Jiang and Hu but reshaped state–society relations by reconstructing the state's repressive machine through institutions and technology. While the state has suffered from less internal fragmentation, repressive power has been strengthened and institutionalised in the face of a rising social sector. This capacity for suppression and control has been a traditional part of the CPC's maintenance of social stability. At the same time, while China still has an exchange system for interests and loyalty, it is no longer being implemented through interpersonal relationships. Instead, the system is based on the monitoring of scientific and technological power, the mastery of big data and the construction of a social credit system for enterprises and local governments, forming a new mode of control.

In terms of their influence, the regime structure, organisation and policy orientation of Xi Jinping's government are vastly different from Hu Jintao's. Xi's regime has also utilised new scientific and technological advances to redirect the regime towards the old ruling system. By doing so, the regime has also tightened its control over the country's political ideology and how people in society think. Although thought management was a major strategy of social control before Xi (Brady, 2008, 2012), it has been intensified in the Xi era. In September 2021, for instance, all elementary and secondary schools in China have included 'Xi Jinping Thought' in their teaching of the national curriculum. According to Chinese officials, they believe that learning Xi Thought will 'help teenagers establish Marxist beliefs' (*Renminwang*, 2021). Undoubtedly, measures like this aim to 'purify' the ideology of society for the party to gain stronger control over it.

The Xi regime is characterised by both traditional CPC suppression and new scientific and technological tools for the maintenance of social stability. This chapter suggests that the Xi era can be described as one of 'institutional autocratisation' for the maintenance of stability. The following is a brief description of the relevant measures that have been taken under Xi's leadership and an exploration of their significance to the changes in China's authoritarian system.

Legislation formulation, institutional adjustment and stability maintenance through science and technology

Intensified legislation for the purpose of stability maintenance

After Xi Jinping assumed power, he began to intensify the introduction of stability-related legislation under a 'holistic approach to national security'. The primary purpose of this was to bolster CPC rule. In the National Security Law promulgated in July 2015, Article 4 states explicitly that 'all national security work shall adhere to the leadership of the CPC and a centralised, unified, efficient and authoritative national security leadership system shall be established'. Article 15 mentions that 'the state shall adhere to the leadership of the CPC and maintain a socialist system with Chinese characteristics'. In addition to Article 26 of the National Security Law that provides for 'increased internet management', the Cyber Security Law was also adopted in November 2016 to legalise government internet control. The law aims to legalise cyberspace sovereignty and raise it to the national strategic level. Aside from responding to the threat of an international cyberwar, it also includes internal considerations such as consolidating political power and maintaining social stability (Quanguo Renmin Daibiao Dahui, 2016c).

The Charity Law adopted in March 2016 also restricts the development of social organisations. For example, Article 4 states that 'charitable activities … shall not endanger national security' while Articles 15 and 104 stipulate that charitable organisations shall not engage in or fund such activities (Quanguo Renmin Daibiao Dahui, 2016a). The Law on the Administration of Domestic Activities of Overseas Non-Governmental

Organisations (NGO) adopted in January 2017 also restricts the activities of overseas NGOs in China by essentially cutting off their links with local NGOs. More specifically, the regulatory authority of international NGOs in China was transferred from the Ministry of Civil Affairs to the Ministry of Public Security. Public security bodies have been given tremendous power to supervise these organisations, which includes interviewing responsible persons, terminating temporary activities, inspecting documents, freezing account funds and announcing 'unwelcome lists' (Quanguo Renmin Daibiao Dahui, 2016b). In order to effectively control public opinion that is disruptive to social order, the National People's Congress also passed the Ninth Amendment to the Criminal Law of China in late August 2015, increasing the criminal liability of 'spreading rumours' and sparking controversy over the freedom of speech (Quanguo Renmin Daibiao Dahui, 2015).

Adjustments to the stability maintenance system

The CPC's stability maintenance system can broadly be divided into the following three phases: (1) 'four-in-one' phases: monopoly by the Political and Legal Affairs Commission; (2) the top-level design phase: establishment of the National Security Commission; and (3) the consolidation and shaping phase of stability maintenance institutions.

'Four-in-one' phases: Monopoly by the Political and Legal Affairs Commission

This phase was during the Hu Jintao era. Stability maintenance institutions were mainly led by the Central Political and Legal Affairs Commission of the CPC together with the Central Commission for the Comprehensive Management of Public Security (中央社会治安综合管理委员会, *zhongyang shehui zhian zonghe guanli weiyuanhui*), the Central Leading Group for Stability Maintenance Work (中央维护稳定工作领导小组, *zhongyang weihu wending gongzuo lingdao xiaozu*), the Central Leading Group for Preventing and Dealing with Heretical Religions (中央防范和处理邪教问题领导小组及其办公室, *zhongyang fangfan he chuli xiejiao wenti lingdao xiaozu ji qi bangongshi*) and its office (commonly known as the 610 Office). The Central Political and Legal Affairs Commission secretary, Zhou Yongkang (周永康), was a member of the Politburo

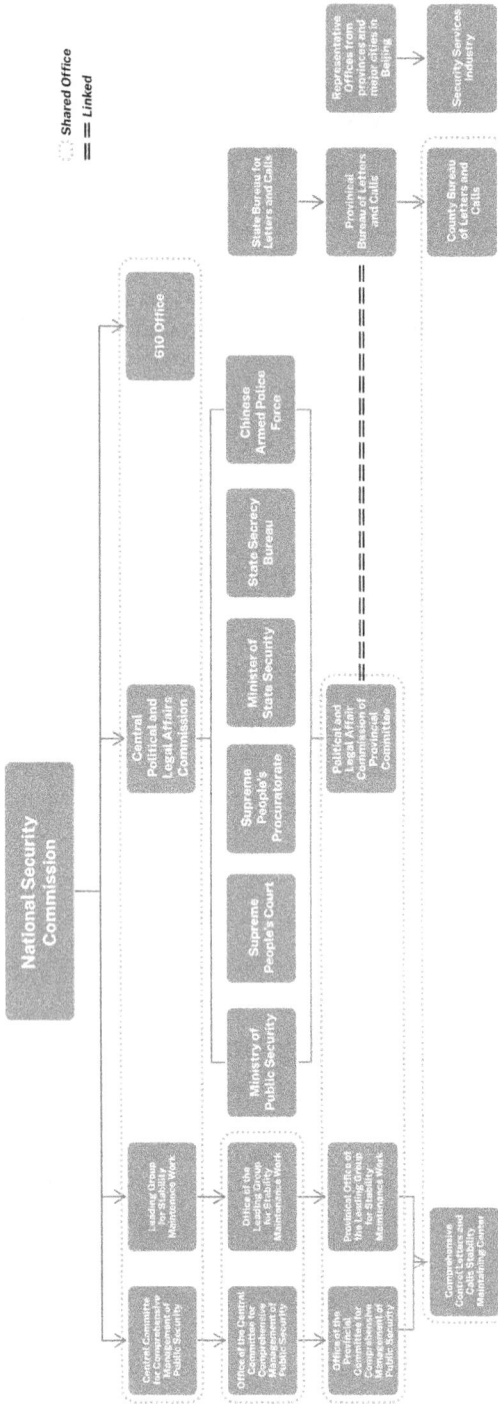

Figure 8.2: Xi's top-level design for the National Security Commission and stability maintenance

Source: Created by authors.

Standing Committee. Most of the secretaries of the Political and Legal Affairs Commissions were also members of local party standing committees at the local level. Even some chiefs of provincial and municipal public security bureaus were also members of the standing committees. Members of the political and legal system occupied key positions in both the central government and local governments, while the power of the Central Political and Legal Affairs Commission extended to almost all departments, even earning the title of 'Second Party Central Committee' (*DW News*, 2019). In addition, stability maintenance institutions also included the Public Complaints and Proposals Administration (信访局, *xinfangju*) in both central and local levels of government as well as 'Beijing Offices' stationed by local governments in Beijing and their entrusted 'security companies' (see figure 8.2 for details).

The top-level design phase: Establishment of the National Security Commission

The top-level design phase occurred after Xi Jinping came to power at the 18th National Congress of the CPC. It includes two major changes. First, the secretary of the Central Political and Legal Affairs Commission no longer served as a member of the Politburo Standing Committee and was only a Politburo member, while the powers of the secretaries of local Political and Legal Affairs Commissions had also weakened. Second, the National Security Commission of the CPC was established. The commission was proposed during the Third Plenary Session of the 18th Central Committee in November 2013 and the Central Politburo reached a decision on its establishment in January 2014 with General Secretary Xi Jinping as its chairman. Since then, the National Security Commission has been the top-level institution for national security work, including stability maintenance (see figure 8.2). Although stability maintenance institutions continued to retain their 'four-in-one' organisation during this phase, the Central Political and Legal Affairs Commission was demoted in both its rank and authority.

The consolidation and shaping phase of stability maintenance institutions

As figure 8.3 presents, the most important change during this phase was the Plan on Deepening the Reform of Party and State Institutions passed by the National People's Congress and National Committee of the Chinese People's Political Consultative Conference in 2018. Its impact on stability

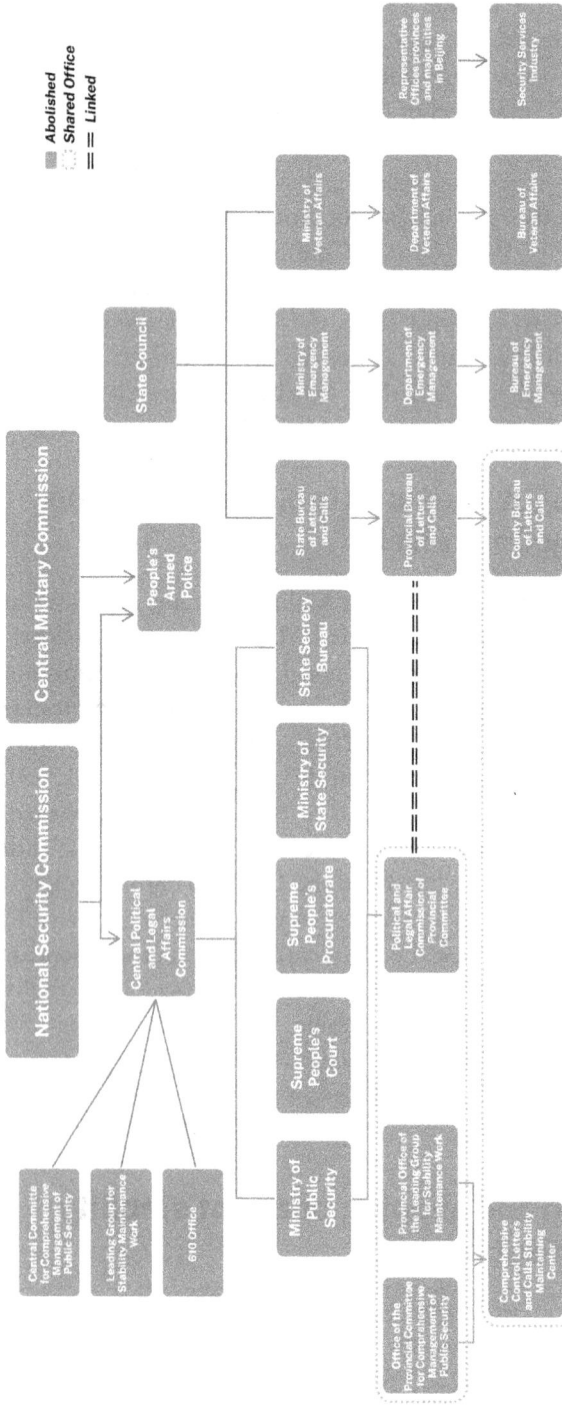

Figure 8.3: China's mechanisms of stability maintenance under Xi Jinping

Source: Created by authors.

maintenance institutions was mainly twofold. The first was to merge the three institutions in the 'four-in-one' organisation with the Political and Legal Affairs Commission, ending collaboration among the four institutions. The second was to establish two new ministry-level units under the State Council, namely the Ministry of Veterans Affairs (退役军人事务部, *tuiyi junren shiwubu*) and Ministry of Emergency Management (应急管理部, *yingji guanlibu*). The former was modelled after the US Department of Veterans Affairs and is involved in the protection and re-employment of veterans, mainly in response to the growing number of veterans joining protests. While the Ministry of Emergency Management is primarily focused on fire prevention, disaster relief and production security, it also includes functions such as 'establishing linking mechanisms in emergency coordination' and 'connecting the People's Liberation Army and armed police forces to participation in emergency rescues'. Two departments related to stability maintenance were newly created in response to the consolidation of numerous party and state institutions in the new institutional reform plan, reflecting the importance of this issue.

This phase also includes the incorporation of the Armed Police Force under the unified leadership of the Central Military Commission in 2018, as it ceased to be under the jurisdiction of the Political and Legal Affairs Commission. The 'Regulations on the Political and Legal Work of the CPC' promulgated in January 2019 also emphasised that the central government has absolute leadership over political and legal work, stipulating that political and legal units must be supervised by the Party Central Committee and report directly to the general secretary. It can be seen that the power of the Political and Legal Affairs Commission has been continuously weakened and increasingly institutionalised. The secretaries of the Political and Legal Affairs Commission in all 31 provinces, municipalities and autonomous regions ceased to serve concurrently as Public Security Bureau chiefs (*Zhongguo Jingjiwang*, 2015) by the time of the 19th National Congress, and the entire cohort was replaced with Xi Jinping's men.

Scientific and technological stability maintenance

In addition to constructing new regulations and institutions, Xi Jinping has strengthened the state's capacity to suppress social resistance, control the internet and limit dissent (Wang, Wang & Tzeng, 2019). At the same time, he has made use of science and technology to strengthen social control through the construction of a social credit system, the establishment of a Skynet project and DNA databases, and a party-state monopoly on big data.

The Social Credit System

Issued in 2014 by the State Council of China, the Planning Outline for the Construction of a Social Credit System (2014–20) was an important start in the implementation of this system (Tsai, Wang & Lin, 2021). It mentions the construction of a national social credit system in 2020 to improve trust and integrity in society through reward and punishment mechanisms. Its actual operations are divided into two major categories. The first category is through the two major internet giants Alibaba (阿里巴巴) and Tencent (腾讯, *tengxun*). For example, Sesame Credit (芝麻信用, *zhima xinyong*) belongs to the Ant Financial Services Group (蚂蚁金服, *mayi jinfu*) under the Alibaba Group, and China Rapid Finance is a partner of Tencent. The second category has been designed by local governments to classify citizens into different credit ratings that determine the different treatment and restrictions they experience. According to the 2018 Annual Analytical Report on the Blacklist of Dishonest Persons issued by the National Public Credit Information Centre, a total of 12.77 million persons were cumulatively listed by the end of 2018, and purchases of 17.46 million air tickets and 5.47 million high-speed rail tickets were banned (Guojia Gonggong Xinyong Xinxi Zhongxin, 2019).

The Skynet Project

The Skynet Project was launched by the Political and Legal Affairs Commission under the joint promotion of the Ministry of Public Security, the Ministry of Industry and Information Technology, and other relevant ministries and commissions. The initial stages of the project saw the gradual formation of urban public security prevention, control systems and demographic informatisation. Developed from artificial intelligence and related technologies, Skynet is an image surveillance system that integrates GIS maps, image acquisition, transmission, control, display and other equipment to perform real-time monitoring and information recording of a fixed area. Its facial recognition system technology is claimed to have an accuracy of more than 99.8 per cent. Together with the aforementioned credit scores, the information acquired by Skynet has formed a social control network. This network has gradually expanded its monitored targets to include enterprises, and has even been exported to South-East Asian countries as the 'smart city'.

DNA collection

The Ministry of Public Security has established a National Public Security Agencies DNA Database Application System in recent years with three main targets:

1. key personnel: dissidents, activists, petitioners and individuals with criminal records who constitute a threat to the regime
2. the floating population: individuals with non-local household registration, such as migrant workers
3. ethnic minorities: especially Uyghurs in Xinjiang.

China intends to use this system to create an expansive DNA database, which can be used for biotechnology research on the one hand and social control on the other.

The key to the technological stability maintenance described above is 'party-managed data'. All information is managed by the state, which has established three national-level big data centres in Beijing, Guiyang in Guizhou and Ulanqab in Inner Mongolia since 2015. In addition, a national credit information-sharing platform was established in 2016 to lay the foundation for the social credit system. It encompasses a data network that spans 44 ministries and more than 60 market institutions. In the context of public security, the state makes use of a 'police cloud system'. The Ministry of Public Security integrates the information and can rapidly mine personal information, including addresses, family relations, birth control methods and religious beliefs. Although these technological developments and institutional innovations claim to be weaving a more complete safety network for society and offering greater convenience, they are in fact a net cast onto society to achieve stronger social control.

There are pros and cons to the development of information and communications technologies (ICTs), of course. As advances in information technology, ICTs help to reduce the cost of participation in public affairs by increasing the channels for individuals to voice their demands to the government, furthering the development of democracy in a country (Buchstein, 1997; Hague & Loader, 1999). Despite the positive influence of ICTs on political development, they can also be exploited by authoritarian rulers to tighten their grip on power. In China, for instance, the state's firm hold of ICTs has made information technology into a tool for the government to control population migration and residency or to monitor messages exchanged online. This social control through ICTs clearly results in the intrusion of the state into individual privacy. It also reinforces the digital divide between farmers and urbanites. Chinese citizens with low credit scores do not usually manage to improve them, becoming marginalised. In other words, an authoritarian government controlling society through ICTs could also lead to increasing social inequality.

The health code system

The outbreak of COVID-19 became a global public health crisis at the end of 2019. As China was the most seriously hit country in the world at the beginning of the outbreak, the government developed a 'health code' system to track people's movements and record their health condition as a tool to manage the pandemic. The health code is an electronic pass used to identify citizens' risk of infection that is issued using data stored on a 'health code platform', which contains information such as personal ID numbers, telephone numbers, residential addresses and work units. As the system has developed, all people in China must register and carry a mobile device with their own health code as a travel permit when they move into public facilities, thus strengthening the government's capability to collect information on social dynamics and control the mobility of its citizens.

Clearly, the outbreak of COVID-19 did not weaken the CPC's ability to maintain social stability. Instead its emphasis on disease prevention and control has been part of its efforts to learn new technologies like the health code system in order to strengthen the maintenance of social stability and consolidate its rule.

Analysis and evaluation

According to the process of institutional autocratisation discussed in this chapter, the CPC has not abandoned its methods of repression and control during the process of reform and opening up. These have instead been reinforced since Xi Jinping took office, as illustrated in the establishment of the numerous regulations and institutions for stability maintenance. In principle, a certain tension should exist between traditionalism and the development of science and technology, which might create new political opportunities for democratisation. In China, however, the party-state system's monopoly over the development of science and technology has both strengthened its capacity to monitor its people and provided incentives for them to obey, resulting in the aforementioned system of 'scientific and technological stability maintenance'. As national governance and state-society relations during the Xi era have been marked by an overcorrection of the internal fragmentation and relative social autonomy in the Jiang and Hu eras, we would also like to discuss whether such an overcorrection has given rise to new problems.

Figure 8.4 presents our observations on changes in the authoritarian system during the Xi era. Based on the policies described in the previous section, we believe that the recentralisation, organisational solidification and policy orientation of China's power structure during the Xi era have ceased to emphasise negotiation or coordination, indicating that the regime is indeed moving towards institutional autocratisation. This will be explained point by point in the following paragraphs.

Authoritarian Institution	Features in the Xi era
Structure	Recentralisation
Organisation	Rigidificaiton
Policy Orientations	Non-bargained ICT Stability Maintenance

→ Institutional autocratisation

Figure 8.4: Institutional features of authoritarianism in the Xi era
Source: Authors' summary.

A top-level design to change a decentralised structure

Studying how the CPC formulates and implements its policies, we can often observe fragmented authoritarianism in the form of conflict between the interests of different departments where affairs that are being managed by different party and government ministries and commissions appear to have different objectives. To combat this fragmentation, Xi Jinping has proposed a top-level design that establishes several institutions through centralisation and attempts to transcend departmental sectionalism and vested interests. This includes the aforementioned National Security Commission, the Cyberspace Affairs Commission and the Comprehensively Deepening Reforms Commission. These three commissions are closely related to the work of stability maintenance.

The National Security Commission is naturally closely related to stability maintenance, and it coordinates the Political and Legal Affairs Commission and various departments related to this goal (see figure 8.3).

The Cyberspace Affairs Commission is primarily responsible for coordinating departments related to cyberspace management, including the Ministry of Industry and Information Technology, the Ministry of Public Security, the Ministry of Science and Technology, the Ministry of Culture, the Ministry of Finance, the Information Office and even the Ministry of Foreign Affairs and the CPC Publicity Department. It aims to improve the response speed and ability of the central government to monitor and guide public opinion.

The Deepening Reforms Commission mainly wields 'soft' power in stability maintenance by promoting the reform of livelihood construction and social undertakings. For instance, the commission reviewed and passed the 'Opinions on Further Promoting the Reform of the Household Registration System' (关于进一步推进户籍制度改革的意见, *guanyu jinyibu tuijin huji zhidu geige de yijian*), which relaxes the criteria for the settlement of migrant workers in cities and has a significant impact on population mobility and social stability. When the Lei Yang Incident (雷洋事件, *Lei Yang shijian*) garnered public attention throughout society, the commission also passed the Opinions on Deepening the Standardisation of Public Security Law Enforcement (关于深化公安执法规范化建设的意见, *guanyu shenhua gongan zhifa guifanhua jianshe de yijian*) in order to deal with the unaddressed problems of law enforcement in public security (Xinhuawang, 2016).

Rule by law and technological stability maintenance drastically reduce organisational flexibility

This chapter argues that the CPC's tools for stability maintenance not only involve explicit state violence but also reinforce 'legal construction'. This was also true as mentioned previously when Xi Jinping accelerated the formulation of laws related to stability maintenance upon taking office. This has been seen as carrying out the principle of 'rule by law', as it has been presented as a campaign to safeguard the people's rights through legislation. In reality, however, it has both legalised social control and incorporated it into the framework of a 'holistic approach to public security'. The above laws and regulations all elevate 'national security' to a level above all other values, which is a tremendous blow to the rights and interests of both citizens and non-citizens in China. In the aforementioned Amendment to the Criminal Law, the provisions for 'spreading rumours' make it more effective in combatting 'Big V' bloggers and limiting online speech. In this regard, China is contributing to rule *by* law and not the rule *of* law for the purpose of rationalising and legalising social control.

In either a totalitarian or authoritarian system, social control may involve the authoritarian use of the judiciary, the army, the police and even the secret police to instil fear in people. At the same time, the maintenance of social stability involves having incentives for people to consent voluntarily. Both coercion and consent are important abilities of contemporary states. This is what Antonio Gramsci has called hegemony, which implies the ideological advantage of the dominant class over social subordinates (Carnoy, 1984, pp. 65–88). Where traditional authoritarian regimes exert direct control from the outside to the inside, today's China can better analyse people's habits and preferences through information technology and instantly grasp behaviour and trajectories. This has certainly allowed the CPC to strengthen the state's capacity to identify radical opponents, which further decreases the costs for the regime to target and repress the opposition (Xu, 2021). Sesame Credit, for example, has analysed personal credit scores using credit histories, behavioural preferences, contractual capacities, identity traits and personal connections. While it appears to be a financial credit rating system, the public's usage of mobile phones, social media posts, online transactions and electronic payment transactions are all within its grasp.

More importantly, while Big Brother monitoring once required a proactive state and collecting information was expensive, the public in the new credit system willingly sends and updates their personal information with companies in the pursuit of higher credit ratings and more favourable shopping discounts. These companies in turn are fully connected to the state behind the scenes, affording it access to the relevant information. The so-called tech crackdown has allowed the party-state to utilise information technology to penetrate the private sector (Koss, 2021). Ringen (2016) believes that China's current model of social control has made it an unprecedented, even 'perfect' dictatorship. This is also why there has been a decrease in organisational flexibility with the rapid advancement of science and technology and the gradual development of social control tools.

A substantial reduction in policy negotiation and responsiveness

If we observe the institutional changes in China during the Xi era from the perspectives of party–government, central–local and state–society relations, a process of power centralisation emerges from the government to the party, from the local to the central and from society to the state. As mentioned above, it was once possible to believe that China would be able to maintain its flexibility, institutionalisation, high responsiveness, decentralisation and other important characteristics of political stability, but these characteristics began to disappear after Xi Jinping took office. While he has attempted to solve the problem of power separation within the system through centralisation and the establishment of top-level institutions, their effectiveness has yet to be evaluated. On the other hand, he has also strengthened social control. Although this has brought stability to society in the short term, it has also caused the regime to lose its past flexibility and resilience while simultaneously reducing the willingness of the government to consult, bargain with and respond to the social sector. The vitality of society and local governments is also suffering under this pressure. We cite the following examples to support this claim.

First, the Chinese Local Government Innovation Award (中国地方政府创新奖, *Zhongguo difang zhengfu chuangxin jiang*) was established in 2000 by the Central Compilation and Translation Bureau, the Central Party School of the CPC and Peking University. As the organisers had official authority and were associated with civil impartiality and professionalism, they quickly received responses from local governments. Judging from the list of previous awards, there have indeed been several initiatives in local and social institutional innovations that have received the attention of official media such as Xinhua News Agency and their evaluation results have even affected the promotions of local officials. Although there were discussions about 'innovation for winning' or 'political death', the related policy innovation and diffusion have also attracted considerable attention (Zhu, 2014). Since Xi Jinping took office, however, a shifting of power towards the upper levels of government has meant greater restrictions on the actions of local officials, drastically reducing the momentum of local innovations. Yu Keping (俞可平), the former director of the Central Compilation and Translation Bureau and now the current dean of the School of Government at Peking University, is the founder of the award. He stated: 'One of the prominent difficulties we currently face is the significant weakening of the momentum in local government innovations. Compared to the sixth award, applications for the seventh award were reduced by one-third and the enthusiasm for local government innovation has been declining.' (*Fenghuang Zixun*, 2015.)

Faced with the booming development of social organisations, the CPC has strengthened its authoritarian regime through an 'absorption' approach (Teets, 2014) alongside more familiar repressive means to quell their voices. In Guangdong, for example, the leaders of several worker rights NGOs were arrested and detained successively in 2015 (Chen, 2015). The liberal political magazine *Yanhuang Chunqiu* (炎黃春秋) was forced to suspend its publication in July 2016, and the civil think tank Unirule Institute of Economics (天则经济研究所, *tianze jingji yanjiusuo*) was forced to close owing to continuous government pressure in August 2019 (*Washington Post*, 2019). In 2018 and 2021, China launched a campaign to toughen its clampdown on illegal social organisations, which led to the shutdown of hundreds of unregistered social organisations. This crackdown has further squeezed Chinese civil society, as it signals that only organisations that receive official approval can survive. During Hu Jintao's rule, many NGOs provided relief after the 2008 Sichuan earthquake (Shieh & Deng, 2011); several volunteers participated in the Beijing Olympics; civil organisations and local governments achieved contingent symbiosis (Spires, 2011); and grassroots organisations implemented survival strategies (Fulda, Li & Song, 2012). The political opportunities that emerged during this period have virtually disappeared during the Xi Jinping era, and this short-lived civil society is suffocating.

Conclusion

This chapter has analysed the transition of China's authoritarian regime between the Hu and Xi eras and explored whether existing theories continue to be applicable to our understanding of the Chinese regime and its institutional stability from the three dimensions of structure, organisation and policy orientation. From a policy or theoretical perspective, it is not difficult to recognise that China has undergone a comprehensive evolution during the Xi era where the recentralisation of the power structure, the new rigidity of organisation and management, and the weakening of policy negotiations and absorption functions have all changed the nature of the Chinese political system. Therefore this chapter began by discussing the theoretical dialogue between authoritarian regimes and state–society relations. We showed that on the one hand, laws and regulations related to stability maintenance were intensively introduced to the system, stability maintenance departments were integrated and the centralised construction of top-level institutions such as the National Security Commission was undertaken. On the other hand, Xi also strengthened the suppression of power and reinforced the maintenance of stability through science and technology to prevent the rise of social forces. In the circumstances discussed, this no longer resembles the 'innovative social governance' proposed in the early days of Xi's presidency. This is not only in terms of its political centralisation but also in terms of the suppression of social forces and the regulation of speech. Drawing from the dialogue between theory and practice, this chapter therefore makes the following observations on current social governance and state–society relations in China and comes to the following conclusions.

Firstly, concerning state–society relations in China, the social sector currently lacks effective organisation. Social resistance is limited to small-scale rioting characterised by a lack of engagement across classes and issues, maintaining the party-state's absolute advantage. While signs of development appeared briefly in 2018, these were quickly suppressed. They therefore did not pose a threat to the regime and merely formed a situation that was 'stable but restless'. Nevertheless, the strengthening of social control has not eliminated the diversification of social power but has instead forced it into hibernation, further increasing the tension between stability maintenance and the protection of civil rights in China.

Secondly, the case of China can further verify the claim that authoritarian systems develop non-linearly and may transition from one authoritarian system to another rather than move towards democratisation (Hadenius & Teorell, 2007). China's political and social development in recent years has revealed that social control in the Hu and Wen eras was relatively relaxed. While China's political system is described in this chapter as consultative, bargained, flexible, responsive and one of soft authoritarianism, these adjectives are applicable only before the Xi era. Developments since his taking office have not only been a return to the old system but have also introduced science and technology into the government's system of social control. The current US–China trade war, the downward pressure on the domestic economy, the collapse of small- and medium-sized private enterprises, the rising unemployment rate and the increase in social autonomy are all factors that have placed more pressure on the government's stability maintenance. It is clear that institutional autocratisation will become increasingly prominent in China.

Finally, this chapter contends that while stability maintenance in the Xi era emphasises institutional construction and power centralisation, the system fails to protect human rights and legalises their suppression by government departments. This involves two risks. First, the system lacks resilience and innovation, rendering the regime vulnerable and unable to cope with sudden environmental changes. Second, Xi's 'cleaning up' of social organisations and the suppression of social power have caused difficulties for the survival of real NGOs. This evidently stems from considerations for the stability of the CPC regime, but undoubtedly adds to the risks for society as a whole. The fact that no national organisations are allowed to exist outside the CPC ensures that 'without the CPC, there would be chaos'. This can also be understood as the result of the state's abduction of society. When the state fails and there is no civil society to support it, further social disorder will ensue.

The world view of the CPC can be understood by its often-mentioned statement: 'the world is undergoing profound changes unseen in a century'. Under these circumstances, Xi has steered the party towards the changing world by building centralised political institutions with a strong capacity to control society coercively. At the Sixth Plenary Session (六中全会, *liu zhong quanhui*) of the 19th Central Committee on 11 November 2021, the CPC approved a rare Resolution on History that further strengthened Xi's hold on power in the party. It is only the third of its kind since the founding of the party—the first was passed by Mao Zedong in 1945 and the second by Deng Xiaoping in 1981. In the resolution, Xi has been characterised as having 'decisive significance' in the rejuvenation of the Chinese nation, and his position in the party has been elevated to a status similar to the two charismatic CPC leaders Mao and Deng. This recent case has shown again that the trend of building a hyper-stability structure seems to have reached the point of no return. If this is the case, future researchers who attempt to unravel politics in China will need to prepare to meet greater challenges when looking into a regime with a political contour that is wholly distinct from the China with which we are currently familiar.

References

Barnett, A. (1960) *Communist China and Asia: Challenge to American Policy.* Harper & Brothers

Brady, A. (2008) *Marketing Dictatorship: Propaganda and Thought Work in Contemporary China.* Rowman & Littlefield

Brady, A. (ed.) (2012) *China's Thought Management.* Routledge

Buchstein, H. (1997) 'Bytes that bite: The Internet and deliberative democracy.' *Constellations* 4(2): 248–63. doi.org/10.1111/1467-8675.00052

Carnoy, M. (1984) *The State and Political Theory.* Princeton University Press

Chen, M. (2015) 'China's latest crackdown on workers is unprecedented.' *Nation*, 15 December. www.thenation.com/article/chinas-latest-crackdown-on-workers-is-unprecedented

Dickson, B. (2021) *The Party and the People: Chinese Politics in the 21st Century.* Princeton University Press

DW News (2019) 'Say goodbye to powerful political and legal affairs commission: CCPRed Header Document shows the changing power structure.' *DW News*, 19 February. news.dwnews.com/china/big5/news/2019-02-01/60116357_all.html

Fenghuang Zixun [凤凰信息, Phoenix News Media] (2015) 'Zhengfu chuangxin juyou shifan zuoyong' [政府创新具有示范作用, Government innovation has a demonstrative effect]. 17 April. news.ifeng.com/a/20150417/43571890_0.shtml

Fewsmith, J. (2021) *Rethinking Chinese Politics.* Cambridge University Press

Fewsmith, J., & Nathan, A. (2019) 'Authoritarian resilience revisited: Joseph Fewsmith with response from Andrew J. Nathan.' *Journal of Contemporary China* 28(116): 167–79. doi.org/10.1080/10670564.2018.1511390

Friedrich, C., & Brzezinski, Z. (1956) *Totalitarian Dictatorship and Autocracy.* Harvard University Press

Fulda, A., Li, Y., & Song, Q. (2012) 'New strategies of civil society in China: A case study of the network governance approach.' *Journal of Contemporary China* 21(76): 675–93. doi.org/10.1080/10670564.2012.666837

Guojia Gonggong Xinyong Xinxi Zhongxin [国家公共信用信息中心, National Public Credit Information Centre] (2019) *2018 nian shixin heimingdan niandu fenxi baogao fabu* [2018年失信黑名单年度分析报告发布, Release of the annual analysis report of the blacklisting system for dishonesty, 2018]. 19 February. www.gov.cn/fuwu/2019-02/19/content_5366674.htm

Hadenius, A., & Teorell, J. (2007) 'Pathways from authoritarianism.' *Journal of Democracy* 18(1): 143–57. doi.org/10.1353/jod.2007.0009

Hague, B., & Loader, B. (1999) *Digital Democracy: Discourse and Decision-Making in the Information Age.* Routledge

Koss, D. (2021) 'Party building as institutional bricolage: Asserting authority at the business frontier.' *China Quarterly* 248(S1): 222–43. doi.org/10.1017/S0305741021000692

Landry, P. (2008) *Decentralized Authoritarianism in China: The Communist Party's Control of Local Elites in the Post-Mao Era.* Cambridge University Press

Lee, C., & Zhang, Y. (2013) 'The power of instability: Unraveling the microfoundations of bargained authoritarianism in China.' *American Journal of Sociology* 118(6): 1475–508. doi.org/10.1086/670802

Lewis, J. (1963) *Leadership in Communist China.* Cornell University Press

Lieberthal, K. (1992) 'Introduction: The fragmented authoritarianism model and its limitations.' In *Bureaucracy, Politics and Decision-Making in Post-Mao China*, ed. K. Lieberthal & D. Lampton, pp. 1–30. University of California Press

Lieberthal, K., and Oksenberg, M. (1988) *Policy Making in China: Leaders, Structures and Processes.* Princeton University Press

Linz, J. (1975) 'Totalitarian and authoritarian regimes.' In *Handbook of Political Science (3): Micropolitical Theory*, ed. F. Greenstein & N. Polsby, pp. 175–412. Addison-Wesley

—— (2000) *Totalitarian and Authoritarian Regimes.* Lynne Rienner

Linz, J., & Stepan, A. (1996) *Problems of Democratic Transition and Consolidation: Southern Europe, South America, Post-Communist Europe.* Johns Hopkins University Press

Mann, M. (1993) *The Sources of Social Power: The Rise of Classes and Nation-States, 1760–1914.* Cambridge University Press

Mertha, A. (2009) '"Fragmented authoritarianism 2.0": Political pluralization in the Chinese policy process.' *China Quarterly* 200: 995–1012. doi.org/10.1017/S0305741009990592

Nathan, A. (1992) 'Totalitarianism, authoritarianism, democracy: The case of China.' In *Case Studies in the Social Sciences*, ed. M. Cohen, pp. 235–56. M.E. Sharpe

—— (2003) 'China's changing of the guard: Authoritarian resilience.' *Journal of Democracy* 14(1): 6–17. doi.org/10.1353/jod.2003.0019

Petracca, M., & Xiong, M. (1990) 'The concept of Chinese neo-authoritarianism: An exploration and democratic critique.' *Asian Survey* 30(11): 1099–117. doi.org/10.2307/2644692

Petrova, T., & Tarrow, S. (2007) 'Transactional and participatory activism in the emerging European polity: The puzzle of East-Central Europe.' *Comparative Political Studies* 40(1): 74–94. doi.org/10.1177/0010414006291189

Quanguo Renmin Daibiao Dahui [全国人民代表大会, National People's Congress] (2015) *Zhonghua Renmin Gongheguo Xingfa Xiuzhengan (Jiu)* [中华人民共和国刑法修正案(九), Amendment (IX) to the Criminal Law of the People's Republic of China]. 29 August. npc.people.com.cn/n/2015/1126/c14576-27857512.html

—— (2016a) *Zhonghua Renmin Gongheguo Cishan Fa* [中华人民共和国慈善法, Charity Law of the People's Republic of China]. 19 March. www.npc.gov.cn/zgrdw/npc/dbdhhy/12_4/2016-03/21/content_1985714.htm

—— (2016b) *Zhonghua Renmin Gongheguo Jingwai Feizhengfu Zuzhi Jingnei Guanli Fa* [中华人民共和国境外非政府组织境内活动管理法, Law of the People's Republic of China on the Administration of Domestic Activities of Overseas Non-governmental Organisations]. 29 April. www.xinhuanet.com//politics/2016-04/29/c_1118765888.htm

—— (2016c) *Zhonghua Renmin Gongheguo Wanglu Anquan Fa* [中华人民共和国网络安全法, Cyber Security Law of the People's Republic of China], 7 November. www.xinhuanet.com/politics/2016-11/07/c_1119867015.htm

Renminwang [人民网, People.cn] (2021) 'Jiaoyubu: Ba Xi Jinping Xin Shidai Zhongguo Tese Shehui Zhuyi Sixiang quanmian rongru kecheng jiaocai' [教育部：把习近平新时代中国特色社会主义思想全面融入课程教材, Ministry of Education: Comprehensively incorporating Xi Jinping Thought on Socialism with Chinese Characteristics for a New Era into the Curriculum]. 24 August. edu.people.com.cn/BIG5/n1/2021/0824/c1006-32205602.html

Ringen, S. (2017) *The Perfect Dictatorship: China in the 21st Century*. Hong Kong University Press

Saich, T. (2021) *From Rebel to Ruler: One Hundred Years of the Chinese Communist Party*. Harvard University Press

Schurmann, F. (1966) *Ideology and Organisation in Communist China*. University of California Press

Shambaugh, D. (2008) *China's Communist Party: Atrophy and Adaptation.* University of California Press

Shieh, S., & Deng, G. (2011) 'An emerging civil society: The impact of the 2008 Sichuan earthquake on grass-roots associations in China.' *China Journal* 65: 181–94

Spires, A.J. (2011) 'Contingent symbiosis and civil society in an authoritarian state: Understanding the survival of China's grassroots NGOs.' *American Journal of Sociology* 117(1): 1–45. doi.org/10.1086/660741

Teets, J. (2013) 'Let many civil societies bloom: The rise of consultative authoritarianism in China.' *China Quarterly* 213: 1–20. doi.org/10.1017/S0305741012001269

—— (2014) *Civil Society under Authoritarianism: The China Model.* Cambridge University Press

Tsai, W.H., Wang, H.H., & Lin, R. (2021) 'Hobbling big brother: Top-level design and local discretion in China's social credit system.' *China Journal* 86: 1–20. doi.org/10.1086/714492

Walder, A.G. (1986) *Communist Neo-Traditionalism: Work and Authority in Chinese Industry.* University of California Press

Wang, S.S., Wang, H.H., & Tzeng, W.F. (2019) 'The nature of popular protest and the employment of repressive state capacity in China.' *Issues and Studies* 55(1): 1950004. doi.org/10.1142/S1013251119500048

Washington Post (2019) 'The shutdown of a liberal think tank is a huge setback for China.' 30 August. www.washingtonpost.com/opinions/the-shutdown-of-a-liberal-think-tank-is-a-huge-setback-for-china/2019/08/30/87a0c8a0-ca72-11e9-a1fe-ca46e8d573c0_story.html

Wright, T. (2010) *Accepting Authoritarianism: State–Society Relations in China's Reform Era.* Stanford University Press

Xinhuawang [新华网, Xinhua Net], 'Xi Jinping zhuchi zhaokai zhongyang quanmian shenhua gaige lingdao xiaozu di 24 ci huiyi' [习近平主持召开中央全面深化改革领导小组第二十四次会议, Xi Jinping chairs the 24th meeting of Central Leading Group for Comprehensively Deepening Reforms] (2016), 20 May. www.xinhuanet.com/politics/2016-05/20/c_1118904441.htm

Xu, X. (2021) 'To repress or to co-opt? Authoritarian control in the age of digital surveillance.' *American Journal of Political Science* 65(2): 309–25. doi.org/10.1111/ajps.12514

Zhongguo Jingjiwang [中国经济网, China Economic Net] (2015) '31 wei yuanshengji zhengfawei shuji quanbu xieren gongan tingzhang (biao)' [31位省级政法委书记全部卸任公安厅长(表), 31 secretaries of the Provincial Political and Legal Affairs Commission have left the office of the Director of the Public Security Department]. 24 July. district.ce.cn/newarea/sddy/201507/24/t20150 724_6033983.shtml

Zhu, X. (2014) 'Mandate vs championship: Vertical government intervention and diffusion of innovation in public services in authoritarian China.' *Public Management Review* 16(1): 117–39. doi.org/10.1080/14719037.2013.798028

9

Maintaining stability and authoritarian rule: Xi era in Xinjiang

Stefanie Kam Li Yee

This chapter contributes to the broader discussion on social and political control under the Xi Jinping administration by examining the party's evolving policies towards Xinjiang. It explains a dual-track approach to counterterrorism that underpins the Chinese party-state's increasingly repressive policies in the region. While most of the works on Xinjiang focus attention on the coercive aspects of the policies in Xinjiang, this book chapter draws attention to the security logics of the policy in Xinjiang with reference to the literature on regime type and counterterrorism. Specifically, it finds that in the Chinese case, the dual-track approach involves both a reactive counterterrorism that stresses the swift imposition of force and a more pre-emptive and preventive approach that encourages mass mobilisation to neutralise potential threats. The Xi administration has begun to pay significantly more attention to the second track, particularly since 2014 following a spate of attacks that included a bombing at an Urumqi railway station while Xi Jinping was visiting the region, which was blamed on Uyghur separatists. Since 2017, Xinjiang has witnessed the rise of a security state in the form of intensified securitisation, digital surveillance and the introduction of 're-education' centres (Kam & Clarke, 2021).

This chapter first proceeds with an overview of the connection between the party-state's view of the real and perceived threat of instability along its periphery and the background of the global War on Terror. China's approach to counterterrorism emphasises the construction of 'social stability and enduring peace' (社会稳定和长治久安, *shehui wending he changzhi jiuan*) while ensuring the legitimacy of the political regime's control over the region. The distinctive features of the CPC's stability maintenance approach to counterterrorism and how this approach is operationalised on the ground are addressed in the second section. It examines how the party-state has localised global counterterrorism approaches and combined coercion and surveillance for the purposes of immediate social and political control, employing social engineering programs that are designed to shape attitudes, identities and loyalties over the longer *durée*. This section also discusses how China responded to Xinjiang-related sanctions from the United States, the United Kingdom and Canada with tit-for-tat, defensive counter-retaliatory sanctions in its efforts to legitimise and rationalise its security approach in Xinjiang between 2020 and 2021 (Xinhuawang, 2021a; Council of the EU, 2021; Mai, 2021). While insights into China's counterterrorism strategy from the perspective of its domestic institutional structures have been well illustrated in a number of works, this chapter provides further insights into the peculiar features of the Chinese approach. In the third section, the chapter examines the challenges that have arisen during China's efforts to integrate the traditional model of reactive counterterrorism with a more pre-emptive and preventive approach, which emphasises mass mobilisation and the prosecution of a 'people's war on terror'.

Preserving stability in Xinjiang

In the post-Tiananmen era, the CPC has empowered its security apparatus to increase its capacity to suppress instability and social and political challenges that would challenge its hold on power. Since coming to power, Xi Jinping has sought to strengthen and consolidate state power by establishing a 'hyper-stability structure' augmented by new technologies (H.H. Wang & Tzeng, 2021). In parallel with these efforts, China has been grappling with the issue of how to integrate its ethnic minorities into the Chinese body politic in its quest to engineer the Chinese nation and state. These concerns about territorial integrity have been particularly acute along its borderland regions of Xinjiang, Tibet and Inner Mongolia. In the context of Xinjiang, the survival of the communist state is tied to the state's institutional capacity to prevent and suppress potential contestations that would pose a threat to its legitimate rule over the territory. Indeed, the Leninist predisposition of the Chinese communist system makes ruling elites particular sensitive to any mobilising processes that function outside its control (Saich, 2000).

Episodes of unrest such as the riots and inter-ethnic violence in Lhasa in March 2008 and Urumqi in July 2009 have challenged the state's exercise of control over society in China's peripheral regions (Hillman & Tuttle, 2016). Between 1990 and 2005, Xinjiang experienced more than 200 violent incidents ranging from terrorist attacks, assassinations, gunfights between Uyghur militias and local police, and large-scale ethnic riots (Cao et al., 2018). In the years following the Urumqi bombing on 5 July 2009, Xinjiang continued to experience violence and deadly clashes. In 2013 and 2014, authorities indicated that both an SUV attack in Tiananmen Square and an attack at a Kunming railway station were linked to the unrest in Xinjiang.

According to the Chinese government's data, ethnic separatists, religious extremists and terrorists have planned and carried out thousands of attacks in the period from 1990 to 2016. These include bombings, assassinations, poisonings, arson, assaults and riots in Xinjiang, and have resulted in the deaths of hundreds and enormous property losses (State Council Information Office of the People's Republic of China [SCIO], 2019). In a March 2019 white paper on Xinjiang, the Chinese government stated that 'since 2014, Xinjiang has destroyed 1,588 violent and terrorist gangs, arrested 12,995 terrorists, seized 2,052 explosive devices, punished 30,645 people for 4,858 illegal religious activities and confiscated 345,229 copies of illegal religious materials' (SCIO, 2019). According to a data chart of the number of terrorist incidents each year from 1990 to 2016 released by the Chinese government on 13 December 2021, the number of recorded terrorist incidents climbed from 111 in 2008 to 1,100 in 2015, a nearly tenfold increase (Guancha, 2021).

Since the start of the global war on terror, China's domestic counterterrorism and stability maintenance efforts are primarily directed towards containing the threat of the 'three forces' (三股势力, *san gu shi li*) of separatism, extremism and terrorism (SCIO, 2002). After the US withdrawal from Afghanistan, Beijing's principal security interest in Afghanistan has been to prevent the destabilisation of Xinjiang province, which could arise from the cross-border infiltration of what the Chinese government officially identifies as terrorist groups, including the East Turkistan Islamic Movement (ETIM). It is also interested in the protection of Chinese assets and nationals in Afghanistan. In this regard, the CPC believes the prevention, monitoring and eradication of real and potential challenges arising from terrorist threats along its periphery to be of critical importance to the broader preservation of stability (维稳, *weiwen*).

In the extant literature on counterterrorism, there is a consensus that regime type heavily conditions the outcomes of terrorism in a country. There is a relative consensus that authoritarian regimes possess an important counterterrorism tool owing to their ability to engage in counterterrorism efforts rapidly, given the relatively few restrictions on administrative power as compared to democracies (Wilson & Piazza, 2013). The PRC's counterterrorism strategies exhibit similarities with those of other governments in its ability to maximise the range of coercive and co-optive strategic responses to political conditions that foster terrorism. However, China's counterterrorism strategy also exhibits key departures from both liberal and authoritarian governments. This is exhibited in the strong political will of the CPC and the emphasis on internal stability, a vertical top-down control from the central level of government down to the provincial level, which constrains and shapes the types of action that can be taken by China's governmental agencies.

Counterterrorism approaches can be broadly categorised as operating within two models. The 'war' model stresses the actual restraint of terror through reactive operations, while the 'criminal justice' model relies on the retrospective deployment of criminal laws.

According to Crelinsten (2014), counterterrorism approaches can be analysed along coercive, proactive, persuasive, defensive and long-term dimensions, all of which may overlap with one another. Coercive counterterrorism approaches tend to rely on the use of force by state agents such as the police or military against combatants who are chosen on the basis of their political or ideological motives rather than a criminal justice approach, which stresses the importance of handling them according to criminal law proceedings. One such example would be the war model of counterterrorism, which deals with terrorism as an act of war or insurgency and emphasises the use of maximal force to overpower enemy combatants.

The rise of proactive counterterrorism approaches that stress the importance of preventing terrorism before it occurs has seen an increased focus on artificial intelligence (AI) in surveillance. This approach stresses the importance of expanding proactive measures in the realm of criminal justice, intelligence, criminal law and military operations as well as the importance of coordination across previously distinct domains, jurisdictions and agencies.

In contrast to coercive and proactive counterterrorism, persuasive counterterrorism involves understanding and dealing with the ideas that underpin the use of terrorism in social and political life. This approach stresses the importance of counterterrorism discourse and propaganda to win the 'hearts and minds' of the public in addition to counter-radicalisation efforts aimed at potential recruits and communities at risk and deradicalisation efforts aimed at active or imprisoned combatants.

Defensive counterterrorism emphasises both preventing terrorist attacks and mitigating the impact of successful ones. Lastly, long-term counterterrorism approaches stress the importance of addressing root causes and structural factors that create conditions for the growth and spread of terrorism.

These various dimensions noted by Crelinsten suggest the need to examine the nuances in the actual approaches and implementation chosen by states. Studies on the development of China's approach to counterterrorism indicate an evolution in its strategy, revealing the state's cognisance of the need for a more comprehensive counterterrorism model in response to increasing threats and concerns about the legitimacy of its counterterrorism practices. For instance, E. Li (2019) notes that China has relied on reactive responses to terrorist violence through crackdowns and criminalisation as well as control and cooperation. Similarly, Xie and Liu (2021) observe that China's securitisation of Xinjiang involves not only stability-focused counterterrorism operations but also the use of 'a performance-based, pre-emptive approach' that relies on civic participation. In this light, an examination of the CPC's exercise of political power in the context of its counterterrorism strategy in Xinjiang provides key insights into the CPC's mechanisms of governing in the global war on terror. It may perhaps even contribute to comparative political studies of the exercise of social and political control in a non-democratic context.

Surveillance, coercion and social engineering

The Chinese state has localised global counterterrorism approaches, adopting a dual-track approach to counterterrorism by integrating high-tech surveillance for the purposes of social and political control with coercion. This has been achieved through the expansion of the policing apparatus in Xinjiang and the introduction of new counterterrorism laws and regulations to promote the sinicisation of religion. Complementing surveillance and coercion is the Chinese party-state's reliance on more nuanced social engineering policies and programs such as deradicalisation through re-education and vocational training and the embedding of party cadres at the grassroots in the pursuit of stability along its periphery. The following paragraphs will provide a systematic overview of this dual-track approach to counterterrorism by disaggregating its specific features.

Surveillance: Prevention and control through the grid-management model

The Chinese party-state's securitisation and surveillance of Xinjiang are informed by its embrace of a techno-scientific planning and administrative mentality. Functioning to support and strengthen the central power's institutional capacity, surveillance technologies deployed in the service of counterterrorism and stability preservation allow authorities to prevent, monitor, control and regulate religious and cultural expression and to eradicate real and potential challenges arising from terrorist threats. The accelerated development of technologies has buttressed the Chinese party-state's institutional capacity by enhancing its strategies and techniques of control and management of the Xinjiang population and territory, which is seen as a core interest. Big-data surveillance functions as a coercive model of simplification, making society more amenable to 'knowing' by means of cataloguing, managing and disciplining the population and the space they live in.

Surveillance networks also strengthen the capacity for the state to bring previously independent information systems already in place in closer coordination with each other. To improve its counterterrorism intelligence in Xinjiang, authorities have put in place an integrated joint operations platform to enhance the Chinese state's capability for integrated joint combat operations (一体化联合作战, *yitihua lianhe zuozhan*) (D. Wang, 2016).

The Xinjiang model of anti-terrorism combines the 'intelligence war model' used by the US Army with the criminal model (both are aimed at eradicating the roots of terrorism and religious extremism) and a public security and governance model that is focused on achieving a normal social order. The intelligence war model of the United States emphasises 'full-spectrum intelligence; placing people in categories of insurgent, neutral and pro-regime change populations; breaking up social networks through targeted detentions; and "winning the hearts and minds" of those who remained' (D. Wang & Shan, 2016). This model has integrated Chinese policing elements and practices, reflecting a counterterrorism strategy that selectively draws on governing principles in Western contexts to supplement indigenous socialist practices tailored to local conditions. This point was highlighted in a 2016 article by two Chinese researchers from Xinjiang Police University, who point to how China's counterterrorism model incorporates key strengths from its own crime model, the public security model, the social governance model and the Xinjiang model (D. Wang & Shan, 2016). High-tech surveillance technologies supplement the party-state's reliance on enhanced coercive capacities to expand its reach across Xinjiang.

As a system of policing, the concept of grid-style social management was first implemented in the early 2000s in multiple cities in the mainland, including Shanghai and Beijing, where the system was used to prevent and control social order problems, like unrest. Throughout the early 2000s, pilot 'grid' policing programs implemented in multiple cities focused on harnessing modern technology to engage in the prevention and control of social order problems. Between 2014 and 2015, party officials recruited more than 10,000 new security personnel, including informal policing staff, and expanded the use of 'grid-style social management' (社会网络化管理, *shehui wangluohua guanli*) at the community-level, emphasising 'community grid-management work' (社区网络化管理工作, *shequ wangluohua guanli gongzuo*). This approach relies on dividing urban communities into smaller units and social management through strengthening and innovating social governance at the grassroots level. Key innovations in grid management included the use of CCTV cameras, mobile internet technologies and big data analytics to monitor each portion of the grid (M. Chen, 2017; Jing, 2013).

The reach of the party-state in Xinjiang further increased under Chen Quanguo, who was appointed Xinjiang's party secretary in August 2016. Chen began a process of expanding the grid-style management system by further incorporating surveillance technologies to supplement grassroots security patrols (Leibold, 2020). One key innovation under Chen was the introduction of 'convenience police stations' (便民警务站, *bianmin jingwu zhan*) within geometrically organised spatial zones. Functioning as critical nodes in each zone, they enhanced the state's capacity to control society through a network of surveillance in cities and villages.

Coercion: Sinicising religion through the law

The CPC has also increased its coercive powers via the implementation of new counterterrorism laws in conjunction with new regulations for regulating religious expression. In this case, the party-state's instrumental use of politico-legal discourse is reflected in the use of counterterrorism laws and regulations on religious expression to control and monitor spaces of religious thought and expression. They are also used to communicate the degree of severity that central authorities expect politico-legal functionaries to apply to terrorist crimes.

In the Chinese context, legal codes and legislative procedures are imbued with a political function as they are designed to preserve stability and ensure the CPC's legitimacy (Trevaskes, 2016). The law has been described as a 'frail weapon' that has not weakened administrative arbitrariness in the everyday exercise of control and particularly in the CPC's efforts to fashion a domestic rule of law (Keith & Lin, 2003, p. 623; O'Brien & Li, 2004, p. 76). The development of counterterrorist politico-legal instruments reflects the CPC's capacity to deploy legal instruments to deal with real and perceived threats to instability. One example of the Chinese party-state's efforts to promote the sinicisation of religion was its May 2013 issuance of Document No. 11, entitled 'Several Guiding Opinions on Further Governing Illegal Religious Activities and Curbing the Infiltration of Religious Extremist Thought in Accordance with the Law' (关于进一步依法治理非法宗教活动、遏制宗教极端思想渗透工作的若干指导意见, *guanyu jinyibu yifa zhili feifa zongjiao huodong, ezhi zongjiao jiduan sixiang shentou gongzuo de ruogan zhidao yijian*). The document defined the boundaries between ethnic customs, normal religious practices and extremist expressions. It contained a list of 75 signs of illegal religious activities, including abstaining from alcohol and cigarettes, listening to unauthorised religious teachings, not attending mandatory political ideology classes, not attending mandatory flag-raising ceremonies and not publicly grieving at funerals (G. Pan, 2014). Document No. 11 was updated in 2014 by Document No. 28, entitled 'Several Opinions on Further Strengthening and Improving the Work with

Regard to Islam' (关于进一步加强和完善伊斯兰教工作的若干意见, *guanyu jinyibu jiaqiang he wanshan yisilanjiao gongzuo de ruogan yijian*). The detailed contents of both documents are unavailable to the public.

In November 2014, Xinjiang legislators revised an existing regional law called the XUAR Regulations on Religious Affairs (新疆维吾尔自治区宗教事务条例, *xinjiang weiwuer zizhiqu zongjiao shiwu tiaoli*). In July 2017, following the passage of the national counterterrorism law in December 2015, regional authorities adopted a new regional law referred to as 'Measures for the Implementation of the "Counter-Terrorism Law of the People's Republic of China" in Xinjiang Uygur Autonomous Region' (新疆维吾尔自治区实施《中华人民共和国反恐怖主义法》办法, *xinjiang weiwuer zizhiqu shishi 'zhonghua renmin gongheguo fan kongbu zhuyi fa' banfa*). In October 2018, authorities in Xinjiang revised an existing piece of legislation that was passed in March 2017, effective the following month, entitled 'XUAR Regulations on De-extremisation' (新疆维吾尔自治区去极端化条例, *xinjiang weiwuer zizhiqu qujiduanhua tiaoli*).

The regulations were announced at the 12th National People's Congress and specifically define the terms 'radicalisation' (极端化, *jiaduan hua*) and radical extremism (极端主义, *jiduan zhuyi*). Radicalisation is defined as a condition of being under the influence of extremism and tainted by religious extremist thought and ideas to the extent where one's speech and behaviour become disruptive to normal life and productiveness. Radical extremism is defined as claims and actions that distort religious doctrines or the use of methods to incite hatred, discrimination and violence. More importantly, the regulations also provide directives to mobilise Xinjiang's functionaries into action, allowing local governments to utilise 'vocational training centres' to 'educate and transform' individuals who are found to harbour extremist thinking.

Social engineering: Deradicalisation through 're-education' and 'vocational training'

Deradicalisation in Xinjiang serves as a means for the Chinese state to re-engineer Uyghurs socially through re-education and vocational training as a form of 'counterterrorist stability maintenance' (反恐维稳, *fankong weiwen*) and 'de-extremisation'(去极端化, *qu jiduan hua*) aimed at preventing radicalisation, educating and preventing the radicalised from committing terrorist attacks, treating the 'symptoms and the root' (Xinhua News, 2019). The basic premise for undertaking deradicalisation has been the realisation that current efforts that merely employ military and law enforcement techniques are insufficient to deter a vulnerable segment of the population from becoming radicalised and recruited by terrorists (Rabasa, 2010). In the 2000s, deradicalisation strategies introduced in such countries as Yemen, Saudi Arabia, Pakistan and Indonesia ranged from a reliance on community engagement methods to engaging terrorist detainees in theological debates in order to debunk radical extremist ideologies and disengage them from violence (Azam & Fatima, 2017; Casptack, 2015; Horgan & Braddock, 2010; Porges, 2010).

With the outbreak of the Syrian civil war in 2011 and the emergence of ISIS in mid-2014, there has been a renewed emphasis on deradicalisation (Honig & Yahel, 2019). Countries have focused their strategies on preventing the radicalisation and recruitment of fighters returning from Syria and Iraq. With a global discourse of deradicalisation and growing evidence that Uyghurs had travelled abroad to take part in militancy, Chinese officials and academics began to understand that global deradicalisation strategies needed to be tailored to the Chinese context to fight domestic violent extremism (Z. Zhou, 2019). The CPC proposed that detention and re-education would make the population psychologically and politically resilient to religious extremism (Mao & Cui, 2017). The focus therefore would be on inoculating a vulnerable section of the population to avoid becoming radicalised and recruited by terrorist and extremist groups abroad. Physical counterterrorism operations would in turn selectively draw on counterinsurgency principles and Western law enforcement models in combination with domestic policing practices suited to local conditions, enabling the state to thwart terror plots through traditional counterinsurgency tactics and intelligence aimed at militarily degrading the physical existence of terrorist groups on Chinese soil.

On 16 August 2019, China's State Council Information Office released a White Paper titled 'Vocational Skills Education and Training in Xinjiang' (新疆的职业技能教育培训工作, *xinjiang de zhiye jineng jiaoyu peixun gongzuo*) outlining terrorism and extremism as 'common enemies of human society' and the shift in the threat landscape defined by 'new circumstances'. With Xinjiang as the 'main battlefield of China's fight against terrorism and de-extremisation', the document asserted that Beijing must not only deal with 'terrorist crimes in accordance with the law' but also 'educate and rescue personnel infected with religious extremism and minor crimes' in order to treat 'both symptoms and the root causes' (Xinhua News, 2019). According to the document, education and training would promote development and increase the overall income of its targets and help Xinjiang 'achieve social stability and lasting peace'. Such efforts complement civic projects such as Visit, Benefit and Gather (访惠聚, *fang hui ju*) in which the party-state embeds cadres in Uyghur villages across Xinjiang as a way of engineering stability at the grassroots. These cadres are tasked with a range of responsibilities that include serving as propagandists for government policies, providing training and basic legal education, and conducting home visits to local villagers to provide individual aid.

China's legitimisation of its deradicalisation strategy in Xinjiang

Beijing has adopted a range of responses within the international community for its policies in Xinjiang. It has engaged in conflict avoidance through denial; established a status quo through the legalisation and institutionalisation of its vocational and educational training centres; and pursued a proactive defence through the rationalisation of its policies and de-escalation of the issue into the realm of 'normal politics' through defensive rhetorical and legal measures in the form of propaganda, official statements, counter-sanctions and its passage of an anti-foreign sanctions law. China has made use of this law along with counter-sanctions as it responds to international criticism and unilateral sanctions by the United States, United Kingdom and Canada.

Phase 1: 'Conflict avoidance' through denial of the existence of vocational and educational training centres

Initially, China responded to international scrutiny over its vocational and educational training centres by denying their existence. By avoiding direct confrontation with the international community, its initial response was one of conflict avoidance. At the Committee on the Elimination of Racial Discrimination on 13 August 2018, the permanent representative of China to the United Nations Office at Geneva, Yu Jianhua, specifically stated that 'there were no such things as re-education centres or counterterrorism training centres in Xinjiang' and that authorities in Xinjiang had 'undertaken special campaigns to clamp down on violent terrorist activities according to the law and had put on trial and imprisoned a number of criminals involved in severe offences'. Those involved in 'minor offences' were 'provided with assistance and education to assist them in their rehabilitation and reintegration'. Yu also stated that those in attendance were not denied legal rights or subject to arbitrary detention or ill-treatment (Office of the High Commissioner of Human Rights, 2018). The United Front Work Department official Hu Lianhe asserted that 'criminals involved only in minor offences' were assigned to 'vocational education and employment training centres to acquire employment (*China Daily*, 2018).

Phase 2: Establishing the status quo through the legalisation and institutionalisation of the vocational and educational training centres

Following the initial denial of the existence of the centres, the Chinese government's normalisation of securitisation in Xinjiang was reflected in its legalisation. In October 2018, Xinjiang authorities revised the March 2017 'XUAR Regulations on De-extremisation'. A new clause was added specifically to state that 'Governments at the county level and above can set up education and transformation organisations and supervising departments such as vocational training centres to educate and transform people who have been influenced by extremism' (Gan & Lau, 2018). The law specified that under the education and transformation program, participants at the training centre would undergo training in spoken and written Chinese and in aspects of the law and other regulations, receive ideological education to eliminate extremism, and treatment and behavioural correction to transform their extremist ideologies before returning to society and their families.

The regulations provided directives to mobilise Xinjiang's functionaries into action, allowing local governments to utilise 'vocational training centres' to 'educate and transform' individuals found to harbour extremist thinking in line with efforts to eliminate religious extremism in three areas. The first was to educate individuals in the common language of the country to increase their 'civic awareness', which would prepare the way to bridge their employment skills, enhance their acceptance of new things and strengthen their mastery of science and technology. The second was to educate them in legal knowledge in areas including criminal law, national security, anti-terrorism, the XUAR's anti-extremist regulations, civil law, marriage and compulsory education. The third was to provide professional skills training in areas such as garment processing, repair and construction, beauty salons and food processing. The White Paper 'Vocational Skills Education and Training in Xinjiang' of August 2019 outlined the state's intent to 'educate' and 'rescue' those infected by radical ideologies (Xinhua News, 2019).

Phase 3: De-escalating the Xinjiang issue into the realm of 'normal' politics

In the third stage, the Chinese government endeavoured to de-escalate the securitisation of the Uyghurs. Following the approval in the US Congress of the Uyghur Human Rights Policy Act in December 2019, Xinjiang's deputy party chief Shohrat Zakir at a State Council Information Office press briefing dismissed the bill as 'crude meddling in China's internal affairs'. Without disclosing the numbers currently or previously held in the centres, Zakir stated that attendees had 'graduated' and found stable jobs while village officials, farmers and unemployed high school graduates continued to enrol on a rolling basis in programs that allowed them to 'come and go freely' (Y. Wang, 2019).

On 5 and 7 December 2019, the Chinese state media channel CGTN also released two documentaries on its 'anti-terrorism efforts in Xinjiang' and the role of the East Turkistan Islamic Movement (ETIM) in 'plotting terrorist attacks in China' titled *Fighting Terrorism in Xinjiang* and *The Black Hand— the ETIM and Terrorism in Xinjiang*. At the Third Xinjiang Central Work Forum held on 25 and 26 September 2020, Xi emphasised the importance of 'casting Chinese collective consciousness as the main line' (以铸牢中华民族共同体意识为主线, *yi zhulao zhonghua minzu gongtongti yishi wei zhuxian*) while stressing that since the vocational and educational training centres were introduced there had been 'no terrorist attacks in Xinjiang in the last three years' (Xinhuawang, 2020).

Finally, China has also adopted defensive countermeasures in response to sanctions by the United States, the United Kingdom and Canada. From Beijing's perspective, these have been in defence of its response in Xinjiang to counter unilateral sanctions initiated by foreign countries against China and to safeguard China's sovereignty, security and development interests. This is reflected in the following exchanges. On 13 July 2020, Beijing responded with a tit-for-tat measure over US sanctions on Chinese individuals and entities. On 22 March 2021, Beijing responded to US sanctions on Chinese government departments and individuals by banning four UK entities and 10 UK individuals from entering China. On 26 and 27 March 2021, Beijing responded to sanctions by the United Kingdom, the United States and Canada on Chinese individuals and entities by banning entry, restricting businesses and freezing the assets of entities and individuals in those countries. On 21 December 2021, Beijing also utilised its newly passed anti-foreign sanctions law of 10 June 2021, by imposing countersanctions in response to US sanctions on Chinese individuals.

The dilemmas of a dual-track counterterrorism strategy

This chapter has so far discussed the CPC's reliance on coercion, surveillance and social engineering efforts in Xinjiang and its legitimisation of counterterrorism and deradicalisation policies there. The following section explains the dilemma that has emerged in the course of China's stability maintenance and counterterrorism efforts. It is now endeavouring to introduce a traditional model of reactive counterterrorism, which stresses a strike first and strike hard approach via the imposition of force. It is striving to integrate and implement this with a pre-emptive and preventive approach that fuses high-tech surveillance and monitoring capabilities with mass mobilisation similar to that of the Mao era.

In the pursuit of greater political and social control in Xinjiang, the Chinese party-state has implemented a dual-track counterterrorism strategy, integrating the traditional model of reactive counterterrorism with a more pre-emptive and preventive approach. It is endeavouring to rely on coercive capacities, surveillance and monitoring while also pursuing whole-of-society efforts to engineer stability through mass mobilisation like that of the Mao era. As a result of this unique strategy, several unintended consequences have arisen at the grassroots level.

This is first evident in the practice of implementing whole-of-society counterterrorism efforts. Notably, Article 5 of the Anti-Terrorism Law of the People's Republic of China (中华人民共和国反恐怖主义法, *zhonghua renmin gongheguo fan kongbuzhuyi fa*), which took effect in 2016, states that the work of anti-terrorism should 'adhere to the principle of combining specialised work with the mass line, focusing on prevention, combining punishment and prevention and pre-emptive control of the enemy and maintaining the principle of being proactive'. It therefore requires the integration of 'elite task forces' (专门工作, *zhuanmen gongzuo*) with 'mass line' (群众路线, *qunzhong luxian*) in counterterrorism work.

Mao's strategy of the 'people's war' emphasised the vital importance of relying on grassroots movements in asymmetric warfare to battle foreign invaders and bring about class emancipation. In the context of China's counterterrorism strategy in Xinjiang, the discourse of the people's war has surfaced in official speeches linking it to the struggle against terrorism (Xinhuawang, 2014). In 2013, Xinjiang's party secretary, Zhang Chunxian, called for the party to improve its abilities in 'publicising, educating, organising and serving the masses' and to 'unite all ethnic groups' in the 'people's war on terror'. The participation of the masses is also inscribed in several sections of the aforementioned Anti-Terrorism Law (notably, articles 5 and 44) (Xinhuawang, 2015).

As a vital element of China's counterterrorism strategy, the mass-line approach hinges on the reconfiguration of Mao's strategy of the 'people's war' in the context of Xi's 'people's war on terror'. For Mao, the crux of the strategy's efficacy lay in the ability to mobilise grassroots movements in asymmetric warfare to battle foreign invaders and to bring about class emancipation. The launch of the 'people's war on terror' in 2014 occurred in parallel with the campaign to 'strike hard' in Xinjiang. The combined force of these two campaign strategies generated an all-out approach to security and stability focusing on 'proactive combat against terrorism' and a subsequent expansion in the state's coercive capabilities in Xinjiang. This was evident in the rise in the number of contract-based police and security-related positions being advertised in Xinjiang during this period (Zenz & Leibold, 2020, p. 4) and a tangible increase in arrests. Xinjiang authorities reported 27,164 arrests in 2014, a rise of 95 per cent from the previous year's figures and a 59 per cent total increase in the number of criminal cases handled by Xinjiang courts since 2013 (*Wall Street Journal*, 2015).

The people's war on terror encompasses the three aspects of building understanding and awareness of the dangers of extremism and terrorism through mass deradicalisation propaganda, counteracting extremism and terrorism through grassroots deradicalisation activities, and providing reward mechanisms to incentivise tip-offs about extremism and terrorism (Xinlang Xinwen, 2017; Global Times, 2016; Renminwang, 2015). The people's war employs a mass line system to apprehend terrorists and to gather and report vital information about suspects and alleged terrorists to authorities through a mobilisation of the local population, including Uyghurs.

A dilemma has arisen from this strategy owing to the assumption that the agentive potential of citizens in counterterrorism is and should be fused with the state's. In this context, the term 'people's war on terror' is underpinned by the lack of clear boundaries between the state and society, and performances of security often merely reproduce the logic that subjects are passive docile bodies produced through the micro-physics of disciplinary (state-led) power. However, there is very little room or incentive for the masses to become actively involved with the counterterrorism decision-making and implementation process.

Another area where the party-state has encountered challenges in the practice of surveillance, coercion and social engineering is in the effective integration of data collected under the grid-management system (Y. Li, 2016). Governance through the grid-management system is more fragmented than assumed for several reasons. There is an absence of a precise legal framework concerning the regulation of grid management, a lack of clear administrative boundaries across the relevant departments at the lower level, and a weakness in the administrative powers of grassroots and social organisations to help advance grid-management work at the community level (C. Zhou, 2016).

Kevin O'Brien and Li Lianjiang have observed the dynamic interplay at work between the local party-state and its societal challengers in administrative litigation procedures. In this regard, the fragmentation of the surveillance apparatus in Xinjiang reflects the nature of the Chinese bureaucracy, which is characterised by multilayered dimensions and 'less a monolith than a hodgepodge of disparate actors, some of whom have multiple identities and conflicting interests' (O'Brien & Li, 2004, pp. 93–4). As Cabestan (2020) observes, this is manifested in the tensions between China's 'digitalised society and surveillance system that is more repressive in some localities and more flexible in others, as is the case with the Chinese bureaucracy in general'. These observations on the 'segmented and layered structure' of the party-state are essential for understanding the nature of the state's everyday exercise of control in its counterterrorism and stability maintenance work in Xinjiang.

A third dilemma that has arisen during the Chinese state's dual-track approach to counterterrorism is the effective mobilisation of the masses in the people's war on terror owing to constraints posed by China's domestic institutional structures. Their influence on the country's counterterrorism strategy is well noted in a number of studies. For instance, Pokalova (2013) notes that political regime types heavily shape counterterrorism procedures and policies, which include accountability to the electorate and the use of repression to narrow political opportunities for terrorist consolidation. Similarly, Wayne (2009, pp. 253–5) argues that the CPC's approach in Xinjiang is defined by its strong political will. This is underpinned by the party's emphasis on self-preservation, the close connection between how the party-state views both internal and external security threats, and the popular demand for internal stability. In addition, Odgaard and Nielsen (2014, pp. 539, 554) have noted that owing to vertical top-down control from the central to the local levels, which has created 'constraints and possibilities that define the types of actions that can be taken by governmental agencies', the tendency for the top-down imposition of policies via assimilation or exclusion by force can also occur at the expense of human rights and dignity.

In the context of Xinjiang, the cadre accountability system acts as an important constraint on cadre behaviour and shapes the development and implementation of security policies in Xinjiang in several ways. As stability is one of the most important criteria for evaluating cadres, local officials focus on measurable and quantifiable outcomes rather than meaningful engagement with the local population. In Xinjiang, this is evident in the way local officials perform stability maintenance tasks largely to meet required quotas for re-education detainees. Local officials in Xinjiang respond to the demand for stability maintenance by pursuing quick-fix solutions to meet short-term goals as a means of securing their careers. They therefore display a preference for the war model of counterterrorism, which relies on intrusive measures in the pursuit of 'social stability and long-term peace'. As noted by Hillman and Tuttle (2016), local officials in subsidised regions are not only opportunistic with fiscal transfers but also display their fidelity to the policy regime in self-promotion and criticise competitors for not making adequate contributions.

Conclusion

An examination of China's dual-track counterterrorism strategy in Xinjiang reveals that the Chinese party-state has increased its coercive powers through expanded policing, the introduction of new counterterrorism laws and regulations for controlling religious expression, and high-tech surveillance. At the same time, this approach has been augmented by the integration of more pre-emptive and preventive approaches designed to engineer stability at the grassroots. As can be seen in the Chinese party-state's social engineering efforts, the latter has led to the 'people's war on terror', a campaign in the Xi era to revive the Mao-era mass line approach that relies on mobilising the masses. This partnership of stability is forged through top-down institutionalised 're-education' and 'vocational training' and by embedding party cadres at the grassroots. These cadres serve to transform their targets through education and persuasion as they are positioned to serve as propagandists for government policies. They are tasked with providing skill training and basic legal education and conducting home visits to Uyghur households in rural villages to provide individual aid.

At the same time, counterterrorism and stability preservation have engendered unintended consequences. The party-state's dual-track strategy has implemented surveillance and coercion on the one hand and social engineering programs on the other. Surveillance and coercion entail a range of measures that include high-tech surveillance technologies, 'grid-style social management' in the form of 'convenience police stations', education and persuasion. Social engineering programs involve the embrace of a populist approach that allows the state to penetrate the grassroots by co-opting the masses, including Han cadres and Uyghurs alike, to gather information on villagers and engineer stability at the grassroots. These pre-emptive and preventive approaches appear to encourage civic participation by fostering partnerships between the government and community in line with the principle of 'combining specialist work with the mass line'. As the cadre accountability system emphasises stability as a key performance indicator, a key dilemma for the Chinese party-state is to exert sovereign control over the territory through force while ensuring a genuine and organically driven 'partnership of stability' with the masses in the fight against terrorism.

The role of the masses in the people's war on terror has been obscured by impediments to the upward flow of opinions and a more agentive role of the public in shaping its conceptualisation, implementation and experience. It is also hampered by the cadre accountability system's constraints. Contrary to the prevailing assumption that the state operates like a well-oiled and coherent machine, authorities continue to be encumbered in the implementation of big-data surveillance by practical limitations and hurdles as well as fragmentation at the horizontal level This makes community-based surveillance difficult to realise. Local officials have responded to the demand for observable, quantifiable and attributable performance tasks and criteria by conceptualising security in terms of performative acts—that is, the repetitive enactment of activities and capabilities that are merely equated with security as an outcome.

Despite the dilemmas that have emerged in the course of the Chinese party-state's implementation of its counterterrorism and stability maintenance work in Xinjiang, a greater challenge to the CPC's legitimacy appears to be coming from the potential erosion of the partnership of stability (Cliff, 2012). Some of the tensions observed between local officials in their performance of security work and local communities highlight the gaps in this partnership and its asymmetrical nature at the level of grassroots implementation. Han Chinese have been migrating out of Xinjiang, showing a decrease from 8.83 million (40 per cent of the region's total population) in 2010 to 8.6 million in 2015 (Lau, 2019). In many of these instances, Han Chinese are motivated to move to the interior provinces where there are more job opportunities and fewer restrictions on their personal freedoms. The unintended consequence of China's pursuit of counterterrorism and stability maintenance has been an increased atmosphere of hostility and communal mistrust towards the Uyghurs, which has affected inter-societal trust and solidarity. In the long term, this could evidently influence future generations of Han settlers in Xinjiang by undermining the extent to which they can be relied on to serve as a bridge between their ethnic minority counterparts and the state.

After Chen Quanguo's high-pressure stability maintenance approach to governance in Xinjiang from 2017 to 2021, the incoming Xinjiang party secretary aims to restore economic growth and to 'normalise' (常态化, *changtaihua*) Xinjiang's counterterrorism and ethnic stability issues according to the 'rule of law' (法治化, *fazhihua*) (Byler, 2022). In December 2021, the central government appointed former Guangdong governor Ma Xingrui as Xinjiang's new party secretary (Xinhuawang, 2021b). The appointment of a new party secretary in Xinjiang came on the heels of the Biden administration's passage of the Uyghur Forced Labour Prevention Act. The personnel reshuffling signalled that Ma had effectively secured a seat on the Politburo's 25-member panel in the months before China's 20th Party Congress in 2022 (Lee, 2021).

While Ma's governing approach to Xinjiang has not evinced a stark departure from the previous policy emphasis on stability, his approach subtly differs from Chen Quanguo's. For instance, Ma has reportedly refrained from formalism and bureaucratic tendencies, removed controversial stability maintenance measures and sought to restore vitality to society in order to bring back a sense of normalcy (Mu, 2022).

Ma's experience as the governor of Guangdong and his background in the defence and technology sectors are also believed to be helpful in guiding Xinjiang's economic development in line with Xi Jinping's emphasis on 'high-quality economic development', which was stressed at the Third Central Symposium on Xinjiang Work. In the months following his appointment, Xinjiang reportedly signed cooperation agreements with central enterprises worth a total of RMB 611.706 billion with plans to invest RMB 108.62 billion in various industries involving petrochemicals, coal, clean energy, equipment manufacturing and infrastructure construction by the end of 2022 (Mu, 2022). Under Xi Jinping's stewardship, Ma confronts an uphill task in governing Xinjiang: he must demonstrate competency in restoring economic growth and ensuring stability in line with the rule of law in the region while proving his loyalty to the leadership.

References

Azam, Z., & Fatima, S.B. (2017) 'Mishal: A case study of a deradicalisation and emancipation program in Swat Valley, Pakistan.' *Journal for Deradicalisation* 11: 1–29

Byler, D. (2022) 'In Xinjiang, a new normal under a new chief—and also more of the same.' SupChina, 2 March. supchina.com/2022/03/02/in-xinjiang-a-new-normal-under-a-new-chief-and-also-more-of-the-same

Cabestan, J.P. (2020) 'The state and digital society in China: Big brother Xi is watching you!' *Issues and Studies* 56(1): 2040003. doi.org/10.1142/S101325 1120400032

Cao, X., Duan, H., Liu, C., Piazza, J.A., & Wei, Y. (2018) 'Digging the "ethnic violence in China" database: The effects of inter-ethnic inequality and natural resources exploitation in Xinjiang.' *China Review* 18(2) 121–54. www.jstor.org/stable/26435650

Casptack, A. (2015) 'Deradicalization programs in Saudi Arabia: A case study.' Middle East Institute, 10 June. www.mei.edu/publications/deradicalization-programs-saudi-arabia-case-study

Chen, M. [陈梦媛] (2017) 'Xinjiang wanggehua zhili tixi de youhua yanjiu' [新疆网格化治理体系的优化研究, Construction on the optimization of the grid-based management system in Xinjiang]. Master's thesis. Xinjiang Normal University

China Daily (2018) 'Slandering Xinjiang as "no rights zone" against fact, Chinese official told UN panel.' 14 August. www.chinadaily.com.cn/a/201808/14/WS5b7260a6a310add14f385a92.html

Cliff, T. (2012) 'The partnership of stability in Xinjiang: State-society interactions following the July 2009 unrest.' *China Journal* 68: 79–105. doi.org/10.1086/666581

Council of the EU (2021) 'EU imposes further sanctions over serious violations of human rights around the world' (press release, 22 March). www.consilium.europa.eu/en/press/press-releases/2021/03/22/eu-imposes-further-sanctions-over-serious-violations-of-human-rights-around-the-world

Crelinsten, R. (2014) 'Perspectives on counterterrorism: From stovepipes to a comprehensive approach.' *Perspectives on Terrorism* 8(1): 2–15. www.jstor.org/stable/26297097

Gan, N., & Lau, M. (2018) 'China changes law to recognise "re-education camps" in Xinjiang.' *South China Morning Post*, 10 October. www.scmp.com/news/china/politics/article/2167893/china-legalises-use-re-education-camps-religious-extremists

Global Times (2016) 'Xinjiang zhongjiang 6 ming jubao baokong zhongda xiansuo qunzhong jiangjin da 220 wan' [新疆重奖6名举报暴恐重大线索群众 奖金达220万, Xinjiang rewards 6 people who report major clues about violence and terrorism]. 9 October. mil.huanqiu.com/article/9CaKrnJXXxI

Guancha (2021) 'Duoduan Xinjiang baokongan huamian shouci pilu! Baotu shenzhi kansha ziji shoushang tonghuo' [多段新疆暴恐案画面首次披露！暴徒甚至砍杀自己受伤同伙, Multiple scenes of Xinjiang violence and terror cases revealed for the first time! The thugs even slashed and killed their wounded accomplices]. 14 December. www.guancha.cn/politics/2021_12_14_618407_3.shtml

Hillman, B., & Tuttle, G. (eds) (2016) *Ethnic Conflict and Protest in Tibet and Xinjiang: Unrest in China's West*. Columbia University Press. doi.org/10.7312/hill16998

Honig, O., & Yahel, I. (2019) 'A fifth wave of terrorism? The emergence of terrorist semi-states.' *Terrorism and Political Violence* 31(6): 1210–28. doi.org/10.1080/09546553.2017.1330201

Horgan, J., & Braddock, K. (2010) 'Rehabilitating the terrorists? Challenges in assessing the effectiveness of deradicalisation programs.' *Terrorism and Political Violence* 22(2): 267–91. doi.org/10.1080/09546551003594748

Jing, X. [井西晓] (2013) 'Tiaozhan yu biange: Cong wanggehua guanli dao wanggehua zhili—jiyu chengshi jiceng shehui guanli de biange' [挑战与变革：从网格化管理到网格化治理—基于城市基层社会管理的变革, Challenges and changes: From grid management to grid governance—based on the transformation of urban grassroots social management]. *Lilun Tansuo* [理论探索, Theoretical Exploration] 1(199): 102–5

Kam, S., & Clarke, M. (2021) 'Securitisation, surveillance and "de-extremization" in Xinjiang.' *International Affairs* 97(3): 625–42. doi.org/10.1093/ia/iiab038

Keith, R., & Lin, Z. (2003) 'The "Falun Gong problem": Politics and the struggle for the rule of law in China.' *China Quarterly* 175: 623–42. doi.org/10.1017/S0305741003000377

Lau, M. (2019) 'Wanted: Chinese cadres to hold Beijing's line in Xinjiang as Han Chinese head for the exits.' *South China Morning Post*, 4 December. www.scmp.com/news/china/politics/article/3040628/wanted-chinese-cadres-hold-beijings-line-xinjiang-han-head

Lee, L.C. (2021) 'What can we expect from Xinjiang's new Party boss Ma Xingrui?' SupChina, 29 December. supchina.com/2021/12/29/what-can-we-expect-from-xinjiangs-new-party-boss-ma-xingrui

Leibold, J. (2020) 'Surveillance in China's Xinjiang region: Ethnic sorting, coercion and inducement.' *Journal of Contemporary China* 29(121): 46–60. doi.org/10.1080/10670564.2019.1621529

Li, E. (2019) 'Fighting the "three evils": A structural analysis of counter-terrorism legal architecture in China.' *Emory International Law Review* 33(3): 311–65. scholarlycommons.law.emory.edu/eilr/vol33/iss3/1

Li, Y. [李宇] (2016) 'Hulianwang + shehui zhili yingyong tansuo' [互联网+社会治理应用探索, Probing the uses of the internet for social governance]. *Renminwang* [人民网, People.cn], 1 September. theory.people.com.cn/n1/2016/0901/c40531-28682384.html

Mai, J. (2021) 'China sanctions four US officials after Washington's measures over Xinjiang.' *South China Morning Post*, 21 December. www.scmp.com/news/china/diplomacy/article/3160567/china-sanctions-four-us-officials-after-washingtons-measures

Mao, W., & Cui, J. (2017) 'New Xinjiang regulation aims to prevent extremism.' *China Daily*, 31 March. www.chinadaily.com.cn/china/2017-03-31/content28747922.htm

Mu, Y. (2022) 'Zhuzheng Xinjiang san ge yue: Ma Xingrui gaibianle shenme' [主政新疆三个月：马兴瑞改变了什么, Three months in charge of Xinjiang: What has Ma Xingrui changed?]. Hong Kong 01, 29 March. www.hk01.com/about #corp

O'Brien, K.J., & Li, L. (2004) 'Suing the local state: Administrative litigation in rural China.' *China Journal* 51: 75–96. doi.org/10.2307/3182147

Odgaard, L., & Nielsen, T.G. (2014) 'China's counterinsurgency strategy in Tibet and Xinjiang.' *Journal of Contemporary China* 23(87): 535–55. doi.org/10.1080/10670564.2013.843934

Office of the High Commissioner of Human Rights (2018) 'Committee on the Elimination of Racial Discrimination reviews the report of China.' 13 August. www.ohchr.org/EN/NewsEvents/Pages/DisplayNews.aspx?NewsID=23452& LangID=E

Pan, G. (2014) 'Learning to identify 75 religious extremist activities in some areas of Xinjiang can be reported to the police.' *Observer Network*, 24 December. web.archive.org/web/20210212200916/www.cssn.cn/zjx/zjx_zjsj/201412/t2014 1224_1454905.shtml

Pokalova, E. (2013) 'Authoritarian regimes against terrorism: Lessons from China.' *Critical Studies on Terrorism* 6(2): 279–98. doi.org/10.1080/17539153.2012. 753202

Porges, M.L. (2010) 'Deradicalisation, the Yemeni way.' *Survival* 52(2): 27–33. doi.org/10.1080/00396331003764553

Rabasa, A. (ed.) (2010) 'Deradicalising Islamist extremists.' RAND Corporation. www.rand.org/content/dam/rand/pubs/monographs/2010/RAND_MG1053.pdf

Renminwang [人民网, People.cn] (2015) 'Zhang Chunxian: Yong fazhi yueshu, wenhua duichong de fangfa "qu jiduan hua"' [张春贤：用法治约束、文化对冲的方法「去极端化」, Zhang Chunxian: Legal restraint and cultural methods of 'deradicalisation']. 16 February. politics.people.com.cn/n/2015/ 0216/c70731-26575784.html

Saich, T. (2000) 'Negotiating the state: The development of social organisations in China.' *China Quarterly* 161: 124–41. doi.org/10.1017/S0305741000003969

State Council Information Office of the People's Republic of China (SCIO) (2002) '"East Turkistan" terrorist forces cannot get away with impunity' (press release). www.china.org.cn/english/2002/Jan/25582.htm

—— (2019) 'Full text: The fight against terrorism and extremism and human rights protection in Xinjiang' (press release), 18 March. english.www.gov.cn/archive/white_paper/2019/03/18/content_281476567813306.htm

Trevaskes, S. (2016) 'Using Mao to package criminal justice discourse in 21st-century China.' *China Quarterly* 226, 299–318. doi.org/10.1017/S0305741016000266

Wall Street Journal (2015) 'Xinjiang arrests nearly doubled in 14 year of "strike-hard" campaign.' 23 January. www.wsj.com/articles/BL-CJB-25742

Wang, D. [王定] (2016) 'Fankong qingbao shizhanhua wenti yanjiu' [反恐情报实战化问题研究, Research on the operationalization of anti-terrorism intelligence]. Fankong Qingbao Jishu Yanjiu [反恐情报技术研究, Police Technology: Research on Anti-Terrorism Techniques], 6, 7–10

Wang, D. [王定], & Shan, D. [山丹] (2016) 'Fankong yanjiu yu xinjiang moshi' [反恐研究与新疆模式, Studies on anti-terrorism and the Xinjiang model]. *Qingbao Zazhi* [情报杂志, Intelligence Magazine] 35(11): 20–35

Wang, H.H., & Tzeng, W.F. (2021) 'Building a hyper-stability structure: The mechanisms of social stability maintenance in Xi's China.' *Issues and Studies* 57(1): 2150002. doi.org/10.1142/S1013251121500028

Wang, Y. (2019) 'China claims everyone in Xinjiang camps has "graduated".' Associated Press, 9 December. apnews.com/article/27f00e4feaa2755f25ab514cecda7add

Wayne, M.I. (2009) 'Inside China's war on terrorism.' *Journal of Contemporary China* 18(59): 249–61. doi.org/10.1080/10670560802576018

Wilson, M.C., & Piazza, J.A. (2013) 'Autocracies and terrorism: Conditioning effects of authoritarian regime type on terrorist attacks.' *American Journal of Political Science* 57(4): 941–55. doi.org/10.1111/ajps.12028

Xie, G., & Liu, T. (2021) 'Navigating securities: Rethinking (counter-)terrorism, stability maintenance and non-violent responses in the Chinese province of Xinjiang.' *Terrorism and Political Violence* 33(5): 993–1011. doi.org/10.1080/09546553.2019.1598386

Xinhua News (2019) 'Full text: Vocational education and training in Xinjiang.' 16 August. www.xinhuanet.com/english/2019-08/16/c138313359.htm

Xinhuawang [新华网, Xinhua Net] (2014) 'Xi Jinping: Yao shi baoli kongbu fenzi chengwei "guojie laoshu renren handa"' [习近平：要使暴力恐怖分子成为「过街老鼠 人人喊打」, Xi Jinping: To make violent terrorists become like 'rats crossing the street with everyone shouting and beating']. 26 April. www.xinhuanet.com/politics/2014-04/26/c_1110426869.htm

—— (2015) 'Zhonghua renmin gongheguo fankongbuzhuyi fa' [中华人民共和国反恐怖主义法, Anti-terrorism law of the People's Republic of China], 27 December. www.xinhuanet.com/politics/2015-12/27/c_128571798.htm

—— (2020) 'Xi focus: Xi stresses building Xinjiang featuring socialism with Chinese characteristics in new era.' 26 September. www.xinhuanet.com/english/2020-09/26/c_139399549.htm

—— (2021a) 'China announces sanctions against European individuals, entities.' 22 March. www.xinhuanet.com/english/2021-03/22/c_139827908.htm

—— (2021b) 'Xinjiang weiwuer zizhiqu dangwei zhuyao fuze tongzhi zhiwu tiaozheng Ma Xingrui ren Xinjiang weiwuer zizhiqu dangwei shuji' [新疆维吾尔自治区党委主要负责同志职务调整 马兴瑞任新疆维吾尔自治区党委书记, Adjustments to the XUAR party committee: Ma Xingrui appointed as party secretary of the XUAR Party Committee], 25 December. www.news.cn/politics/2021-12/25/c_1128200313.htm

Xinlang Xinwen [新浪新闻, Sina News] (2017) 'Kaiban yishi shang zhongbang xin jigou zhongyang tongzhanbu jiu ju lingdao xianshen' [开班仪式上 重磅新机构中央统战部九局领导现身, New agency unveiled at the opening ceremony of the 9th Bureau of the Central United Front Work Department]. 13 July. news.sina.cn/gn/2017-07-13/detail-ifyiakur8830418.d.html?isJump=0&universallink=1&from=wap

Zenz, A., & Leibold, J. (2020) 'Securitizing Xinjiang: Police recruitment, informal policing and ethnic minority co-optation.' *China Quarterly* 242: 324–48. doi.org/10.1017/S0305741019000778

Zhou, C. [周春花] (2016) 'Xinjiang Kashen shi shequ zhili fazhan qingkuang he moshi ji xianshi kunjing' [新疆喀什市社区治理发展情况和模式及现实困境, Developments and challenges in the model of community governance in Kashgar, Xinjiang]. *Shishi Qiushi* [实事求是, Seek Truth From Facts] 2016(2): 54–7

Zhou, Z. (2019) 'Chinese strategy for deradicalisation.' *Terrorism and Political Violence* 31(6): 1187–1209. doi.org/10.1080/09546553.2017.1330199

10

Sinicisation or 'xinicisation': Regulating religion and religious minorities under Xi Jinping

Ray Wang

What do taking down Christian crosses, banning Islamic symbols and removing Buddhist classics from library bookshelves have in common? These have all taken place during the rule of a single man. Since Xi took power in 2012 and began his 'Sinicisation of Religion' (宗教中国化, *zongjiao zhongguohua*) campaign, there has been a steady increase in alarming headlines and shocking images regarding religious persecution in China. The nature and extent of this campaign have turned religion into one of the major human rights disputes between Beijing and the international community. Although China's human rights record has long faced criticism owing to the 1989 Tiananmen massacre and imprisonment of such political dissidents as Liu Xiaobo, the recent trend of religious sinicisation marks a new wave of political repression. Xi's religious policy demonstrates a different kind of approach from that of his predecessors and one that deserves careful scrutiny.

On the surface, Xi's attitude to religion seems to be a continuation of that of other Chinese Communist Party (CCP/CPC) leaders and has shown little innovation. The term 'sinicisation' borrows from the old anti-Christianity movement of the 1920s, and the rhetoric demanding that religions be more 'Chinese' or 'patriotic' differs little from what was implemented in the

1950s when the country expelled Western missionaries. Xi has published no concrete policy guidelines like Deng Xiaoping's 'Document 19' except to update an existing administrative decree titled the *2004 Regulations on Religious Affairs* in 2018. In most of his public speeches, he has simply repeated well-known phrases such as 'rule by law', 'religious harmony' and 'guiding religion to accommodate socialist society', just as Jiang Zemin and Hu Jintao before him.

Nonetheless, it would be a mistake to think that Xi is on the same path as Deng, Jiang or Hu. Three misunderstandings often prevent observers from comprehending what is really happening with religions and religious minorities in Xi's China. First, it is not as if China had once tolerated religious freedom and things suddenly turned worse after he took power in 2012. Evidence from independent expert assessments such as Freedom House's annual freedom index shows little difference, with China scoring 0 out of 5 in religious freedom from the 1980s until 2022 (Cook, 2017a).

Second, it would be equally wrong to assume that these expert reports have captured the complexity of church–state relations. Outside critics have often labelled Xi the instigator of this new wave of repression, but actions of religious repression have always been common in China even while religious activity flourishes throughout the country. It is often overlooked that the Chinese Communist Party has maintained a unique narrative and elaborate system of social control since the 1950s, one that has been largely successful in mobilising social elites to support its policies or marginalise its critics (Groot, 2003; Wang, 2019; Wang & Groot, 2018).

One often overlooked piece of evidence for this continuation is the puzzling 'popularity' of Xi's religious and minority policies among regular Chinese citizens. In today's China, for example, it is not hard to find numerous WeChat or Weibo posts condemning Christians or Muslims for not being 'patriotic' or requesting even tougher regulations on believers. Outsiders would be surprised that most of those intolerant opinions are not in fact state propaganda or at least are not directly sponsored by the CPC. While dissatisfaction has risen after various social challenges such as the housing bubbles and the COVID-19 crisis, the CPC still enjoys high overall popularity through its 'earned legitimacy' (Cunningham, Saich & Turiel, 2020, p. 14).

Third, it is not as if China is overhauling its policies and agencies on religion and minority affairs in response to Xi's reaching new conclusions. While it is often stated by foreign critics or in Chinese propaganda that Xi has created a new method or 'thought' (思想, *sixiang*) regarding religion and minority affairs, he has made surprisingly few 'contributions' to the field other than brutal tactics such as the cross demolition campaigns in Zhejiang and the re-education camps in Xinjiang. Neither can these actions be conceived as 'new' in the CPC's history. Xi's method has largely been to learn, borrow from and rejuvenate old party traditions, and his rhetoric and tactics cannot be fully understood without understanding the nature of 'united front work' (统一战线工作, *tongyi zhanxian gongzuo*) in the CPC's playbook.

While the persecution of religious minorities was also common in the Jiang and Hu periods, social spaces for certain types of innovation, activism and even disobedience could be observed before 2012. Although the overall party policy on religious and minority affairs continues, Xi has clearly changed the tactics and priorities in order to limit these spaces more effectively, especially through his new religious regulations and institutional reforms on united front work.

To better explain Xi's policies on religion and religious minorities, this chapter includes five sections. First, it identifies the core focus behind Xi's policy of religious sinicisation. In short, it is less about religious faith and minority groups and more about rejuvenating the aged regulatory system in charge of managing religions and minority affairs. After decades of political campaigns and sinicisation from Mao to Xi, the major religions of China have been fully regulated, organised and financially administrated by Chinese-only patriotic associations for some time. Each is closely supervised by the United Front Work Department (UFWD). All limit membership to Chinese citizens, are ministered by Chinese clergymen and use only government-sanctioned texts. As such, there is little more that could be done to make these religions more 'Chinese'.

While the persecution of underground congregations, illegal texts and religion-fuelled activism has existed for decades, it is important to ask why this has changed in the present. The historical context indicates that Xi is bringing back old tactics. The second section will review the sociopolitical background of religion and religious minority affairs in which diverse 'religious markets' and faith-based activism are born. A growing prevalence of civil resistance (or the tolerance of it) that began in the late 1990s and reached its peak from 2008 to the early 2010s was interpreted by party hardliners as evidence that the control system was broken and that the regime was facing a life-or-death moment. Before Xi began the Party Rectification (anti-corruption) Movement in 2013 (his first campaign), rumours had spread through local and overseas Chinese communities that Xi had expressed a deep worry in several speeches about the 'disapproval relating to the life and death of the Party' (Xi, 2013). The fear of 'peaceful evolution' from within stopped Xi from continuing Jiang and Hu's more lenient policies on religion and religious minorities.

Toughening social control was a logical result of this fear, but it does not explain why the new regulations target not only disobedient individuals but also obedient organisations and their party administrators. The third section reviews the Great United Front (大统战, *da tong zhan*) campaign, the counter-strategy that Xi has promoted (X. Zhang, 2016). Since 2013, it is evident that Xi's version of Sinicism has been expending enormous effort on his loyal subjects; that is, sanctioned churches, mosques, temples, museums, seminaries, schools and various civic organisations. All united front work-based establishments are now under heavy scrutiny. Particularly in the cases of Zhejiang and Xinjiang, we have seen credible reports that local officials of religion and minority affairs were severely punished for being too close to their subjects (Ramzy & Buckley, 2019). Does the supreme leader think his party comrades are not 'Chinese' enough? Reaching a better understanding and hopefully a better counter policy for this new wave of repression necessitates looking beyond the rhetoric and digging into the institutional layers of these new developments.

The fourth section will examine the cross-removal campaign in Zhejiang, and the fifth will discuss the radical anti-extremist campaign in Xinjiang, two prominent cases that reveal the unique traits of the Great United Front. Although many news articles and human rights reports have covered these cases, few have connected these incidents with larger regulatory and institutional changes. Without comprehending Xi's grand strategy, the above three misunderstandings will persist in our analysis and thus prevent decision-makers from providing an effective response. Connecting Protestants and Muslims with the same Great United Front lens is crucial as daily intolerance and systematic atrocities of both are motivated by the same logic and manufactured by the same apparatus. Most important of all, what was implemented in Zhejiang and Xinjiang has been gradually spreading to other provinces and regions, and the Great United Front arguably deserves more scrutiny as its central mechanism.

The argument in brief

In order to understand the similarities and differences of Xi's approach from his post-reform predecessors and other authoritarian dictators who do not see religion as a direct threat to their regimes, it is necessary to recognise that ever-changing, contentious spaces for religious freedom in China have always existed and have been occupied by religious believers, advocated by policy entrepreneurs and sanctioned by programmatic front-line officials in the post-reform era (Wang, 2019). These spaces are occupied by a wide range of practitioners that include religious protesters, crusaders and martyrs who would fight openly with the regime to their deaths and 'reluctant' activists who are mostly lay believers who pretend to cooperate while cultivating a network of friendly alliances, accumulating support from society and waiting for the right moment to initiate their demands for policy reform. The literature calls them solidary groups (Tsai, 2007), policy entrepreneurs (Mertha, 2009) and transnational advocates (Wang, 2019). The 'Boss Christians' (老板基督徒, *laoban jidutu*) in Wenzhou and 'Mazuers' (妈祖人, *mazuren*) in Xiamen are well-known examples in the post-reform era (Cao, 2008; Clark, 2015).[1]

This chapter argues that Xi's ultimate goal is to constrain and shrink these spaces by adding legal pressure (i.e. through sinicisation and the regulations) on practitioners and political pressure (e.g. united front work reform and anti-corruption campaigns) on administrators. He is driving them to prevent an outcome like the 1989 revolutions in Eastern Europe or the colour revolutions in the Arab world, which are understood to be sparked or facilitated by religion (Martin, 2014). Xi is convinced that religion and other elements of civil society are credible threats that must be firmly contained.

Furthermore, Xi's religious policy is not meant to recreate Mao's Cultural Revolution, although many incidents, such as re-education camps, burning religious texts, bulldozing mosques or giving military training to monks and priests, have brought back memories of that painful period (Nikkei Asia, 2021).[2] Yet Xi's policy lacks any clear ideological traits compared to Mao's, and he seems so far to have less of an interest in eliminating religious faith than in repressing the faithful and their administrators by further shrinking their space and liberty to act independently.

---

1   Both phenomena have been widely recorded in studies of Chinese religions.
2   Observers have argued that Xi so admired Mao's approach that he refused to condemn the Cultural Revolution, one of Mao's most controversial 'achievements', as most of his predecessors have done.

While the Great United Front, a supposedly more comprehensive strategy to alter the dangerous 'peaceful evolution' that emerged from previous, more lenient societal policies, appears to be at the centre of these new developments, it had received little attention from scholars until events that have dominated international news in the last five years. The discussion is also currently limited to residents of Xinjiang, Tibet, Hong Kong, Taiwan and sometimes overseas Chinese in Western countries who are suspected of engaging in espionage (Brady, 2017; Hamilton & Ohlberg, 2020; Nye, 2018). This view of united front work overlooks the long-lasting and overreaching influence of the party's strategy since the 1930s and Xi's evident reverence for the legacy of Mao Zedong.[3]

In 2012, the UFWD announced that it was hiring an additional 40,000 cadres; in 2014, the number of groups declared to be UFWD priorities increased from 11 to about 14; and in 2015, Xi invested significant personal capital in a long-delayed national United Front Work Conference, raising its importance for party leaders nationwide (Groot, 2016, pp. 168–9). The 2018 regime reconstruction made the UFWD one of the most powerful party-state agencies in China with a global reach. There is even a new united front 'law', first published in 2015 and formalised on 6 January 2021.

While Xi is influenced by Mao's obsession with constant struggle, he realises that this struggle is mainly between himself and other party leaders and that victory can be determined by their skill to rally cadres and regular citizens around their agenda. As a direct victim of Mao's anti-party campaign in the 1960s and 1970s, Xi is also convinced that the real threat exists within the ranks of his own party. During the Cultural Revolution, Mao mobilised regular citizens and especially young students to attack and purge party officials, including Xi's father. While his father was under military detention, Xi's home was attacked by student Red Guards and he was forced to leave Beijing and lived in a village during the latter part of the Cultural Revolution to relearn how to be a 'good communist' (Buckley & Tatlow, 2015). As such, he now views it as his turn to re-educate fellow party members.

---

3   Xi's interest in united front work might have another more intimate source in addition to Mao's influence. It is well known in China that his father Xi Zhongxun had built a reputation as a pragmatic united front work leader before 1962 and after 1978. One of his 'mistakes', which cost him his job in the 1960s, was his close friendship with the Tibetan united front celebrity Choekyi Gyaltsen, the 10th Panchen Lama (第十世班禅喇嘛额尔德尼) (Reynolds, 2015). Groot (2003) provides a detailed account of the united front's history, definition, organisation and revival since the reform and opening-up period.

From this alternative understanding, the sinicisation campaign can be seen as one largely directed towards religious leaders, minority elites and administrative officials who have been involved in a working relationship with the united front that was too cosy in the past; that is, officials who have allowed too many churches and mosques to be built, too much diversity within Chinese society and too much foreign involvement. The top leader now wishes for them to be re-examined, re-educated and punished if necessary in order to ensure that every cadre knows how to behave like 'good communists', being tough enough to genuinely defend the 'red lines' (红线, *hongxian*) on religion and minority affairs. In Xi's own words: 'We urge them [cadres] to strengthen their consciousness of the need to maintain political integrity [政治意识, *zhengzhi yishi*], think in big-picture terms [大局意识, *daju yishi*], follow the leadership core [核心意识, *hexin yishi*] and keep in alignment [看齐意识, *kanqi yishi*].' As such, cadres are expected to be mindful of the risks posed by religion and minority affairs. They are tasked with re-educating their subordinates 'to uphold the authority of the Central Committee and its centralised, unified leadership' (Xi, 2017).

Triple religious markets and rising social activism

The 'big picture terms' in regulating religion and minority affairs concern how to deal with rising social activism and the leadership's core fear that the party is losing control of it. Since the reform and opening-up period of the late 1970s, the CPC's social policy has gradually changed in response to new developmental goals, giving religious minorities and their organisations more social space as long as they are able to keep their operations purely 'Chinese'. This can be understood using its policy towards Christianity and the 'three-self' (三自, *san zi*) principle: self-propagation, self-governance and self-support. The principle and the institutions enforcing it were created in the 1950s by Mao and have been applied equally to other religions in China since (Cook, 2017b).

The three-self policy draws three distinct 'red lines' between legal and illegal religious activities that both practitioners and researchers have learned from the church–state experience in today's China: (1) no evangelism—churches are forbidden from expanding beyond permitted sites or offering fellowship to non-believers and minors; (2) foreigners are forbidden from working inside Chinese religious organisations or worshipping alongside Chinese citizens; and (3) foreign donations or missions of any kind are prohibited in local religious gatherings.

According to the celebrated sociologist Yang Fenggang, the policy has created 'triple religious markets' in which Falun Gong, Eastern Lightning and other groups who rebel against the above rules are labelled as cult religions (邪教, *xiejiao*) and are forced to operate secretly in the 'black' market. Meanwhile, conformists of organisations such as the Three-Self Patriotic Movement Church (TSPM) and the Chinese Patriotic Catholic Association (CPCA) enjoy legal recognition as well as financial and policy assistance from the state as long as they follow all of the party's rules (Yang, 2006), operating in the 'red' market. Deng Xiaoping's reforms largely relaxed these rules, causing an enlarged 'grey' market to emerge. Reforms allowed local officials to take a lenient attitude to illegal religious activities if this tolerance could help them attract more outside investment, human resources and modern business know-how to accommodate the growing needs of China's path to capitalism (Tamney, 2005).

For the purposes of united front work, certain provincial leaders were also encouraged to relax the red lines when overseas Chinese from Hong Kong, Taiwan, South-East Asia and North America were involved. Many of these early homecoming investors were Christian businessmen from Hong Kong or Malaysia who saw Deng's reform and opening up as an opportunity both for capital gains and to revive evangelism in China. The Australian political scientist Gerry Groot has documented how the UFWD used various diaspora connections to bring in the first buckets of capital in the early stage of reforms (Groot, 2003). In interviews with the author, elders of Protestant churches also spoke about how overseas Chinese (华侨, *huaqiao*) donated money to build the first churches and how local religious affairs officials turned a blind eye or even encouraged this because these foreigners also donated money to local schools, hospitals or benevolent centres (Wang, 2019).

Religious regulation in China since 1949 has been strict, and every religious activity, including weekly worship, theological training, festival gatherings or the mere receiving of an outside visitor, has required official approval up to a certain level. Without leniency in these policies, both foreigners and local officials would be severely punished by the authorities, and locals would be deterred from welcoming overseas involvement. For post-reform local leaders eager to produce stronger economic growth, the chances were better that religious organisations would be tolerated or even encouraged by local authorities (Wang, 2019, p. 112).

As political scientist Lily Tsai has described in her book on the provision of local public services in rural villages, religious and other local associations—referred to as 'solidary groups'—can often channel better policy choices to hometowns with their capital and human resources if they are allowed to exist (Tsai, 2007, p. 355). A closed system would have prevented such transnational achievements as the Tzu Chi Foundation's monumental headquarters in Suzhou; Chongyi Church, the largest Protestant Chinese church in Hangzhou; or the colossal Mazu pilgrimage to Meizhou Island, which has drawn tens of thousands of participants each year and garners international attention to this day.

For at least three decades, China's policy had shown selected levels of tolerance and target-specific flexibility towards both mainstream religions and religious minorities, with irregular outbreaks of harassment and crackdowns on political anniversaries like June 4th or against 'cult religions'. The rapid growth of religious populations in all religions is evidence of this selected tolerance and flexibility. Scholars have noticed that these religious revivals became manifest in every religion beginning in the late 1980s, starting from villages and spreading to big cities all over China (Bays, 2003; Dean, 2003; Lai, 2003; Madsen, 2003). Although scholars are sceptical about these numbers, official statistics show that followers of major religions have increased from double to more than tenfold over the past 40 years. The number of Protestants grew from 3 million in 1983 to 38 million in 2018, Catholics from 3.5 million in 1988 to 6 million in 2018 and Muslims from 13 million in 1980 to 20.3 million in 2018 (Zhonghua Renmin Gongheguo Guowuyuan Xinwen Bangongshi, 2018).

Such growth in the post-reform era would be even more astonishing if underground populations were included. These rapid increases indicate that China's religious policy of containment is broken. Although Document 19 and the Constitution promise that citizens may enjoy freedom of worship (信仰自由, *xinyang ziyou*), they have never guaranteed the freedom to convert millions of non-believers. Article 36 of the Constitution declares the freedom to 'believe in or do not believe in any religion', implying that religious freedom to the atheist CPC in fact is one of freedom *from* religion rather than a right to it (PRC State Council, 2019).

Even more, the rhetorical language of religious freedom has incited an unexpected consequence: practitioners and their overseas supporters are beginning to leverage this language of freedom to resist government interference. Once forbidden, missionaries returned to China illegally but received little punishment. There emerged an activism for religious freedom that was transnationally based. Not only were Western media, governments and NGOs empowering local practitioners but also people in the red market saw through the tough skin of Beijing's language. The red lines became 'cheap talk', and exceptions became normal practices (Wang, 2019, pp. 56–7).

Consequently, observers began to witness the normalisation of the violation of religious red lines. Tens of thousands of missionaries from every global faith entered the country each year on tourist, business or educational visas to build strongholds in China. Organisations in both the red and black markets received donations from overseas partners, and official establishments opened their doors to foreigners to participate, worship, serve and even deliver forbidden messages at their gatherings. More and more faith-based groups engaged in various social engagement activities such as bookselling, coffee-making and charity-giving, launching evangelical projects to attract young, urban and talented citizens to their faiths (Wang, 2017, pp. 558–60).

These developments must have concerned Xi and other hardline communist leaders. Things became even more urgent when religious activists, especially Christians, began collaborating with other civil society activists.[4] According to the estimates of some insiders, six out of the top 10 most wanted student leaders of the June 4th movement have become Christians over the past 30 years.[5] Nearly all of the top Chinese human rights lawyers, including Chen Guangcheng (陈光诚), Gao Zhisheng (高智晟), Wang Quanzhang (王全璋), Qin Yongpei (覃永沛), Deng Xiaoyun (邓晓云) and Chang Weiping (常玮平), have revealed religious affiliations and/or defended

---

4   The well-known case of the 'barefoot lawyer' Chen Guangcheng demonstrates how a harmless local practitioner can become an international human rights star who brings wide criticism to the regime. In November 2013, the author interviewed Guo Yushan, civil rights activist and founder of the Open Constitution Initiative (公盟, *gong meng*). Guo was one of the key people involved in Chen's escape. He told the author that during repeated interrogations, he told authorities that Guo had escaped on his own but had received assistance from Christian activists such as He Peirong, who drove him around before arriving at the embassy. Guo was also arrested in 2014. Chen's story is transcribed in Ian Williams's article in NBC News (2012).

5   This is based on the author's personal interviews with exiled dissidents in the United States on 4 June 2019.

clients who are devoted believers, such as members of Falun Gong or the underground church. Two of the three leaders of the Hong Kong Occupy Central Movement (Benny Tai Yiu-ting, 戴耀廷 and Reverend Chu Yiu-ming, 朱耀明)—some would argue all three—are Christians.

Christians amount to less than 2 per cent of the total Chinese population, and these Christian activists are motivated by their own personal convictions with no church organisation behind them. Nevertheless, the CPC has seen enough overproportioned faith-based activism to see religion as a credible threat.

The empire strikes back: The Great United Front reforms

This social activism has forced the top leaders to face deep-rooted social cleavages that involve not only the above-mentioned social activists but also embarrassingly negligent, easily corrupted and ideologically disloyal administrators. After three decades of Deng's reforms, China was suffering from a wide range of difficulties. One of the most hated beasts has been irresponsible and corrupt local politics fostered by crony capitalism and covered up by the one-party dictatorship. Social resistance waged by numerous civil rights activists gained widespread support during the mid-1990s and the 2000s because they spoke for the weak and the hopeless amid the widening income gap, fast-changing urbanisation and absolute authoritarianism. The almost uncensored internet and rising social media at that time gave them platforms to speak up for the marginalised against party-state domination.[6]

To manage these rising social problems, Xi's first move was to target his own party comrades, vowing to crack down on corruption almost immediately after ascending to power in November 2012. This time, the Chinese leader meant it. Only one month into his term, Xi published an 'eight-point' austerity guide in December 2012 that listed strict rules to curb excessive and wasteful spending such as on luxury banquets and gift-giving during

---

6   There are many fruitful studies on social resistance during this period. Two of the most cited descriptions are from Kevin O'Brien and Li Lianjiang's *Rightful Resistance in Rural China* (2007) and Andrew Mertha's *Fragmented Authoritarianism* (2009), which provide explanations of such cases as urban housing disputes and opposition to the construction of dams from both societal and political perspectives. However, the mainstream literature seems to have overlooked the role of religious activism in this process.

official party business (Andrew, 2013). In January 2013, Xi personally attended the meeting of the Central Commission for Discipline Inspection (CCDI), a then trivial party organ in the post-reform era that had rarely made the news before his time. During the meeting, he vowed that his anti-corruption campaign would root out 'tigers and flies'; that is, both ordinary party functionaries and high-ranking officials would be under the close scrutiny of the newly reformed CCDI.

This brief history of Xi's early term is noteworthy because it demonstrates how Mao's social control strategy of 'three magic weapons' (三大法宝, *san da fabao*) has influenced his social policy. The centre of this strategy is party-building (党建, *dang jian*), a principle that emphasises the centrality of consolidating power and the command chain within the regulatory system. As Mao's famous phrase goes, '*dasao ganjing wuzi zai qingke*'(打扫干净屋子再请客, 'Clean up the house and then invite and treat'). After a series of anti-corruption purges that began in 2013, Xi had gradually put his own people into every department of the party and government ministries. However, he could not yet be sure that these appointees would do his work, especially the difficult task of cutting ties with the religious establishment and seriously implementing the old red line policies. In the regulation of China's religious landscape, the PLAC is generally used to identify and repress a relatively small number of disobedient activists in the religious black market. It is the CCDI's function to prosecute the few party cadres who have continued to maintain improper involvement, those who have in essence failed to clean their hands upon removing them from the black and grey market cookie jar.

To manage successfully the general religious and minority population, and particularly those in the sanctioned red market, Xi needed to transform the ageing UFWD. He therefore began the Great United Front in 2014, a campaign that reached its peak in 2018 when the UFWD had absorbed several key governmental agencies in religious and minority affairs. The range and scale of the Great United Front machine had clearly surfaced by the time the UFWD had expanded from nine divisions to 12 (Joske, 2019; Wang & Groot, 2018).

The reform's final step was the highly symbolic drafting and publishing of the first United Front Law. Led by Xi's leading working group, the UFWD drafted the Regulations on the Work of the United Front of the Communist Party of China (Trial Implementation) (2015) through a Committee of the Central Politburo on 30 April 2015 and formalised them on

6 January 2021. While most of the document's content was a summary and re-emphasis of established united front concepts, Xi's imprimatur placed new responsibilities on all cadres.

The regulations clarified the obligations of united front work at the provincial level. This work was rarely viewed as a priority during the reform era, and it was seldom used to evaluate the performance of cadres with the exception of Xinjiang, Tibet and Special Economic Zones. The common practice was for governors and mayors to place the work in the hands of career UFWD staff led by seasoned, pre-retirement-age senior officials. Local party chairs participated in united front work only when it involved central-level visits or high-value targets (e.g. celebrities or political figures from Taiwan or Hong Kong). According to the regulations (Article 6, Section 7), local leaders are now to assume direct responsibility:

> The principal leader of each local Party committee (organ) is the primary responsible person for United Front work. The leading members of each local Party committee (organ) shall take the lead to learn, propagate and implement the Party's united front theories, policies and regulations; they shall take the lead to participate in important united front events and make more non-Party friends. (Zhonguo Gongchandang Xinwen Wang, 2021)

The wording is clear. Xi's new Great United Front requires local party chairs to add its tasks to their schedules and performance evaluations. While it is not clear how much they will take this policy to heart, united front work demands rigorous effort and connections with diverse targets. It is also difficult to set suitable goals and evaluation criteria. Nevertheless, there are reports that provincial leaders have begun assigning deputies to run UFWD offices. Since August 2015, there have been 35 provincial UFWD appointments, 30 of which have been filled with incumbents of Provincial Standing Committees. Only four appointees are older than 60. Some provinces have gone further to have their 'number 1' take the lead (e.g. Sichuan, Tibet, Shanxi, Shaanxi and Henan). These have mimicked the centre by establishing or proposing United Front Work Leading Groups above existing united front structures to better coordinate different offices and improve effectiveness (Wenweipo, 2015).

The speedy expansion of the UFWD in 2018 is another strong message that Xi seeks a more powerful, centralised and effective system. The UFWD absorbed the full staff and functionalities of three key state apparatus in charge of overseas, religious and minority affairs: the State Administration for Religious Affairs (SARA), State Ethnic Affairs Commission (SEAC) and the Overseas Chinese Affairs Office (OCAO) (Joske, 2019).

It should not be misconstrued that the UFWD is 'replacing' these agencies or 'regaining' leadership over these affairs. The UFWD has always been the superior of these agencies and the final decision-maker of overseas, religious and minority affairs. This institutional reconstruction is rather a removal of the nominal party/state division that was once the highlight of Deng's reforms but has been seen to be the cause of red tape, delays, buck-passing (推诿, *tui wei*) and wrangling (扯皮, *che pi*) in bureaucratic processes. The author's interviews and other sources all indicate that this restructuring is simply intended to remove another excuse for cadres to shirk their responsibilities to other departments (Si, 2019).

The Great United Front is becoming a handy tool in Xi's construction of a united front bandwagon. United Front work was once taken seriously only in the provinces of Fujian, Guangdong, Tibet and Xinjiang owing to their geographical significance and relevance to issues of internal stability, Taiwan and Hong Kong, India, South-East and Central Asia. With the new Great United Front doctrine, this work might well extend to every corner of the nation.

Testing the Great United Front on Protestant Christians

After consolidating his power and overhauling the united front work system, it was no surprise that Xi chose Zhejiang Province to field test his new campaign of sinicisation. Xi had served as governor and party secretary of Zhejiang from 2002 to 2007, and his faction is often called the New Zhijiang Army (之江新军, *zhijiang xinjun*) (NZA) for this reason. Xia Baolong (夏宝龙), for example, was deputy party secretary when Xi governed Zhejiang and was a well-known NZA celebrity. As acting governor in 2011 and party secretary of Zhejiang in 2012, Xia was the key figure to implement Xi's new tactics on religion and other united front work subjects. He ordered the infamous campaign to demolish church crosses (DCC) in Zhejiang from 2014 to 2016, which forced around 1,500 to 1,800 Protestant churches to remove their crosses and/or demolish all or parts of their church buildings (Ying, 2018).

The DCC campaign attracted both international condemnation and local criticism because it was not targeted towards underground 'house church' congregations as before but placed sanctions on TSPM establishments that had registered, paid their full taxes and dues to the party and followed every command from their UFWD officers since day 1. Experts believe that Zhejiang and particularly Wenzhou City was targeted owing to its having the highest concentration of Protestant Christians in China (Wenzhou is often nicknamed the Chinese Jerusalem among Christians). This made it the ideal place to send the message (Cao, 2010, pp. 2–3) that the new leadership was unhappy about the current united front work arrangement and needed a new 'Wenzhou Model' that would be more in line with its interests. In essence, church leaders were forced to 'bend the knee' and declare fealty to the state over their beloved churches. Compelling churchgoers to allow the government to take away their crosses in order to keep their status was an intentionally unreasonable demand for a show of loyalty to the state.

Xi and his NZA clique had good reason to choose Protestant Christians and their crosses. Besides their dubious connections to civil rights lawyers like Chen Guangcheng and Gao Zhisheng and foreign human rights advocates (e.g. China Aid from Midland, Texas, Chinese Human Rights Defenders and CHRD from Washington, DC), the Great United Front understood that the key problem with Protestant Christians was the overly comfortable relationship between these social elites and their administrators: the officers tasked with 'uniting with' and 're-educating' (再教育, zaijiaoyu) and 'transforming' (改造, gaizao) these potential enemies had instead become friends. The patriotic associations built to contain religious and minority crowds had become the engine of transnational activism, harbouring underground collaboration and facilitating illegal religious activities. Both underground 'black' groups and legal 'red' congregations were emboldened by the UFWD's inaction and actively engaged in otherwise forbidden evangelism in the post-Reform era (Ma & Li, 2017; Vala, 2017; Wang, 2019).

The author's field research indicates that underground churches, sanctioned churches and foreign missionaries formed networks of evangelism that directly violated the 'no foreigners' rule and the other red lines above while local administrators looked the other way.[7] Zhejiang's 2014 cross and church demolitions targeted a cherished Christian symbol: crosses both represent

---

7   The author has conducted interviews and participant observation since 2010, the major findings of which are presented in Wang (2019).

the sacrifice and redemption of Christ and function as unifying banners for foreign donations, missions and other causes. The DCC campaign bluntly asked: 'Is this God's universe, or the Party's?' (这是十字架的天下，还是共产党的天下, *zhe shi shizijia de tianxia, haishi gongchandang de tianxia*) (Yang, 2018).[8]

Observers were shocked by these demands because Zhejiang was seen by many as one of few positive examples of policy innovation, a bright spot in an uneasy religious tolerance that had existed since the late 1980s. There had been an ongoing discussion in the region about legalising house church congregations in the 2000s. At first, the provincial government denied that the 'Three Rectifications and One Demolition' campaign (as it was officially known) was targeting Protestant churches, but numerous eyewitness reports confirmed that tens of thousands of Protestant believers had resisted demolition teams and riot police for weeks or months in front of cameras, although this had rarely developed into violent confrontations (Yang, 2018). Leaders of the TSPM spoke up in public, criticised the provincial government and requested the top leadership to respect their freedoms (China Change, 2015).

For law-abiding Zhejiang Christians, the DCC came as an unwelcome surprise. Believers had tried every channel, including complaints to the Chinese People's Political Consultative Conference (CPPCC), group petitions to the UFWD and central-level officials and signing open letters to the media. Such actions had never occurred among TSPM congregations before because open criticism was considered 'unpatriotic' under the rule of united front work. While there were proper consultative channels where patriotic citizens could defend their legal rights without questioning the authorities, all legal and consultative efforts had failed, and church leaders had to seek unprecedented alternatives. At the end of 2016, Zhejiang's Protestant Christian Council disclosed that more than 1,500 churches and crosses had been demolished or removed, and they openly demanded a correction. Zhejiang's Protestant leaders aired their objections and publicly shamed the authorities because many believed that the government's actions might herald a nationwide anti-Christian movement with authorities increasingly accusing Christians of being a front for malicious foreign forces to destabilise China (Guo & Liu, 2015).

---

8   The quote was from Xia Baolong (Yang, 2018).

The contrast between the old United Front and the Great United Front can be seen in the case of Joseph Gu (顾约瑟), the former senior pastor of Chongyi Church in Hangzhou City, Zhejiang Province. Chongyi is believed to have been one of the largest churches in China and arguably the largest Chinese Protestant congregation in the world. Pastor Gu was a legendary figure in the church who had successfully fundraised RMB 4,200 million in two years. His team transformed a historic British Overseas Missionary Fellowship church into a 5,500-seat megachurch in 2005. From the perspective of the Great United Front, Pastor Gu's 'mistake' was failing to think in 'big-picture terms', which meant giving up his own interests in order to remain in alignment with the core leadership.

Pastor Gu had been the poster boy of the old system. Under the old United Front policy, Protestant churches and their leaders who joined the TSPM and pledged their loyalty to the party could legally register and enjoy many institutional privileges, which included housing permits, zoning licenses and official endorsements for their grand openings, and local officials were happy to attend the successful united front work ceremonies. Chongyi Church represented the success of the United Front policy, and Pastor Gu was awarded a leadership position in the TSPM system, selected as a City CPPCC council member in 2007, elected head of the Zhejiang Christian Council in 2010 and appointed a Provincial CPPCC council member and the official representative of all Zhejiang Christian Groups in 2014. There was much to indicate that the party viewed Pastor Gu as its faithful representative, at least before 2014 (Ying, 2016).

In 2013, when the DCC policy was announced, Gu and the other TSPM leaders faced a tough choice. Under the existing united front work arrangement, their churches had satisfied all the major legal requirements, although the rapid growth of their congregations had led to several building code violations and irregularities. While not directly opposing the DCC, they asked for more time to deliberate.

As both model patriotic Christians and standing members of the CPPCC, they initially tried to argue with their superiors following the regular united front work process and promised to fix the irregularities. For example, Gu and others deliberated with Deputy Director Chen Zongrong (陈宗荣) of the State Administration for Religious Affairs in Hangzhou on 25 May 2014, but Chen's response was terse and disheartening (Tsang, 2016, pp. 25–61).

In mid-2014, Gu and his fellow TSPM leaders began to realise that conventional channels had failed because the directive had come from the top and was non-negotiable. He therefore decided on a response that was provocative and unprecedented among sanctioned churches. The Zhejiang Christian Council released an open letter online on 10 July, which declared the DCC to be a direct violation of religious freedom that had to be stopped. Gu used his UFW position as leverage to pressure the authorities: 'Party and state guiding policy regarding religious work is: "Protect, Serve, Manage, Lead". Only the "management" function has recently been on display within our province, however, and this "management" has been so unreasonable and violent that it makes it impossible for our council to fulfil its role as a "bridge"' (China Change, 2015).

The reluctant Christian activists insisted: 'In view of this … We hereby request that you observe the constitution and the law, consider the special and complex nature of religion and immediately cease this mistaken policy of removing crosses that is tearing the Party and the masses apart' (China Change, 2015).

The authorities rejected these demands, and the campaign persisted violently for another year as the practice of cross removal reportedly spread to several other provinces. Gu and other collaborators paid a price for this minor 'disobedience'. Bao Guohua (包国华), another member of the China Christian Council and a pastor at a local TSPM church, was sentenced to 14 years in prison in February 2016 (BBC Zhongwen Wang, 2016). Gu was removed from the Christian Council, and the authorities secretly detained him from January to March 2016 (Cook, 2017b). Without any warning or explanation, the DCC campaign was abruptly and quietly halted in April 2016. Pastor Gu was released from house arrest at the end of 2017. Many optimistic observers believe that the termination of the campaign was due to unremitting resistance by local Christians in Zhejiang and elsewhere, red market collaborators becoming protestors and an unexpected consequence that 'the church–state equilibrium in China may be approaching a tipping point' (Yang, 2018, pp. 5–25).

It is noteworthy that relatively few people were formally prosecuted and sentenced to jail during this two-year-long campaign despite the scale of local resistance and violent clashes between believers and the authorities. The CPC could certainly have contained this resistance harshly, as it has done with Falun Gong and other social resistance movements (O'Brien

& Li, 2007; Perry, 2001). A spatial empirical analysis of DCC sites also revealed that the campaign affected relatively small areas of the province and most of the Protestant landscape remained intact (Yang, 2018, p. 5).

Under Xi's rule, it is evident that the regime is making greater use of extralegal methods such as house arrests, residence surveillance, forced televised confessions, forced disappearances, harassing relatives and friends in their places of work or study and using TSPM-like United Front organisations to dilute resistance. These represent a range of alternatives to sending activists directly to jail (Caster, 2017). Zhejiang's DCC story is consistent with this trend. The relatively 'softer' ending of resistance in this case indicates neither a tolerance for sanctioned groups nor a victory for their cause. Instead, it happened in this way because Xi's Great United Front prefers rescinding the reputations, willpower and social bases of dissenters rather than making them into martyrs of the opposition. As such, it was loyal TSPM clergymen instead of secret police who were the first to discourage the activists from continuing their demonstrations. Arrested demonstrators would often be sent to nearby TSPM facilities instead of police stations for their re-education. Without costly large-scale repression, these softer tactics could still effectively send a message to participants.

Government officials were the other recipients of this message. Reportedly, local Zhejiang officials were also punished for their tolerance and inaction towards the growing Protestant activism (Yang, 2018; Ying, 2018). Top UFWD officials such as Chen Zongrong were sent to 'hot zones' including Hangzhou and Wenzhou to supervise the DCC campaign. While many see the DCC as a total disaster, which incited an unnecessary rebellion from the inside, the masterminds of the policy have been handsomely rewarded by the top leadership. For his loyal service on the incident of Zhejiang, Chen Zongrong was later promoted to chief secretary of the UFWD in 2018.

After he left Zhejiang in 2017, 66-year-old former governor Xia Baolong was moved into the Environment and Resource Protection Council of the People's Congress as one of its deputy directors, a 'secondary position' that implied the end of his career and the beginning of his pre-retirement stage, according to precedents set in the Deng Xiaoping era (Kou & Tsai, 2014). However, he was later promoted to vice chairman and secretary general of the CPPCC in 2018 and director of the Hong Kong and Macau Affairs Office in 2020, two prominent top UFW leadership positions (Shi, 2020). Xia's rising career shows that the Great United Front is never only about religion or religious control; it incentivises cadres to show absolute resolve during difficult offensives against the party's potential enemies even when doing so might hurt their own people and change the existing united front order.

Testing the Great United Front on ethnic minorities

In terms of reconstructing the existing order for the purposes of the Great United Front, there would be no better example than the case of Xinjiang. Xi's new policy towards the Xinjiang Uyghur Autonomous Region (XUAR) is a radical departure from the 'united multi-ethnic state' of his predecessors. This was a policy that legally and institutionally encouraged a bilingual and multicultural environment, generous career and educational subsidies and more lenient enforcement of a wide range of socioeconomic policies (Permanent Mission, 2004).

When the UFWD created a new Xinjiang Division in 2017, there were soon rapidly increasing reports about 'anti-extremist' and Great United Front measures in XUAR and other Uyghur-populated regions. They described local Uyghurs as having to turn in their passports to authorities, register their kitchen knives at police stations, dress and speak like their Han counterparts, and avoid using Arabic or Islamic texts online or in public lest they face fines or worse. Today, more than a million Uyghurs have been imprisoned in 'vocational education and training centres' against their will, and their family members at home and relatives overseas have been intimidated by various united front methods, preventing them from speaking out against these injustices and mistreatment (Cook, 2017a).

The traditional ethnic and minority control tactics of the CPC are very similar to its religious ones: with generous legal and institutional benefits, the party supports legitimate, government-sanctioned ethnic and religious groups and leaders while co-opting, containing or delegitimising all others. The united front 'successes' of the 1950s were duplicated in the 1980s, and the minority-state relationship had been largely stable for 20 years (Leibold, 2012; Potter, 2003). Nonetheless, recent developments in religious and minority affairs show that local leaders like Xia Baolong and Chen Quanguo (陈全国) were promoted in their careers for being tough enough to say no to the old arrangements in order to further contain religious organisations and ethnic minorities.

By 2018, the world was finally made aware that the XUAR was going through religious and ethnic repression on a horrifying scale. What happened in XUAR was manufactured by Xi's loyalists like Chen Quanguo, who were selected and promoted by Xi Jinping exactly because of their extremely repressive records on religious minorities.[9] Chinese authorities detained up to a million Uyghurs in re-education camps for trivial code violations such as having a full beard, reading religious texts or downloading ethnic songs online. Families and overseas relatives have also been monitored, harassed and banned from talking to the press. Shocking testimonies from victims and leaked documents discuss systematic torture, rape and mental abuses taking place in camps that are hidden under such names as 'career skill training', 'Mandarin language education' or 'de-extremism' programs. Uyghurs were forced to go through these against their will and without a court order at least from 2017 to the end of 2019, at which point the Chinese authorities claimed that 'all participants had "graduated" and left the programs' (BBC Zhongwen Wang, 2019).

Human rights watch groups have described this as ethnic cleansing, a term that brings to mind the Final Solution of the Nazis. China's minority policy rapidly expanded from targeting small cells of religious extremists to banning Arabic texts, Islamic symbols and halal eating practices among regular citizens of both Xinjiang and Tibet, Sichuan, Ningxia and other areas where many minorities live. It seems that the current plan is to fully assimilate minorities through militant indoctrination programs in order to force them to be not only Chinese citizens but also culturally 'real Chinese' (Yu, 2018). Testimonies describing forced sterilisations and the systematic rape of minority women are especially powerful in shattering any doubt (Hill, Campanale & Gunter, 2021).

This new wave of ethnic repression is believed to have begun around mid-2016 when Xi appointed former Tibet Party Secretary Chen Quanguo to govern XUAR and the Xinjiang Production and Construction Corps (XPCC). The corps is a state-owned economic and paramilitary organisation formed from discharged People's Liberation Army soldiers and their families who run cities, settlements and farms in Xinjiang and have served as 'stabilisers' in this minority-populated region since 1954. The XPCC controls the most

---

9   In other words, they are tough enough to say no to the more flexible and lenient policies and demand local cadres to adapt a new, much more repressive one; the same story we saw in the 'Zero COVID' controversy. Xi promoted Li Qiang to be premier in last October, because he rejected his own best instinct and locked down the whole city of Shanghai, cruelly and harshly, for three months. This is the kind of leadership quality Xi Jinping truly values.

profitable areas of production in Xinjiang, such as cotton and fruit. Xi chose Chen because his resolve in putting down the slightest disobedience inside and outside the party and his 'successful' pacification tactics in Tibet had won him the reputation of being a man with an iron fist.

Soon after Chen became party secretary of Xinjiang in August 2016, he began using similar 'magic weapon' tactics to Xi. He purged disobedient party cadres, revitalised the provincial united front work task forces and militarised the law and order system as he had done in Tibet. Before his infamous re-education camps were exposed to the public in 2017, Chen had been known for controversial tactics such as confiscating the passports of all Tibetans, stationing law enforcement and/or armed soldiers on the street corners of major cities and hiring more than 3 million Neighbourhood Watch personnel to run 81,140 surveillance posts all over the autonomous region in the name of 'grid-style social management' (社会网格化管理, *shehui wanggehua guanli*) (Zenz & Leibold, 2017).

What differentiates Chen from Xi's other lieutenants is the way he has revitalised united front work and taken it to the next level. He demanded that the local UFWD apparatus implement aggressive assimilation policies, including closing religious schools, taking over religious activities, making frequent visits to the homes of minority leaders, pairing up (结对子, *jie duizi*) Han cadres with united front targets in close contact and, in some cases, marrying off their daughters when possible. 'Cadre-family pairing' (结对认亲, *jiedui renqin*) is a united front work policy that arranges for minority or disadvantaged Han families to be matched with the families of local civil servants to form a fabricated 'kinship'. The aim is to monitor the whole clan, control their behaviour and ensure unshakeable loyalty to the party (Liao & Tsai, 2019).[10] The designated families are forced to host assigned civil servants at their homes for a few weeks per year, which in the case of Xinjiang are middle-aged party cadres from the XPCC. Eventually, the female members of the families have no choice but to 'sleep with' these men under the same roof—even sharing the same beds, according to some reports—when their husbands, brothers or sons are behind bars or locked up under the re-education programs (Kang & Wang, 2018).

---

10   Pairing up is a commonly used method not only to control minorities but also for poverty alleviation, disaster relief and other social affairs involving local and central collaboration.

Although the Chinese propaganda machine continues to deny these allegations, claiming that they are lies 'from a defamation campaign … in an attempt to discredit and suppress China' (China Change, 2021), the CPC's own internal propaganda has confirmed that pairing up is a common practice for 'helping' minorities in Tibet and Xinjiang. The CPC has felt no shame in telling Chinese people how thoroughly these intrusive practices have been enforced on minority families. On 2 January 2019, the Central UWFD's WeChat account published a post online revealing that '1.12 million cadres from city governments, state-owned enterprises, central government liaison offices in Xinjiang, PLA divisions, armed police garrisons and XPCC have established "pairing up" marriages with 1.69 million local families all with ethnic backgrounds in Xinjiang' (Qiaoyi, 2019). On 8 January 2021, the Tibet Autonomous Region (TAR) government published a statement on state-owned media announcing that 160,000 cadres, including TAR officials, work teams and staff stationed in villages, and Tibet aid workers from the central government, have 'paired up poor families and households' in Tibet (Lasa Ribao, 2021).

Initially, the chilling securitisation and militarisation in Tibet and Xinjiang did not stir a lot of attention outside China except for occasional news articles reported by religious freedom and ethnic rights watch groups. The turning point came in November 2019 when the International Consortium of Investigative Journalists (ICIJ) and the *New York Times* released a joint report based on a collection of hundreds of pages of internal documents. The leaked documents revealed secret discussions between CPC general secretary Xi Jinping and his Xinjiang administrators, extensive manuals on how to run the camps and prevent people escaping, and details about how some local administrators were punished because they refused to obey these brutal orders (Austin & Chris, 2019). With this concrete evidence, legislators of several nations proposed or passed Xinjiang-related bills that have since led to the international boycotting of Xinjiang slave labour and China's 2022 Winter Olympic Games.

In response, Xi mobilised his Great United Front machine to counter international condemnation. China's global news channel CGTN released at least two documentaries about the party's achievements in Xinjiang on YouTube while countless 'pink' netizens posted on Twitter, Facebook and Instagram in support of Xinjiang cotton and other products. Press conferences were held to defend China's position on Xinjiang by an unprecedented number of government agencies and government-controlled non-governmental organisations (GONGOs) such as the China Society for Human Rights Studies (CSHRS), Islamic Association of China (ISA) and China Foundation for Human Rights Development (CFHRD).

Among the Chinese campaigns is a particular counterargument that since there are more mosques in Xinjiang than in the United States, Uyghurs enjoy more religious freedom than US Muslims. An analysis of 2,158 accounts removed by Twitter shows that the Chinese government sponsored private groups like Changyu Culture (张裕文化, *zhangyu wenhua*) and Xinjiang Online (新疆网, *xinjiang wang*) to spread positive 'testimonials' from Uyghurs talking about their colourful culture and prosperous lives in China (e.g. #新疆好生活 [*xinjiang haoshenghuo*]) in order to influence public views about Xinjiang (Ryan et al., 2021).

One result of these formal and informal influence operations was an international community that was divided on the Xinjiang issue: the Third Committee of the United Nations General Assembly at UN headquarters in New York issued two separate statements on 29 October 2019. One was drafted by 23 countries, including the United Kingdom, the United States, France, Germany, Canada, Australia and Japan, and expressed serious concerns about the human rights violations, while another 54 countries, including Russia, Belarus, Iran and mostly developing and Muslim nations, praised China's achievements in economic development, poverty alleviation and anti-terrorism in Xinjiang (BBC Zhongwen Wang, 2019). Chinese media proudly quoted the opinions of 'foreign media' from Russia or Iran and 'human rights experts' with government backgrounds to support the idea that China had won this global human rights battle.

For example, the *Global Times* often quoted the Chinese scholar Qian Jinyu (钱锦宇), executive dean of the Human Rights Institution of Northwest University of Political Science and Law in Shaanxi province and a council director of the CSHRS: 'From the contrasting numbers, we can see that more countries support China's Xinjiang policy and gave an objective and fair judgement on Xinjiang's development on human rights. However, Western countries led by the US and UK are using human rights issues or truth-twisting methods for their political purposes' (Liu & Xie, 2019).

Conclusion: From resilient to sharp authoritarianism

As Xi enters his third term in 2022, China will continue to promote a party-central and militant policy on religion and religious minorities that is strengthened by the Great United Front. Xi and his propaganda machine have called this sinicisation, a Chinese version of ultra-nationalism that puts party loyalty above all. Yet this 'freedom with Xi Jinping characteristics' is moving away from both the universal standards of religious freedom and the CPC's own practical approach in the post-1979 reform era.

In comparison, Xi's approach is a rejuvenation of Mao's united front concept with updated tactics interplaying brutal internal purges, intensified legal regulations and a steroid-injected party organ for its implementation. Cleaning one's own house is the top priority and is highly characteristic of this process. The cross-removal campaign and radical anti-extremist campaigns show that Xi was dissatisfied with the old United Front arrangement represented by the 'Wenzhou Model' in Zhejiang and the 'united multi-ethnic state' in Xinjiang, and his lieutenants were eager to create new methods to flush out incompetent cadres and impudent religious and minority elites, in order to keep potential social resistance at bay. The new cadres and updated standards were followed by new laws, programs and concentration camps and the rest is history.

For this reason, we are seeing a notable continuation of older religious and minority control tactics. We continue to see Xi's officials taking group pictures with pastors and monks, attending grand religious ceremonies and funding conferences and summits as long as they help out the party's Great United Front on such issues as Tibet, Xinjiang, Hong Kong and Taiwan, or foreign policies like the Belt and Road Initiative. At the same time, its core doctrine, which had been much more tolerant and flexible in the Deng, Jiang and Hu eras, has been replaced—the party is now above all. Furthermore, the Great United Front is 'greater' because its responsibility now knows no bounds. United Front cadres who used to consist more of educators, researchers and conference organisers in relevant fields are now also taking the lead in maintaining community security, persecuting defiant participants and monitoring hostile overseas individuals and groups. In other words, Xi's China is less preoccupied with boosting its popularity than with eliminating threats to its legitimacy. A summary of the contrast between the old and the new methods is offered in table 10.1.

Table 10.1: Regulating religion and minority affairs: Before and after

	Doctrine	Tactics	Cases
Old United Front	Document 19: 'guide religions in adapting to socialist society' (*zongjiao yu shehui zhuyi xiang shiying*), managing religions by law (*yi fa guanli zongjiao*), a united multi-ethnic state (*tongyi de duo minzu guojia*)	Co-optation through legalising patriotic associations and marginalising unsanctioned groups; micro-managing affairs through central SARA and local UFWD staff	Zhejiang's TSPM and Christian Council churches, the building of China's Jerusalem Xinjiang's XUAR and multi-ethnic schools, markets and working environment
Xi's Great United Front	Political integrity (*zhengzhi yishi*), think in big-picture terms (*daju yishi*), follow the leadership core (*hexin yishi*) and keep in alignment (*kanqi yishi*), sinicisation of religion (*zongjiao zhongguohua*)	Internal purging, re-education and reconstruction; tougher regulations and more extralegal control methods; de-Islamisation (*qu yisilanhua*): militant assimilation and radical anti-extremism programs	Zhejiang's DCC campaign, Joseph Gu and Chongyi Church Xinjiang's 'grid-style social management' (*shehui wang hehua guanli*) Tibet: 'cadre-family pairing' (*jiedui renqin*)

Source: Author's summary.

While the new wave of the Great United Front is supposed to facilitate more inter-provincial and centre–local collaboration in the enforcement of religious and minority regulations (which had become cracked and weakened in the post-reform era), it might just as easily frighten cautious cadres, create more self-censorship and, ironically, hamper further collaboration. United front work in ethnic and religious communities is a core task for the UFWD, but there is an obvious reason why it cannot work well: how can religious and minority populations trust promises from the authorities after what has been happening in Zhejiang and Xinjiang? Without genuine cooperation from their constituencies, local officials have little choice but to keep delaying, wrangling and passing the buck.

Cases of persecution and prosecution are more frequently reported in troubled regions like Tibet and Xinjiang. Promotion-minded cadres who have paid close attention to Xi's rhetoric of sinicisation may be responsible for the most aggressive acts of religious repression, defeating the purpose of long-term United Front efforts. Provincialism has proven itself to be one of the most dangerous challenges to the effectiveness of the United Front (Tong, 2014). The United Front's failure to win over target groups is demonstrated by harsh local securitisation and militant policies such as the demolition of mosques and churches, the banning of religious education and publications, re-education camps, frequent ID checking and the requiring of citizens to have their names and IDs engraved on their own kitchen knives.

The story of religion and religious minorities under Xi Jinping presents a lesson that is central to the study of comparative authoritarianism. It has long been argued that the CPC's success came from its institutional resilience and ideological flexibility to overcome a wide range of sociopolitical challenges (Nathan, 2003). After witnessing its wolf-warrior diplomacy and the Great United Front abroad, international relations scholars such as Joseph Nye now call this 'sharp power' and argue that strong authoritarian regimes like the CPC have a unique ability to exploit the freedoms and democratic institutions in liberal democracies while using their authoritarian means to defend against the soft power of these democracies (Nye, 2018).

Yet the author has found that as one of the CPC's key institutions, the UFWD has both been overlooked and overestimated at the same time by our literature for some time. The literature has rarely discussed the department's centrality to many aspects of the CPC's discourses of legitimacy, and United Front methods and tactics have seldom been used to explain the party's longevity.

This analysis has revealed that while the party's overall legitimacy remains strong owing to its economic performance, the legitimation strategies conducted by its agencies are suffering significant difficulties and setbacks. However, these challenges have not prompted Xi to retreat but instead to strengthen the UFWD and radicalise its policies towards religion and religious minorities. One reasonable explanation for this dilemma is that Xi's true concerns are not really with religion or minorities; instead, he intends for the UFW to be used to ensure both the loyalty of its own elites and the ideological purity of party cadres. This echoes the way Mao repeatedly played this game before his Cultural Revolution destroyed all of the above.

Xi's tough regulations on religion and religious minorities are meant to shrink the collaborative space between social elites and party cadres, but he is also less likely to repeat Mao's mistakes. This is because Xi does not aim to convert religious believers completely, as Mao did. He also seems to distrust his administrators less. His main strategy has so far been to rely on legal and institutional means. Nonetheless, his top-performing lieutenants such as Xia Baolong and Chen Quanguo have managed to produce some deeply disturbing human rights incidents and bring international condemnation that the CPC cannot easily expunge. Religious and minority affairs will remain one of the toughest challenges for Xi and other Chinese leaders to come.

This chapter concludes that any examination of the party's regulation of religion and religious minorities should include the United Front. It may also be able to provide insights into the CPC's survival as well as its future prospects. While Xi is reconstructing the discourse, militarising tactics and launching a total overhaul of the institutions of the United Front, will he strengthen or weaken this magic weapon? After an examination of Xi's reforms of the UFWD and his new policies on religion and religious minorities, the fundamental limitations of this system are hard to miss. As the author and Gerry Groot have argued, the United Front is a self-defeating weapon because its power relies on the party's ability to lie to its constituency (Wang & Groot, 2018). As the tragic fate of Chinese Christians and Xinjiang's Uyghurs has shown us, the promise of freedom and prosperity can be taken away in an instant. How many incidents are needed before the United Front's targets seek to unplug themselves from the CPC's reality and finally realise the truth: that there is no spoon?

References

Andrew, J. (2013) 'Elite in China face austerity under Xi's rule.' *New York Times*, 27 March

Austin, R., & Chris, B. (2019) '"Absolutely no mercy": Leaked files expose how China organised mass detentions of Muslims.' *New York Times*, 16 November

Bays, H.D. (2003) 'Chinese Protestant Christianity today.' *China Quarterly* 174: 488–504. doi.org/10.1017/S0009443903000299

BBC Zhongwen Wang [BBC中文网, BBC Chinese] (2016) 'Zhejiang jiao an: Bao Guohua, Xing Wenxiang mushi fuqi zao zhong pan' [浙江教案：包国华、刑文香牧师夫妻遭重判, Zhejiang religious case: Husband and wife co-pastors Bao Guohua and Xing Wenxiang given heavy sentences]. 26 February. www.bbc.com/zhongwen/simp/china/2016/02/160226_china_church_trial

—— (2019) 'Zhongguo Xinjiang renquan wenti, lianheguo liang da zhenying ruhe duili' [中国新疆人权问题 联合国两大阵营如何对立]. 30 October. www.bbc.com/zhongwen/trad/world-50234021

Brady, M.A. (2017) 'Magic weapons: China's political influence activities under Xi Jinping' (paper presentation). Conference on the Corrosion of Democracy under China's Global Influence, Arlington, VA, 16–17 September. www.wilson center.org/article/magic-weapons-chinas-political-influence-activities-under-xi-jinping

Buckley, C., & Tatlow, K.T. (2015) 'Cultural revolution shaped China's leader, from schoolboy to survivor.' *New York Times*, 24 September

Cao, N. (2008) 'Boss Christians: The business of religion in the "Wenzhou Model" of Christian revival.' *China Journal* 59: 63–87. doi.org/10.1086/tcj.59.20066380

—— (2010) *Constructing China's Jerusalem: Christians, Power and Place in Contemporary Wenzhou*. Stanford University Press

Caster, M. (2017) *The People's Republic of the Disappeared: Stories from Inside China's System for Enforced Disappearances*. Safeguard Defenders

China Change (2015) 'Christian sentiment in Zhejiang against cross removal: Three statements.' 7 August. chinachange.org/2015/08/07/christian-sentiment-in-zhejiang-against-cross-removal-three-statements

China Daily (2021) 'Things to know about all the lies on Xinjiang: How have they come about?', 30 April. www.chinadaily.com.cn/a/202104/30/WS608b 4036a31024ad0babb623.html

Clark, R.H. (2015) 'What makes a Chinese god? Or, what makes a god Chinese?' In *Imperial China and Its Southern Neighbours*, ed. V. Mair & L. Kelley, pp. 111–39. ISEAS–Yusof Ishak Institute

Cook, S. (2017a) 'The battle for China's spirit: Religious revival, repression and resistance under Xi Jinping.' Freedom House. freedomhouse.org/report/special-report/2017/battle-chinas-spirit

—— (2017b) 'Christianity: Religious freedom in China.' Freedom House. freedom house.org/report/2017/battle-china-spirit-christianity-religious-freedom

Cunningham, E., Saich, T., & Turiel, J. (2020) 'Understanding CCP resilience: Surveying Chinese public opinion through time.' Ash Centre for Democratic Governance and Innovation. ash.harvard.edu/files/ash/files/final_policy_brief_7.6.2020.pdf

Dean, K. (2003) 'Local communal religion in contemporary South-east China.' *China Quarterly* 174: 338–58. doi.org/10.1017/S0009443903000214

Groot, G. (2003) *Managing Transitions: The Chinese Communist Party, United Front Work, Corporatism and Hegemony*. Routledge

—— (2016) 'The expansion of the united front under Xi Jinping.' In *China Story Yearbook 2015: Pollution*, ed. G. Davies, J. Goldkorn & L. Tomba, pp. 168–77. ANU Press. doi.org/10.22459/CSY.09.2016

Guo, B.S. [郭宝胜], & Liu, Y. [刘贻] (2015) 'Guo Baosheng, Liu Yi mushi zai "xi zhengquan xia buduan ehua de zongjiao pohai" xinwen hui shang de fayan' [郭宝胜、刘贻牧师在「习政权下不断恶化的宗教迫害」新闻会上的发言, Remarks by pastors Guo Baosheng and Liu Yi at the press conference on 'The Worsening Religious Persecution under Xi's Regime']. China Aid, 24 September. www.chinaaid.net/2015/09/blog-post_81.html

Hamilton, C., & Ohlberg, M. (2020) *Hidden Hand: Exposing How the Chinese Communist Party is Reshaping the World*. Hardie Grant Books

Hill, M., Campanale, D., & Gunter, J. (2021) '"Their goal is to destroy everyone": Uighur camp detainees allege systematic rape.' BBC News, 2 February. www.bbc.com/news/world-asia-china-55794071

Joske, A. (2019) 'Reorganising the United Front Work Department: New structures for a new era of diaspora and religious affairs work.' *China Brief* 19(9): 6–13

Kang, D., & Wang, Y.N. (2018) 'China's Uighurs told to share beds, meals with party members.' AP News, 1 December. apnews.com/article/ap-top-news-international-news-prayer-weddings-occasions-9ca1c29fc9554c1697a8729bba4dd93b

Kou, C.W., & Tsai, W.H. (2014) '"Sprinting with small steps" towards promotion: Solutions for the age dilemma in the CCP cadre appointment system.' *China Journal* 71: 153–71. doi.org/10.1086/674558

Lai, C.T. (2003) 'Daoism in China today, 1980–2002.' *China Quarterly* 174: 413–27. doi.org/10.1017/S0009443903000251

Lasa Ribao [拉萨日报, Lasa Daily News] (2021) 'Xizang jin 16 wan ming ganbu yu pinkun qunzhong jiedui renqin' [西藏近16万名干部与贫困群众结对认亲, Nearly 160,000 cadres in Tibet have undergone family pairing with the poor]. 8 January. www.xizang.gov.cn/xwzx_406/ztzl_416/cxzt/fpgj/202101/t20210108_186605.html

Leibold, J. (2012) 'Toward a second generation of ethnic policy?' *China Brief* 12(13): 7–9. jamestown.org/program/toward-a-second-generation-of-ethnic-policies/

Liao, X.M., & Tsai, W.H. (2019) 'Clientelistic state corporatism: The united front model of "pairing-up" in the Xi Jinping era.' *China Review* 19(1): 31–56. www.jstor.org/stable/26603249

Liu, X., & Xie, W.T. (2019) '54 countries renew support for China's Xinjiang policy.' *Global Times*, 21 October. www.globaltimes.cn/content/1168522.shtml

Ma, L., & Li, J. (2017) *Surviving the State, Remaking the Church: A Sociological Portrait of Christians in Mainland China*. Pickwick Publications

Madsen, R. (2003) 'Catholic revival during the reform era.' *China Quarterly* 174: 469–87. doi.org/10.1017/S0009443903000287

Martin, D. (2014) 'Nationalism and religion; collective identity and choice: The 1989 revolutions, evangelical revolution in the global south, revolution in the Arab world.' *Nations and Nationalism* 20(1): 1–17. doi.org/10.1111/nana.12034

Mertha, A. (2009) 'Fragmented authoritarianism 2.0: Political pluralisation in the Chinese policy process.' *China Quarterly* 200: 995–1012. doi.org/10.1017/S0305741009990592

Nathan, J.A. (2003) 'Authoritarian resilience.' *Journal of Democracy* 14(1): 6–17. doi.org/10.1353/jod.2003.0019

Nikkei Asia (2021) 'Full text of the Chinese Communist Party's new resolution on history.' 19 November. asia.nikkei.com/Politics/Full-text-of-the-Chinese-Communist-Party-s-new-resolution-on-history

Nye, S.J. (2018) 'China's soft and sharp power.' Project Syndicate, 4 January. www.project-syndicate.org/commentary/china-soft-and-sharp-power-by-joseph-s--nye-2018-01

O'Brien, K., & Li, L. (2007) *Rightful Resistance in Rural China*. Cambridge University Press

Permanent Mission of the People's Republic of China to the United Nations and Other International Organisations in Vienna (2004) *National Minorities Policy and Its Practice in China* (White Paper). www.fmprc.gov.cn/ce/cgvienna/eng/ljzg/zfbps/t127407.htm (page discontinued)

Perry, E. (2001) 'Challenging the mandate of heaven: Popular protest in modern China.' *Critical Asian Studies* 33(2): 163–80. doi.org/10.1080/14672710122544

Potter, B.P. (2003) 'Belief in control: Regulation of religion in China.' *China Quarterly* 174(2): 317–37. doi.org/10.1017/S0009443903000202

PRC State Council (2019) 'Constitution of the People's Republic of China.' english.www.gov.cn/archive/lawsregulations/201911/20/content_WS5ed8856ec6d0b3f0e9499913.html

Qiaoyi [乔伊] (2019) 'Jingbao Xinjiang baiwan nan peidui jihua: Qiangzhi shaoshu minzu funu 1 nian peishui 36 tian' [惊爆新疆百万男配对计划: 强制少数民族妇女1年陪睡36天, Shocking news about Xinjiang Million Men Matching Plan: Forces minority women to sleep with them for 36 days a year]. *Aboluowang* [阿波罗新闻网], 9 November. hk.aboluowang.com/2019/1109/1366857.html

Ramzy, A., & Buckley, C. (2019) '"Absolutely no mercy": Leaked files expose how China organised mass detentions of Muslims.' *New York Times*, 16 November

Reynolds, A. (2015) 'The 10th Panchen Lama and Xi Jinping's father.' Chinese Leaders, 25 January. chinese-leaders.org/blog/xi-zhongxun-panchen-lama

Ryan, F., Bogle, A., Zhang, A. & Wallis, J. (2021) '#StopXinjiang rumours: The CCP's decentralised disinformation campaign.' Australian Strategic Policy Institute

Shi, J.T. (2020) 'Xia Baolong—From toppling church crosses to overseeing Hong Kong affairs.' *South China Morning Post*, 13 February. www.scmp.com/news/china/politics/article/3050540/xia-baolong-toppling-church-crosses-overseeing-hong-kong

Si, Li [思力] (2019) 'Fangzhi zhengchu duomen, dujue tuiwei chepi' [防止政出多门、杜绝推诿扯皮, Prevent bureaucratic overlaps, put a stop to buck passing and wrangling]. Qiu Shi [求是], 26 November

Tamney, J.B. (2005) 'Introduction.' In *State, Market and Religions in Chinese Societies*, ed. J.B. Tamney & F. Yang, pp. 1–17. Brill

Tong, J. (2014) 'The devil is in the local: Provincial religious legislation in China, 2005–2012.' *Religion, State and Society* 42(1): 66–88. doi.org/10.1080/09637494.2014.887359

Tsai, L.L. (2007) *Accountability Without Democracy: Solidary Groups and Public Goods Provision in Rural China*. Cambridge University Press

Vala, C.T. (2017) *The Politics of Protestant Churches and the Party-State in China: God Above Party?* Routledge

Wang, R. (2017) 'Authoritarian resilience versus everyday resistance: The unexpected strength of religious advocacy in promoting transnational activism in China.' *Journal for the Scientific Study of Religion* 56: 558–76. doi.org/10.1111/jssr.12366

—— (2019) *Resistance under Communist China: Religious Protesters, Advocates and Opportunists*. Palgrave Macmillan

Wang, R., & Groot, G. (2018) 'Who represents? Xi Jinping's grand united front work, legitimation, participation and consultative democracy.' *Journal of Contemporary China* 27(112): 569–83. doi.org/10.1080/10670564.2018.1433573

Wenweipo [文汇网] (2015) 'Shiba da hou 18 sheng diao tongzhanbu zhang 24 sheng you changwei jianren' [十八大后18省调统战部长 24省由常委兼任, After the 18th National Congress of the CPC, 18 provinces fill UFWD chairs with standing committee members]. 10 August. news.wenweipo.com/2015/08/10/IN1508100004.htm

Williams, I. (2012) 'Why did blind activist Chen Guangcheng anger Chinese authorities?' NBC News Beijing, 5 May. www.nbcnews.com/news/world/why-did-blind-activist-chen-guangcheng-anger-chinese-authorities-flna753595

Xi, J. [习近平] (2013) 'Dang de qunzhong luxian jiaoyu shijian huodong gongzuo huiyi zhaokai, Xi Jinping fabiao zhongyao jianghua' [党的群众路线教育实践活动工作会议召开 习近平发表重要讲话, The Party's Mass Line Education and Practice Movement Work Conference convenes, Xi Jinping makes important speech]. China Copyright and Media, 19 June. chinacopyrightandmedia.word press.com/2013/06/19/xi-jinping-launches-party-rectification-movement

—— (2017) 'Dang de shijiu da baogao shuang yu quanwen' [党的十九大报告双语全文, Bilingual full text of the Party's report to the 19th National Congress of the Communist Party of China]. *China Daily*, 16 November. www.chinadaily.com.cn/interface/flipboard/1142846/2017-11-06/cd_34188086.html

Yang, F. (2006) 'The red, black and gray markets of religion in China.' *Sociological Quarterly* 47(1): 93–122. doi.org/10.1111/j.1533-8525.2006.00039.x

—— (2018) 'The failure of the campaign to demolish church crosses in Zhejiang province, 2013–2016: A temporal and spatial analysis, 2013–2016.' *Review of Religion and Chinese Society* 5(1): 5–25. doi.org/10.1163/22143955-00501002

Ying, F.T. [邢福增] (2016) 'Chai shi fengbao zhong de Gu Yuese mushi' [拆十风暴中的顾约瑟牧师, Pastor Joseph Gu in the ten demolitions storm]. *Duanchanmei* [端传媒, Initium Media], 3 February. theinitium.com/article/20160203-opinion-yingfuktsang-cross

—— (2018) 'The politics of cross demolition: A religio-political analysis of the "Three Rectifications and One Demolition" campaign in Zhejiang Province.' *Review of Religion and Chinese Society* 5(1): 43–75. doi.org/10.1163/22143955-00501004

Yu, M.M. (2018) 'China's final solution in Xinjiang.' *Caravan* 1819, 9 October. www.hoover.org/research/chinas-final-solution-xinjiang

Zenz, A., & Leibold, J. (2017) 'Chen Quanguo: The strongman behind Beijing's securitisation strategy in Tibet and Xinjiang.' *China Brief* 17(12): 16–24. james town.org/program/chen-quanguo-the-strongman-behind-beijings-securitization-strategy-in-tibet-and-xinjiang/

Zhang, P. (2022) 'Former Chinese justice minister expelled from Communist Party, accused of corruption.' *South China Morning Post*, 1 April. www.scmp.com/news/china/politics/article/3172654/former-chinese-justice-minister-expelled-communist-party

Zhang, X. (2016) 'Zhongyang tongzhanbu yuan fu mishu zhang: Zhongguo "datongzhan" geju chubu xingcheng' [中央统战部原副秘书长：中国「大统战」格局初步形成, UFWD former deputy secretary-general: China's 'Great United Front' setup has taken shape]. *Ta Kung Pao* [大公报], 30 September. news.takungpao.com/mainland/focus/2016-09/3375185.html

Zhonguo Gongchandang Xinwen Wang [中国共产党新闻网, CPC News] (2015) 'Zhongguo gongchandang tongyi zhanxian gongzuo tiaoli (shixing)' [中国共产党统一战线工作条例（试行）, Regulations on the work of the United Front of the Communist Party of China (trial implementation)]. 23 September. cpc.people.com.cn/n/2015/0923/c64107-27622040.html

—— (2021) 'Zhongguo gongchandang tongyi zhanxian gongzuo tiaoli' [中国共产党统一战线工作条例, Regulations on the work of the United Front of the Communist Party of China]. Zhonguo Gongchandang Xinwen Wang, 6 January. politics.people.com.cn/BIG5/n1/2021/0106/c1001-31990197.html

Zhonghua Renmin Gongheguo Guowuyuan Xinwen Bangongshi [中华人民共和国国务院新闻办公室, State Council Information Office of the People's Republic of China] (2018) 'Zhongguo baozhang zongjiao xinyang ziyou de zhengce han shijian bai pi shu' [《中国保障宗教信仰自由的政策和实践》白皮书, China's policies and practices on safeguarding freedom of religious belief] (White Paper)

11

Revolutionary-style campaigns and social control in the PRC: The campaign to Sweep Away Black and Eliminate Evil

Ben Hillman[1]

During the Mao era, the CPC mobilised the masses through campaigns to achieve rapid social and economic change. It also used these campaigns as tools of political and social control—either to reform or to annihilate the party's perceived enemies. Although the party's present-day governing style is more rational and bureaucratic than revolutionary, the party continues to use campaigns in support of priority political and policy goals. The CPC has used campaigns to achieve policy goals such as the nationwide campaign to combat poverty (Zeng, 2020) and the 'building the socialist countryside' campaign, which sought to transform rural economy and society (Perry, 2011). Campaigns are also deployed for political and social control purposes, and some campaigns combine policy and political and social control objectives. By targeting official corruption as well as political rivals, Xi Jinping's anti-corruption campaign was one such example.

1   This chapter is a revised and updated version of the article that first appeared as B. Hillman (2021) 'Law, order and social control in Xi's China.' *Issues and Studies* 57(2), Article 2150006. doi.org/10.1142/S1013251121500065. Reprinted with permission.

Another example of a campaign that combines policy and social and political control objectives is the campaign of 2018–20 to Sweep Away Black and Eliminate Evil (扫黑除恶, *saohei chue*). On the surface, Sweep Away Black was a law enforcement campaign targeting criminal syndicates known as 'black societies' (黑社会, *hei shehui*) and activities typically associated with gangsters such as gambling, prostitution, drug trafficking, protection rackets, extortion and coercive monopolies that distorted local markets. The stated goals of the campaign were to eradicate a variety of crimes that bedevilled local communities and corrupted local economic activity. As the campaign unfolded, however, it became clear that targets included a wider number of 'deviant' elements within society who had previously eluded control. Campaign documents called on party branches to work with local Public Security Bureaus to confront a wide range of threats to social order and party authority.

Drawing on an analysis of policy documents and official reports as well as 31 interviews with government officials, police and citizens in Yunnan Province, this chapter examines the way the Sweep Away Black campaign was used for purposes of political and social control beyond its stated law enforcement goals. The design and implementation of the campaign highlight a new approach to political campaigns, one that is more managerial than revolutionary and integrated with party efforts to institutionalise a rules-based society and economy in accordance with notions of 'rule by law' (依法治国, *yifa zhiguo*). It also complements ideological campaigns such as the 'core socialist values' program, which are designed to shape citizen values and behaviour and integrate moral values into the law.[2] This study provides insights into emerging techniques of political and social control, notably the way the party harnesses the revolutionary traditions of the Mao era and fuses them with legal and rational modes of governance.

The campaign to Sweep Away Black and Eliminate Evil has to date received scant scholarly attention, arguably because it was launched at a time of rising censorship and restrictions on academic freedom within China (Barmé, 2019; Zhao, 2016) and increasingly limited access to the field for foreign scholars and journalists. Despite the lack of media and academic coverage, it has been one of the most significant domestic political

2   The 'core socialist values' program is an official interpretation of Chinese socialism and was introduced at the 18th Party Congress in 2012. The 12 values include the national values of prosperity, democracy, civility and harmony; the social values of freedom, equality, justice and the rule of law; and the individual values of patriotism, dedication, integrity and friendship. See Lin and Trevaskes (2019).

initiatives of Xi Jinping's second term. The evidence for this can be seen in the campaign's leadership structure and in the ubiquity of its promotion, which at least in 2018 and 2019 had overwhelmed previously dominant street propaganda about the 'Chinese dream' and the CPC's 'core socialist values'. The campaign's propaganda and information materials covered the country, including major urban centres.

The Leading Small Group for the Special Struggle to Sweep Away Black and Eliminate Evil was established to oversee the campaign. Similar to a task force, leading small groups (领导小组, *lingdao xiaozu*) are key hubs of power at the top of China's party-state. Typically led by a member of the Politburo, they bring together heads of agencies that are responsible for the achievement of high-level political and public policy goals. Since becoming CPC secretary general, Xi Jinping has personally chaired many of the existing leading small groups as a way of consolidating his power over the party-state apparatus. He has also established new ones under his direct control, including the National Security Commission, which oversees law enforcement and national security. The most powerful leading small groups are established as permanent commissions (委员会, *weiyuanhui*). Leading Small Groups may be established under the party, the State Council or the People's Liberation Army.

The Leading Small Group for the Special Struggle to Sweep Away Black and Eliminate Evil was established within the party's powerful Central Political and Legal Affairs Commission, headed by Xi Jinping protégé Guo Shengkun (郭声琨). A member of the Politburo and former minister of public security, Guo is also the director of the Leading Small Group for the Special Struggle to Sweep Away Black and Eliminate Evil. Other members of the high-powered group at the time of its creation were Deputy Director Zhao Kezhi (赵克志), the minister of public security; Chief Justice of the Supreme Court Zhou Qiang (周强); Chief Prosecutor General Zhang Jun (张军); Deputy Party Secretary of the Central Commission for Discipline Inspection Li Shulei (李书磊), who is also known as a top adviser to and confidant of Xi Jinping; the then deputy chief of the party's Organisation Department, Qi Yu (齐玉); and Secretary General of the Central Commission for Discipline Inspection Chen Yixin (陈一新), who also serves as deputy director of the powerful Central Commission for Comprehensively Deepening Reform.

The composition of the Leading Small Group reflects the state agencies coordinating the implementation of the campaign: the Supreme People's Court, the Supreme People's Procuratorate, the Public Safety Bureau (police) and the Ministry of Justice. Every province, district, municipality, county and township in China has established a Sweep Away Black Office (扫黑版, *saoheiban*) to coordinate the activities of party and law enforcement organs. The office is responsible for educating party and government cadres about the objectives of the campaign and how to identify and apprehend those suspected of carrying out 'black and evil' deeds.

In several counties in Yunnan visited by the author in 2019, there were more party and government meetings about Sweeping Away Black and Eliminating Evil than any other policy issue. A scan of provincial and subprovincial government websites suggests this pattern was repeated across the country, underscoring the political priority Xi Jinping placed on the campaign. To reinforce the political importance of the campaign, its implementation was accorded 'veto' status (一票否决, *yipiao foujue*) in cadre performance evaluations conducted by the party's Organisation Department—hence the department's prominent representation in the Leading Small Group. If a task has veto status, officials who fail to deliver on its goals will not be considered for promotion regardless of their performance and achievements in other areas. The veto is an administrative mechanism that is widely used in China to motivate officials to throw themselves into key political campaigns (Hillman, 2010, 2014).

The strategies for implementing the campaign to Sweep Away Black and Eliminate Evil were articulated in detail in documents issued by the Leading Small Group and by justice agencies such as the People's Procuratorate and the Supreme Court. The documents illustrate the party's new tightly controlled, managerial and sequenced approach to such campaigns. According to the documents, the campaign was to be implemented in three, year-long phases. In the first phase in 2018, law enforcement officials were to 'treat the symptoms' of 'black' and 'evil'. That is, their task was to crack down on criminal organisations and activities and round up as many offenders as possible, including those officials and agents of law enforcement who served as 'protective umbrellas' (保护伞, *baohusan*) for criminals and criminal organisations. The targeting of these protective umbrellas is where Sweep Away Black intersects with Xi Jinping's anti-corruption campaign and can be seen in some regards as an extension of it.

In the second phase in 2019, law enforcement was tasked with digging through the available evidence and investigating tougher, more complex cases of black and evil, for example those involving criminal syndicates. In the third phase in 2020, law enforcement was to tackle the 'root cause' of black and evil by establishing 'long-lasting mechanisms' to suppress criminal activity and 'strengthen party organisation' at the grassroots. Here we see the intersections between the campaign and parallel efforts to strengthen local party branches; namely, the capacity of party branches to influence policy, administration and law enforcement at the local level, especially at the community level of rural villages and urban neighbourhoods. Party cadres were expected to 'achieve an overwhelming victory in the special struggle to combat evil and eliminate evil'.

During several visits to China in 2018 and 2019, I observed that there was no topic more widely covered in public propaganda than the campaign to Sweep Away Black and Eliminate Evil. Beginning in 2018, giant billboards about the campaign greeted arrivals at airports, trains and bus stations, and city streets were adorned with a multitude of signs explaining the campaign and giving the public instructions on how to report someone suspected of having committed a black and evil deed, a concept illustrated by graphic posters depicting gangsters beating up people and extorting money.

In nearly every café and restaurant in Yunnan I visited in 2019, there was a small sign on the table explaining the list of offences the campaign was targeting and listing a police hotline for reporting transgressions. A reward was promised to anyone who led the police to uncover a black or evil deed. In one hotel I stayed in, the room was adorned with a 20-page glossy brochure that outlined all the misdeeds that the campaign sought to rectify. These included (1) Gangland Vice: gambling, opening casinos, forcing women to work in public entertainment venues such as karaoke bars, dance halls, spas and chess and card rooms; (2) Extortion and Protection: bullying, pressure buying and selling, extortion, protection rackets and the disturbance of the normal order of business at markets, wharves, tourist attractions and other places by such undesirables as 'vegetable tyrants' (菜霸, *caiba*), 'city tyrants' (市霸, *shiba*) and 'transport tyrants' (行霸, *xingba*) who used mafia tactics to monopolise services and distribution; (3) Loan Sharking and Usury: 'trick loans' (套路贷, *taoludai*), campus loans (校园贷, *xiaoyuandai*), 'nude loans' (裸贷, *luodai*) and other forms of illegal loans in addition to assault, illegal detention and threats and intimidation in debt collection.[3]

---

3   The details are reproduced from CPC documents. See 'Zhonggong Zhongyang Guowuyuan' (2018).

In addition to highlighting the campaign's importance, the extensive propaganda also serves to remind people that the party is being tough on crime and implicitly respond to public perceptions that the police are derelict or corrupt in discharging their duties. As Peng Wang (2020) has noted, both authoritarian and democratic parties routinely promote themselves as defenders of law and order. He further suggests that the emphasis on law and order in both cases serves to distract public attention from other social ills and policy shortcomings such as economic slowdowns and social instability. I argue that the campaign also establishes a mechanism by which the party can reassert its control at the grassroots after decades of community empowerment that has seen its influence recede, particularly in rural areas (Hillman, 2004).

The campaign's origins: The Chongqing prototype

The PRC has a long history of using 'strike hard' (严打, *yanda*) campaigns to demonstrate that the party-state is tough on crime (Bakken, 2005; Trevaskes, 2006). This has been particularly so since the 1980s when organised crime made a resurgence (Broadhurst, 2012). Although party documents do not spell this out, the campaign to Sweep Away Black and Eliminate Evil has obvious roots in past campaigns. Most notable is the Strike Black campaign (打黑, *dahei*) launched in Chongqing in 2009 by the now disgraced (and imprisoned) former municipal party leader and Politburo member Bo Xilai (薄熙來). Following his appointment as Chongqing party secretary, the ambitious Bo began work on a set of social and economic policies designed to address growing inequalities in the south-western municipality while promoting revolutionary ('red') culture, making him a star among China's New Left (neo-Maoist) intellectuals. Bo Xilai is best known, however, for tackling crime and corruption in the city via a ruthless anti-crime campaign that targeted the city's gangs and their corrupt official networks.

In 2009, Bo appointed an ally from his previous tenure as mayor of Dalian City in Liaoning Province as Chongqing's new chief of police. They expanded the police force, removing rotten cops and rotating beats to undermine established networks of police and crooks. Within two years, Bo and his police chief oversaw the arrest of an estimated 5,700 criminals along with corrupt businesspeople, policemen, judges and government officials (P. Wang, 2013). The campaign was hugely popular in Chongqing and soon became famous around the country, especially as powerful gangsters and law enforcement officials who had once been considered untouchable were pulled into the city's dragnet. The city government seized luxurious cars, properties and businesses from those they arrested, flooding city coffers with funds that could be used to support Bo's social programs such as increased spending on public housing.

Described by insiders as a pilot for an eventual nationwide campaign,[4] Strike Black also struck at 'red–black' collusions between gangsters and party-state officials. This included official protection for criminal activities as well as local monopolies such as those that forced construction projects to purchase materials from a single supplier. The campaign's most prominent arrest was Wen Qiang (文強), head of the city's Justice Bureau, who was convicted and executed for bribery, shielding gangs, and being unable to explain how he came to accumulate millions of dollars in assets and cash. News media reported on multiple cases in which victims of crime had been denied justice because the perpetrators had connections in the police force and courts—a widespread problem and the source of much public anger in China.

By combatting crime and being seen to dispense justice more equitably, Bo Xilai's Strike Hard campaign was immensely popular with the public. However, it was also criticised for its ruthless disregard of legal procedures, including the extraction of confessions through torture (Lubman, 2012). Famously, Bo's prosecutors charged a defence attorney representing one of the mafia bosses with falsifying evidence, a move that was widely seen as a politically motivated attack on the defence attorney and the legal profession at large (Cabestan, 2011).

Upon its launch in 2018, Xi's Sweep Away Black and Eliminate Evil followed the Strike Black playbook by making sweeping arrests of organised criminals. Sweep Away Black also targeted anti-competitive practices such as stand-over tactics, manipulated tendering, illegal land occupation and illegal monopolies in industries and such fields as construction, building supplies, transport, mining, manufacturing, warehousing and logistics. The first round of Bo Xilai's Strike Hard campaign busted a network of organised crime that monopolised the sand-mining industry in one of Chongqing

---

4   'It is a pilot project in the plans for a nationwide push, adopted at the recent central leadership meeting', said Sidney Rittenberg, who has personally known every Chinese leader since Mao Zedong (Moore, 2009).

Municipality's towns. Xi Jinping's Sweep Away Black specifically targets 'sand tyrants' (沙霸, *shaba*), a term that has come to refer to any coercive monopolist of building materials.

Other similarities between the campaigns include the targeting of corrupt land deals. Sweep Away Black targets 'evil forces' (恶势力, *e shili*) in real estate development, forcibly charging 'site fees', 'management fees' and 'protection fees' in the process of land acquisition, land leases, demolition and construction. Other offences include the recruitment of 'hoodlums' (流氓, *liumang*)—a word with a broad application but that here signifies local thugs—to monopolise the market, disrupt production, take over work sites and violently destroy property. Developers often employ *liumang* to intimidate people who do not cooperate with projects that demand the requisition or demolition of their land, homes or property. Often, such activities involve collusion between businesspeople, gangsters and officials (their 'protective umbrellas'). Bo Xilai's Strike Black garnered attention for striking at these 'red–black' networks, a criminal version of the broader 'relationship networks' (关系网, *guanxi wang*) that permeate party, state and society and are the common pathways along which so much in China gets done.

Unlike the Chongqing prototype, however, the party-state more tightly regulated and controlled law enforcement targets and activities under Sweep Away Black, providing detailed and evolving policy guidelines.[5] Although authorities apprehended and imprisoned those who were swept up in the campaign's dragnet for extended periods while their cases were being investigated, party documents emphasised that charges and punishments had to be in accordance with established laws. I confirmed this in conversations with law enforcement and local officials and by first-hand observation. In one Yunnan village I had visited many times, locals confirmed that the village chief had been apprehended and investigated for corruption on at least three occasions during the campaign but was ultimately released for lack of evidence (personal communication, December 2019). This evidence-based approach to prosecution notwithstanding, a tarring with the 'black' brush could have devastating consequences. As discussed later in greater detail, this is one reason why such campaigns are effective tools of social and political control.

---

5 See for example *Opinions on Several Issues Concerning the Handling of Criminal Cases of Black and Evil Forces*, which was jointly released by the Supreme People's Court, the Supreme People's Procuratorate, the Ministry of Public Security and the Ministry of Justice (*Zhonghua Renmin Gongheguo Zuigao Renmin Jianchayuan*, 2019).

Sweep Away Black: Results and response

Understanding Sweep Away Black to be a top party priority and that their performance would be closely monitored, local officials mobilised their law enforcement agencies to begin making arrests soon after its launch in early 2018. The state news agency Xinhua reported that by the end of March 2019, the campaign had uncovered 14,226 cases of 'black and evil' activity involving 79,018 people nationwide (Yin, 2019). At the National Meeting to Promote the Special Struggle to Sweep Away Black and Eliminate Evil held in Xi'an on 13 October 2019, it was further revealed that 29,571 criminal gangs had been eliminated nationwide (Lu, 2019).

Media outlets gave extensive coverage to Sweep Away Black cases, especially those that involved the arrests of protective umbrellas (Hillman, 2020). In April 2019, Liaoning Province's Office for Discipline Inspection announced that it had investigated and responded to more than a thousand 'black and evil' cases, including some involving 'big fish' such as Ji Hongsheng (季洪生), the former deputy chief of Dandong City Public Security Bureau. Ji was sentenced to 10 years for helping criminals avoid prosecution. In the dock, Ji said, 'I thought was helping out a friend—no big deal. I didn't think it was a crime, but now I regret it' (Fan, 2019).

Political campaigns such as Sweep Away Black secure local compliance through the oversight and management of local officials charged with their enforcement (Burns & Zhou, 2010), but the campaign offered an additional incentive to cash-strapped local governments in the contribution to their coffers of confiscated properties and assets. Borrowing again from the Chongqing playbook, convicted crooks and their protective umbrellas could be subject to large fines as well as the confiscation of their cash, cars, businesses and property, with the proceeds flowing into local government coffers. On 8 May 2019, the People's Intermediate Court in Xiangyang City, Hubei Province convicted 12 gangsters guilty of offences under Sweep Away Black that included usury, kidnapping, extortion and intimidation. The court noted that it had carefully screened their property and assets and confiscated 'black monies' from the gang's ringleader to the value of 48 million yuan (US$6.7 million). All of his convicted associates were given jail terms and fines starting from 460,000 yuan (US$64,000). This was just one of 37 gangland cases sent to the courts by Sweep Away Black operations in Xiangyang in early 2019 (Hubei Sheng Renmin Zhengfu, 2019). In August 2019, Heilongjiang Province reported the smashing of 46 gangs and accompanying asset seizures totalling 2.17 billion yuan (US$300 million), almost eight times the average monthly value of such seizures in the period before the 'special struggle' began (Feng, 2019).

As with many other high-level national campaigns, Sweep Away Black encouraged competition among provinces and localities. In Yunnan Province, authorities boasted to me in interviews that they had smashed more than 5,000 criminal gangs. One high-profile case involved convicted rapist Sun Xiaoguo (孙小果), also known in the media as the 'Kunming Bully'. Despite being handed a death sentence in 1998, Sun was discovered by a journalist in April 2019 to be living freely in Kunming and a shareholder in multiple entertainment venues. He was also believed to be the head of a criminal gang. Subsequent investigations into the handling of his commuted prison sentence charged his parents and 17 others in connection with his evasion of justice. Sun's mother Sun Heyu (孙鹤予) was sentenced to 20 years, and his stepfather Li Qiaozhong (李桥忠) received 19 years for accepting and offering bribes. Others sentenced for helping Sun evade punishment included a former inspector at the provincial Justice Department Luo Zhengyun (罗正雲), as well as a former judge of the Yunnan People's Higher Court, Liang Zi'an (梁子安) (Zhongguo Ribaowang, 2019). Like the case of Ji Hongsheng in Liaoning Province, Sun's case received much attention in the media because it addressed a popular source of frustration in Chinese society: the unequal treatment that people receive in their encounters with law enforcement.

As with Xi Jinping's anti-corruption drive, the appeal to public opinion was part of the point of Sweep Away Black. The campaign targeted crimes such as loan sharking that were stirring public indignation. As China's economy cooled over several years and credit restrictions tightened across China, many ordinary citizens in need of money for various reasons, including access to health care, fell victim to loan sharking (Hillman, 2020). Loan sharks charge a high rate of interest for fast cash, and loan terms are typically short. Chinese law prohibits interest rates above 24 per cent per annum on any form of credit, but loan sharks will sometimes charge this amount and more per month. Borrowers find themselves in serious trouble if they fail to repay the loans on time. One loan shark offering is the 'nude loan'. These require borrowers (who are typically young and female) to provide the loan shark with nude photos of themselves that the loan shark will post on the internet in the event of default. Law enforcement in China calls such offences 'soft violence' (软暴力, *ruan baoli*). Debtors can experience hard violence, too. According to a local policeman I interviewed in Yunnan Province, 'gangs will do anything to terrorise people who owe them money [including] flushing people's heads in the toilet and making them eat shit. Sometimes loan sharks imprison people in a room until they come up with a plan for repayment' (personal communication, 2019). False (illegal) imprisonment is apparently so common that it has been specifically identified as one of the 'black and evil' acts to be eradicated. China's Ministry of Public Security announced in February 2018 that in just the first year of the Sweep Away Black campaign, it had arrested 16,249 suspects and seized 3.53 billion yuan ($US527 million) in connection with loan scams (Ren, 2019).

In a Yunnan village I visited in March 2019, locals confirmed the policeman's report and offered many examples of people who had met such fates. In several villages and towns that I visited, I found the police crackdown on loan sharking to be extremely popular among ordinary citizens. Many also reported satisfaction with the arrests of village tyrants behind coercive monopolies in the construction industry. In one village I visited, the village head and 21 of his associates had been arrested in connection with offences relates to uncompetitive practices. 'The gangs are quiet now', a former township head told me. 'They know this [crackdown] is serious' (personal communication, March 2019).

As Peng Wang (2020) notes, the campaign's targeting of unpopular gang activities has helped to bolster the legitimacy of the police and by extension the party. People I interviewed also expressed satisfaction with Sweep Away Black's crackdown on scams and rip-offs. In many parts of Yunnan Province, the local economy was highly dependent on tourism (Hillman, 2003, 2010). However, the province had attracted a bad name for tourism-related scams, and many in the industry perceive the widespread nature of such scams to be detrimental to the long-term health of the regional economy (Hillman, 2018). Yunnan had become notorious for cut-price holiday packages that unscrupulous operators often sold below the actual cost to unsuspecting domestic tourists. Sellers of souvenirs and local produce at inflated prices would in turn offer commissions in exchange for their delivery of busloads of tourists, enabling them to recoup a profit. In interviews in 2018 and 2019, local industry insiders confirmed that these roadside shopping centres had been closed and that this practice has now stopped. Many locals I interviewed were happy that authorities were cracking down on these illegal activities and scams because it was giving their region a bad name and driving tourist numbers down. According to one local entrepreneur, 'the crackdown might hurt the economy in the short-term, but I think it will be good for us in the long term. The party is doing the right thing' (personal communication, December 2019).

However, the public reaction to Sweep Away Black was not always favourable. During a second visit to China at the end of 2019, I noticed a shift in public attitudes in the same communities I had visited earlier in the year. Although citizens remained satisfied with the crackdown on loan sharks, many reported that the crackdown on gambling, a popular pastime in rural areas, had gone too far. As one man reported, 'Both of my sons were "swept away" [arrested] for gambling and spent one month in the town lockup. But they were just playing for fun. The police should focus on the gangsters and not the gamblers' (personal communication, December 2019).

I discovered in many places I visited that as part of the Sweep Away Black crackdown, the police were handing out short-term extrajudicial sentences to anyone caught participating in illegal activities. In another village I visited in the same county, I learned that the police had arrested more than 30 men for using illicit drugs. One policeman told me that they were under pressure to meet quotas and needed to arrest as many people as possible. In a once-sleepy township I had visited many times over the years—a place where police and township officials often enjoyed long midday siestas, police were working extra hours to meet the demands of the campaign. One woman whose brother was a police officer said he often did not return home from work until after 11 o'clock each evening. In one prefectural city, I learned that an additional 'black' (extrajudicial) prison had been constructed on the edge of town to accommodate all those swept up in the campaign, including many who were being detained (i.e. not formally arrested) for days or even weeks as extrajudicial punishment for their alleged connection to illegal activities.

The extrajudicial element also has parallels in the Chongqing experience: Bo Xilai's Strike Black force reportedly relied on forced confessions—an illegal but common *modus operandi* of China's Public Security Bureau—and abused those who questioned the campaign's legality. In a similar vein, Peng Wang (2020, p. 1) argued that the Sweep Away Black campaign 'distorts the criminal justice system by demanding that criminal justice organs deliver severe and swift justice'.

Peng Wang (2020) also sounded the alarm about Sweep Away Black's seizure of property, which was also a hallmark of Bo Xilai's crackdown in Chongqing. It was well known that Bo wanted a stronger state role in the economy, and many observers in China perceived his actions as being anti-private enterprise. Once the richest man in Chongqing, Li Jun (李俊) went on the run when the Public Security Bureau seized 700 million yuan (US$100 million) of his assets. From his place of hiding (presumably somewhere in China), the fugitive businessman described Strike Black as a violent struggle over property and power (Higgins, 2012).

Sweep Away Black was launched at a time when entrepreneurs in China were already nervous about Xi Jinping's preferential treatment of state-owned enterprises (SOEs) at the expense of private enterprise. Under Xi, the government was awarding SOEs an increasing proportion of government contracts and granting them easier access to finance than their private counterparts. The trend acquired its own epithet: 'the state advances, the private [sector] retreats' (国进民退, *guojin mintui*) (Hillman, 2019a). Just like in Chongqing in the late 2000s, businesspeople became nervous that officials—sometimes with the encouragement of business rivals—would use the excuse of Sweep Away Black to destroy their operations and seize their assets arbitrarily. 'The problem', as one businessperson in Yunnan's provincial capital of Kunming explained, 'is that any who's done business of any size in China has had interactions with officials and regulations that weren't always clear cut from a legal point of view. Everyone is vulnerable' (personal communication, March 2019).

Several business people and officials I interviewed expressed concern that it was unclear who might be targeted and when. The political power of the terms 'black' and 'evil' lie in their ambiguity. Although the campaign's guiding documents outlined specific offences, they also specified vague categories of offenders to give party officials and local law enforcement room to apply the 'black' label without limitation.

The label 'black' has a long history in Chinese political and legal discourse that goes well beyond the sense of a 'gangster' or 'miscreant'. In CPC rhetoric and propaganda, the terms 'black and evil forces' and 'black hand' are often used as shorthand for critics, dissidents and its enemies. Official media frequently referred to prominent pro-democracy activist Liu Xiaobo, for example, as a 'black hand' (Buckley, 2017). State media also described the Hong Kong protests of 2019 as having been orchestrated by 'black hands' with support from 'foreign black hands'. It used similar language to characterise protests in China's Tibetan areas a decade ago.[6]

Not surprisingly, then, the party has used the Sweep Away Black campaign to extend its control over certain discordant elements of society, which includes certain online bloggers, those who participate in protests and other activists. The campaign also targets such people as 'vigilantes and self-appointed mediators' who act as 'underground law enforcement' (地下执法队, *dixia zhifadui*) in the streets, railway stations, urban villages, urban–rural integration areas and on public transport. It targets villagers who engage in protests such as those blockading buildings or roads or activists who are accused of mobilising the public to 'disturb public order and endanger public security'. Finally, it targets 'evil forces' that organise or recruit 'water armies' (水军, *shuijun*) on the internet to threaten, intimidate, insult, defame and harass others as well as 'evil forces across borders'— a warning to those exchanging politically sensitive information with parties outside China (Renminwang, 2018).

Internet-related cases tend to focus on cyber attacks, especially those involving the extortion of enterprises and individuals through the posting of malicious articles and commentary (Y. Wang, 2019). The regulations also covered the spreading of online rumours, which can include any information authorities find inconvenient or 'politically sensitive'. Although such actions were already classified as crimes, their inclusion in the campaign signalled to local party branches and law enforcement agencies that such offences were priority targets.

Political and social control

The Sweep Away Black and Eliminate Evil campaign's political and social control objectives set it apart from the Chongqing prototype. In 2019, campaign documents began increasingly to exhort law enforcement to focus on issues related to social disorder (乱, *luan*) in addition to black and evil forces, a clear signal that Sweep Away Black was no ordinary anti-crime campaign. The expanded mandate was reflected in campaign propaganda

---

6   For the mainland Chinese media's portrayal of the Hong Kong protests, see Hillman (2019b). On the Chinese Communist Party characterisations of the Tibetan protests of 2008 and 2009 and the Uyghur protests of 2009, see Hillman and Tuttle (2016). On the party's dark formulas for dehumanising enemies, see also Barmé (2019).

across the country. A telling slogan commonly found on billboards and banners in 2019 read: 'Where there is black, sweep it, where there is no black, eliminate evil and where there is no evil, cure disorder'. Security forces were put on notice that there would always be someone to catch. Party documents and propaganda suggest that the inclusion of 'disorder' was a natural extension of the campaign and reflected the emphasis on 'rule by law' and China's new social governance systems (Shan, 2018). Nanjing City, for example, announced in 2019 that it was strengthening its grid-based social management system[7] to ensure that 'evil forces', including village, city and transport 'tyrants', had nowhere to hide (Ding, 2019).

With Sweep Away Black and Eliminate Evil campaign committees established at all levels of administration, security agencies mobilised and 'undesirables' filling police detention centres, the tightening of the campaign's grip on society and the economy under Xi proved very useful for the party. The persistence of 'evil forces' provided justification for the expansion of authoritarian social control systems such as surveillance and social credit schemes. The campaign also coincided with *zhengshen* (政审), for college applicants and job seekers. One's political record[8] matters more for life chances in the Xi Jinping era than at any time since the end of the Mao era. People expressed fears to me that their association with or family ties to someone swept up in the Sweep Away Black campaign could land them in trouble. Villagers told me that a young village woman was expelled from a corporate recruitment program when her father was 'swept up'. When I mentioned this to a local businesswoman and asked for her thoughts, she told me, 'Sweep Away Black and Eliminate Evil is the party's latest initiative to make us more obedient' (听话, *tinghua*) (personal communication, March 2019).

By 2020, campaign documents routinely referred to 'comprehensive governance' (综合治理, *zonghe zhili*), a term the CPC uses to describe its strategic approach to the maintenance of social order. According to the documents, this involves the integrated deployment of legal, political,

---

7   Local police authorities in China divide communities into segments in accordance with a grid pattern and appoint managers to collect information about the community, including complaints and grievances. The managers perform a community monitoring function, which the party uses as a tool of social control. See Pei (2021).

8   Local governments and public employers in China maintain permanent records (档案, *dang'an*) of the activities and attitudes of citizens, which include school reports, professional credentials, job performance and political history. As they cannot be easily accessed, the dossiers are used as tool of political and social control.

economic, administrative, educational, cultural and other means to punish crimes while educating and rehabilitating other offenders. It aims to prevent crimes, maintain social order, safeguard people's 'happy lives' and ensure the smooth progress of socialist modernisation. Overseeing all of this are party committees and governments at all levels with support from other political and legal organs (Zhonghua Renmin Gongheguo Zhongyang Renmin Zhengfu, 2001).

The design and implementation of Sweep Away Black reflect the party's comprehensive governance approach complete with guidelines for how officials should understand and communicate its purposes. A handbook distributed to officials in one county in Yunnan Province provided 30 standard language formulations known as *biaozhun yongyu* (标准用语) for discussing and promoting Sweep Away Black. They describe the campaign's primary purposes as 'maintaining long-term social order', 'creating a safe and stable social environment guaranteeing peace and order for the people and long-term stability for the nation' and enhancing the people's sense of well-being and security.

Despite the strict guidelines, the campaign afforded local authorities a degree of flexibility in how they identified what was 'black and evil' in their area. Not surprisingly, they sometimes overreached. In March 2019, the government of Xiangtan City, Hunan Province, announced that 'members of families that have lost an only child' and 'serious cases of mental illness' would be 'priority targets' for the campaign on the logic that such categories of people could be prone to disorderly behaviour. In Jinan, Shandong Province, the Public Security Bureau announced that 29 types of behaviour including 'wearing big gold chains, sporting tattoos or displaying rude and unreasonable attitudes' were considered 'expressions of black and evil forces' (Andelie, 2019). Guidelines introduced in 2019 expanded the campaign's targets to unauthorised religious organisations and activities, including gatherings and the running of religious schools. This development posed additional risks for ethnic and religious minorities that were already under pressure, subjecting them to additional repression and abuse by security forces.

Anecdotal evidence suggests that local party and government organs continued to use the campaign to squash dissent. In Yunnan, I learned of one case in which villagers who complained about an exploitative land deal—itself a rightful target of the campaign—were detained under the auspices of the campaign after assembling in a group of 30–40 people to protest. As one village elder told me: 'Previously when we had a problem with the government, we could often resolve it by going in a group to the township or county government and waiting for the leaders to agree to hear our complaint. Nowadays people do not act together like this out of fear they will be targeted by the Sweep Away Black Office.' In another village, a single police raid swooped up 23 people. One of the campaign's explicit targets has been 'thuggery in grassroots politics', including the activities of 'clan forces'. This has empowered local authorities to clamp down on the power of local families, which is seen as an obstacle to party influence in the countryside. When I returned to Yunnan later in 2019, villagers who had previously celebrated the campaign's takedown of gangland activities expressed concern at its mission creep. As one villager explained to me, 'We worry because someone only needs to report you to the committee for you to be investigated. People have started making false reports against their enemies. It's like the Cultural Revolution' (personal communication, March 2019).

Although the campaign formally ended in 2020, the party declared that the crackdown would continue and be 'normalised' into government and law enforcement work under the supervision of the National Anti-Corruption Office. The National Anti-Corruption Office reports that it maintained the intensity of the crackdown in 2021, destroying 195 underworld-related organisations and 1,086 'protective umbrella' networks nationwide. It also claimed to have overseen the disqualification of 93,000 candidates for village head and village party secretary positions across the nation (Zhongguo Chan'anwang, 2022). The National Anti-Corruption Office further announced in 2022 that the mission of the campaign will be upheld through continuous publicity and popular films and television dramas such as 'Sweeping Black Storm', the storylines of which draw on real cases from the campaign such as the case of Sun Xiaoguo (Zhongguo Chan'anwang, 2022). In its 'normalised' form, the campaign to Sweep Away Black continues to reinforce party efforts to shape a loyal and obedient citizenry that behaves in accordance with party-sanctioned norms and values.

Conclusion

The campaign to Sweep Away Black and Eliminate Evil built on the anti-corruption campaign that preceded it and drew heavily on the Chongqing prototype of crime-busting spearheaded by the disgraced former party leader Bo Xilai. Unlike the Strike Black campaign in Chongqing, however,

Sweep Away Black was much more than an anti-organised crime campaign. The use of the politically loaded terms 'black' and 'evil' created a semantic scope for local party committees and party bosses to target political enemies and nuisances as well as ordinary citizens who might embarrass authorities through in-person or online protests about government policies and actions. This instilled a sense of fear among ordinary citizens in the same way the anti-corruption campaign instilled a sense of fear in party and government officials. In this way, the campaign has served as an important means of expanding party power and reach at the grassroots.

Sweep Away Black reminds us that revolutionary-style campaigns remain an important tool for the CPC to extend its political and social control. The party continues to use such campaigns to achieve rapid cultural and attitudinal change and to signal serious intent for certain governance or policy reforms. However, unlike the Maoist-era political campaigns, contemporary political campaigns mobilise officials rather than 'the masses'. Whereas Mao mobilised people against elements of the state apparatus that he perceived to be impeding his revolutionary agenda, campaigns such as Sweep Away Black are bureaucratic initiatives that limit the role of the masses to serving as informers, an important feature of CPC strategies to discipline and punish. Campaigns such as Sweep Away Black serve as a clear reminder that the party is the ultimate arbiter of right and wrong in the People's Republic of China and that the party is increasingly determined to enforce its own moral codes of conduct to crush perceived obstacles to policy initiatives or threats to the party's monopoly of power.

The broadening of the meaning of 'black and evil' to include political enemies has led to overreach in many instances, but anecdotal evidence suggests that although there has been disgruntlement at the degree of intrusion into the community and private lives, the campaign's visible impact on gangland activity has been broadly popular. The campaign therefore bolstered the party's legitimacy while expanding its social and political control at the grassroots. The campaign has also expanded the scope for domestic security agencies to punish behaviour the party considers deviant, disobedient or inconvenient. By integrating moral values into the law, the campaign has provided an impetus for combatting organised crime and official corruption. At the same time, it has furnished the party and law enforcement agencies with additional tools of political and social control.

Sweep Away Black is a further example of a 'managed' campaign or 'campaign-style' social management. It has become characteristic of party rule under Xi Jinping for the party to draw on its revolutionary traditions to mobilise its agents. However, unlike in the Maoist past, the party seeks to mobilise its members and officials rather than the masses. Also, unlike the Maoist past, the party ensures that its campaigns are tightly managed with targets, quotas and guidelines to ensure greater central control of local agents and to allow for adaptive tinkering with campaigns as they are rolled out. Guidelines and targets for Sweep Away Black were updated and expanded regularly throughout the three years of the campaign, and local committees were tasked with communicating and overseeing tweaks to the program. The Sweep Away Black campaign therefore provides helpful insight into the hybrid revolutionary and legal rational modes of governance being used to secure political and social control in Xi's China.

References

Andelie [安德烈] (2019) 'Qingwen Xi zongshuji, zhe shi saohei haishi mohei' [請問習總書記 這是掃黑還是抹黑, General Secretary Xi, is this sweeping black or smearing [black]?]. Faguo Guoji Guangbo Diantai [法國國際廣播電台, Radio France International], 12 April

Bakken, B. (ed.) (2005) *Crime, Punishment and Policing in China.* Rowman & Littlefield

Barmé, G. (2019) 'Sweep away all professors! Make China's universities safe spaces.' China Heritage. chinaheritage.net/journal/sweep-away-all-professors-make-chinas-universities-safe-spaces

Broadhurst, R. (2012) 'Black societies and triad-like organised crime in China.' In *Handbook of Transnational Organised Crime*, ed. F. Allum & S. Gilmour, pp. 151–71. Routledge

Buckley, C. (2017) 'Liu Xiaobo, Chinese dissident who won Nobel while jailed, dies at 61.' *New York Times*, 13 July. www.nytimes.com/2017/07/13/world/asia/liu-xiaobo-dead.html

Burns, J.P., & Zhou, Z. (2010) 'Performance management in the government of the People's Republic of China: Accountability and control in the implementation of public policy.' *OECD Journal on Budgeting* 10(2): 1–28. doi.org/10.1787/budget-10-5km7h1rvtlnq

Cabestan, J.P. (2011) 'The implications of the Chongqing model for the reform of China's legal system.' In *One or Two Chinese Models?*, ed. F. Godement, pp. 8–11. European Council on Foreign Relations

Fan, C. [范春生] (2019) 'Liaoning ji qi hei e shili "baohusan" yunzuo guiji guancha' [遼寧幾起黑惡勢力「保護傘」運作軌跡觀察, Observations on the operational tracks of several 'evil umbrellas' in Liaoning]. Xinhuawang [新華網, Xinhua Net], 21 May. www.xinhuanet.com/legal/2019-05/21/c_112452 3669.htm

Feng, X. [熊豐] (2019) 'Gao qing dudao "li jian" zai xian qiangda gongshi (saohei chue jinxing shi)—Zhongyang saohei chue dier, disan lun dudao zongshu' [高擎督導「利劍」再掀強大攻勢（掃黑除惡進行時）—中央掃黑除惡第二、第三輪督導綜述, Holding high the 'sharp sword' of supervision to unleash a powerful offensive (while the Sweep Away Black and Eliminate Evil campaign is in progress)—Summary of the second and third rounds of supervision]. *Renminwang* [人民網, People.cn], 17 August. politics.people.com.cn/n1/2019/ 0817/c1001-31301047.html

Higgins, A. (2012) 'Fugitive Chinese businessman Li Jun details struggle over power and property.' *Washington Post*, 4 March. www.washingtonpost.com/world/asia _pacific/fugitive-chinese-businessman-details-struggle-over-power-and-property/ 2012/03/03/gIQATIJqqR_story.html

Hillman, B. (2003) 'Paradise under construction: Minorities, myths and modernity in northwest Yunnan.' *Asian Ethnicity* 4(2): 177–90. doi.org/10.1080/1463136 0301654

—— (2004) 'The rise of the community in rural China: Village politics, cultural identity and religious revival in a Hui hamlet.' *China Journal* 51: 53–73. doi.org/ 10.2307/3182146

—— (2010) 'Factions and spoils: Examining political behavior within the local state in China.' *China Journal* 64: 1–18. doi.org/10.1086/tcj.64.20749244

—— (2014) *Patronage and Power: Local State Networks and Party–State Resilience in Rural China.* Stanford University Press

—— (2018) 'Shangri-La and the curse of Xi Jinping.' In *China Story Yearbook 2017: Prosperity*, ed. J. Golley & L. Jaivin, pp. 70–5. ANU Press. doi.org/10.22459/ CSY.04.2018

—— (2019a) 'The state advances, the private sector retreats.' In *China Story Yearbook 2018: Power*, ed. J. Golley, L. Jaivin, P.J. Farrelly & S. Strange, pp. 294–307. ANU Press. doi.org/10.22459/CSY.2019

—— (2019b) 'Hong Kong protests in the Mainland eye.' *East Asia Forum*, 20 October

—— (2020) 'Xi's war on black and evil.' In *China Dreams: China Story Yearbook*, ed. J. Golley, L. Jaivin, B. Hillman & S. Strange. ANU Press. doi.org/10.22459/CSY.2020

Hillman, B., & Tuttle, G. (eds) (2016) *Ethnic Conflict and Protest in Tibet and Xinjiang: Unrest in China's West*. Columbia University Press

Hubei Sheng Renmin Zhengfu [湖北省人民政府, People's Government of Hubei] (2019) 'Zuigao Renmin Fayuan Zuigao Renmin Jianchayuan Gonganbu Sifabu guanyu banli e shili xingshi anjian ruogan wenti de yijian' [最高人民法院 最高人民檢察院 公安部 司法部關於辦理惡勢力刑事案件若干問題的意見, Opinions of the Supreme People's Court, the Supreme People's Procuratorate, the Ministry of Public Security and the Ministry of Justice on several issues concerning handling criminal cases by evil forces] (press release). www.hubei.gov.cn/hbfb/szsm/201905/t20190510_1549714.shtml

Lin, D., & Trevaskes, S. (2019) 'Creating a virtuous leviathan: The party, law and socialist core values.' *Asian Journal of Law and Society* 6(1): 41–66. doi.org/10.1017/als.2018.41

Lu, J. [盧俊宇]. (2019) 'Quanguo saohei chue zhuanxiang douzheng huo zhongda jieduan xing chengguo, xia yibu zhugong fangxiang mingque' [全國掃黑除惡專項鬥爭獲重大階段性成果 下一步主攻方向明確, Major phase results of the national Sweep Away Black and Eliminate Evil campaign]. *Xinhuawang* [新華網, Xinhua Net], 13 October. www.xinhuanet.com/legal/2019-10/13/c_1210310440.htm

Lubman, S. (2012) 'Bo Xilai's gift to Chongqing: A legal mess.' *Wall Street Journal*, 12 April. www.wsj.com/articles/BL-CJB-15614

Moore, M. (2009) 'China corruption trial exposes capital of graft.' *Telegraph*, 17 October. www.telegraph.co.uk/news/worldnews/asia/china/6357024/China-corruption-trial-exposes-capital-of-graft.html

Pei, M. (2021) 'Grid management: China's latest institutional tool of social control.' *China Leadership Monitor*, 1 March. www.prcleader.org/pei-grid-management

Perry, E. (2011) 'From mass campaigns to managed campaigns: "Constructing a new socialist countryside".' In *Mao's Invisible Hand: The Political Foundations of Adaptive Governance in China*, ed. E.J. Perry & S. Heilmann, pp. 30–61. Harvard University Press

Ren, Q. (2019) '$527 million seized, 16,200 arrested in loan shark crackdown.' *Caixin Global*, 26 February. www.caixinglobal.com/2019-02-26/527-million-seized-16200-arrested-in-loan-shark-crackdown-101384297.html

Renminwang [人民網, People.cn] (2018) 'Zhonggong Zhongyang Guowuyuan fachu "guanyu kaizhan sao hei chu e zhuanxiang douzheng de tongzhi"' [中共中央國務院發出《關於開展掃黑除惡專項鬥爭的通知》, The Central Committee of the Communist Party of China and the State Council issue the 'Notice on Launching a Special Campaign to Fight Crime and Eradicate Evil']. CPC.people.com.cn/n1/2018/0124/c64387-29784940.html

Shan, W. (2018) 'Social control in China: Towards a "smart" and sophisticated system.' *East Asian Policy* 10, 47–55. doi.org/10.1142/S1793930518000041

Trevaskes, S. (2006) 'Severe and swift justice in China.' *British Journal of Criminology* 47: 23–41. doi.org/10.1093/bjc/azl032

Wang, P. (2013) 'The rise of the Red Mafia in China: A case study of organised crime and corruption in Chongqing.' *Trends in Organised Crime* 16: 49–73. doi.org/10.1007/s12117-012-9179-8

—— (2020) 'Politics of crime control: How campaign-style law enforcement sustains authoritarian rule in China.' *British Journal of Criminology* 60(2): 422–43. doi.org/10.1093/bjc/azz065

Wang, Y. [王陽]. (2019) 'Jingzhun daji wangluo hei e shili "shuijun" zhili "wumai" chengqing wangluo kongjian' [精準打擊網絡黑惡勢力「水軍」治理「霧霾」澄清網絡空間, Accurately combat the 'water army' of the cyber underworld, manage the 'smog' and cleanse cyberspace]. *Renminwang* [人民網, People.cn]. media.people.com.cn/n1/2019/1009/c40606-31388218.html

Yin, S. [尹深]. (2019) 'Quanguo Saoheiban: Jiezhi 3 yuedi quanguo qisu she hei she e fanzui an 14226 jian' [全國掃黑辦：截至3月底全國起訴涉黑涉惡犯罪案14226件, Anti-crime Office: As of the end of March, 14,226 criminal cases involving the black and evil have been prosecuted nationwide. Xinhuawang [新華網, Xinhua Net], 9 April. www.xinhuanet.com/2019-04/09/c_112434 3704.htm

Zeng, Q. (2020) 'Managed campaign and bureaucratic institutions in China: Evidence from the Targeted Poverty Alleviation Program.' *Journal of Contemporary China* 29(123): 400–15

Zhao, S. (2016) 'Xi Jinping's Maoist revival.' *Journal of Democracy* 27(3): 83–97. doi.org/10.1353/jod.2016.0051

Zhongguo Chan'anwang [中國長安網, Chinapeace.gov.cn] (2022) 'Chang'an daolun: Zhong Zhengsheng: 2022 nian changtaihua saohei chue yao jixu dahao zuhequan' [（長安導論）鐘政聲：2022年常態化掃黑除惡要繼續打好組合拳, (Introduction to Chang'an) Zhong Zhengsheng: In 2022, we must continue to fight well in combination]. 24 March. www.chinapeace.gov.cn/chinapeace/c100007/2022-03/24/content_12609374.shtml

Zhongguo Ribaowang (2019) '19 sentenced for ties to Sun Xiaoguo crime case.' 15 December. www.chinadaily.com.cn/a/201912/15/WS5df5ce27a310cf3e3557 e33a.html

Zhonghua Renmin Gongheguo Zhongyang Renmin Zhengfu [中華人民共和中央人民政府, Central People's Government of the People's Republic of China] (2001) 'Zhonggong Zhongyang Guowuyuan guanyu jinyibu jiaqiang shehui zhian zonghe zhili de yijian' [中共中央國務院關於進一步加強社會治安綜合治理的意見, Opinions of the Central Committee of the Communist Party of China and the State Council on further strengthening the comprehensive management of social security] (press release). 5 September. www.gov.cn/gongbao/content/2001/content_61190.htm

Zhonghua Renmin Gongheguo Zuigao Renmin Jianchayuan [中華人民共和國最高人民檢察院, Supreme People's Procuratorate of the People's Republic of China]. (2019) 'Zuigao Renmin Fayuan, Zuigao Renmin Jianchayuan, Gonganbu, Sifabu guanyu banli eshili xingshi anjian ruogan wenti de yijian (quanwen)' [最高人民法院 最高人民檢察院 公安部 司法部關於辦理惡勢力刑事案件若干問題的意見（全文）, Opinions of the Supreme People's Court, the Supreme People's Procuratorate, the Ministry of Public Security and the Ministry of Justice on several issues concerning handling criminal cases by evil forces (full text)] (press release). April. www.spp.gov.cn/zdgz/201904/t2019 0409_414134.shtml

www.ingramcontent.com/pod-product-compliance
Lightning Source LLC
Chambersburg PA
CBHW051952270326
41929CB00015B/2627

9 7 8 1 7 6 0 4 6 6 1 9 0